Encountering early America

Encountering early America

Rachel Winchcombe

MANCHESTER UNIVERSITY PRESS

Copyright © Rachel Winchcombe 2021

The right of Rachel Winchcombe to be identified as the author of this work has been asserted by them in accordance with the Copyright, Designs and Patents Act 1988.

Published by Manchester University Press
Oxford Road, Manchester M13 9PL

www.manchesteruniversitypress.co.uk

British Library Cataloguing-in-Publication Data
A catalogue record for this book is available from the British Library

ISBN 978 1 5261 4577 2 hardback
ISBN 978 1 5261 7174 0 paperback

First published 2021
Paperback published 2023

The publisher has no responsibility for the persistence or accuracy of URLs for any external or third-party internet websites referred to in this book, and does not guarantee that any content on such websites is, or will remain, accurate or appropriate.

Typeset by
Servis Filmsetting Ltd, Stockport, Cheshire

Contents

List of figures	vi
Acknowledgements	viii
Introduction: Early English encounters with the New World	1
1 Understanding America: The theoretical origins of English colonialism	26
2 Commercialising America: Religion, trade, and the challenges of English colonialism	71
3 Dressing America: Clothing, nakedness, and the foundations of civility	112
4 Eating America: Bodily discourse in the early English colonial imagination	155
Conclusions	202
Bibliography	210
Index	235

Figures

1 Unknown, woodcut, 'Feathered Native Americans', in Anonymous, *Of the Newe La[n]des and of ye People Founde by the Messengers of the Kynge of Porty[n]gale* (Antwerp, 1520). RB 18704 pt. 1, The Huntington Library, San Marino, CA. Public domain. 117

2 Theodore de Bry, copper engraving, 'The Manner of Makinge Their Boates', in Thomas Harriot, *A Briefe and True Report of the New Found Land of Virginia* (Frankfurt, 1590). Courtesy of the John Carter Brown Library, CC BY-SA 4.0. 136

3 Theodore de Bry, copper engraving, 'Their Manner of Fishynge in Virginia', in Thomas Harriot, *A Briefe and True Report of the New Found Land of Virginia* (Frankfurt, 1590). Courtesy of the John Carter Brown Library, CC BY-SA 4.0. 137

4 Theodore de Bry, copper engraving, 'A Chieff Ladye of Pomeiooc', in Thomas Harriot, *A Briefe and True Report of the New Found Land of Virginia* (Frankfurt, 1590). Courtesy of the John Carter Brown Library, CC BY-SA 4.0. 138

5 Theodore de Bry, copper engraving, 'A Weroan or Great Lorde of Virginia', in Thomas Harriot, *A Briefe and True Report of the New Found Land of Virginia* (Frankfurt, 1590). Courtesy of the John Carter Brown Library, CC BY-SA 4.0. 139

6 Theodore de Bry, copper engraving, 'A Younge Gentill Woeman Doughter of Secota', in Thomas Harriot, *A Briefe and True Report of the New Found Land of Virginia* (Frankfurt, 1590). Courtesy of the John Carter Brown Library, CC BY-SA 4.0. 140

7 Theodore de Bry, copper engraving, 'The True Picture of a Women Picte', in Thomas Harriot, *A Briefe and True Report of the New Found Land of Virginia* (Frankfurt, 1590). Courtesy of the British Library. Public domain. 141

List of figures

8	Theodore de Bry, copper engraving, 'The True Picture of a Yonge Dowgter of the Pictes', in Thomas Harriot, *A Briefe and True Report of the New Found Land of Virginia* (Frankfurt, 1590). Courtesy of the British Library. Public domain.	142
9	Theodore de Bry, copper engraving, 'The True Picture of One Picte', in Thomas Harriot, *A Briefe and True Report of the New Found Land of Virginia* (Frankfurt, 1590). Courtesy of the British Library. Public domain.	143
10	Theodore de Bry, copper engraving, 'The Browyllinge of their Fishe over the Flame', in Thomas Harriot, *A Briefe and True Report of the New Found Land of Virginia* (Frankfurt, 1590). Courtesy of the John Carter Brown Library, CC BY-SA 4.0.	187
11	Theodore de Bry, copper engraving, 'Their Seetheynge of their Meate in Earthen Pottes', in Thomas Harriot, *A Briefe and True Report of the New Found Land of Virginia* (Frankfurt, 1590). Courtesy of the John Carter Brown Library, CC BY-SA 4.0.	188
12	Theodore de Bry, copper engraving, 'Their Sitting at Meate', in Thomas Harriot, *A Briefe and True Report of the New Found Land of Virginia* (Frankfurt, 1590). Courtesy of the John Carter Brown Library, CC BY-SA 4.0.	189

Acknowledgements

In the course of writing this book I have been lucky enough to have had the support of numerous people, at both a personal and a professional level. I must thank the Arts and Humanities Research Council for funding the initial research for this book. The Huntington Library, the John Rylands Library, John Carter Brown Library, and the British Library have provided essential resources for this project and I thank all the staff at these institutions for sharing their time and expertise with me. Their knowledge and advice have been invaluable.

I could not have successfully completed this book without the support of many colleagues and friends. I have learned a great deal from friends at the University of Manchester including Natalie Zacek, Misha Ewen, Steven Mossman, and Stefan Hanβ, as well as from colleagues at other institutions, including John Morgan and Rebecca Earle. Special thanks go to Jenny Spinks and Sasha Handley. Jenny, your wealth of knowledge and constant encouragement have been critical to the completion of this book, and you continue to provide me with support from the other side of the world! Sasha, you've been the best mentor I could have ever hoped for, as well as a great friend. This book has undoubtedly been enriched by your various insights and unwavering generosity.

I have had a number of opportunities to share my research in various forums and my work has benefitted immeasurably from the feedback I have received at these events. I am grateful to the North West Early Modern Seminar, the Sixteenth Century Society Conference, the Hakluyt Society Conference, the European Early American Studies Association Conference, the 'Bites Here and There': Literal and Metaphorical Cannibalism Across Disciplines Conference, and the John Rylands Seminar "Print and Materiality in the Early Modern World" for allowing me to present my research and learn from the research of others.

I would also like to thank my editor Meredith Carroll for her constant guidance throughout the publication process and to the reviewers who commented on the initial draft of the manuscript. Their thoughtful critiques and helpful suggestions not only helped me improve the book, but made the process of publishing much less stressful than it otherwise could have been.

My thanks go to my family and friends, especially my mum and dad, who continue to support me and encourage me in everything I do. My final thanks go to Suraj. I couldn't have written this book without you. You have been with me every step of the way and I'm lucky to have you.

Introduction:
Early English encounters with the New World

In 1606 King James I of England and VI of Scotland chartered two joint-stock companies that would become known collectively as the Virginia Company. In December 1606 one of these companies, the Virginia Company of London, set sail to establish an English colony in North America. As every American school child knows, this colony, named Jamestown by its founding members, would become the first permanent English settlement in the New World. For authors of American history school textbooks, the establishment of the Jamestown colony in 1607 represents a defining moment in the history of North America, marking the very beginning of Anglo-American history.[1] But why did these men and boys set sail for the New World at the end of 1606? What convinced them to uproot their lives in England and to settle in Virginia? What promises and beliefs fuelled their departure? Fundamentally, what happened between Christopher Columbus's so-called discovery in 1492 and the settling of Jamestown in 1607 that encouraged English men and women to start a new life in the Americas?

These questions remain largely unanswered and the story of the first century of English encounters with the New World largely untold. The dominant narrative of English beginnings in the Americas has condemned the sixteenth century to relative historical obscurity. For historians interested in the development of English colonial ideology, and indeed identity, it was in the period of permanent English settlement in the New World, ushered in with the survival of the Jamestown colony, that the origins of Anglo-America have been most clearly discerned.[2] As this book will show, however, the experiences of English explorers, merchants, and colonisers in America in the sixteenth century, and indeed their interest in the experiences of other European colonising nations, did not merely reflect a pre-history or prologue for what was to come later. It was in the sixteenth century that English men and women first grappled with what the 'discovery' of 1492 meant for them; the period witnessed the first sustained English attempts at exploration, settlement, and colonisation in the Americas, and the first

English endeavours to understand and define the new lands across the Atlantic. As this book argues, the sixteenth century represents a discreet and influential period in the history of English encounters with the Americas that is characterised by a multiplicity of approaches. The sixteenth-century English encounter with the New World was at times inconsistent, often dynamic and adaptive, and always grounded in a set of European, as well as distinctly English, cultural assumptions.

This book is not primarily concerned with the *reality* of the New World and its peoples, but with English *perceptions* of them. Important work has been undertaken that attempts to recover Indigenous voices from colonial texts.[3] However, the objective of this book is to uncover the many European voices, and the many cultural influences, involved in the construction of early English perceptions of the Americas. While the encounters described in the printed materials that form the basis of this book are grounded in real-life Indigenous communities and distinct historical groups, the Indigenous peoples referred to in early English Americana are also representational. English explorers and colonisers, and those who wrote about them, although encountering diverse Indigenous groups, created, to varying degrees, a number of 'imagined' and largely homogenised Indigenous communities who conformed to a range of English expectations and cultural frameworks. These imagined groups functioned as 'representational machines', shaping both English perceptions of the New World and early approaches to overseas expansion and colonisation.[4] Due to the representational and imagined nature of many English depictions of Indigenous people, selecting appropriate terminology is not straightforward. This book uses, where possible, the correct tribal affiliation, or wider ethnic group, of the various Indigenous communities that the English encountered. As English descriptions of Indigenous people, and the European representations that influenced them, are in many cases homogenous and non-specific in nature, this is not always possible. Where more generic terms need to be used to reflect the tone of English and translated European sources, 'Indigenous people' has been chosen as a more expansive term than 'American Indian' or 'Native American'.[5]

The sixteenth century was a time of increased trans-national rivalry and competition, and an era of English social upheaval and cultural change. These shifts in both the international and domestic landscape played a critical role in shaping early English perceptions of the New World and its peoples and attempts to establish English territorial authority in the region. The English legitimised their colonial and explorative exploits by employing diverse and well-known intellectual and religious frameworks, from classical climatology to early modern humoralism, religious schemes of providentialism, and Christian morality. English writers, editors, and explorers embedded New World projects within the changing domestic landscape of sixteenth-century England, using these ventures to comment on international relations, the nature of the English Reformation, fears and anxieties surrounding foreign travel, and economic stagnation. Harnessing this vast array of knowledge, and placing it within the context of the domestic concerns of sixteenth-century England, those writing about the new American lands explained both failure and success, and created an assortment of flexible images of America and its peoples that were used to their own cultural, political, and colonial advantage.

Continental European perceptions of America also played an integral role in the development of English New World projects. Writers utilised accounts of French experiences in America to reflect on their own disappointments and mistakes. The exploits of Spain were arguably even more influential, becoming central to English understandings of their own projects. While the Catholic Mary I still sat on the throne between 1553 and 1558, the English consumption of Spanish descriptions of America fostered a colonialism of emulation. As Anglo-Spanish relations deteriorated, English ventures in the Americas began to develop in opposition to the Spanish model, using the flexibility of English categorisations of America to simultaneously attack the Spanish and justify their own methods.

To understand how the English interpreted American lands in the sixteenth century, and how they came to settle there, English encounters with America must be situated in a trans-Atlantic context. The relationship between America and England, as well as the wider European continent, was symbiotic. Just as events taking place in England and the rest of Europe impacted explorative and colonial decisions taking place across the Atlantic, encounters between English explorers, merchants, sailors and colonisers, and the peoples and lands of America contributed to changing ideas of morality, religious practice, economic vigour, and state building back in Europe. These issues and connections have provided rich pickings for both Atlantic historians and historians of American borderlands. Recent Atlantic scholarship has demonstrated the various ways in which ideas, commodities, and people moved between and around the broader Atlantic world. This scholarship, by tracing this movement back and forth across the Atlantic in the early modern period, has demonstrated the interconnectedness of European colonising states and Indigenous and African societies.[6] A criticism levelled at Atlantic history has been its tendency to focus on the core, and most especially nation states, rather than on peripheries.[7] In contrast, borderlands scholarship has emphasised the importance of peripheries to our understanding of colonial history. Studying interactions in the borderlands, i.e. the contested spaces where nations 'frayed at the edges' and where peoples, things, and ideas flowed, has enabled scholars to de-centre European colonising nations and 'epic' narratives of imperial history. Instead, this scholarship emphasises the autonomy of Indigenous people in contested borderlands and demonstrates how the study of peripheries, whether geographic or metaphorical, can reveal early America to be a 'tangled web' of imperial, national, and Indigenous cultural journeys.[8]

Both Atlantic and borderlands historians have more recently suggested that, whether focusing on cores or peripheries, the history of America and its connection to the wider world is a deeply entangled one. Jorge Cañizares-Esguerra, for example, has argued that studying historical phenomena that are in essence trans-Atlantic and trans-national within the constraints of national narratives is futile. Instead, he proposes that these national narratives are intrinsically entangled and need to be studied as such.[9] In particular, Cañizares-Esguerra's work argues that the colonial histories of Spain and Britain are entangled and the Iberian Atlantic is the core of this entanglement.[10] Responding to Cañizares-Esguerra's call for an entangled history that works from the centre out, Eliga Gould has argued that the exercise of power at the centre cannot be disentangled from how power operates at the margins. In doing so, Gould suggests that it is impossible to separate the entangled histories of colonial peripheries from metropolitan histories, as the former is integral to the latter.[11] It is to this understanding of entangled history, in which peripheries and the core are radically intertwined, that this book ascribes. By considering how early English projects functioned within a broader Atlantic framework that incorporates the domestic and the international, and the core and the periphery, this book demonstrates the extent to which early English understandings of the Americas are entangled with the projects of rival European countries and with the encounters English explorers experienced in the New World.

In analysing this foundational era of English exploration and settlement in the New World, this book transforms our understanding of the origins of the British Empire in America, placing it within an international framework of competition, rivalry, and shared cultural heritage, and a domestic context of substantial cultural, religious, economic, and political change. Early English perceptions of America were the product of a century-long engagement with the colonialism of other nations, the transference and adaptation of ideas and theories first proposed in continental Europe, and the concerted English effort to carve out an approach to America that was substantially different to that of their European rivals. This resulted in a set of English images of America that both converged with and diverged from those created by other European nations. English explorers and colonisers appropriated images of America that they found helpful for achieving their own ambitions, while simultaneously creating their own images that allowed for the condemnation of the Spanish approach and the celebration of their own. Sixteenth-century English representations of America and its people were thus the product of a set of ever-changing cultural influences, born at home, in continental Europe, and in the new lands across the Atlantic. The history of England's first century in America is a story of both England and America, a tale of both the local and the international, and a record of England's dynamic and adaptive, if often unsuccessful, messy, and abortive, approach to overseas expansion.

Sixteenth-century English encounters with America

The English encounter with America undoubtedly came in fits and starts. England's entry into the race to secure New World colonies was belated in comparison to her European neighbours, but despite this, the sixteenth century nonetheless witnessed a variety of projects directed towards the Americas. These ventures sought to establish England on the international stage and rival the settlements, trade partnerships, and missionising zeal of the Spanish, Portuguese, and French. It is these English projects, and their various setbacks, adaptations, and influences that form the focus of this book.

To date, these earlier English ventures in America have received relatively little scholarly attention, especially when compared with their seventeenth-century counterparts. While individual projects, and the individuals and texts related to them, have, of course, been analysed in detail, the various English approaches to America that developed across the sixteenth century have not been explored in any real depth.[12] The sixteenth century has not been analysed as a discreet period in the history of English overseas expansion, but rather as a preface to the projects that developed in the seventeenth century. While discussions on the development of Anglo-America have often begun with a glance towards the late sixteenth century, particularly the failed attempt at settlement at Roanoke, this period of English engagement with America has mostly been dismissed as precursory rather than foundational.[13]

When the wider sixteenth-century English approach to America has been analysed in more detail, the diversity and changeability of English understandings of America across the century has been largely flattened or obscured. For example, although Joyce Chaplin, in her excellent study of science and technology on the early modern Anglo-American frontier, has explored the sixteenth century, she has nonetheless implied that English attitudes towards America remained consistent throughout the century, arguing that 1500 to 1585 represented a phase of English colonisation in which the English were uncertain of their ability to master nature.[14] Likewise, the influential work of both Mary Fuller and Andrew Fitzmaurice has suggested that the sixteenth-century English approach to America was underpinned by a consistent rhetorical and intellectual strategy, whether the discourse of 'failure' for Fuller or the language of humanism for Fitzmaurice.[15] One exception to this tendency of portraying the sixteenth-century English approach to America as largely consistent is Karen Kupperman's extensive work on the Jamestown colony in a global context. Kupperman demonstrates the 'messy' origins of the colony and the various global influences that helped shape its development.[16] However, important questions remain unanswered. While the global contexts in which English projects in America were situated are, of course, important, so too are the fluctuating domestic conditions of sixteenth-century England and how they impacted English projects in America across the century. As this book argues, by examining both the domestic and trans-Atlantic contexts of English ventures in the Americas, and by analysing the changing attitudes towards America across the sixteenth century, it becomes clear that English approaches to New World projects were not just messy and unsuccessful, but also adaptive, dynamic, and crucial to later success.

This tendency to omit or flatten the varied sixteenth-century English approaches to the New World, or focus on other overseas contexts that influenced English colonisation in America, has led to the assumption that English interest in the new lands across the Atlantic was limited in the sixteenth century and of little historical consequence for how English colonies in the Americas would ultimately develop. Despite this, and as this book will argue, the English did in fact begin machinations for the Americas almost immediately after Columbus first made landfall in October 1492. Henry VII had famously passed on the opportunity to fund Columbus's explorations, which had meant that England had narrowly missed out on being the benefactor of what very quickly became a highly profitable and lucrative discovery. In an attempt to correct this oversight, the English Crown hastily sought to establish its authority in the region. As we shall see, across the sixteenth century, English writers interested in the Americas lamented the fact that England had missed out on this early opportunity, something that they would continually try to correct in the following decades.

England's first foray into New World exploration came in the 1490s and early 1500s with the voyages of John and Sebastian Cabot. In 1497 John Cabot, an Italian navigator, had garnered the support of Henry VII for a voyage to the New World. This venture, although not widely publicised either in print or manuscript, resulted in the first English navigation of the North American coast. Spurred on by his father, Sebastian Cabot would later lead an expedition to find a Northwest Passage to Asia, something that had been the intended aim of Columbus and would also become a key objective for English merchants throughout the sixteenth century.[17] Neither of these early English ventures was capitalised on, however, and English interest in New World exploration retreated with the ascension of Henry VIII and the ensuing domestic instability of the country.[18]

It would not be until the 1550s that English interest in establishing New World colonies would once again be piqued. In particular, it was the work of Richard Eden, an English translator and one-time secretary to William Cecil, that reminded English readers of how profitable American colonies could be and encouraged England's courtiers and merchants to establish their own links overseas. Through his translations of key European texts relating to the Spanish and Portuguese explorations of the New World, Eden brought the first detailed images of America to an English readership as well as the first sustained calls for English activity in the region. Eden's abridged and greatly condensed versions of the Italian historian Peter Martyr's *De Orbe Novo Decades*, the Spanish historian Gonzalo Fernández de Oviedo's *La Historia General y Natural de las Indias*, and the German cosmographer Sebastian Münster's *Cosmographia*, illustrated to English readers for the first time both the benefits and dangers of European travel to the New World, themes that would continue to dominate English texts on America throughout the sixteenth century.[19] Through these texts, Eden showed how wealth and natural resources could be successfully extracted from the new American environments and how the 'savage' and 'ungodly' Indigenous peoples of the region could be raised to European civility and converted to the true Christian faith. At the same time, Eden's translations also highlighted the somewhat uneasy relationship between European bodies and the American environment, recounting tales of European sickness and Indigenous resistance and violence. Despite calling on his fellow Englishmen to make overseas exploration and exploitation of America a reality, Eden's work, for the most part, remained theoretical as English overseas expansion continued to lag behind that of the Iberian powers.

As the sixteenth century wore on, other interested parties began printing texts in a bid to describe the lands and the peoples that they had encountered across the Atlantic and to promote their burgeoning explorative, trade, and colonial projects. In the 1560s the voyages and exploits of John Hawkins in the Caribbean demonstrated to English readers the many calamities that could befall a traveller in foreign and distant lands. As Hawkins explained in his own account of his 1567 voyage, the animosity of the Spanish and their unwillingness to trade with the English, coupled with appalling weather that hampered the fleet's return home, had been detrimental to the voyage, resulting in the crew facing starvation and extreme sickness.[20] Accounts of Hawkins's voyages also illustrated to English readers the priorities of those engaged in travel to the New World. The purpose of these voyages, among others undertaken by the likes of Francis Drake, was to accumulate vast amounts of wealth through acts of privateering and piracy aimed at both the Spanish and French.

It was also in the 1560s that English translators and printers first began looking to the French for information on the new lands across the Atlantic. In 1562 the French Huguenot Jean Ribault undertook his first exploration of Florida, returning through England the following year.[21] An account of his voyage appeared in English in 1563 and introduced a highly positive assessment of the Floridian people and environment.[22] English interest in the hotly contested region of Florida was short-lived, however, as in 1566 another account of Ribault's exploits in Florida was published in England that highlighted the dangers of engaging in colonial activity in this region of America, because it had already been claimed by the Spanish Crown. Nicolas Le Challeux, a member of Ribault's crew, recounted the disastrous events of the 1565 voyage to Florida. The venture ended with the destruction of the French settlement by the Spanish and with the execution of Ribault, putting an end to both French and potential English plans for the region.[23]

A third influential French text was translated into English in 1568, providing more detailed information on the various regions of the New World and implicit suggestions as to where prudent European settlement may take place in the future. Thomas Hacket's translation of André Thevet's 1557 work, *Les Singularitez de la France Antarctique*, drew important distinctions between the Indigenous peoples of South America and those of the more northerly regions. While the Indigenous peoples of the south lived, according to Thevet, like 'brutish beasts', those in the north were considered more civilised.[24] This more positive assessment of the people of North America, coupled with the demonstrable dangers of attempting settlement in the Spanish sphere of influence, arguably encouraged the English to focus their efforts on the more northerly regions of the Americas. Indeed, from the 1570s onwards, English attention was squarely directed towards the North American continent.

It was in the 1570s that the English undertook their first sustained attempts to settle in the New World. Towards the end of the decade accounts of Martin Frobisher's voyages to the Far North began appearing on the booksellers' stalls of London. The narratives of these voyages highlighted the frustrations of these early English colonial projects and the perceived reasons behind their failures. For one member of Frobisher's crew who wrote an account of his time in Meta Incognita, Dionyse Settle, the harsh climate and lack of critical natural resources, combined with the hostility of the Inuit, made English settlement in this region of America a near impossibility.[25] If English colonialism in America was to be successful, it was imperative that explorers find a region of the New World that not only suited them in terms of climate, but also provided ample profitable commodities that could be exploited by investors back home.

The 1580 English translation of Jacques Cartier's account of his three voyages to Canada in the 1530s and 1540s set out what had gone wrong in the explorations of Meta Incognita and encouraged future English settlers and potential colonists to set their sights on the more temperate, southerly regions of North America in the future.[26] Three years later, and offering similar advice, George Peckham and Christopher Carleill penned tracts that encouraged English settlement and the establishment of Anglo-Indigenous trade links in Newfoundland. Making similar arguments to those that had been expressed in the English edition of Cartier, both Peckham and Carleill argued that Newfoundland represented a suitable region for English settlement due to the fact that it shared a similar climate to that of England and was home to a number of critical commodities that could be exploited for profit by England's merchants.[27] This optimistic view of the North American continent would continue to be expounded throughout the 1580s with the English attempt at colonisation in Virginia, orchestrated by Walter Ralegh. In the promotional texts related to this project, most notably Thomas Harriot's *Briefe and True Report of the New Found Land of Virginia*, Virginia was presented as a region of the New World that was perfect for English habitation. Not only was Virginia home to a vast array of profitable merchandise, the Indigenous population was also believed to have great potential for receiving English civility and religion.[28] Having ostensibly learned from the mistakes of the 1570s voyages to the Far North, and despite the difficulties faced by the early settlers at Roanoke, English advocates of New World colonisation would continue to encourage English settlement in Virginia well into the seventeenth century.

By the end of the sixteenth century a significant number of English courtiers, merchants, and gentlemanly speculators were increasingly outward-looking, willing to learn from past explorative and colonial mistakes, and prepared to learn from and adapt the approaches used by their European rivals. Indicative of this process of collation, assessment, and adaptation is Richard Hakluyt the younger's colossal text *The Principal Navigations* which was first published in 1589, with an extended version appearing between 1598 and 1600.[29] Bringing together an extensive range of sources, Hakluyt's text synthesised European knowledge and experience of the New World in the hope that it would encourage the continuation of English exploration and colonisation in America. In doing so, Hakluyt brought together various accounts and narratives that had appeared throughout the sixteenth century, whether positive or negative, and whether demonstrating explorative and colonial failure or success. *The Principal Navigations* is thus a testament to the messy, adaptive, but ultimately optimistic, English approach to America in the first century after the 'discovery'.

By the time Jamestown was settled in 1607 there had already been over a century of English engagement with the new lands across the Atlantic. These varied experiences, which were often characterised by failure and a need to adapt, shaped the trial-and-error approach that would continue to dominate English American projects in the seventeenth century. Continued flexibility, adaptivity, and experimentation would allow English settlements in the New World to flourish and would result in a multiplicity of English colonies, spanning the Caribbean to Canada, and being formed around a diverse set of objectives, whether economic, religious, or a mixture of the two. The sixteenth-century English approach to America thus combined influences from other European colonising nations with domestic, English cultural, and economic priorities. It was these fluctuations in both international relations and domestic circumstances that made sixteenth-century English projects in America so dynamic, adaptive, and ultimately influential to how English settlements in the New World would continue to develop.

Trans-national influences

These voyages and projects did not take place in a vacuum, nor were they merely shaped by what was found in the lands across the Atlantic Ocean or by the individual motivations of particular key players. English endeavours to explore, exploit, and settle the new lands of America were undoubtedly conceived within a trans-European context.[30] In the chapters that follow, the European influences that helped English commentators explain the American lands and its peoples will be traced in detail. English approaches to New World exploration and settlement were by no means exceptional. They were shaped by the successes of other European colonising nations and constructed around knowledge and information first gleaned from translations of European travel narratives and early colonial histories. Of equal importance, however, English projects in the Americas were also created in opposition to the imperial models cultivated by England's European rivals, most notably Spain. European knowledge about the New World could therefore be used by English commentators, explorers, and advocates of an English overseas empire, as both a template for how to succeed economically, politically, and culturally in the New World, and as a medium through which English plans for the region could be distinguished from those of their political and religious enemies.

The trans-national cultural influence on early English empire building in the Americas has, of course, already received a great deal of scholarly attention. Historians such as David Quinn, Nicholas Canny, and John Patrick Montaño have long since discussed the connections between English colonisation in Ireland and the English conceptualisation of America in the early modern period. In particular, this body of work has demonstrated that many of those who were involved in projects in Ireland were likewise the early proponents of English activity in the Americas and that experience gained in Ireland throughout the sixteenth century later proved useful for those who undertook colonial ventures in America.[31] While it is undoubtedly true that patterns of settlement and methods of colonial control first developed in Ireland were recreated in the Anglo-American colonies, it is less clear whether the two colonial contexts were directly compared, especially in the sixteenth century. Indeed, analysing the sixteenth century as a discreet period in English explorative and colonial history, challenges some of the assumptions that have been made about the connection between colonisation in Ireland and exploration and settlement in America. Firstly, many of the projects and ventures directed towards the Americas in the sixteenth century were not explicitly colonial in nature, making a direct and sustained connection to the Irish plantations difficult to maintain. English voyages to the Americas ranged from privateering ventures in the Caribbean, to explorative missions to discover a Northwest Passage to Asia in the Far North and attempts to establish trading partnerships with Indigenous people in North America. Secondly, even when the English did advocate specifically colonial projects in the sixteenth century, it was not the Irish plantations that they turned to for inspiration. Instead, and as this book will demonstrate, it was the experiences of other European nations in the New World that they looked towards when planning and assessing their own ventures. Nicholas Canny, who has perhaps done most to advance the Irish-North American colonial connection, has in fact suggested that it was literature about the New World, including the works of José de Acosta and Peter Martyr, that helped shape English approaches to Ireland, particularly those employed by Henry Sidney.[32] These same influences can be found in the sixteenth-century English literature about America.[33] Both English colonisation in Ireland, and English explorative and colonial ventures in the Americas, are thus indebted to wider European influences. As Andrew Hadfield has neatly summarised, American 'colonialism does not have to be read as a trans-Atlantic phenomenon based on first-hand experience in Ireland; it can be read more comprehensively as a European development'.[34] It is this more comprehensive, European approach that this book engages with and shows to be most fruitful for understanding early English approaches to the New World.

English enterprises in the Americas emerged within an Atlantic and broader European framework, with ideas about the New World travelling between the New World, England, and her European neighbours.[35]

The influence of various other colonising nations fluctuated across the sixteenth century, but it was the experiences of the Spanish, the French, and the Portuguese that influenced English approaches to overseas expansion in America most explicitly.[36] Early Portuguese and French experiences in the New World served as important points of reference for many early proponents of English colonial activity. French ventures in North America, in particular, became important blueprints for English endeavours to settle Virginia in the 1580s. Translations of French travel narratives provided English readers with crucial information on the kinds of resources that could be found in North America and suggested how European bodies might respond to this new environment. French experiences in Canada had proven that European bodies could survive in North America and that the Indigenous peoples of the region were largely tractable and easily brought to European standards of civility, spurring English advocates of colonisation onwards in their attempts to settle in more southerly regions of the North American continent.

While French experiences has demonstrated that the English focus on North America was expedient, the influence of Spanish conquest and colonisation in the Americas was far more fraught. England's relationship with Spain in the sixteenth century was complex, changing dramatically across the century. In the wake of the Dutch Revolt, the Armada, and the ensuing Anglo-Spanish war, the relationship between the English and the Spanish deteriorated significantly which in turn impacted how English explorers and colonisers engaged with Spanish models of New World imperialism.[37] This book traces these changing English attitudes towards Spanish imperialism over the course of the sixteenth century, from one of admiration and imitation in the 1550s, to one of criticism and opposition in the 1580s. The transplantation of Spanish ideas about America were therefore anything but straightforward. At points in the sixteenth century, English writers advocated emulation, while at others the Spanish model of imperialism was condemned and derided.[38] Spanish attitudes towards America were not easily subsumed into English ones. While English advocates of overseas expansion undoubtedly looked towards the Spanish for information, this information was often critically received and used as a tool to compare the morally upright, if economically less impressive, approach of the English, with the avaricious and violent conquest conducted by the Spanish.

The cultural apparatus of sixteenth-century England

This book also offers new insights into the various domestic dimensions of early modern England that shaped approaches to New World exploration and colonisation. These English voyages of discovery, failure, and adaptation played out in print and were constructed around the vacillating social and cultural concerns of the era. The sixteenth century was a period of immense cultural and social change in England. The century was characterised by religious dispute, growing international hostility, economic downturn, particularly in the English cloth trade, and a sustained English anxiety surrounding their ability to compete with other European nations on a global stage. These domestic concerns shaped English responses to America and coloured the various approaches taken to English projects and ventures in the New World. As the following chapters illustrate, a variety of societal forces shaped English expeditions in the Americas, influencing how trade and settlement should be conducted and how American peoples and lands should be firstly understood and secondly incorporated into English explorative and colonial schemes.

The interaction between English voyages of exploration and the domestic conditions that shaped their development has garnered considerable attention from historians. Recent scholarship has explored a range of issues in relation to the impact that English exploration and colonisation in the New World had on English society and culture in the late sixteenth and seventeenth centuries. This research has demonstrated that English colonisation in Virginia had a profound impact on English political life, especially notions of commonwealth; that accounts of New World projects were part of a broader domestic conception of English nationhood; that English travel writing participated in contemporary domestic debates, whether surrounding fears of religious toleration and persecution, or the protection of individual liberty; and that New World travel and imperialism transformed the tastes and social lives of English statesmen, and in turn their political fortunes.[39] Working in the other direction, a number of scholars have recently highlighted how political and intellectual changes taking place in England shaped the development of English overseas colonies. Humanist thought, notions of providential power, and fluctuating approaches to political thought have all been shown to have impacted the development of the British Empire.[40] While this rich scholarship has identified the two-way relationship between American colonisation and English and British political identities, it has not analysed other critical domestic societal forces that were at play in English understandings of the New World.

Moving beyond the influence of political thought and the history of ideas, this book demonstrates that a variety of cultural apparatus was employed by those Englishmen who were either interested in, or involved with, exploration and colonisation in the Americas during the sixteenth century.[41] English understandings of the body, human diversity, the history of the British Isles, correct religious observation, and contemporary worries over the moral decay of civilisation were all collected together and redeployed in the context of English colonial activity in the Americas. This complex composite of cultural influences, based around distinctly English interpretations of wider European conceptual frameworks, was employed both consciously and unconsciously by English writers and explorers. While some English representations of America were undoubtedly motivated by a need to justify English territorial expansion, others were more unconscious reflections of the precarious economic situation of sixteenth-century England and contemporary anxieties related to religious reform and moral conduct. Whether consciously or unconsciously articulated, it is clear that English attitudes towards America were very much a product of sixteenth-century English culture.

Not only was this cultural apparatus varied, it also fluctuated across the sixteenth century. Just as England experienced volatile relationships with her European neighbours, the country was also embroiled in a number of domestic difficulties across the sixteenth century that would go on to reshape how the English engaged with the New World. Changing domestic religious practice collided with English experience in America, influencing how the pursuit of profit in the New World was conceptualised and moving the English towards an increasingly distinct form of colonialism across the sixteenth century. While Catholicism remained the religion of the realm, English commentators could happily advocate an imperial model that sought to bolster Spanish processes of conquest and conversion in the New World. With the establishment of the Church of England, and with Elizabeth I's tacit support for the Dutch rebels against their Spanish rulers, godly-minded advocates of expansion called for an approach that differed significantly to their Spanish rivals. Domestic economic concerns also infiltrated English accounts of America. Merchants whose trade with other parts of the Eurasian continent, most notably Muscovy, had contracted in the sixteenth century looked increasingly westwards for new economic opportunities. Likewise, as the English cloth trade dwindled, and as levels of poverty spiralled out of control, the notion that America was home to an Indigenous population who would become vociferous consumers of English wares was articulated time and again. The new lands across the Atlantic were increasingly viewed as the answer to England's economic and social ills. Those suffering poverty in England could be put to productive work in the New World, producing commodities to be traded with the Indigenous communities of North America.

Sources

English Americana of the sixteenth century, which is the focus of this research, is comprised of a relatively broad spectrum of genres, from cosmographies and histories, to texts aimed at promoting English New World projects to investors and potential future colonists back home, to travel narratives penned by inquisitive explorers and merchants. These examples of 'public writing' about the Americas appeared in both printed and manuscript form and represent invaluable sites where rhetoric, intertextual influences, and cultural and social priorities intersect.[42] These works were produced in order to be consumed by a relatively large number of individuals, and were more often than not created to spread ideas and opinions about the Americas and England's plans to exploit the region. The study of this material offers a unique insight into the ways in which English explorers, translators, and editors consciously chose to present America, and the cultural, political, and religious forces that implicitly influenced and shaped English responses to the new lands across the Atlantic.

The role of print in the dissemination of ideas about foreign lands, and its use in promoting overseas expansion is, of course, well established. As this rich scholarship has demonstrated, printed texts played an active role in generating England's entry into New World exploration and settlement.[43] Printed material did not merely *reflect* how English projects in America were developing, it was crucial for *provoking* these developments. Printed works were the means by which English advocates of overseas expansion not only encouraged their fellow countrymen to get involved, but also spread the notion of an English territorial claim to North America across the European continent. For example, the 1590 edition of Thomas Harriot's account of English plans for Virginia, published by the Frankfurt-based printer and engraver Theodore de Bry, was produced in part to remind European readers that the English claim to these lands was legitimate. As well as allowing for a wide dissemination of English claims to North American lands, the printed word also ensured that negative accounts of certain English projects that had circulated in manuscript form could be quashed and replaced with the permanency of more positive printed reports. This is clear to see, for example, in the documentary material relating to the Roanoke Colony. In 1588 Thomas Harriot published his *Briefe and True Report of Virginia* as an answer to malicious reports about the colony's fortunes. Although we know that the colony had been abandoned and the whole affair had been rather disastrous, Harriot's printed account told a different story, a story that was to encourage continued attempts to settle in Virginia for decades to come.

In the early modern period printed texts also increasingly conferred a level of authority that was not necessarily present in manuscripts. This was also true for texts detailing explorations and voyages in the Americas. As Margaret Small has recently argued, Richard Hakluyt revered the authority of the printed book and sought, therefore, to produce faithful renditions of the eye-witness testimony he translated, even if it meant presenting information that appeared contradictory to what he had written previously.[44] The proliferation of English printed texts that claimed to present 'truthful' accounts of the New World points to the fact that those commenting on America harnessed the power of print in a bid to make their narratives and ideas for exploration and colonisation more plausible. Perhaps most importantly, it was the increase of English-penned and translated travel narratives that provided the environment in which the English trial-and-error approach to overseas expansion could flourish. Information that could only be accessed via the printed word, such as that derived from travel accounts written by French and Spanish explorers and colonisers, allowed English advocates of expansion to assess the successes and failures of previous voyages and to suggest correctives for future English plans. Without the public circulation of both printed and manuscript sources, it is likely that English projects in the New World would have continued to flounder. Texts aimed at a wider public helped shape English approaches to America and ensured that adaptation, dynamism, and reassessment would become the hallmarks of English activity in the Americas.

This study uses a combination of translated continental European works alongside English-penned travel accounts from the sixteenth century. The majority of these sources will be familiar to scholars interested in both English and European colonialism, but the use of these disparate sources in tandem will offer new insights into early printed English encounters with the Americas, highlighting earlier European influences on English thinkers and examining divergences between English texts and those written by authors from other nations equally eager to establish New World colonies. These sixteenth-century sources are undoubtedly remarkable in their content, providing genuine insights into early English views of America and English plans for exploration and colonisation. They are, however, limited in number, especially when compared to the plethora of books that appeared in England with American themes in the seventeenth century.[45] While the English population in general may not have been particularly interested in the discoveries made across the Atlantic in 1492, a small, yet highly influential group of men, including Richard Eden, Humphrey Gilbert, Walter Ralegh, and Richard Hakluyt, were nonetheless committed to promoting America and potential future English colonies to their readers throughout the sixteenth century. Despite the limited number of texts dealing with America in sixteenth-century England, and despite the fact that these texts were increasingly produced by a close circle of interconnected interested parties, they nevertheless had a profound effect on the way in which English understandings of America developed well into the seventeenth century.

Structure

Throughout the book, English approaches to the New World are traced in relation to the main cultural influences that helped shape them. These influences range from the everyday to the profound, the domestic to the international, and the religious to the economic. Continuities and changes in English understandings of the New World are charted within each chapter to highlight the effects of domestic social, cultural, economic and religious change, and fluctuating intra-European political dynamics on specific English ventures in the Americas. Chapter 1 analyses how a range of European conceptual frameworks were put to work in the context of English exploration and attempted settlement in the New World. By examining English uses of theories of American origins, ideas of monstrosity and foreign 'others', and early modern understandings of climatology, the chapter demonstrates that English commentators and explorers expertly manipulated and adapted these intellectual frameworks to meet a range of discursive demands. Challenging the notion of a monolithic early modern mind that was ill equipped to deal with the radical difference of America, this chapter instead contends that Old World frameworks of knowledge were concsiously employed and adapted by English writers to justify their explorative and colonial approaches to the New World. In doing so, I argue that English explorers and writers viewed the new American lands selectively, seeing not what was really there, but what was most advantageous to the political, economic, cultural, and colonial aims of the viewer. This type of 'selective appopriation', which was grounded in both a shared European and distinctly English cultural heritage, shaped early English understandings of the New World and helped define and validate sixteenth-century English colonial decisions.

Chapter 2 moves beyond English theories about exploration and settlement in America to explore the very real challenges faced by those who undertook ventures to the New World in the sixteenth century. The chapter examines how English advocates of overseas expansion dealt with the various failures and setbacks that characterised sixteenth-century English projects in America, tracing the interplay between religious and economic motivations for overseas expansion across the century. In particular, the chapter highlights the tension in English travel and colonial literature between the desire to seek wealth and riches in the New World and the need to advance the glory of God, demonstrating how and why at certain points across the sixteenth century, either religious or economic motivations were emphasised. In tracing this complex relationship between the religious and the economic, the chapter argues that by the end of the sixteenth century, and in response to the failures that had characterised English activity in America, the two had been successfully combined, with financial gain in the Americas being interpreted as a reward from God. This blending of commercial incentives and pious intentions would remain indicative of how the English undertook colonial projects in the New World throughout the seventeenth century.

Just as English conceptions of religiously inspired settlement were bound up with the economic dimensions of overseas expansion, so too were English ideas relating to day-to-day culture. Chapters 3 and 4 focus on the everyday practices of dressing and eating and their role in shaping early English approaches to the New World. Unlike other daily pursuits, such as religious devotions and sociable activities, dressing and eating are referred to time and again in the literature from the sixteenth century. It was these particular daily activities that preoccupied English explorers and writers in the period before permanent English settlement in the Americas. As this book will demonstrate, this was in part due to the fact that eating and dressing had broader implications for English conceptions of the body, climate, cultural difference, and economic potential, ideas that in turn impacted English projects in the New World significantly. These chapters, then, not only stake a claim to the embodied nature of early colonisation but also argue that cultural markers of dress and diet played a significant role in shaping English responses to Indigenous peoples and approaches to exploration and settlement. English perceptions of clothing and diet, whether European or Indigenous, shaped where English explorers, merchants, and colonisers should place their focus; they encouraged investment, both from merchants and gentlemen more interested in establishing English colonies; and they informed understandings of Indigenous peoples and how successfully they could be manipulated and controlled by the English. Chapter 3 focuses on the significance of clothing for early English enterprises in America, arguing that English beliefs surrounding clothing and appearance validated and justified a range of English projects in the New World, both intellectually and commercially. Descriptions of Indigenous clothing and nakedness in English print varied throughout the sixteenth century and performed a variety of functions, from shaping English approaches to trade and colonisation in the New World, to informing and framing moral and religious debates taking place back home. Chapter 4 also argues that corporeality was vital to the formation and dissemination of English representations of America, this time through an investigation into the role played by diet in English overseas projects. Eating and the effect of food on the body became, when placed in an American context, indicative of successful and profitable ventures or unsuccessful and troublesome ones. English ideas about the human body and how it functioned in different environments were integral to the encounter between England and America. This bodily discourse allowed for the defence of failed attempts at settlement, the celebration of English explorative and colonial projects as providential, and for the establishment of a set of beliefs about the American environment that had ideas about food and the body at its centre.

This book provides a crucial chapter in the larger history of the development of the British Empire. It reminds us that the march of British imperialism was by no means inevitable, nor exceptional. The emergence of English overseas colonies in the Americas was the result of a century-long engagement with the imperial practices of other European nations, and was the consequence of a dynamic and adaptive approach to exploration and settlement that was often born from previous failure.

Notes

1 Gerald A. Danzer et al. eds., *The Americans: Reconstruction to the 21st Century* (Sacramento, CA: McDougal Littell, 2006), 21; Joyce Appleby et al. eds., *The American Vision* (New York: McGraw Hill Education, 2001), 102–103; Paul S. Boyer et al., eds., *The Enduring Vision: A History of the American People* (Boston, MA and New York: Houghton Mifflin Company, 2006), 29–30.

2 Studies that have neglected the sixteenth-century English approach to America include: Jack P. Greene, *Pursuits of Happiness: The Social Development of Early Modern British Colonies and the Formation of American Colonies* (Chapel Hill and London: University of North Carolina Press, 1988); W. W. Abbot, *The Colonial Origins of the United States, 1607–1763* (New York: Wiley, 1975); Warren M. Billings, *Jamestown and The Founding of the Nation* (Gettysburg, PA: Thomas Publications, 1990); L. H. Roper, *The English Empire in America, 1602–1658: Beyond Jamestown* (London: Pickering & Chatto, 2009).

3 Works that have set about recovering Indigenous voices through colonial era texts include: Inga Clendinnen, *Ambivalent Conquests: Maya and Spaniard in Yucatan, 1517–1570* (Cambridge: Cambridge University Press, 2003); Caroline Dodds Pennock, *Bonds of Blood: Gender, Lifecycle, and Sacrifice in Aztec Culture* (Basingstoke: Palgrave Macmillan, 2008); Camilla Townsend, "Burying the White Gods: New Perspectives on the Conquest of Mexico," *The American Historical Review* 10, no. 3 (June, 2003): 659–687; Neil Whitehead, "The Discoverie as Ethnological Text," in *The Discoverie of the Large, Rich and Bewtiful Empyre of Guiana*, ed. Neil Whitehead (Manchester: Manchester University Press, 1997), 60–116.

4 The term 'representational machine' is used here to reflect the fact that representations of Indigenous peoples in English print were analytical tools used by English writers to help readers make sense of the New World and to help push forward their visions for overseas expansion and colonisation. For more on this term and its uses see Stephen Greenblatt, *Marvellous Possessions: The Wonder*

of the New World (Oxford: Clarendon, 1991), 4; Surekha Davies, *Renaissance Ethnography and the Invention of the Human* (Cambridge: Cambridge University Press, 2016), 4.
5 This chosen terminology is based on the findings of a study by Michael Yellow Bird. This terminology aims to be respectful towards Indigenous people, while also reflecting the realities of early English representations of New World peoples which were largely homogenising, culturally and geographically non-specific, and often highly pejorative. As well as using ethnic affiliations and the term 'Indigenous people' where possible, the term 'American' (as well as other European names applied to various geographic regions of the continent) is used on occasion as a way of making the location of a particular geographic space in which Indigenous people lived clear to the reader. Occasionally, the term 'Indian' is used in quotation marks to reflect sixteenth-century English terminology. When offensive or inappropriate terms are used to reflect early English attitudes towards Indigenous people, they are given in quotation marks (e.g. 'savage' or 'heathen') or the prose makes it clear that this is a sixteenth-century English viewpoint. For more information on ethnic identity labels see Michael Yellow Bird, "What We Want to Be Called: Indigenous Peoples' Perspectives on Racial and Ethnic Identity Labels," *American Indian Quarterly* 23, no. 2 (Spring, 1999): 1–21; Gregory Younging, *Elements of Indigenous Style: A Guide for Writing By and About Indigenous People* (Edmonton, Alberta: Brush Education, 2018).
6 For recent Atlantic scholarship see Robert Appelbaum and John Wood Sweet, eds., *Envisioning an English Empire: Jamestown and the Making of the North Atlantic World* (Philadelphia: University of Pennsylvania Press, 2005); David Armitage and Michael J. Braddick, eds., *The British Atlantic World, 1500–1800* (Basingstoke: Palgrave Macmillan, 2009); Judith A. Carney and Richard Nicholas Rosomoff, *In the Shadow of Slavery: Africa's Botanical Legacy in the Atlantic World* (Berkeley: University of California Press, 2009); Carla Gardina Pestana, *Protestant Empire: Religion and the Making of the British Atlantic World* (Philadelphia: University of Pennsylvania Press, 2009); María Elena Martínez, *Genealogical Fictions: Limpieza de Sangre, Religion, and Gender in Colonial Mexico* (Stanford: Stanford University Press, 2008); John Thornton, *Africa and Africans in the Making of the Atlantic World, 1400–1800* (Cambridge: Cambridge University Press, 1998).
7 For a detailed and expansive critique of Atlantic history see Jack P. Greene and Philip D. Morgan, eds., *Atlantic History: A Critical Appraisal* (Oxford: Oxford University Press, 2009).
8 The idea of American history as a 'tangled web' is taken from Pekka Hämäläinen and Samuel Truett, "On Borderlands," *The Journal of American History* 98, no. 2 (September, 2011): 361. For recent borderlands scholarship focused on the Americas see Andrew K. Frank and A. Glenn Crothers, eds., *Borderland Narratives: Negotiation and Accommodation in North America's Contested Spaces, 1500–1850* (Gainesville: University Press of Florida, 2017); Alan Taylor, *The Divided Ground: Indians, Settlers, and the Northern Borderland of the American Revolution* (New York: Routledge, 2001); Jean O'Brien, *Dispossession*

by Degrees: Indian Land and Identity in Natick, Massachusetts, 1650–1790 (Cambridge: Cambridge University Press, 1997); Daniel K. Richter, *Facing East from Indian Country: A Native History of Early America* (Cambridge, MA: Harvard University Press, 2001); Kathleen DuVal, "Indian Intermarriage and Métissage in Colonial Louisiana," *William and Mary Quarterly* 65, no. 2 (April 2008): 267–304; Ramon A. Gutiérrez, *When Jesus Came, the Corn Mothers Went Away: Marriage, Sexuality, and Power in New Mexico, 1500–1846* (Stanford: Stanford University Press, 1991).
 9 Jorge Cañizares-Esguerra, "Entangled Histories: Borderland Historiographies in New Clothes?" *The American Historical Review* 112, no. 3 (June, 2007): 787–799.
10 Jorge Cañizares-Esguerra, "Introduction," in *Entangled Empires: The Anglo-Iberian Atlantic, 1500–1830*, ed. Jorge Cañizares-Esguerra (Philadelphia: University of Pennsylvania Press, 2018), 1–15; Jorge Cañizares-Esguerra, *Puritan Conquistadors: Iberianizing the Atlantic, 1550–1700* (Stanford: Stanford University Press, 2006).
11 Eliga H. Gould, "Entangled Atlantic Histories: A Response from the Anglo-American Periphery," *The American Historical Review* 112, no. 5 (December, 2007): 1415–1422.
12 For studies on individual projects and key individuals see Peter C. Mancall, *Hakluyt's Promise: An Elizabethan's Obsession for an English America* (New Haven, CT: Yale University Press, 2007); Shannon Miller, *Invested With Meaning: The Raleigh Circle in the New World* (Philadelphia: University of Pennsylvania Press, 1998); Harry Kelsey, *Sir John Hawkins: Queen Elizabeth's Slave Trader* (New Haven, CT and London: Yale University Press, 2003); Rachel Lloyd, *Elizabethan Adventurer: A Life of Captain Christopher Carleill* (London: Hamish Hamilton Ltd., 1974); James McDermott, ed., *The Third Voyage of Martin Frobisher to Baffin Island, 1578* (London: The Hakluyt Society, 2001); James McDermott, *Martin Frobisher: Elizabethan Privateer* (New Haven, CT and London: Yale University Press, 2001); Robert McGhee, *The Arctic Voyages of Martin Frobisher: An Elizabethan Adventure* (London: British Museum Press, 2001); David B. Quinn, *Set Fair for Roanoke: Voyages and Colonies, 1584–1606* (Chapel Hill and London: University of North Carolina Press, 1985).
13 This is particularly evident in Karen Kupperman's work on early Anglo-America. Kupperman does utilise various sources from the sixteenth century in her analysis, but these tend to be used alongside sources from the seventeenth century to make similar points. For example, in a chapter examining the ways in which English explorers and colonisers 'read' Indian bodies, Kupperman moves seamlessly between examples taken from the writings of David Ingram from the late sixteenth century, to ones written by William Wood during the Pequot War in 1636–37. Kupperman's analysis therefore leaves little room for assessing the difference in representations that can be identified across the sixteenth century; Karen Ordahl Kupperman, *Indians and English: Facing Off in Early America* (Ithaca, NY and London: Cornell University Press, 2000), 47–48. A similar approach to source material can be found in Bernard Sheehan,

Savagism & Civility: Indians and Englishmen in Colonial Virginia (Cambridge: Cambridge University Press, 1980). Indeed, Catherine Armstrong has gone as far as to define the explorations of the English in the sixteenth century as the 'pre-history of English involvement in North America'. Armstrong uses this phrase in the abstract to her PhD thesis; Catherine Armstrong, "Representations of American 'Place' and 'Potential' in English Travel Literature, 1607–1660," PhD Thesis (University of Warwick, 2004), 8. Even though this phrase does not appear in the monograph related to this earlier research, the Elizabethan voyages to America are still condensed into a short chapter of the book entitled 'Prologue', suggesting that the sixteenth-century English experience in America is not central to Armstrong's understanding of the development of the early English colonies; Catherine Armstrong, *Writing North America in the Seventeenth Century: English Representations in Print and Manuscript* (Farnham: Ashgate, 2007), 1–15.
14 Joyce E. Chaplin, *Subject Matter: Technology, the Body, and Science on the Anglo-American Frontier, 1500–1676* (Cambridge, MA and London: Harvard University Press, 2001), 9–21.
15 Andrew Fitzmaurice, *Humanism and America: An Intellectual History of English Colonisation, 1500–1625* (Cambridge: Cambridge University Press, 2003); Mary C. Fuller, *Voyages in Print: English Travel to America, 1576–1624* (Cambridge: Cambridge University Press, 1995).
16 Karen Ordahl Kupperman, *The Jamestown Project* (Cambridge, MA: Harvard University Press, 2007).
17 For a detailed discussion of the Cabot voyages see David B. Quinn, *England and the Discovery of America, 1481–1620* (London: Allen & Unwin, 1974), 93–159.
18 Ibid., 160–191.
19 Peter Martyr, *The Decades of the Newe Worlde or West India*, trans. Richard Eden (London, 1555); Sebastian Münster, *A Treatyse of the Newe India With Other New Founde Landes and Islandes*, trans. Richard Eden (London, 1553).
20 John Hawkins, *A True Declaration of the Troublesome Voyadge of M. John Haukins to the Parties of Guynea and the West Indies* (London, 1569).
21 Fitzmaurice, *Humanism and America*, 33.
22 Jean Ribault, *The Whole and True Discoverye of Terra Florida*, trans. Thomas Hacket (London, 1563).
23 Nicolas Le Challeux, *A True and Perfect Description, of the Last Voyage or Navigation, Attempted by Capitaine John Rybaut* (London, 1566).
24 André Thevet, *The New Found Worlde, or Antarctike*, trans. Thomas Hacket (London, 1568).
25 Dionyse Settle, *A True Reporte of the Laste Voyage into the West and Northwest Regions, &c. 1577* (London, 1577).
26 Jacques Cartier, *A Shorte and Briefe Narration of the Two Navigations and Discoveries to the Northweast Partes called Newe Fraunce* (London, 1580).
27 George Peckham, *A True Reporte, of the Late Discoveries, and Possession, Taken in the Right of the Crowne of Englande* (London, 1583); Christopher

Carleill, *A Breef and Sommarie Discourse Upon the Entended Voyage to the Hethermoste Partes of America* (London, 1583).
28 Thomas Harriot, *A Briefe and True Report of the New Found Land of Virginia* (London, 1588).
29 Richard Hakluyt, ed., *The Principal Navigations, Voyages, Traffiques and Discoveries of the English Nation* (London, 1589); Richard Hakluyt, ed., *The Principal Navigations, Voyages, Traffiques and Discoveries of the English Nation* (London, 1598–1600). Unless expressly stated, further citations for this text will relate to the 1598–1600 edition.
30 Comparative approaches to colonial history have analysed the similarities and divergences between different colonial nations, yet they have not focused on the reciprocal influences between competing nations. J. H. Elliott, *Empires of the Atlantic World: Britain and Spain in America, 1492–1830* (New Haven, CT and London: Yale University Press, 2006); Anthony Pagden, *Lords of All the World: Ideologies of Empires in Spain, Britain and France, c. 1500–c. 1800* (New Haven, CT and London: Yale University Press, 1995); Gordon M. Sayre, *Les Sauvages Américains: Representations of Native Americans in French and English Colonial Literature* (Chapel Hill and London: University of North Carolina Press, 1997).
31 David B. Quinn, *Raleigh and the British Empire* (London: Hodder and Stoughton, 1947); David B. Quinn, *The Roanoke Voyages, 1584–90* (London: The Hakluyt Society, 1955); Nicholas Canny, *Kingdom and Colony: Ireland in the Atlantic World, 1560–1800* (Baltimore, MD and London: Johns Hopkins University Press, 1988); John Patrick Montaño, *The Roots of English Colonialism in Ireland* (Cambridge: Cambridge University Press, 2016).
32 Nicholas Canny, *The Elizabethan Conquest of Ireland: A Pattern Established, 1565–76* (New York: Barnes and Noble, 1976), 45–65.
33 Alongside this recognition of continental European influence, more recent scholarship, including the work of David Armitage, has emphasised the importance of classical works for both Irish and American patterns of colonisation. See David Armitage, *The Ideological Origins of the British Empire* (Cambridge: Cambridge University Press, 2000).
34 Andrew Hadfield, "Irish Colonies and the Americas," in *Envisioning an English Empire: Jamestown and the Making of the North Atlantic World*, eds. Robert Appelbaum and John Wood Sweet (Philadelphia: University of Pennsylvania Press, 2005), 172–191.
35 For scholarship on trans-Atlantic and intra-European influences on English approaches to colonisation see María Fernanda Valencia Suárez, "The Aztecs Through the Lens of English Imperial Aspiration, 1519–1713," PhD Thesis (University of Cambridge, 2010); Gesa Mackenthun, *Metaphors of Dispossession: American Beginnings and the Translation of Empire, 1492–1637* (Norman, OK and London: University of Oklahoma Press, 1997); Jonathan Hart, *Representing the New World: The English and French Uses of the Example of Spain* (Basingstoke: Palgrave, 2001); Cañizares-Esguerra, "Introduction," 1–15; Cañizares-Esguerra, *Puritan Conquistadors*. For additional scholarship see Introduction, note 6.

36 Alison Games has traced English colonial and economic aspirations across the globe to highlight how the British Empire came to pre-eminence. In contrast, this book examines the cultural influences of England's colonial rivals and the changing nature of English society during the sixteenth century, rather than the experiences of English explorers and traders in other parts of the world. Alison Games, *The Web of Empire: English Cosmopolitans in an Age of Expansion, 1560–1660* (Oxford: Oxford University Press, 2008).

37 For a detailed analysis of Elizabethan foreign policy see W. T. MacCaffrey, *Elizabeth I: War and Politics*, 1588–1603 (Princeton, NJ: Princeton University Press, 1992); R. B. Wernham, *The Making of Elizabethan Foreign Policy*, 1558–1603 (Berkeley: University of California Press, 1980).

38 This interpretation is in stark contrast to that set out by Gesa Mackenthun. Mackenthun argues that Spain remained an important ideological and political reference point for English ventures in both North America and the Caribbean, shaping English responses and methods of colonial justification despite increased political animosity. Jorge Cañizares-Esguerra has also argued that the colonial history of Spain and England are deeply entwined and that Iberian America was 'normative' and helped English explorers define their own projects. Like Mackenthun's work, Cañizares-Esguerra's scholarship does not explore the aggressive recalibration of Spanish imperialism by English commentators in the sixteenth century. The work of Jonathan Hart has challenged this interpretation to a certain extent, arguing that both English and French attitudes towards Spain were ambivalent throughout the sixteenth century. Yet Hart also suggests that Spain nonetheless remained an important exemplar for New World exploration and settlement. See Mackenthun, *Metaphors of Dispossession*; Hart, *Representing the New World*; Cañizares-Esguerra, "Introduction," 1–15; Cañizares-Esguerra, *Puritan Conquistadors*.

39 Misha Odessa Ewen, "'To a Foundation of a Common-Wealth': English Society and the Colonisation of Virginia, c. 1607–1642," PhD Thesis (University College London, 2017); Richard Helgerson, *Forms of Nationhood: The Elizabethan Writing of England* (Chicago: University of Chicago Press, 1992); Andrew Hadfield, *Literature Travel and Colonial Writing in the English Renaissance* (Oxford: Oxford University Press, 1998); Lauren Working, *The Making of an Imperial Polity: Civility and America in the Jacobean Metropolis* (Cambridge: Cambridge University Press, 2019).

40 Fitzmaurice, *Humanism and America*; Alexander B. Haskell, *For God, King, and People: Forging Commonwealth Bonds in Renaissance Virginia* (Chapel Hill: University of North Carolina Press, 2017); Armitage, *Ideological Origins*.

41 An exception to this political focus is Malcolm Gaskill's work, although it is largely focused on the seventeenth century: Malcolm Gaskill, *Between Two Worlds: How the English Became Americans* (Oxford: Oxford University Press, 2014). Likewise, Shannon Miller has examined how economic considerations influenced the American projects of Walter Ralegh: Miller, *Invested with Meaning*.

42 This book will utilise Catherine Armstrong's definition of 'public writing' i.e. a document that was 'intended for consumption by a large number of individuals

in order to spread information and opinion'. This definition could therefore include texts aimed at a general reading public or ones aimed at particular groups of individuals. Armstrong, *Writing North America*, 21. This study is also predicated on the notion that early modern travel narratives and promotional texts offer a valuable insight into the workings of early modern culture and its textual imprint. For this reason, this research is indebted to the school of New Historicism in one key respect; the movement's suggestion that culture was in fact text opened up a vast array of marginalised sources for detailed literary criticism. New Historicist scholarship on travel narratives includes Greenblatt, *Marvellous Possessions*; Fuller, *Voyages in Print*; Peter Hulme, *Colonial Encounters: Europe and the Native Caribbean, 1492–1797* (London and New York: Routledge, 1992); Jeffrey Knapp, *An Empire Nowhere: England, America, and Literature from Utopia to The Tempest* (Berkeley: University of California Press, 1992); Louis Montrose, "The Work of Gender in the Discourse of Discovery," in *New World Encounters*, ed. Stephen Greenblatt (Berkeley: University of California Press, 1993), 177–217.

43 For scholarship on the power of print in English colonial thought see Fuller, *Voyages in Print*; Francisco J. Borge, *A New World for a New Nation: The Promotion of America in Early Modern England* (Oxford: Peter Lang, 2007); Michael G. Brennan, "The Literature of Travel," in *The Cambridge History of the Book in Britain*, vol. 4: *1557–1695*, eds. John Barnard and D. F. McKenzie (Cambridge: Cambridge University Press, 2002), 246–273; Daniel Carey and Claire Jowitt, eds., *Richard Hakluyt and Travel Writing in Early Modern Europe* (Farnham: Ashgate, 2012).

44 Margaret Small, "A World Seen Through Another's Eyes: Hakluyt, Ramusio, and the Narratives of the *Navigationi et Viaggi*," in *Richard Hakluyt and Travel Writing in Early Modern Europe*, eds. Daniel Carey and Claire Jowitt (Farnham: Ashgate, 2012), 49.

45 Richard C. Simmons, "Americana in British Books, 1621–1760," in *America in European Consciousness, 1493–1750*, ed. Karen Ordahl Kupperman (Chapel Hill and London: University of North Carolina Press, 1995), 365.

1

Understanding America: The theoretical origins of English colonialism

Tuesday, October 23rd / I wished to-day to set out for the island of Cuba, which I believe must be Cipangu [Japan], according to the indications which these people give me concerning its size and riches.[1]
– Christopher Columbus

With these words from his journal of 1492, Christopher Columbus, the Genoese merchant sailor and somewhat reluctant 'discoverer' of America, made a geographical mistake that he was to repeat consistently until his death. Columbus was convinced that the land he had sailed to in 1492 was not a newly discovered world, but instead the eastern extremities of the Asiatic continent. Columbus's unwavering belief was the product of his understanding of the size of the world, the distance between Europe and Asia, and the proportion of land to sea. Columbus's assumptions were based on his interpretation of Aristotelian and biblical explanations of the earth's formation and on the findings of earlier explorative expeditions such as those of Marco Polo.[2] European perceptions of the new lands across the Atlantic, as illustrated by Columbus, were thus often informed and coloured by European knowledge and Old World tradition. When European eyes gazed upon America, they saw what they expected to see. As J. H. Elliott famously put it, for these explorers, tradition, experience, and expectation were their 'determinates of vision'.[3] This did not mean, however, that this process of viewing, in which expectation and experience were key, was in any way passive or subconscious in nature. Europeans expertly manipulated, adapted, and selectively appropriated a number of intellectual frameworks to make sense of the radical difference of America, and to justify their colonial decisions and responses to Indigenous peoples. By examining the European use of theories of American origins, the discourse of monstrous races, and classical climate theory, in an American context, it becomes clear that ideas about the New World circulated internationally, being adapted and manipulated to serve the particular needs of those employing them. For Spanish *conquistadores* of the early sixteenth century, for example, monstrosity was used to highlight American alterity and exoticism, while for the English it was used to establish political authority and colonial validity. Theories of American origins were used by the Spanish to legitimise their colonial approach to the New World, in which conversion of rational Indigenous people was imperative, whereas for the English, hypotheses about exactly where Indigenous Americans had come from were used to illustrate ancient English ties to the New World and the likelihood of finding a Northwest Passage to Asia. Although a shared European cultural heritage informed many European responses to America, creating the theoretical tools of empire, the ways in which it was employed differed radically. English explorers, authors, translators, and editors borrowed information from their continental European neighbours and adapted it to suit their own needs. The ways in which the English engaged with America and legitimised their own specific approach to settlement and colonisation is the focus of what follows.

The impact of European knowledge, tradition, and experience on the reception of America into early modern European thought has been dominant in the scholarship to date and yet it has tended to portray this European inability to recognise the uniqueness of America as a product of an inflexible and monolithic early modern mind. Lynn Ramey and Margaret Hodgen, for example, have both suggested that early accounts of America were heavily influenced by classical and medieval models of ethnography and fantasy, colouring and distorting the ways in which America was portrayed in the early decades after 'discovery'.[4] Anthony Pagden, in his pioneering work on the origins of comparative ethnology, has also argued that in the early years of European contact with the Americas there was a severe 'problem of recognition' and a strong belief that 'the new could always be satisfactorily described by means of some simple and direct analogy with the old'.[5] In contrast, I contend that Old World knowledge relating to human history, exotic peoples, and climate was consciously employed by English writers to justify their approaches to the New World, rather than being an unconscious reflection of their own incapability to recognise American difference.[6] Anthony Grafton has complicated this image of the inflexible European mind through his analysis of how the shock of the 'discovery' of the New World collided with the enduring power of Old World tradition. As he argues, despite the growing realisation that experience in the New World called into question the validity of hallowed classical texts on geography and natural history, these canonical texts nonetheless proved remarkably resilient, being adapted to incorporate the new knowledge discovered in the Americas.[7] This conscious adaptation of classical theory to meet the new demands of knowledge gained in the Americas became a crucial aspect of English colonial validation. By adapting classical theories on climate, for example, English explorers could promote certain regions of the New World by proving their habitability and fertility.

Old World understandings of both natural and human history were not only utilised to contain the American lands within the bounds of European experience, they were also used to define what European experience in America could and should look like. A number of studies have begun to unpack how some of these conceptual frameworks were applied to the New World, illustrating the peaks in popularity of certain ideas, and the various ways they were employed by different colonising nations.[8] In what follows, I show how traditional European frameworks of religion, natural history, and culture were transformed to meet the needs of England's burgeoning overseas identity. By utilising Old World ideas relating to monstrosity, human diversity, and climate, English writers, explorers, and colonists created a set of tools of empire that could successfully justify and shape their approach to the New World. In adapting European theories that were first applied to the new American lands by Spanish, Portuguese, and French writers and explorers, the men involved in early English colonial projects in America were able to legitimise their claims to territory in the New World, explain their increasingly positive assessment of Indigenous peoples, validate their decision to focus their colonial attention on the lands of North America, and convince potential investors and colonisers of the validity of their projects. In this way, then, Old World frameworks of understanding, rather than being restrictive, became flexible rhetorical tools that made America comprehensible and more importantly open to European manipulation. It was, therefore, not the innocent nor incapable eye, but 'the selective eye' that first viewed America, seeing not what was really there, but what was most advantageous to the political, economic, cultural, and colonial aims of different viewers.[9]

American origins and the legitimisation of empire

In 1520 the English printer, and sometime dramatist John Rastell, put down in print, in the form of a play, a question that was to puzzle Europeans for centuries. The play was composed soon after Rastell's own disastrous colonial venture that aimed to reach the New World.[10] In the play Rastell pondered the nature of the inhabitants of the strange new lands of America, describing how they 'lyve all bestly / For they nother know god nor the devell / Nor never harde tell of hevyn or hell / Wrytynge, nor other scripture'.[11] He also posed an intriguing question about the Indigenous populations of the New World; 'but howe the people furst began In that countrey or whens they cam', i.e. what were the origins of the Indigenous inhabitants of America?[12]

Rastell would not be the last to pose this question. The debate over where the peoples of the Americas had originated became a hot topic for many authors writing about the discoveries in the early decades of the sixteenth century. Unlike Rastell, however, who offered no theory of his own, preferring to leave such questions 'for clerkes', these other writers did propose a variety of theories that would connect the peoples of the New World to the history of the peoples of the Old World.[13] Once the newness of America had been accepted, and Columbus's consistent belief that he had in fact reached Asia had been shed, the recognition that the very existence of Indigenous people in the Americas posed a problem for early modern Europeans began to emerge.[14] In early sixteenth-century Europe Christians believed that all peoples were descended from Adam and Eve, and more specifically from the three sons of Noah: Ham, Shem, and Japhet.[15] To preserve the veracity of the biblical account of the dispersal of humankind, the Indigenous peoples of America had to be linked to the sons of Noah, and by extension, to the peoples of Europe, Africa, and Asia.

To date, the emergence of sixteenth-century European theories on American origins has been interpreted by scholars as being motivated by an urge to reconcile the scriptural account of the dispersal of humankind with the discovery of a continent filled with peoples previously unknown to the Old World. In this reading, then, the debate surrounding the origins of Indigenous Americans was in essence a theological one.[16] While this is undoubtedly true in some cases, it is also clear that Europeans manipulated theories of American origins to meet other political, economic, and colonial objectives. How this was achieved depended heavily on who was writing and for what reason. English responses to American origin theories, while undoubtedly shaped by Spanish views, were presented in a way that emphasised the particular concerns of late sixteenth-century English explorers and potential colonists. As we shall see, the English in particular harnessed these theories, not merely to prove the validity of the Bible, but to prove the validity of the English territorial claim to America and their belief in a Northwest Passage to Asia.[17] English theories of American origins thus reflect the process by which information regarding the new lands was circulated, digested, and transformed to meet specific English needs.

For English readers, their first exposure to theories regarding the origins of the Indigenous peoples of America came, as did much of the early information on the New World, through Richard Eden's 1555 translation of Peter Martyr's *Decades*. First published in its entirety in 1530 under its Latin title, *De Orbe Novo Decades*, Martyr's original lengthy text detailed the early Spanish discoveries and explorations of the New World.[18] Martyr had left his native Italy, in his own words, to 'collecte, these marvelyous and newe thynges, which shoulde otherwyse perhappes have line drowned in the whirlepoole of oblivion'.[19] He quickly rose through the ranks in Spain, becoming a member of the Council of the Indies and a trusted advisor of the Holy Roman Emperor, Charles V.[20] His comprehensive accounts of the early decades of Spanish contact with America proved popular, with subsequent abridged and partial editions of the text appearing in French in 1532, German in 1534, English in 1555, Dutch in 1563, and Italian in 1564.[21] Eden's 1555 edition, however, contained more than just his translation of Martyr's *Decades*. It also included abridged and greatly condensed versions of Francisco López de Gómara's *Historia General de las Indias* and Gonzalo Fernández de Oviedo's *La Historia General y Natural de las Indias*. Both Gómara and Oviedo were closely connected to events taking place in Spanish America, Gómara as secretary and chaplain to Hernán Cortés and Oviedo as a colonial administrator in Santo Domingo, with both later producing chronicles of the events that they had witnessed or heard tell of.[22] Because of the compiled nature of Eden's text, a number of theories relating to American origins were introduced, discussed, and, on occasion, discounted.

In the early years of European exploration in the Americas the methodological approach of writers who wished to deduce the origins of Indigenous American communities was essentially deductive and exegetical.[23] This was also the case for the theories presented in Eden's text. One of the earliest theories relating to the origins of the peoples of the New World was first expounded by Christopher Columbus and later relayed to European readers by Peter Martyr. This theory claimed that America, particularly the island of Hispaniola, was in fact the land of great riches that the biblical King Solomon had purportedly sailed to – the land of Ophir. It is clear from Columbus's own writings that the story of Ophir heavily influenced his engagement with America. Columbus invoked the salient passages from the Old Testament books of Kings and Chronicles dealing with Solomon's voyage in a number of texts, including in his letter to Ferdinand and Isabella from his fourth voyage to the New World in 1503.[24] In the letter, Columbus stated that, in his opinion, the mines that King Solomon had found in Ophir were identical to the mines that he had found in the New World. He concluded by suggesting that 'Jerusalem and Mount Sion are to be rebuilt by the hands of Christians', with the Christians in question being Columbus and the subjects of Spain.[25] Equating Hispaniola with Ophir was not only 'good public relations' as it gave credence to the idea that America, like Ophir, was filled with riches. It also highlighted Columbus's own personal piety and his belief that his discovery represented a providential event on the short road to the End of Days in which the rebuilding of the temple in Jerusalem was key.[26]

Peter Martyr in his retelling of the theory was, however, far from convinced. Martyr restated Columbus's belief that Hispaniola was in fact Ophir on multiple occasions, but he was unwilling to suggest whether or not this belief was true, stating that 'whether it bee soo or not, it lyeth not in me to judge, but in my opinion it is farre of'.[27] If the English readers of Eden's text were in any doubt about the validity of Columbus's claims they need only return to Eden's own preface to find a firm denunciation of this particular theory. In his address to the reader, although claiming in a somewhat similar fashion to Columbus that the Spanish had 'planted a newe Israell muche greater than that whiche Moises ledde throughe the red sea' in America, Eden argued that the fact remained that during the time of Solomon's voyages there was 'no knowlage of Antipodes' and 'neyther dydde any of his [Solomon's] shyppes sayle abowt the hole worlde'.[28] Eden found no evidence that the lands that Solomon had travelled to were in fact the lands of the New World. Eden even suggested that the Spanish explorations of America had actually exceeded Solomon's voyages in terms of wealth and territorial gain. As Eden informed his readers, in the tales of King Solomon we do not read 'that any of his shyppes were so laden with golde that they soonke, as dyd a shyppe of kynge Ferdinandos' and nor could Solomon's dominion that 'extended from the ryuer of Euphrates to the lande of the Philistians' be compared 'with the large Empire whiche the kynges of Spayne have in the west Indies'.[29] In Eden's opinion, then, America was not the Ophir of the Bible but a much more impressive region of the world that was home to far more riches and precious materials than even Solomon could have imagined.

For the English, who had no claim to the territories already taken by the Spanish in the Caribbean, connecting Hispaniola to King Solomon's fabled Ophir held little appeal. With the rejection of this theory in Eden's text, the idea of a clear biblical origin for the peoples of America appeared to wane in the English context. Indeed, Robert Berkhofer has argued that scriptural interpretations of American origins were rarely employed due to the belief in the validity of the Bible's explanation for the dispersal of humankind.[30] The English instead turned to explanations that relied less on scriptural analysis and more on hallowed classical texts and their particular understanding of the history of the British Isles. Once more, we must turn to the work of Richard Eden to identify the root of some of these English explanations. Although Eden had discredited Columbus's theory that America was Ophir, there was another key theory on American origins that was introduced in the section of the book taken from Gómara's history of the Indies; this was the theory that America was in fact the fabled, lost island of Atlantis. Gómara found the hypothesis that America was Atlantis thoroughly convincing, beginning his discussion on the Atlantis theory by exploring the history of the story. As Gómara suggested, the existence of an island named Atlantis was first espoused by the Greek philosopher Plato in his two dialogues Timaeus and Critias. Atlantis, as Gómara explained, was purported to be an island 'greater then Affrica and Asia'. The kings of Atlantis were said to have 'governed a greate parte of Affrica and Europe' until 'a certeyne greate earthequake and tempest of rayne' 'soonke' the island, drowning its people. Whether this story had any truth to it was of course debatable, with Gómara reminding his readers that 'sum take this for a fable' while others 'for a trewe hystorie'.[31] Gómara himself felt that the European discovery of America once and for all proved the veracity of Plato's tale; according to Gómara, there was 'nowe no cause why wee shulde any longer doubte or dispute of the Iland Antlantide, forasmuch as the discoverynge and conquest of the west Indies do plainly declare what Plato hath wrytten of the sayde landes'.[32] Gómara had deduced from Plato's writings that as Atlantis was said to have been located 'in the sea Atlanticke' and after its demise 'that sea Atlantike coulde not bee sayled', the idea that America, hidden in the dangerous and difficult to traverse Atlantic Ocean, was in fact Atlantis looked increasingly likely.[33]

The idea that America was in fact Atlantis became extremely popular among writers attempting to deduce the origins of the peoples that inhabited the New World. Harold J. Cook has suggested some possible reasons for this theory's popularity, arguing that the Atlantis story fit perfectly into a sixteenth-century vision of history in which 'the present was witness to the return of a Golden Age'.[34] Alongside these more theoretical motivations, it can also be argued that for writers such as Gómara making the connection between Atlantis and America served more practical functions. The Spanish imperial project relied heavily on papal support. The papal bull *Inter Caetera*, issued in 1493, stated very clearly that the Spanish claim to the lands of America was entirely bound up with conversion; the Spanish Crown was given the right to seek out 'mainlands remote and unknown and not hitherto discovered by others, to the end that you might bring to the worship of our Redeemer and the profession of the Catholic faith their residents and inhabitants.'[35] In order to convert the Indigenous population to Catholicism it first had to be proven that the peoples of the Americas were indeed rational humans, capable of receiving the gospel.[36] In this context of proving Indigenous rationality, the story of Atlantis was particularly useful. It illustrated that the peoples of the New World were indeed connected to those of the Old through the lineage of the people of Atlantis, without contradicting or misinterpreting Scripture. This not only served to reconcile the biblical account of the dispersal of humankind with the 'discovery' of America, illustrating clearly that all peoples, including those of the New World, were descended from the progenitors of Adam, but also proved that

Indigenous people were capable of receiving the gospel due to their inherent, if not immediately obvious, humanity. By identifying the Indigenous communities of the Americas as lost and degenerate Atlanteans, Spanish writers maintained the unity of humankind and so strengthened their own colonial claims to a land in desperate need of Christian conversion.

While the Spanish arguably used the Atlantis theory to bolster their American conversion project, the English use of the story justified their early approach to the Americas, being variously used to establish English claims to American lands and to make sense of the new geographical discoveries of the sixteenth century.[37] Intellectual understandings of the Atlantis story are undoubtedly critical since they helped shape English responses to a newly expanding world, yet the practical use of the theory in an English context should not be underestimated. It was the work of Humphrey Gilbert, in particular, that reflected the practical use of the Atlantis story for would-be English explorers.[38] Half-brother to the more famous Walter Ralegh, Gilbert, along with many other Englishmen, was convinced of the existence of a Northwest Passage to the wealthy lands of Cathay, now modern-day China.[39] But what does this question of geography have to do with the legend of Atlantis? Atlantis, as has already been suggested, was famously an island. As Gilbert explained in his short pamphlet on the subject from 1576, because 'Atlantis, now called America was ever knowen to be an island, and in those days navigable round about', 'a far greater hope now remaineth of the same by the northwest'.[40] Put simply, if you could sail around the northwest coast of Atlantis, you could sail around the northwest coast of America because they were one and the same. The attempt to find a new passage to Cathay was integral to English aspiration at this time. As Gilbert suggested in a letter to his brother, John, which was printed at the beginning of his pamphlet, the discovery of a new passage to Cathay by the English would open up an abundance of 'wonderful wealth and commodities'.[41] Gilbert also implicitly explained why a Northwest Passage to Cathay would prove most favourable. Not only were the Portuguese in control of the route around the Cape of Good Hope, but the route itself was extremely dangerous as 'the greatest *Armados*' 'cannot without great difficulty passe that way'.[42] Gilbert also rejected the notion of a Northeast Passage, stating that in this part of the world 'no shippe of great burden can navigate in so shallow a sea', with the 'gross thicke ayre' of the region making any navigation extremely difficult.[43] The Northwest Passage, where conditions were believed to be much more favourable, was thus the only logical route for the English to establish.

By connecting America to the lost island of Atlantis, Gilbert was justifying his reasons for believing there to be a navigable Northwest Passage to Cathay. Atlantis, or indeed America, was to be England's door to wealth and European supremacy. With empirical data on the existence of such a passage lacking, and with the dominant belief that true wisdom about the world was to be found in the major works of antiquity, classical theories and philosophical ideas became the only way for Gilbert and his fellow mariners to gain support for their explorations.[44] This reliance on canonical classical literature, a feature that also, as we shall see, influenced to varying degrees English understandings of monstrosity and climate in an American context, was undoubtedly a result of the sixteenth-century English educational system. By the end of the century it was largely agreed among pedagogical theorists that English education, from the grammar school to the university, should be based around the humanist principles of grammar, rhetoric, poetry, history, and moral philosophy. Within this educational scheme the retrieval and preservation of an ancient form of wisdom, derived from the works of classical thinkers, was of profound importance.[45] Andrew Fitzmaurice has contended, moreover, that the humanist imagination in fact dominated early English colonial projects, with many of the men at the forefront of colonisation, including Gilbert, being trained in the *studia humanitatis*.[46] In the hands of the humanist Gilbert, then, the Atlantis theory became less an explanation for the existence of American peoples, as had been the case in Gómara's exposition of the story, and more a tool with which to convince potentially sceptical readers of the validity of his ideas. The Atlantis theory was popular in both Spain and England but the way in which it was utilised differed dramatically. By the latter half of the sixteenth century, when Gilbert's tract was published, the theory had been transformed from one which attempted to explain the existence of an entire continent, to one which hoped to explain the existence of a passage to the rich and prosperous East.

Attempting to prove a lucrative passage to the East through the conflation of America and Atlantis was not the only way in which English writers used theories of American origins for their own ends. Towards the end of the sixteenth century the English were just beginning to form imperialistic ideas about the Americas. One way to justify their involvement in the New World was to illustrate an early English discovery there. Some writers, therefore, wished to prove that the origins of Indigenous Americans could be connected to the British Isles.[47] In texts written to encourage English colonisation in America, authors such as George Peckham, John Dee, and Richard Hakluyt hoped to prove Elizabeth I's territorial claim to the lands of North America by suggesting the region was first populated by a medieval Welsh prince.[48] This attempt to produce a genealogy that linked the people of America with the people of a European colonising nation was not unique to the English. A similar hypothesis had been proposed in Spain in the early decades of the European encounter with America. It claimed that the peoples of the Americas were descendants of the inhabitants of the ancient islands of the Hesperides. According to Oviedo, who first proposed this theory in the 1530s, the Hesperides of the ancient writers were controlled by the Spanish, being named after the twelfth king of Spain, Hespero.[49] Oviedo backed up this theory by employing a number of examples which illustrated this custom of naming territories after their leaders: 'the Romans of Romulus, their king, built the city of Rome' and 'the Alexandrians of Alexander the Great, their king, built that city of Alexandria'.[50] Unfortunately for Oviedo, his contemporaries did not agree with his hypothesis. The theory was met with much derision, with various Spanish authors claiming that Oviedo had utilised discredited authors to invent a story that would flatter and praise the Spanish monarchy.[51] The theory was also lambasted in Eden's translations of Martyr and Gómara, with both writers claiming that the Hesperides were in fact the Cape Verde islands.[52]

The English genealogical claim to the Americas, despite making similar outlandish assertions to those of Oviedo, was met with far more approval. The first printed reference to this claim appeared in 1583 in a text on America written by George Peckham.[53] Peckham was a close associate of Humphrey Gilbert and helped finance Gilbert's first attempt at establishing an English colony in North America in 1578. Peckham, as a Catholic, wished to establish settlements for English Catholics in the New World that, while remaining loyal to the English Crown, would be far enough removed from England to avoid the crippling fines imposed on recusants.[54] Peckham's text appeared at a crucial time for this project because in 1583 Gilbert's voyage to the Americas ended with his death at sea. Peckham's text was thus an attempt to restore confidence in the project after the loss of the enterprise's most well-respected member.[55] A key aspect of this attempt to incite interest and optimism in the project was to establish and prove the English right to explore and settle the region. Rather than simply relying on the 1578 letters patent that gave Gilbert permission to explore and settle North America, Peckham suggested that the English claim to the region was indisputable, given the fact that the lands had first been discovered by a Welsh prince from whom Elizabeth I was directly descended.[56] In a chapter of the book specifically pertaining to 'the lawfull tytle' of Queen Elizabeth, Peckham claimed that 'her Highnesse' was 'lyneally descended from the blood royall, borne in *Wales*, named *Madocke ap Owen Gwyneth*'.[57] Madoc, as Peckham explained, had departed from the coast of England in 1170, arriving and settling himself and his people in the territories of North America that the English were now engaged in exploring. According to Peckham, a Welsh presence in America was still clearly identifiable in the late sixteenth century as there were 'sundrie Welch names' and 'divers other welch wordes' still in daily use in the region.[58]

In the following year, another text appeared that also utilised this theory to justify English claims to the territories of North America. David Powell, in his *Historie of Cambria, now Called Wales*, gave a more detailed account of the Madoc story, likewise claiming that it was clear that America was 'long before by *Brytaines* discovered, afore either *Columbus* or *Americus Vesputius* lead anie *Spaniardes* thither'.[59] After a succession dispute, and subsequent war between siblings, Madoc set sail and 'sought adventures by seas, sailing west'. Eventually Madoc came upon a 'land unknowen, where he saw many strange things'. When Madoc returned home he told tales of a 'pleasant and fruitful' land that was crucially uninhabited. Setting sail once again, Madoc returned to these strange lands with a number of men and women who were 'desirous to live in quietness'.[60] Powell concluded by suggesting the lands that Madoc had settled had been in the region of Mexico, giving two particular explanations for his reasoning. Firstly, according to the inhabitants of that country, 'their rulers descended from a strange nation, that came thither from a farre countrie', a point which was confirmed 'by *Mutezuma* king of that countrie, in his oration made for quieting of his people, at his submission to the king of *Castile*'. Secondly, and as Peckham had also suggested, 'the Brytish words and names of places, sed in that countrie even to this daie, doo argue the same'.[61] Not only, then, did the Madoc story justify English exploration in North America, it also disputed the Spanish claim to Mexico. By invoking a tale of American origins that linked the peoples of the British Isles to those of the New World, writers such as Peckham and Powell were not only expressing England's imperialistic ambitions but also England's increasingly antagonistic attitude towards the Spanish. As we will see in Chapter 2, this was a theme that was to become central to the early English colonial project.

The Madoc story's significance to early English colonial thought is cemented by its inclusion in Richard Hakluyt's *Principal Navigations* of 1589, a colossal text which attempted to bring together information on all English overseas voyages in an effort to popularise the idea of an English empire.[62] In this edited version of Powell's text, Hakluyt too claimed that America 'was by Britaines discovered, long before *Columbus* led any Spanyards thither'. While he removed the section that claimed the lands were in fact those of Mexico, possibly in an attempt to widen the scope of English territorial claims in the North American continent, Hakluyt was still certain that the land that Madoc had voyaged to and settled 'was some part of the *West Indies*'.[63]

The roots of this tale are somewhat difficult to untangle and it is unclear how far its advocates were influenced by the earlier Spanish claim that Indigenous communities of the New World were descended from ancient Spaniards. The first reference to the Madoc story appeared in Humphrey

Llwyd's 1559 manuscript *Cronica Walliae*. In almost identical terms to those expressed by Peckham and Powell, Llwyd explained how Madoc ventured to a land unknown that was believed to be 'some parte of that lande which the Hispaniardes do affirme them selves to be the first finders'.[64] In around 1575 John Dee obtained a copy of Llwyd's manuscript.[65] It is clear from Dee's own writings that the story of Madoc was crucial to his conception of an English empire. In Dee's *Unto your Majesties Tytle Royall to these Forene Regions & Ilandes*, dated May 1578 and most probably presented to the queen shortly thereafter, Dee employed the story of Madoc to illustrate the first example of lands in America being 'discovered, inhabited, and partlie conquered by the subjectes of this *Brytish Monarchie*'.[66] After running through other examples of early English exploration in the New World, Dee concluded by stating that for all the lands north of Florida, 'the tytle royall and supreme governement is due and appropriate unto your most gratious Majestie'.[67] Dee was known to have met with Humphrey Gilbert to discuss English overseas expansion and it is therefore likely that Peckham, who himself was a close associate of Gilbert's, learned of the Madoc story either directly from Dee or via Gilbert. David Powell was also associated with John Dee's circle and likely received Dee's copy of Llwyd's *Cronica*, which he greatly expanded and adapted to form his own history of Wales.[68] It is also clear from John Dee's library that he was not ignorant of some of the debates taking place in Spain over the origins of the Indigenous population and the Spanish legal right to these lands. He is known to have owned a copy of Ferdinand Columbus's *History of the Life and Deeds of the Admiral Christopher Columbus*, a text that explored Ferdinand's father's encounter with the New World.[69] In this text, Columbus disputed Oviedo's claims that the West Indies were in fact the Hesperides. As Álvaro Bolaños has suggested, Columbus's reason for denouncing this claim was clear; 'the proposition that the Caribbean islands had belonged to a Spanish king in ancient times not only undermined the significance of Cristóbal Colón's [Christopher Columbus's] discovery, but also made his heirs' legal suit demanding rights over land in the New World look ridiculous'.[70] While it is unclear whether or not Dee was influenced by this theory when developing his own ideas about Madoc, what is clear is that Dee was well aware of this claim, and other Spanish claims, to the Americas. As William H. Sherman has noted in his analysis of Dee's annotations of this text, it is Ferdinand's frequent assertions of the Spanish right to conquer and settle the Americas that are most vehemently criticised by Dee in the margins of the text.[71] Dee's theory surrounding the English entitlement to settle North America thus combined the medieval history of the British Isles with the denunciation of Spanish claims to the Americas. The Madoc origin story was thus simultaneously influenced by, and created to counter, origin stories first proposed in Spain.

An analysis of the English use of stories relating to American origins highlights the ways in which Europeans utilised, adapted, and manipulated Old World frameworks of knowledge and learning, based on classical texts and the Bible, to advance their colonial programmes. The prevalence of American origin stories in English travel writing was not a response to a set of ostensibly threatened assumptions regarding the dispersal of humankind, but a considered response to complex questions of colonial legitimacy and economic advancement. The content of American origin theories was similar in both Spain and England and yet the ways in which these theories were employed and received differed dramatically. For the English, with their belated entrance into the race for American colonies and their seeming lack of claim to the lands that had already been divided between the Spanish and the Portuguese with the Treaty of Tordesillas of 1494, American origin stories that validated their ideas about American geography and established connections between the new lands and those of the British Isles became indispensable theoretical tools of empire.

Making America monstrous?

Ideas relating to American origins were not the only conceptual frameworks used to legitimise English colonial plans. Beliefs about the nature of the Indigenous inhabitants of the Americas, derived from classical and biblical understandings of humanity and monstrosity, also helped shape English responses to the New World and their place within it. From ancient times, exotic and foreign peoples had been associated with monstrosity in the European imagination. Hermaphrodites, dog-headed Cynocephali, the Blemmyae with their faces in their chests, and large footed Sciapods can all be found wandering through the pages of classical and medieval travel literature. These beings, along with many others, were members of what were commonly referred to, from the Middle Ages onwards, as the monstrous or Plinian races.[72] These 'races' could differ markedly in appearance from the Europeans describing them, while others were proven 'monstrous' through their behaviour. These included the human-flesh-eating cannibals, the cave-dwelling Troglodytes, couples that lived together unmarried, and even men who went about naked.[73] Another feature of these monstrous creatures, aside from their unusual appearance and behaviour, was their location, occupying regions far away from the society of the people describing them, in this case Europeans. In classical and medieval writing, these races were placed in the relatively mysterious lands of India, Ethiopia, Albania, and Cathay. These races not only inhabited lands outside the civil Mediterranean that was home to the classical writers who first described them, they also inhabited lands distant from Christendom. In the immensely popular volume *The Travels of Sir John Mandeville*, the further Mandeville travelled away from the Christian and civilised centre of Jerusalem, the more fantastical and monstrous the people he met became.[74] The further Mandeville moved away from Jerusalem, moreover, the more he encountered societies 'that seem to exist for the sole purpose of flouting such Christian taboos as those against cannibalism, incest, polygamy, public nudity, and human sacrifice'.[75] In late medieval Europe, then, monstrosity was used to describe far-flung peoples who lived in ignorance, or indeed in contempt, of the true faith of Christianity.

With the onset of the Age of Discovery, and as geographical knowledge of the lands in the East grew, the monstrous races were shifted to regions less well known.[76] The races were transported from their traditional homelands in the East, namely India and 'Ethiopia', to the newly discovered and mysterious lands of the West.[77] Lynn Ramey, in her analysis of early modern travel literature, has convincingly argued that Renaissance explorers relied heavily on classical and medieval models of monstrosity to explain the new-found lands of America.[78] The use of monstrosity in descriptions of America did not represent, however, a mere continuation of classical and medieval ethnographic modes of describing exotic peoples. As more recent studies have suggested, monstrosity in the American context served particular cultural and political functions. In an enlightening article on gender in the discourse of discovery, Louis Montrose has highlighted the way in which monstrous Amazonian women were utilised in English travel writing, particularly in the work of Walter Ralegh. According to Montrose, the Amazonian anti-culture 'precisely inverts' European norms of political authority, sexual license, marriage, and child-rearing practices.[79] This recognition of a matriarchal and gynocratic system, which could not be fully contained by European patriarchy, reflected the gender contradictions of Elizabethan England that simultaneously called for loyalty to a female sovereign and the exercising of masculine authority over women.[80] Surekha Davies, in her innovative analysis of the role played by maps in Renaissance ethnology and understandings of human diversity, has also suggested that the relationship between the human and classical concepts of monstrous peoples was integral to European colonialism in the Americas.[81] According to Davies, 'each point on the human-monster graph performed different cultural work'. The identification of monstrous peoples could be a cause for optimism, with suggestions that evangelisation could eradicate their monstrosity. On the other hand, the presence of monstrous peoples could be highly destabilising, causing European explorers to question the effect that an environment that had brought forth monsters might have on their own bodies.[82]

In early English engagements with America, it is clear that monstrosity also served important political and cultural functions. As we shall see, utilising the image of the Indigenous cannibal could legitimise English colonialism, while the suggestion of a female-led Amazonian tribe, who controlled their territory without the aid of a husband, located near the powerful empire of Guiana, could be used as a means to flatter the similarly independent Elizabeth I in an attempt to secure funding for further expeditions. While images of cannibals and Amazons were employed sporadically by English writers to serve particular rhetorical functions, the image of the wild man significantly helped shape English responses to Indigenous people and in doing so informed colonial decisions. By employing the ambiguous figure of the wild man, English writers, explorers, and colonists created a flexible assortment of images of Indigenous people that could be used simultaneously to praise their own enterprise and criticise those of their competitors.

English conceptions of American monstrosity were initially influenced, not by direct English experience in the New World, but by descriptions of America that reached the English through translations of continental texts. In 1553 English readers got their first glimpse of the monstrous Americas through Richard Eden's English translation of Sebastian Münster's *Cosmographia*. The *Cosmographia* first appeared in German in 1544, with a definitive Latin edition going on sale in 1550. Assembled from various avenues of investigation, from personal research to detailed considerations of ancient authorities, and utilising a 'bewildering number of sources', from contemporary travel narratives to the classical works of Ptolemy and Strabo, Münster's text was highly ambitious in scope, ranging from discussions on cartography and geography, to considerations of history and ethnographic description.[83] It is unsurprising that Eden selected this particular text for his first foray into publicising the new discoveries in the west. Münster was committed to the Reformation, leaving the Franciscan order in Heidelberg for Basel in 1529.[84] For Eden, who produced his translation during the reign of the Protestant Edward VI and under the patronage of the Duke of Northumberland, John Dudley, who was also a committed Protestant, Münster's text appeared to be, ideologically speaking, ideal for English translation.[85] However, the English edition of 1553 was, in comparison to Münster's original text, extremely modest. Rather than focusing on the geography and history of the entire globe, as had Münster, Eden's translation was instead limited to the description of the 'new founde landes and islandes', both 'eastwarde as westwarde' that had recently been 'discovered' by the Spanish and Portuguese.[86] It is clear, then, that Eden's real interest lay in these newly discovered parts of the world, rather than in Münster's conception of global history and geography. Originally published in the lands of Reformation Europe, the *Cosmographia* was thus an excellent source for disseminating information on the New World to an English and ostensibly Protestant readership.

A large proportion of the text is focused on early Spanish encounters with America and, in particular, the various voyages of Christopher Columbus and Amerigo Vespucci. According to Münster, the New World appeared to be home to an array of strange and exotic humans, many of whom were reminiscent of the Plinian races and monstrous peoples of Mandeville. In Hispaniola, Columbus heard of a 'people called canibales or anthropophagi, which are accustomed to eate mans fleshe'. There was the intriguing Island of Martinique 'in whyche dwell only women, after the maner of them called Amazones'. There was the land explored by Vespucci and his men that was said to be home to giants of 'so greate stature' that the Spanish 'marveyled thereat' and on their departure 'called that Ilande, the Ilande of Giauntes'.[87]

Two years later, another text appeared in English that repeated these descriptions almost word for word. This text was Eden's 1555 edition of Peter Martyr's *Decades*. Although this text appeared in English after Münster's, it was in fact printed in Latin some fourteen years earlier than the first edition of the *Cosmographia*. Given the similarity of description and Münster's use of a vast array of contemporary source material, it is likely that Münster's accounts of monstrosity were directly influenced by those of Martyr. According to Martyr, and as Münster had also suggested, in America there were 'the wylde and myscheveuous people called Canibales' who were 'accustomed to eate mannes fleshe (and called of the olde writers, Anthropophagi)'.[88] There was the Island of Martinique which was 'inhabited only with women; to whom the canibales have accesse at certen tymes of the yeare', reminiscent in Martyr's mind of the Thracians of the 'owlde tyme' and their access to 'the Amazones in the Islande of Lesbos'.[89] Martyr made it clear that these 'creatures' were not products of his imagination, and nor were they products of the specific environment of America. They were examples of those monstrous races handed down by the 'olde writers' and 'antiquites' of the classical and medieval period to the writers of the Renaissance such as Martyr. The women of Martinique and the man-eating *canibales*, although given new names, were thus part of a European cultural heritage spanning centuries.

New World cannibals

As English experience in the New World from the late 1560s onwards increased, American monstrosity became less a tool for explaining the exoticism of the new lands and more one for justifying and validating specific aspects of English explorative and colonial strategy. This new approach to American monstrosity can be seen in the way in which English writers and explorers adapted and employed the image of the cannibal and, as will be discussed later, the Amazon, and the wild man. As Merrall Llewelyn Price has suggested, reports of cannibalism in the New World served to vilify the 'other' and became a 'convenient screen for European fears and phantasies and for the realities of colonial violence'.[90] From the outset of European contact with America, the division of Indigenous populations between gentle and naïve peoples, and vicious cannibalistic ones became a critical tool for the justification of European conquest and colonial violence.[91] Columbus had been the first to divide the Indigenous peoples of America in this way, between the gentle Taíno and cannibalistic Caribs.[92] According to Richard Eden's preface to Martyr's account of Columbus's voyages, not only did the Caribs, also known among the Spanish as the *Canibales*, consume human flesh, they also enslaved their gentle Taíno neighbours.[93] Up until the arrival of the Spanish, the Taíno 'were ever in daunger to be a pray to those manhuntynge woolves'. Thanks to the Spanish intervention, however, the benign inhabitants of the Greater Antilles were freed from the bondage of that 'develysshe generation' of Caribs and, indeed, from that of 'Sathans tyrannie' more generally.[94] In Eden's understanding of the Indigenous inhabitants of the Caribbean, then, the Spanish were cast as the saviours of the Taíno, freeing them from the intolerable bondage of the Caribs and enlightening them with the word of God. The presence of the cannibalistic Caribs thus enabled the Spanish, and their English admirers such as Eden, to justify both colonial violence and a programme of conquest and conversion; a violent approach in the Caribbean would rid the region of the inhuman practice of cannibalism, while a continual Spanish presence would keep the Taíno safe from their vicious neighbours and enable their conversion to Catholicism.

This early Spanish use of the Indigenous cannibal to validate European conquest and colonialism no doubt influenced English explorers who also employed this image in the late sixteenth century. In George Peckham's 1583 publication that aimed to illustrate the benefits of continued English exploration and settlement in Newfoundland, the spectre of the man-eating cannibal was an important feature. Peckham, as well as running through a number of benefits that the English sought to gain through settlement and trade in America, was also keen to stress that Indigenous groups would benefit from English colonisation too.[95] Not only would they receive the true word of God, saving their souls from eternal damnation, they would also be protected 'from the cruelty of their tyrannicall & blood sucking neighbors, the *Canniballes*, wherby infinite number of their lives shalbe preserved'.[96] Peckham, then, in much the same way that Eden had done in relation to Spanish colonialism, employed the image of the American cannibal to support continued English colonialism in the Americas. The fact that Peckham used the word '*canibale*' also highlights how engrained this notion of the dastardly, man-eating cannibal was. Despite exploring a region that was much further north than the Caribbean, it was still Columbus's *canibale* that was cast as the tyrannical neighbour. At the end of the sixteenth century, then, *canibale* remained a by-word for the inhuman, cannibalistic 'Indian' that preyed upon their gentle neighbours and was identified by various authors in such diverse regions of the continent as Trinidad, Venezuela, Brazil, and Canada.[97] The *canibales* were no longer merely the vicious inhabitants of the Caribbean island of Canibata. They were instead a cruel and depraved group that could be found in all corners of the New World and used to justify the imperialistic ambitions of both the English and the Spanish.

American Amazons

The belief in a tribe of Amazonian women was also transplanted from the Caribbean of Columbus's early expeditions to regions of the Americas that the English hoped to conquer for themselves. In Walter Ralegh's 1596 published account of his 1595 voyage to South America, the Amazonian women are transformed to meet the specific requirements of his text.[98] Unlike many of his contemporaries, Ralegh portrayed the all-female tribe in a rather positive light, rationalising their perceieved perverse behaviour.[99] In order to understand Ralegh's interpretation of the Amazons, it is first crucial to understand the rationale behind the publication of his narrative. Any reader of the text cannot fail to notice how often Ralegh mentions Queen Elizabeth I and how important her image is to the potential success of the project. As Walter Lim has suggested, the ideal reader of Ralegh's text was the Virgin Queen herself who, incidentally, was also the ideal investor for any future expedition.[100] Throughout the narrative, Ralegh explained how he told the Indigenous chiefs of the queen's 'greatenes, her justice, her charitie to all oppressed nations' and all the rest 'of her beauties and vertues'.[101] Shannon Miller has argued that Ralegh's use of stories about the queen and her image reflected how the monarch was presented as a commodity, 'an object, a token, that Ralegh can trade throughout the river villages of Guiana'.[102] In casting the queen as a coin that could be traded, Miller argues that Elizabeth's power in the New World was effectively transferred to Ralegh.[103] This interpretation, however, underestimates the importance that Ralegh placed on his relationship with the queen and his recent fall from grace. Ralegh had been a former favourite of the queen, only finding himself in trouble when he married one of the queen's ladies-in-waiting, Elizabeth Throckmorton, without royal permission. When the marriage was discovered, Ralegh was thrown into the Tower of London. Although he was eventually released, Ralegh was unable to restore his former privileged position at court.[104] Mary Fuller has suggested that Ralegh's exploration of Guiana and his account of the expedition reflected this precarious position in the 1590s. According to Fuller, Ralegh's expedition to Guiana was meant as penance for his sexual indiscretion with Elizabeth Throckmorton; 'the profitable discovery of the other was to overwrite the disgraceful discovery of the self'.[105] Read in this way, then, Elizabeth's image was employed by Ralegh in an attempt to win back the favour of the queen.

Elizabeth's virginity, justness, and imperial prowess are employed time and again in Ralegh's text. Although these symbolic representations of the queen could be used to both praise and criticise the monarch, in Ralegh's case these images are clearly used to flatter Elizabeth, win her support, and convince her of the viability of the venture in Guiana.[106] Ralegh pointed out that he told the Indigenous population of Elizabeth's just nature, explaining how she gave 'charitie to all oppressed nations', and how she 'was an enemy to the *Castelani* in respect of their tyranny and oppression'.[107] Elizabeth's imperial and military prowess is alluded to at various points, with Ralegh telling his readers how he told the Indigenous communities he met about England's stunning success against the Spanish Armada and how the queen had freed all the coast of the northern world from Spanish servitude.[108] Elizabeth's perpetual virginity is also alluded to. Ralegh described her to the Indigenous population as 'the great *Casique* of the north, and a virgin'.[109] The queen's virginity was therefore presented as being central to her ability to lead; she was a great leader or *cacique* because she was a virgin. Elizabeth's impregnable virginity literally fended off foreign princes, preserving England and bolstering Elizabeth's position as a powerful and independent leader.[110] The virtues of the queen thus became the virtues of Ralegh's project in Guiana; by echoing Elizabeth's chastity, fairness, and military power, Ralegh attempted to reingratiate himself with the queen and convince her and her court of the viability of his enterprise.

It is within this context of royal flattery that Ralegh's description of the Amazons should be read. Ralegh's more positive account of the Amazonian tribe can be seen as an attempt to praise Elizabeth's female leadership to secure further investment for a second expedition. Ralegh, despite employing some of the key themes common to all stories of the Amazons such as their apparent cruelty towards prisoners of war, rationalised and to some extent humanised the behaviour of the all-female tribe.[111] In Ralegh's description, the Amazons 'accompanie' with men but once a year, apparently in the month of April. All the kings of the bordering nations gather with the queens of the Amazons, the queens choose their preferred sexual partner, and the rest 'cast lots for their *valentines*'.[112] If the Amazons conceive and bear a son, they return him to his father and if they bear a girl they keep her and 'send unto the beggeters a Present' in thanks.[113] The process by which the Amazons became pregnant is thus portrayed as a ritual performed by all the people of the region, including male leaders, in which there is a clear set of protocols that the women completely control. Although Ralegh admitted that they were rather blood-thirsty towards people who invaded their territory, he highlighted the care they gave to their children and the respect awarded to the men with whom they procreated. This description of the Amazons differs dramatically to others written in the sixteenth century. The French Franciscan explorer André Thevet, for example, portrayed the way in which the Amazons conceived as shambolic and secretive, their treatment of their children cruel and, in many cases, murderous. According to Thevet, rather than meeting at an organised time and place, the Amazons met with unspecified men, 'sometime secrete in the night, or at some appoynted time'. Rather than consistently returning their male children to their fathers they 'kil their male children incontinently after they are delivered'.[114] There are, of course, interesting parallels to be drawn between Elizabeth and the Amazonian women, such as their perpetual unmarried statuses and their ability to lead. It would therefore seem from Ralegh's narrative that he saw Elizabeth as the ultimate Amazonian woman. She had shown that she could successfully defend her own territories without the aid of a husband and, as Ralegh suggested, when the Amazons 'heereby heare the name of a virgin' who is able to do this they would undoubtedly submit themselves to her, making the Virgin Queen their leader.[115] Ralegh transformed the image of the Amazons, from one that epitomised female aberrance and monstrosity, into one that could be used to praise female leadership and in turn help him achieve his imperial objectives. By reworking and manipulating well-known classical models of monstrosity, then, English explorers once again transformed Old World knowledge to match the demands of New World experience. English images of the cannibal and the Amazon, although influenced by continental European writers such as Martyr, Münster, and Thevet, were employed to meet the particular political needs of their authors, legitimising English settlement in Newfoundland and English conquest in Guiana.

New World wild men

Peckham's cannibals and Ralegh's Amazons, despite highlighting how monstrosity could be adapted to function in English theories of overseas expansion, remain isolated examples of the English use of American monstrous peoples. What is particularly notable about English accounts of America written in the late sixteenth century is, in fact, the lack of reference to specific types of monstrous peoples. As John Block Friedman has argued, in the sixteenth century the monstrous men of antiquity were gradually reduced to a single figure, 'the hairy wild man', which was then conflated with the Indigenous peoples of the New World.[116] The wild man, alongside his female counterpart, the wild woman, was the antithesis of the civilised. He wore no clothes, had long, thick, tangled hair, carried a club or tree trunk as a weapon, crawled on all fours, and lived on the outskirts of civilisation in the wilderness of European woods and forests.[117] The wild man was ubiquitous in European society and culture in the medieval and early modern period, with his image not only present in the literature of the time, but also adorning prints and panel paintings, ceramics, coats-of-arms of kings and popes, and even playing cards.[118] In late medieval and early modern Europe, however, the wild man was a deeply ambiguous figure. On the one hand, he represented human regression to an animal state, yet on the other was an idealised image used as justification for rebellion against civilisation.[119] The wild man was thus symbolic of two competing ideas; he was the antithesis of desirable humanity, but also the embodiment of man in his natural state.[120] It was this ambiguity that made the wild man such an important frame of reference for English explorers in the late sixteenth century. By employing this image, English writers commenting on the nature of Indigenous people could portray them as either savage and beyond achieving European civility, or as primitive and living in a state of natural perfection. The employment of the wild man in an American context, then, allowed for the creation of a flexible assortment of English representations of Indigenous peoples, which served to promote certain regions of the Americas, while criticising and condemning others. As we shall see in Chapters 3 and 4, a similarly flexible approach to Indigenous communities is also present in English representations of Indigenous appearance and diet.

It is clear that wildness was seen by Europeans as a key characteristic of Indigenous peoples throughout the sixteenth century, with the adjective 'wild' being employed by a number of authors to describe the various peoples of the New World. The people of Canada were 'wilde and unruly', the *canibales* 'wylde and myscheveuous', those of the Caribbean islands 'wyld and nakte', and the people of Central America 'wilde and savage'.[121] Like the wild men of the medieval imagination, the wild folk of America were often naked and were most at home in the woods, mountains, and wilderness. Early descriptions of America, reaching an English audience through translation, are replete with tales of the Indigenous populations retreating to the woods when faced with the possible threat of European visitors. In Martyr's description of a Spanish skirmish with 'Indians', Indigenous men fled to the woods where they were able to shoot at the Spanish more safely. As Martyr explained, Indigenous people were 'accustomed to the woodes and naked without any lette', being able to pass through the bushes and the shrubs as if they 'had byn wylde bores'.[122] When exploring the lands of modern-day Canada in the 1530s, the French explorer Jacques Cartier also found that the Iroquoians had to be coaxed out of the woods. The arrival of Cartier and his fellow Frenchmen had 'caused all the young women to flee into the wood', only being tempted out again by the promise of French gifts.[123] In a markedly less friendly encounter with the women of the American wilderness, Münster recounted the gruesome tale of a young Spaniard, voyaging with Amerigo Vespucci, who was clubbed to death with a 'great stake' by an Indigenous woman, taken to the mountains, cut into pieces, and roasted on a huge fire.[124]

By far, the clearest comparison between Indigenous Americans and the European conception of the wild man available to English readers in the mid-sixteenth century was to be found in the 1568 translation of André Thevet's work that detailed the early French explorations of America. In Thevet's description, the wild man was synonymous with the Indigenous man, with the term 'wild man' being used most regularly to denote the people of the New World.[125] Not only did Thevet categorise the peoples of America as wild, his description of their behaviour also corresponded to the negative European image of the wild man. Like the wild man of European folklore, the Indigenous peoples of America lived 'without Fayth, without Lawe, without Religion, and without any civilitie: but living like brute beasts, as nature hath brought them out, eating herbes and rootes, being alwayes naked as well women as men'.[126] Thevet's American wild man, then, engaged in the same beastly, uncivilised behaviour as the European wild man and highlighted the need for missionary and colonial activity that would encourage wild Indigenous people to leave their 'brutish living, and lerne to live after a more civill and humayne manner'.[127] While Thevet employed the image of the wild man to highlight the necessity of French civilising and missionary zeal, English writers increasingly used the language of the wild man to promote their own colonial plans, condemn the results of their competitors, and articulate the frustrations of expeditions that did not go according to plan, once again illustrating how pan-European cultural references could be employed in radically different ways.

The articulation of savagery through the image of the wild man was employed by some Englishmen in a bid to explain the dangers of exploring the lands of Spanish America. John Chilton, a merchant sailor who had spent a prolonged period of time in Spain before setting sail for the New World, composed a short but detailed account of his time in New Spain and the West Indies, which was eventually published in Richard Hakluyt's

Principal Navigations.[128] While Chilton suggested that the Spanish had been able to subdue a large number of Indigenous groups, reporting in detail the tribute they paid to the Spanish, it is also clear from Chilton's account that some Indigenous communities were so wild that the Spanish were unable to control them.[129] In New Biscay, now modern-day northern Mexico, Chilton came across a group of 'Indians' who, 'for the most part go naked, and are wilde people'. These wild 'Indians' also had the worrying tendency to 'eate up such Christians as they come by', evidence indeed of their lack of loyalty to the Spanish conquerors.[130] The city of Pánuco, which used to be a 'goodly city, where the king of *Spaine* had his governour', now 'lieth in a maner waste' because 'the Indians there destroyed the Christians'.[131] Having left Pánuco with the intention of returning to Mexico City, Chilton found himself lost in 'a great wood' where he 'fell into the hands of certaine wilde Indians'. The 'Indians' placed Chilton upon a mat and called for a young Indigenous girl to act as translator. According to Chilton, the girl told him that these people would ordinarily eat any Christian that crossed their path. On this occasion, however, Chilton seemed to have been lucky as the girl also told him that 'thou mayest thanke God thou art leane; for they feare thou hast the pocks: otherwise they would eate thee'.[132] After being sent on his way, Chilton, after a short time, came to a town that was inhabited by Christians. After hearing his account of his close encounter with 'Indian' cannibalism, the Christians of the town 'marvelled to heare' that he had come 'from those kinde of Indians alive' as it 'was a thing never seene nor heard of before: for they take a great pride in killing a Christian'.[133]

It is important to note here that Chilton clearly linked notions of wildness with the practice of cannibalism. As has already been suggested, cannibalistic Indigenous Americans were often associated with the maneating anthropophagi of the classical imagination. From accounts such as Chilton's it is also clear, however, that some instances of apparent 'Indian' cannibalism in the sixteenth-century English mind were the product of a parallel cultural trajectory that linked the image of the wild man with the behavioural trait of cannibalism. This is unsurprising, for as Timothy Husband has argued, the medieval image of the wild man, in which cannibalism was a prominent feature, was heavily influenced by the classical monstrous races.[134] Whether associated with the classical anthropophagi or with the medieval wild man, representations of American cannibalism were part of a broader European cultural heritage that correlated the abhorrent practice of eating human flesh with savage, beastly, and monstrous peoples. Chilton's voyages through Spanish America and his deployment of images of wild, cannibalistic 'Indians' had identified some of the shortcomings of the Spanish imperial project and the continuing savagery of some groups of Indigenous people. Some Indigenous populations appeared to be under the control of the Spanish, but there still remained groups of wild 'Indians' that posed a significant threat to the Christians settling in the region. The lands of Spanish America, although filled with unimaginable riches, were also filled with untold dangers.

It was not just in the lands conquered by the Spanish, however, that wild Indigenous people posed a threat. In the 1570s English explorers hoping to claim the very north of the American continent for Elizabeth I also purportedly encountered the savagery of some Indigenous groups. Dionyse Settle, a member of Martin Frobisher's crew that undertook an expedition to Meta Incognita in 1577, was particularly damning of both the region's potential and its Indigenous inhabitants.[135] According to Settle, this region of America was home to 'barren mounteines', 'furious seas', and 'monstrous and great Islandes of yce'.[136] There was 'no grasse', 'no wood at all', or indeed anything 'profitable for the use of man'.[137] Settle's portrayal of the Inuit was closely entwined with this negative opinion of the environment and commodities of the region. As Settle suggested, 'as the Countrie is barren and unfertile, so are they [the Inuit] rude and of no capacitie to culture the same'.[138] The Inuit were 'craftie villains' who would 'lye lurking', waiting to pounce on unsuspecting English visitors.[139] They were 'voyde of humanitie', feasting like beasts on raw and spoiled meat and living in animalistic 'dennes' rather than in houses.[140] This image of the wild, unruly Inuit thus reflected the disappointing nature of the region as a whole. Not only were there no profitable commodities to speak of in Meta Incognita, the Inuit were beyond civility, making English settlement in the region pointless, if not, impossible. The negative image of the wild man, devoid of humanity, was thus employed by English writers to criticise particular regions of the Americas. The wild, cannibalistic 'Indians' of Spanish America highlighted the difficulty of controlling conquered Indigenous populations, while the beastly Inuit reflected the harsh and unprofitable nature of the Far North.

Not all images of American wild men were negative, however. From the 1580s, English writers, although still utilising the language of wildness and savagery, perceived some Indigenous groups as primitive and living in a state of nature, rather than as beastly and inhuman. This more positive assessment of Indigenous people is particularly evident in the early English writing on Virginia, for as Surekha Davies has suggested, the view of Virginian life as primitive and simple 'chimed well with the promotional purpose of early colonial literature, which was aimed at encouraging English settlers'.[141] Writers such as Arthur Barlowe and Thomas Harriot, both of whom had spent time in Virginia, attempted to idealise the figure of the Algonquian, projecting an image of a people who lacked civility and lived without science and culture, but were nonetheless loving, well-natured, and thus easy to control. For those Englishmen and women thinking of making the voyage for themselves, and who had potentially read about the wild, cannibalistic people of Spanish America, this affectionate portrayal of the Algonquians would have been particularly appealing. In Barlowe's account of his reconnaissance voyage to Virginia in 1584, the Algonquians were described as a 'people most gentle, loving, and faithfull, voide of all guile and treason'.[142] This contrasted heavily with the English image of the Indigenous peoples of Mexico and Meta Incognita who were perceived to be treacherous, vicious, and, in many cases, murderous. The Algonquians, despite their loving nature, were still perceived to be somewhat wild and uncivilised compared to the English. As Barlowe suggested, it was as if they lived 'after the maner of the golden age', a time of pre-lapsarian innocence, in which people lived according to the laws of nature rather than the laws of man. They cared not for wealth, being more concerned with 'howe to defend themselves from the cold in their short winter, and to feed themselves with such meat as the soile affoordeth'.[143] This lack of concern for wealth and the many trappings of civilisation would help ensure the success of the English project in the region. English colonisers could exploit the neglected commodities of the region while improving the lives of the primitive and wild Algonquians by exposing them to English civility.

A year after Barlowe's expedition, another English crew set out to Virginia, this time hoping to establish a permanent English settlement in the region. A principal member of this crew, Thomas Harriot, wrote a detailed account of his time in the region that was eventually published in 1588 and then again in 1590. Just like Barlowe, Harriot promoted Virginia as a land of natural resources and innocent people. Harriot found the Virginia Algonquians to be a 'savage people', yet it is important to note that this word did not, in the sixteenth century, necessarily have the negative connotations that it has today.[144] Rather than exclusively meaning fierce or violent, the word savage was a derivation of the French word *sauvage*, meaning wild.[145] The concept of savagery was thus still closely connected to that of wildness in the sixteenth century. Just as the wild man of European folklore could be used in positive and negative ways, so too could the image of the savage Indigenous American. Alongside being somewhat savage and wild, the Algonquians were, according to Harriot, 'a people poore', lacking 'skill and judgement in the knowledge and use of our things'. As well as being deficient in knowledge and skill, the Indigenous population was also rather naïve, esteeming English 'trifles before thinges of greater value'. Despite this obvious primitivism and lack of civility, Harriot also identified a potential for learning. The Algonquians seemed rather 'ingenious', for although they did not have 'such tooles, nor any such craftes, sciences and artes' that were enjoyed by the English, in the things they did have they showed 'excellencie of wit'. This type of savage primitivism, combined with the perceived superior technology and intellect of the English, led Harriot to conclude that because the Algonquians of Roanoke would wish to learn from the English, they would 'desire' the 'friendships & love' of the colonisers and develop 'the greater respect for pleasing and obeying' them.[146] Harriot, therefore, believed that the English could control the Indigenous people of Virginia because of their perceived savage primitivism. Once the Algonquians recognised the superiority of English knowledge, they would undoubtedly 'have cause both to feare and love' their English visitors.[147]

The image of the wild man thus served a number of important functions in early English travel narratives. The negative concept of the wild man, devoid of humanity, engaging in cannibalism, and living in barbarous, beastly and vicious conditions, could be used to identify a lack of colonial control on the part of the Spanish, or the inappropriate nature of some regions for English settlement. Conversely, the more positive figure of the wild man, in which savagery was considered an aspect of the natural primitive state of man, could be used to achieve the exact opposite. The incivility and naivety of the Virginia Algonquians was clear proof that this Indigenous group could easily be controlled by the 'superior' English. The fact that the Algonquians also seemed uninterested by their natural resources of potentially great value also indicated to the English that the lands of Virginia could be successfully exploited for financial gain. Although the language of savagery was, in the words of Peter Hulme, 'honed into the sharpest instrument of empire' by all European colonising nations, in the sixteenth century it was arguably the English, in particular, that were able to mould it into a range of useful and multi-functional forms most successfully.[148] Through redeploying the symbolism of the medieval wild man in an American context, English writers illustrated how wildness and savagery continued to be construed as evidence for both the limitations of civilisation and the worrying potential of man to regress to a beastly and primitive state. Moreover, by employing the image of the wild man, and the associated concept of savagery, those commenting on early encounters with America created an assortment of positive and negative images of Indigenous people that served a variety of important political and colonial functions, from justifying a continued English presence in Virginia to illuminating the perceived failures of Spanish colonialism. The practical utility of these flexible representations of Indigenous people, and how they connect to everyday practices of dressing and eating, and to broader processes of economic expansion and cultural dominance, will be explored in more detail in Chapters 3 and 4.

Climate theory and the location of English colonies

The environment, and particularly the climate, of the New World was also critical to English responses to America in the sixteenth century, with the English understanding of climate becoming a key theoretical tool of empire.[149] In a similar process to that identified in the English use of ideas of monstrosity, certain aspects of classical climatology were manipulated and rejected to conform to New World experience, while others were retained and redeployed for the new American context. The discovery of America challenged the ancient theory that lands located near the equator were unfit for human habitation. The undermining of this theory, through explorative experience in the Americas, meant that the question of climate was now open for debate, being manipulated by English authors to make claims about the suitability of cold, far northern regions for English settlement. Yet at the same time, the climate of America remained a central concern for European colonising nations due to its perceived effects on early modern bodies. While the ancient notion that human habitation was impossible close to the equator due to extreme heat was rejected in the sixteenth century, the classical belief that different nations were suited to particular climates remained a potent one. Although classical climatology came under increasing strain in the sixteenth century, then, certain aspects still remained resilient. Ideas relating to the various climates of the new lands helped English commentators, explorers, and colonisers predict which regions of the New World would be most suitable for English habitation. While the Spanish were at home in the torrid regions of the Caribbean and Central and South America, the English focused their colonial attention on more suitable, cool climates in the north. Ideas about climate, both based on Old World knowledge and New World experience, thus significantly impacted English colonial choices and the location of potential settlements. As Chapters 3 and 4 will demonstrate in more detail, ideas relating to climate, the body, and diet were central to the articulation of English overseas expansion, shaping not only the explorative decisions discussed below, but also influencing how English explorers understood their own ability to survive in the New World and incorporate Indigenous people into their colonial ventures.

First attributed to the Greek philosopher Parmenides, climate theory that identified the Earth's different zones remained valid for centuries. According to the theory, human habitation was only possible in the Earth's 'temperate zones'. The other two zones, the hot 'torrid zone' and the cold 'frigid zone', were uninhabitable due to their extreme climates. Unsurprisingly, Europe could be found sitting comfortably within the temperate zone.[150] As more populated lands were discovered lying within the apparently uninhabitable torrid zone, the theory came under increasingly close scrutiny. In a wide-ranging book that dealt with mathematics, cosmography, geography, and navigation, Thomas Blundeville attempted to set down a collection of treatises that would be 'very necessarie to be read and learned of all yoong gentlemen'.[151] In his section on cosmography, Blundeville reiterated the commonplace belief that the earth was split into five zones, stating that 'the extreme hoat Zone lyeth betwixt the two Tropiques, in the middest of which two Tropiques, is the Equinoctiall line'.[152] Despite repeating the assertions put forward by ancient Greek philosophers, Blundeville later admitted their errors. The ancient writers 'did greatly erre in affirming 3. of the Zones to be unhabitable' due to 'a lacke of experience', having 'never travelled to those regions'.[153] Conversely, the explorers sent to the New World from Spain, England, France, and the Netherlands had travelled through the supposed uninhabitable torrid zone and found it to be 'well inhabited'.[154] Martin Cortés, in his popular manual for navigation, also tackled the issue of the ancient writers' mistake regarding uninhabitable zones.[155] Like Blundeville, Cortés explained how, in times past, cosmographers had believed the 'burnt zone (called *Torrida Zona*)' to be uninhabitable 'by reason of the greate heate thereof'. But also like Blundeville, he highlighted that experience in the New World had proven this to be untrue. The New World was 'well replenyshed wyth people' and to say anything to the contrary was clearly 'a manifest errour'.[156] Writers with first-hand experience of the New World also rejected the notion that the lands beneath the equator were uninhabitable due to the extreme climate. George Best, a captain in the Frobisher fleet that explored the far north of America in the 1570s, for example, found the idea that the land beneath the equator could not sustain life due to the heat almost laughable, declaring that 'under the Equinoctiall, is the most pleasant and delectable place of the worlde to dwell in'.[157] By the end of the sixteenth century, then, and in large part due to European experience in the Americas, the idea that the torrid zone was uninhabitable due to intolerable heat had become obsolete.

With the realisation that the classical writers had been wrong about habitable and uninhabitable zones, sixteenth-century Europeans attempted to explain the reasons behind this mistake. Best, for example, speculated why there was this disagreement between what the ancient writers thought and what the sixteenth-century explorers found.[158] He suggested that the reason America was a temperate, abundant environment, rather than a scorched and meagre one, was down to the position of the sun. Classical writers, according to Best, had focused their attention on the angle of the sun with the earth and how this affected temperature.[159] Best argued that their failure to take into account the length of time the sun spent above the horizon in various locations explained their error regarding the temperature and climate of the torrid zone. Because the sun spent longer beneath the horizon in America, so Best theorised, it was not as hot as expected. For a place to be intolerably hot the sun must 'maketh perpendicularly righte Angles' with the earth *and* the sun must shine above the horizon for a long period of time. When one of these conditions was 'wanting', 'the rigor of the heat is lesse'.[160] Cortés also highlighted the importance of the long American nights in explaining the temperate climate the continent enjoyed as 'the coldnesse of the night doth sufficiently temper the heate of the day'.[161] By observing the difference between the length of days in their native Europe with those in America, Best and Cortés had shown that experience and observation could explain phenomena that Europe's trusted classical works had been unable to.

Writers such as Best, however, were not necessarily interested in the climate of America for purely educational reasons. With the abandonment of the classical theory of habitable and uninhabitable zones, English explorers and colonisers like Best could begin to manipulate ideas about climate to suit their explorative, discursive, and rhetorical needs.[162] For Best, and those other men interested in the far north of the American continent, this meant proving the habitability of the cold, frigid zone. If the classical philosophers had been wrong about the torrid zone, could they have also made a similar mistake about the frozen region to the north? Thomas Churchyard, a soldier and prolific writer, made an impassioned plea for continued English exploration of the Far North in 1578 after Frobisher and his men had abandoned their project to plant a colony in the region. With the failure of the expedition and the spreading of, what Best called, 'sundry untruths' about the venture, texts such as Churchyard's attempted to silence the critics and instil a new sense of optimism for English overseas expansion.[163] Churchyard referred directly to some of these criticisms, particularly those levelled against the climate of the region. According to Churchyard, some of those that had criticised the Meta Incognita project had suggested that there was 'no peece of benefite to bee gotten in a cold climate'.[164] In response, Churchyard had suggested that due to their lack of experience, these critics were in no position to comment; as Churchyard argued, they relied on 'strong reasons and argumentes on their owne sides because thei haue not proued the experience of this journey'.[165] Just as the Spanish explorations in America had proven the lands close to the equator to be far more temperate than the classical authorities had suggested, those 'honourable personages' who had actually experienced Meta Incognita for themselves had shown the region to be beneficial to the English nation.[166]

George Best, one of the 'honourable' explorers that Churchyard had referenced, agreed with this sentiment, arguing that the 'old writers' were 'perswaded by bare conjecture' that the frozen and torrid zones were uninhabitable. According to Best, the ancient geographers, when discussing extreme climates compared them 'to their owne complexions' and thus 'felt them to be hardlie tolerable to themselves'. In concluding that extreme hot and extreme cold climates were intolerable to the temperate Mediterraneans of the classical world, these regions were deemed to be uninhabitable. To explain his point clearly, Best used the following example: 'if a Man borne in *Morochus*, or other part of *Barbarie*, should at the later end of Sommer, upon the suddayne, eyther naked, or with hys thinne vesture, be broughte into *England*, he woulde judge this Region presently not to be habitable, bycause he being broughte up in so warme a Countrey'.[167] Tolerable climates were thus relative to experience, something that Best claimed had been ignored by the classical writers. Having made this point, Best then went on to explain why he thought the Far North was in fact home to a temperate climate, providing a complex theory that explored the length of days and the position of the sun in the region, leading him to conclude that in Meta Incognita 'the Sommers are warme & fruitful, & the Winters nights under the pole, are tollerable to living creatures'.[168] This argument also, rather helpfully, enabled Best to explain away negative English accounts of the region such as Settle's in which monstrous islands of ice and barren, unfertile lands featured heavily.[169] According to Best, the mountains of ice that were created during the cold winter would thaw thanks to the heat of the summer sun. The fact that some areas of the region seemed barren was not problematic as the same could be said for the northern coastal regions of Devon and Cornwall.[170] The frozen zone was not only habitable, then, in summer it was positively temperate. Best also implicitly suggested that the coldness of the winter would not be a problem for the English as 'by little and little by certaine degrees' human beings were able to adapt to new climates, so that eventually the air would seem 'more temperate'.[171] Both Churchyard's and Best's arguments relating to climate thus helped bolster their assertions that Meta Incognita was a suitable region for English habitation. Debates surrounding the validity of classical climate theory, therefore, helped shape English responses to criticism and enabled explorers to reassert the viability of their ventures.

English writers interested in overseas expansion also utilised ideas surrounding climate to explain and justify European patterns of colonisation. Unlike Best, not all writers were happy to suggest that it was possible for humans to adjust to all climates, as there was a strong connection in the early modern period between climate and national character. Not only was it believed, by the late sixteenth century, that all regions of the world were in fact habitable, it was also believed, and had been for centuries, that different nations suited different climates. In the early modern period it was believed that national temperaments and character were shaped by a country's physical environment and most notably its climate.[172] This notion of climate being connected to national character had its origins in the climatic and medical theories of Aristotle, Hippocrates, and Galen.[173] In sixteenth-century Europe, Hippocratic and Galenic humoral theory remained the most common way of explaining how the human body functioned. According to these theories, the human body was made up of four different humours: blood, phlegm, black bile, and yellow bile. When the humours remained in equilibrium, the body remained healthy, but when the humours became unbalanced, due to the effect of external forces such as diet and climate, the body became unhealthy.[174]

Early modern explorers were particularly concerned with the American climate due, in large part, to this understanding of the human body and national temperament. A consideration of the differing climates of various parts of the Americas could serve to highlight the suitability of particular regions for English settlement while also providing legitimate reasons for avoiding hostility in lands already occupied by other European nations. It was, once again, the texts relating to Frobisher's voyages to the Far North that first articulated these ideas relating to climate. Dionyse Settle, in the preface to his account of the second English voyage to Meta Incognita, clearly identified the effect that climate had on European colonisation patterns in the New World. It was Settle's belief that God had deemed it appropriate that these new lands 'should be found out by those people, which for the temperature of their habitation, are most apt to achive the same'. For Settle, then, success in the New World was rooted in climate theory. The Spanish were 'the most apte men for the injoying of the habitation of the West Indies', for 'continual heate' 'is agreeable to their temperature'.[175] Likewise, God was also content that the Portuguese, who shared a similar climate to the Spanish, 'have explored Africa, even through the burning zone'. The French, who enjoyed cooler climes to those of the Spanish and Portuguese, discovered New France as the Spanish had thought other parts of America 'not apt for their temperature'.[176] In a logical conclusion to his argument, Settle posited that the English should seek out regions more 'septentrional than those before rehearsed' as they would be 'more agreeing' to the English natural temperament.[177] In Settle's opinion, then, the success of European colonial ventures was intrinsically linked to how well the colonisers were able to deal with the climate of the lands they set out to conquer.

Despite Best's and Churchyard's attempts at convincing readers that the northerly regions of North America were suitable for English settlements, interest in Meta Incognita largely failed to reignite after the abandonment of the proposed colony in 1578. The content of these accounts of Meta Incognita had belied the arguments that Best and Churchyard had set out in their prefaces; the region was barren, cold, and held little colonial potential.

Just as Settle had advocated, the focus of English colonial ambition moved further south, concentrating on the regions of Newfoundland and Virginia, with climate once again being a key tool with which to prove the viability of particular ventures. George Peckham, for example, described the climate of Newfoundland as 'mylde and temperate, neither too hotte not too colde', making it a most 'convenient place to plant and inhabite in'.[178] Peckham suggested that this region was particularly suited to the English as the 'countrey dooth (as it were with arme advaunced) aboue the climats both of *Spayne* and *Fraunce*, stretche out it selfe towardes *England* onelie'.[179] Newfoundland was thus on a similar latitude to England, enjoying a cooler, more northerly climate than both France and Spain.

In the 1580s, as the English moved still further south to Virginia, climate theory was once again adapted to fit the needs of English colonists. Rather than claiming that Virginia enjoyed a similar climate to England, however, some writers suggested that it actually had a superior one. According to Thomas Harriot, Virginia benefitted from an 'excellent temperature of the ayre there at all seasons', being 'much warmer then in England, and never so violently hot, as sometimes is under & between the Tropikes'.[180] The quality of a country's air and climate was central to English understandings of bodily health. As Chapter 4 discusses in more detail, in the healthcare system of the six non-naturals, external forces such as climate and diet were believed to affect a person's humoral balance and thus in turn their health.[181] The primary principle in need of regulation within this system was that of air. As the physician Andrew Boorde claimed, 'no thynge excepte poyson' was more detrimental to a person's health than a 'corrupte and a contagyous ayre'.[182] Proving that Virginia was home to wholesome and temperate air was thus critical for establishing the region's suitability for English habitation. John Brereton, in his account of his voyage to northern Virginia, concurred with Harriot's description, claiming that the climate of the region agreed with the English, even making the explorers 'fatter and in better health' than when they had left England.[183] Brereton agreed with Harriot that Virginia was a place 'temperat and well agreeing with our [the English] constitution', being located 'betweene 40. and 44. degrees of latitude, under the Paralels of *Italy* and *France*' and yet not as hot as these countries 'by reason that the suns heat is qualified in his course over the Ocean, before he arriveth upon the coasts of *America*'.[184] Virginia was thus warmer than England, but not as hot as the countries of the Mediterranean and equatorial America.

This shift towards promoting warmer climates over the cooler ones of Meta Incognita and Newfoundland is particularly interesting and surprising given the prevalence of the belief that a change in climate could harm the body and the fear of the effect of heat on English bodies in particular.[185]

This fear of the heat of the tropics is exemplified in a medical tract of 1598 written by George Wateson. In Wateson's opinion, the cause of many of the diseases found in America was an excess of heat. The *Espinlas*, an inflammatory skin condition, takes hold 'after great heat or travell', the *Erizipila*, another acute skin infection, proceeds from the 'unholesome aires and vapours, that hot climates doo yeelde', while one of the principal causes of *las Cameras*, also known as the Bloodie Flux, was simply 'being hot'.[186] The heat, so Wateson's diagnosis suggested, caused an imbalance of humours which needed to be corrected in order to cure the disease. Wateson recommended that patients should be 'purged' and have 'the corrupted humour' drawn out from their bodies, while, of course, 'continuing in colde places'.[187] Despite Wateson's determination that heat was incredibly dangerous, English attitudes towards hot weather were in fact highly ambivalent. While it was accepted that heat could do damage to bodies used to cold climates, it was also widely believed that hotter countries enjoyed more abundant crops and higher volumes of precious commodities.[188] This belief led Roger Barlow, an English merchant and early investor in English enterprises in America, to lament the fact that much of South America had already been claimed by the Spanish, leaving only the north of North America for the English. In this part of America, according to Barlow, 'it is to be presupposed that ther is no riches of gold, spyces nor precious stones, for it stondeth farre aparted from the equinoctial'.[189] In early accounts of Virginia, then, the suggestion that the country enjoyed a warmer climate than England served to bolster the common assertion that Virginia was an abundant, fertile land, home to an array of profitable commodities. By suggesting that Virginia was warm, but not too warm, Harriot and Brereton were not only able to reassure their fellow countrymen and women that their bodies would survive in such a climate, they were also able to convince colonisers that their move across the Atlantic would be a profitable one.

The English use and adaptation of climate theory thus served a number of important functions, influencing English explorative decisions directly in the latter half of the sixteenth century. The reworked version of classical climate theory, in which all lands were now habitable, enabled explorers involved in the Meta Incognita project to assert that the lands in the frigid north were in fact temperate and suitable for English habitation. The retention of the belief that climate shaped national temperament also allowed English colonisers to justify their focus on the northerly regions of the North American continent. Commentators argued that it was in this part of the Americas that English colonialism, and indeed, as Chapter 4 will demonstrate, English bodies would prove most successful and resilient. By the late 1580s ideas about the climate of the Americas had shifted once more, with explorers and writers now suggesting that the English would not only retain their natural complexions and characteristics in America, but would in fact improve them, becoming healthier and more robust. By looking to the unclaimed territories of the North American continent, and by utilising climate theory to validate this focus, the English would not only diminish the risk of skirmishes and territorial conflicts with Spanish and other European colonisers in parts of America that had already been claimed, they would also ensure the retention, and even improvement, of English natural temperament and bodily health. Climate had thus become a key tool of empire, validating colonial decisions and convincing potential investors and colonisers that they would be able to survive and even thrive in the temperate and abundant regions of the northern American lands. How these theories of the body, climate, and environment played out in practice will be the focus of Chapters 3 and 4.

* * *

Throughout the sixteenth century, English writers, explorers, and colonisers created a set of theoretical tools, based on Old World intellectual frameworks of knowledge and understanding, which helped shape and define English responses to America. These ideas relating to human diversity, monstrosity, and climate were first articulated in an American context by Spanish, Portuguese, and French explorers who had travelled to and settled in America in the early decades of the sixteenth century. These writers had illustrated how useful these conceptual ideas were for European colonising nations. Monstrosity could help elucidate European fear, and indeed interest, in exotic others; theories of American origins could serve to justify European conquest and conversion; and the adaptation of classical climate theory could stimulate debate on how the world worked and what could be learned from exploring the new lands across the Atlantic.

When placed in the hands of English writers, however, these theories were remodelled to meet the needs of burgeoning English colonial projects. Rather than merely translating the ideas of their continental neighbours, then, the English transformed them. Through the selective appropriation of the Spanish theory that America was in fact Atlantis, and through the creation of their own origin myth that linked the people of the New World to the Tudor dynasty, English writers were able to convince their readers of the likelihood of a Northwest Passage to the East and assure potential investors and colonisers of the English legal entitlement to lands in the newly discovered West. English images of monstrous Americans and New World wild men allowed for the creation of flexible portrayals of Indigenous people, both positive and negative, which could be used to justify continued English colonialism in Newfoundland, flatter the queen in an attempt to win financial backing for explorative projects in Guiana, illustrate the dangers of journeying through Spanish America, and highlight the natural, primitive, and thus easily controllable, state of the Virginia Algonquians. Beliefs surrounding climate, based both on classical learning and New World experience, informed English decisions to focus their attention on the lands to the north of those already conquered by Imperial Spain and validated beliefs that this region of the Americas would not only be particularly suitable for English habitation, but would also be home to a vast array of precious commodities that could be exploited by those making the journey across the Atlantic. By employing these Old World theoretical frameworks, then, those men involved in the early English attempts to explore and colonise America were able to justify and validate a range of explorative and colonial decisions. However, it was not just the theory behind English overseas expansion that helped frame English responses to America in the late sixteenth century. As the next chapter illustrates, the reality of these early colonial ventures, in which failure and disappointment were common themes, served to reshape English approaches to exploration and settlement in the New World, creating an English colonial model in which godly conquest, rather than material gain, became the most prominently articulated goal.

Notes

1 Christopher Columbus, *The Journal of Christopher Columbus*, trans. Cecil Jane (London: Anthony Blond & the Orion Press, 1960), 42.
2 Edmundo O'Gorman, *The Invention of America* (Bloomington: Indiana University Press, 1961), 54–61.
3 J. H. Elliott, *The Old World and the New: 1492–1650* (Cambridge: Cambridge University Press, 1970), 20.
4 Lynn Ramey, "Monstrous Alterity in Early Modern Travel Accounts: Lessons from the Ambiguous Medieval Discourse on Humanness," *L'Esprit Créateur* 48, no. 1 (Spring 2008): 81–95; Margaret Hodgen, *Early Anthropology in the 16th and 17th Centuries* (Philadelphia: University of Pennsylvania Press, 1964), 30–32.
5 Anthony Pagden, *The Fall of Natural Man: The American Indian and the Origins if Comparative Ethnology* (Cambridge: Cambridge University Press, 1982), 10–11.
6 Historians have noted, however, a transformation of European understandings of America towards the end of the sixteenth century in which the novelty of the New World was increasingly recognised. On the rise of comparative ethnology see Pagden, *Fall of Natural Man*; Hodgen *Early Anthropology*. On the growing acceptance of American alterity see Elliott, *The Old World*; Inga Clendinnen,

"'Fierce and Unnatural Cruelty': Cortés and the Conquest of Mexico," in *New World Encounters*, ed. Stephen Greenblatt (Berkeley: University of California Press, 1993), 12–47.

7 Anthony Grafton, *New Worlds, Ancient Texts: The Power of Tradition and the Shock of Discovery* (Cambridge, MA and London: Harvard University Press, 1992), 10.

8 A variety of studies have looked at particular European intellectual frameworks and how they were applied in an American context. For work on theories of monstrosity see Surekha Davies, "The Unlucky, the Bad and the Ugly: Categories of Monstrosity from the Renaissance to the Enlightenment," in *The Ashgate Research Companion to Monsters and the Monstrous*, eds. Asa Mittman and Peter J. Dendle (Farnham: Ashgate, 2012), 49–75; Persephone Braham, "The Monstrous Caribbean," in *The Ashgate Research Companion to Monsters and the Monstrous*, eds. Asa Mittman and Peter J. Dendle (Farnham: Ashgate, 2012), 17–47; Montrose, "The Work of Gender," 177–217; Stanley L. Robe, "Wild Men and Spain's Brave New World," in *The Wild Man Within: An Image in Western Thought from the Renaissance to Romanticism*, eds. Edward Dudley and Maximillian E. Novak (Pittsburgh, PA: University of Pittsburgh Press, 1972), 39–53. For studies on theories of American origins see Richard H. Popkin, "The Rise and Fall of the Jewish Indian Theory," in *Menasseh ben Israel and his World*, eds. Henry Méchoulan and Richard H. Popkin (Leiden: Brill, 1989), 63–82; Álvaro Félix Bolaños, "The Historian and the Hesperides: Gonzalo Fernández de Oviedo and the Limitations of Imitation," *Bulletin of Hispanic Studies* 72, no. 3 (1995): 273–287; Harold J. Cook, "Ancient Wisdom, the Golden Age, and Atlantis: The New World in Sixteenth-Century Cosmography," *Terrae Incognitae* 10, no. 1 (1978): 27–29; Amy H. Sturgis, "Prophesies and Politics: Millenarians, Rabbis, and the Jewish Indian Theory," *The Seventeenth Century* 14, no. 1 (1999): 15–23; Richard W. Cogley, "'Some Other Kinde of Being and Condition': The Controversy in Mid-Seventeenth-Century England over the Peopling of Ancient America," *Journal of the History of Ideas* 68, no. 1 (January, 2007): 35–56; Richard W. Cogley, "John Eliot and the Origins of the American Indians," *Early American Literature* 21, no. 3 (Winter, 1986/87): 210–225.

9 The term 'selective eye' is taken from Cook, "Ancient Wisdom," 43.

10 Rastell set sail for the New World in the summer of 1517, hoping to settle the lands that had been claimed by the English in 1497 and to find a Northwest Passage to Asia. The venture was a disaster as Rastell's crew abandoned him in Waterford and sold Rastell's cargo in Bordeaux. Rastell remained in Ireland for two years, where he is believed to have composed *A New Interlude*; Cecil H. Clough, "John Rastell," *Oxford Dictionary of National Biography*, last accessed 21 June, 2016, www.oxforddnb.com/view/article/23149?docPos=1.

11 John Rastell, *A New Interlude and a Mery, of the Nature of the iiij Elements* (London, 1520), sig. C2r.

12 Ibid., sig. C2v.

13 Ibid.

14 Lee Eldridge Huddleston, *Origins of the American Indians: European Concepts, 1492–1729* (Austin: University of Texas Press, 1967), 6.
15 Ibid., 9.
16 Huddleston, *Origins of the American Indians*, 9–11; and Robert F. Berkhofer Jr., *The White Man's Indian: Images of the American Indian from Columbus to the Present* (New York: Knopf, 1978), 34–35.
17 Theories of American origins were of course not the only means through which Europeans justified territorial expansion. For the legal dimensions of English overseas expansion see Ken MacMillan, *Sovereignty and Possession in the English New World: The Legal Foundations of Empire, 1576–1640* (Cambridge: Cambridge University Press, 2006); Armitage, *Ideological Origins*; Braddick, *State Formation in Early Modern England* (Cambridge: Cambridge University Press, 2000).
18 Elizabeth M. Nugent, ed., *The Thought & Culture of the English Renaissance: An Anthology of Tudor Prose, 1481–1555* (The Hague: Martinus Nijhoff, 1969), 2:511.
19 This quotation is taken from Martyr's preface to the extended edition of *Decades of the Newe Worlde* from 1516. This is cited in Andrew Hadfield, "Peter Martyr, Richard Eden and the New World: Reading, Experience and Translation," *Connotations* 5, no. 1 (1995/96): 9.
20 Nugent, *Thought & Culture*, 2:511.
21 Huddleston, *Origins of the American Indians*, 7.
22 Lesley Byrd Simpson, "Introduction," in *Cortés: The Life of the Conqueror by His Secretary Francisco López de Gómara*, ed. and trans. Lesley Byrd Simpson (Berkeley and London: University of California Press, 1964), xx; Antonello Gerbi, *Nature in the New World: From Christopher Columbus to Gonzalo Fernández de Oviedo*, trans. Jeremy Moyle (Pittsburgh, PA: University of Pittsburgh, 2010), 140–141.
23 Huddleston, *Origins of the American Indians*, 10–11.
24 James Romm, "Biblical History and the Americas: The Legend of Solomon's Ophir, 1492–1591," in *The Jews and the Expansion of Europe to the West, 1450–1800*, eds. Paolo Bernardini and Norman Fiering (New York and Oxford: Berghahn Books, 2001), 28–31.
25 Christopher Columbus, "A Letter Written by Don Christopher Columbus, Viceroy and Admiral of the Indies, to the Most Christian and Mighty Sovereigns, the King and Queen of Spain," in *Christopher Columbus, With Other Original Documents Relating to the Four Voyages to the New World*, ed. and trans. R. H. Major esq. (London: The Hakluyt Society, 1847), 197.
26 Romm, "Biblical History and the Americas," 30–31.
27 Quotation from Martyr, *Decades of the Newe Worlde*, fol. 22. Martyr asserts Columbus's belief that Hispaniola is in fact Ophir on fol. 2, fol. 10 and fol. 22.
28 Ibid., sig. A4r.
29 Ibid.
30 Berkhofer, *White Man's Indian*, 35.

31 Martyr, *Decades of the Newe Worlde*, fol. 31. For a summary of the debates surrounding the veracity of the Atlantis story see Cook, "Ancient Wisdom," 28.
32 Martyr, *Decades of the Newe Worlde*, fol. 310.
33 Ibid.
34 Cook, "Ancient Wisdom," 27.
35 Papal Bull, "Inter Caetera, 1493," American History from Revolution to Reconstruction and Beyond, the University of Groningen, last accessed 30 June, 2016, www.let.rug.nl/usa/documents/before-1600/the-papal-bull-inter-caetera-alexander-vi-may-4-1493.php.
36 Pagden, *Fall of Natural Man*, 104–119; Patricia Seed, "'Are These Not Also Men?': The Indians' Humanity and Capacity for Spanish Civilisation," *Journal of Latin American Studies* 25, no. 3 (October, 1993): 635–637.
37 Harold J. Cook argues, for example, that the Atlantis story became conflated with other tales, most notably the belief that Queen Elizabeth I was a descendant of the Trojans, in an attempt to validate English exploration and colonisation in the Americas: Cook, "Ancient Wisdom," 27–42. In contrast to Cook, Margaret Small has suggested that the theory was also utilised to make sense of the rapidly expanding world of the sixteenth century, especially by the Elizabethan polymath and early advocate of English imperialism, John Dee, whose use of the theory illustrates the influence of Neoplatonic thought on geography after the discovery of America. Dee believed in the Platonic principle that there was an underlying unity and balance in the world. Within this framework, Atlantis-as-the-Americas represented an inhabited world that acted as a 'counterpart and counterweight to the known world', providing mathematical balance and thus terrestrial unity. According to Small, it was these philosophical interpretations of Plato's work, rather than the physical geography of the Atlantis myth, that convinced audiences well-versed in humanism of the merits of projected English voyages like those to discover a Northwest Passage to the East: Margaret Small, "From Thought to Action: Gilbert, Davis, And Dee's Theories Behind the Search for the Northwest Passage," *Sixteenth Century Journal* 44, no. 4 (Winter, 2013): 1044–1058.
38 Cook, "Ancient Wisdom," 39–40; Small, "From Thought to Action," 1055–1056.
39 Rory Rapple, "Sir Humphrey Gilbert," ODNB, last accessed 30 June, 2016, www.oxforddnb.com/view/article/10690.
40 Humphrey Gilbert, *A Discourse of a Discoverie for a New Passage to Cataia* (London, 1576), sig. B2v.
41 Ibid., sig. ¶¶¶4v.
42 Throughout this book, italics in quotes appear as in the original texts except where stated otherwise; Ibid., sig. D4v.
43 Ibid., sigs. E3r–F1r.
44 Small, "From Thought to Action," 1057–1058.
45 Quentin Skinner, *Reason and Rhetoric in the Philosophy of Hobbes* (Cambridge: Cambridge University Press, 1996), 20–24. For other studies of humanist

education in theory and practice see Anthony Grafton and Lisa Jardine, *From Humanism to the Humanities: Education and the Liberal Arts in Fifteenth- and Sixteenth-Century Europe* (Cambridge, MA: Harvard University Press, 1986); Rebecca W. Bushnell, *A Culture of Teaching: Early Modern Humanism in Theory and Practice* (Ithaca, NY and London: Cornell University Press, 1996).

46 Fitzmaurice, *Humanism and America*, 1–19.
47 L. Sprague de Camp, *Lost Continents: The Atlantis Theme in History, Science, and Literature* (New York: Dover, 1970), 124.
48 For more on the legal underpinnings of this theory see MacMillan, *Sovereignty and Possession*.
49 Gonzalo Fernández de Oviedo, *Historia General y Natural de las Indias* (Madrid: La Real Academia de la Historia, 1851), 14.
50 Ibid., 15. Original Spanish reads: 'los romanos de Rómulo su rey, que edificó la cibdad de Roma' and 'los alexandrines de Alexandre Magno su rey, que edifice aquella cibdad de Alexandria'.
51 Gerbi, *Nature in the New World*, 272; Bolaños, "Historian and the Hesperides," 280.
52 Martyr, *Decades of the Newe Worlde*, fol. 12 and fol. 310.
53 Peckham, *A True Reporte*.
54 James McDermott, "Sir George Peckham," ODNB, last accessed 30 June, 2016, www.oxforddnb.com/view/article/21743.
55 Ibid.
56 Gilbert's letters patent can be found in "The Letters Patents Graunted by her Maiestie to Sir Humfrey Gilbert Knight, for the Inhabiting and Planting of our People in America," in *Principal Navigations*, 3:135–137; information on Elizabeth I's ancestors from Peckham, *A True Reporte*, sig. D4r.
57 Peckham, *A True Reporte*, sig. D4r.
58 Ibid., sig. D4r–D4v.
59 David Powell, *The Historie of Cambria, Now Called Wales* (London, 1584), 228.
60 Ibid., 227–229.
61 Ibid., 229.
62 For more detail on the significance of the Madoc story in the work of Richard Hakluyt see Mancall, *Hakluyt's Promise*, 136–138.
63 David Powell, "The Most Ancient Discovery of the West Indies by Madoc the Sonne of Owen Guyneth Prince of North-Wales, in the Yeere 1170," in *Principal Navigations*, 3:1.
64 Humphrey Llwyd, *Cronica Walliae*, ed. Ieuan M. Williams (Cardiff: University of Wales Press, 2002), 168.
65 Ieuan M. Williams, "Introduction," in *Cronica Walliae*, 4.
66 John Dee, "Unto your Majesties Tytle Royall to these Forene Regions & Ilandes," in *The Limits of the British Empire*, eds. Ken MacMillan and Jennifer Abeles (Westport, CT and London: Praeger, 2004), 43.
67 Ibid., 48.
68 Ronald H. Fritze, "David Powell," ODNB, last accessed 6 June, 2016, www.oxforddnb.com/view/article/22643.

69 This book is listed in the additions and corrections to the bibliographical society's catalogue of John Dee's library. Julian Roberts and Andrew G. Watson, "John Dee's Library Catalogue: Additions and Corrections," The Bibliographical Society, last accessed 30 June, 2016, www.bibsoc.org.uk/sites/www.bibsoc.org.uk/files/John%20Dee%27s%20Library%20Catalogue%204.pdf, 11.
70 Bolaños, "Historian and the Hesperides," 280.
71 William H. Sherman, "John Dee's Columbian Encounter," in *John Dee: Interdisciplinary Studies in English Renaissance Thought*, ed. Stephen Clucas (Dordrecht: Springer, 2006), 136.
72 For more on the discourse of the monstrous in medieval Europe see Bettina Bildhauer and Robert Mills, eds., *The Monstrous Middle Ages* (Toronto: University of Toronto Press, 2003); Jeffrey Jerome Cohen, *Of Giants: Sex, Monsters and the Middle Ages* (Minneapolis: University of Minnesota Press, 1999); Lorraine Daston and Katherine Park, *Wonders and the Order of Nature*, 1150–1750 (New York: Zone Books, 1998); Asa Simon Mittman, *Maps and Monsters in Medieval England* (New York: Routledge, 2006); Lisa Verner, *The Epistemology of the Monstrous in the Middle Ages* (New York: Routledge, 2005); David Williams, *Deformed Discourse: The Function of the Monster in Mediaeval Thought and Literature* (Montreal: McGill-Queen's University Press, 1999); Robert Bartlett, "Medieval and Modern Concepts of Race and Ethnicity," *Journal of Medieval and Early Modern Studies* 31, no. 1 (Winter, 2001): 39–56; Francois Hartog, *Mirror of Herotodus: The Representation of the Other in the Writing of History*, trans. Janet Lloyd (Berkeley: University of California Press, 1988).
73 John Block Friedman, *The Monstrous Races in Medieval Art and Thought* (Syracuse, NY: Syracuse University Press, 2000), 1–24; Ramey, "Monstrous Alterity," 86.
74 As Iain Macleod Higgins has argued, the popularity of Mandeville's text is attested to by the fact that 300 manuscripts of the early version of the book remain extant. Its success continued into print, with the book appearing in eight languages before 1515. By 1600 there had been sixty printings of the text; Iain Macleod Higgins, *Writing East: The 'Travels' of Sir John Mandeville* (Philadelphia: University of Pennsylvania Press, 1997), 8. The popularity of Mandeville's book among early English explorers of America is also clear. A copy is known to have been taken on the Martin Frobisher voyages to Baffin Island and Walter Ralegh explicitly cites the text in his printed narrative of his expedition to Guiana; William C. Sturtevant and David Beers Quinn, "This New Prey: Eskimos in Europe in 1567, 1576, and 1577," in *Indians & Europe: An Interdisciplinary Collection of Essays*, ed. Christian F. Feest (Lincoln and London: University of Nebraska Press, 1999), 115; Walter Ralegh, *The Discoverie of the Large, Rich, and Bewtiful Empire of Guiana* (London, 1596), 70.
75 Martin Camargo, "*The Book of John Mandeville* and the Geography of Identity," in *Marvels, Monsters, and Miracles: Studies in the Medieval and Early Modern Imaginations*, eds. Timothy S. Jones and David A. Sprunger (Kalamazoo, MI: Medieval Institute Publications, 2002), 81.
76 Friedman, *The Monstrous Races*, 1.

77 Ethiopia is placed in inverted commas because in the medieval and early modern periods the term was, as Friedman illustrates, a 'vague literary term rather than one denoting a specific place'; Friedman, *The Monstrous Races*, 8.
78 Ramey, "Monstrous Alterity," 81–95.
79 Montrose, "The Work of Gender," 202.
80 Ibid., 201–210.
81 Davies, *Renaissance Ethnography*, 20.
82 Ibid., 15.
83 Matthew McLean, *The Cosmographia of Sebastian Münster: Describing the World in the Reformation* (Aldershot: Ashgate, 2007), 1–3.
84 Ibid., 2.
85 David Loades, "John Dudley," ODNB, last accessed 11 August, 2016, www.oxforddnb.com/view/article/8156?docPos=1.
86 Münster, *Treatyse of the Newe India*, title page.
87 Ibid., sigs. G6r, H2v and L4r–v.
88 Martyr, *Decades of the Newe World*, fol.3.
89 Ibid., fol.6.
90 Merrall Llewelyn Price, *Consuming Passions: The Uses of Cannibalism in Late Medieval and Early Modern Europe* (New York and London: Routledge, 2003), 83–84.
91 Persephone Braham has also suggested that the inference of cannibalism in the Caribbean became a convenient justification for conquest, enslavement, and abuse. Braham, "The Monstrous Caribbean," 22.
92 Robe, "Wild Men and Spain's Brave New World," 44–45.
93 The word cannibal itself is derived from the Spanish word *canibales*. The *canibales* were the peoples of the land of *Caniba* or *Canibata*. As one of the defining features of these peoples was their penchant for consuming human flesh, the word '*canibale*' quickly became synonymous with the eating of humans, eventually being adopted as the word to describe this very phenomenon. Information taken from Robe, "Wild Men and Spain's Brave New World," 45.
94 Martyr, *Decades of the Newe World*, sig. a2v.
95 Peckham, *A True Reporte*, sigs. E2r–E4r.
96 Ibid., sigs. F2v–F3v.
97 For Trinidadian and Venezuelan '*canibale*s' see Ralegh, *The Discoverie*, 29 and 47; For Brazilian '*canibales*' see Jan Huygen van Linschoten, *John Huighen van Linschoten. His Discours of Voyages Into ye Easte & West Indies*, trans. William Phillip (London, 1598), 242; For Canadian '*canibales*' see George Best, *A True Discourse of the Late Voyages of Discoverie, for the Finding of a Passage to Cathaya* (London, 1576), sigs. M1r–M1v.
98 Ralegh, *The Discoverie*, 23–24 and 100–101.
99 For a wholly negative interpretation of South American Amazons see: Thevet, *New Found Worlde*, fol. 74.
100 Walter S. H. Lim, *The Arts of Empire: The Poetics of Colonialism form Ralegh to Milton* (Newark and London: University of Delaware Press and Associated University Presses, 1998), 45.

101 Ralegh, *The Discoverie*, 62.
102 Miller, *Invested with Meaning*, 175.
103 Ibid., 181.
104 Quinn, *Raleigh and the British Empire*, 175–177.
105 Fuller, *Voyages in Print*, 74.
106 Susan Doran, "The Queen," in *The Elizabethan World*, eds. Susan Doran and Norman Jones (London and New York: Routledge, 2011), 49.
107 Ralegh, *The Discoverie*, 62 and 7.
108 Ibid., 7 and 52.
109 Ibid., 7.
110 Knapp, *An Empire Nowhere*, 67.
111 Ralegh, *The Discoverie*, 24.
112 Ibid., 23.
113 Ibid., 23–24.
114 Thevet, *New Found Worlde*, fol. 74.
115 Ralegh, *The Discoverie*, 101.
116 Friedman, *The Monstrous Races*, 197.
117 Alixe Bovey, *Monsters & Grotesques in Medieval Manuscripts* (Toronto: University of Toronto Press, 2002), 55.
118 Timothy Husband, *The Wild Man: Medieval Myth and Symbolism* (New York: The Metropolitan Museum of Art, 1980), 4.
119 Hayden White, "The Forms of Wildness: Archaeology of an Idea," in *The Wild Man Within: An Image in Western Thought from the Renaissance to Romanticism*, eds. Edward Dudley and Maximillian E. Novak (Pittsburgh, PA: University of Pittsburgh Press, 1972), 22–23.
120 Ibid., 28.
121 Cartier, *Shorte and Briefe Narration*, 7; Martyr, *Decades of the Newe World*, 3; Thomas Greepe, *The True and Perfecte Newes of the Woorthy and Valiaunt Exploytes, Performed and Doone by that Valiant Knight Syr Frauncis Drake* (London, 1587), sigs. B2v; Job Hortop, *The Rare Travailes of Job Hortop* (London, 1591), title page.
122 Martyr, *Decades of the Newe World*, 33–34.
123 Cartier, *Shorte and Briefe Narration*, 20.
124 Münster, *Treatyse of the Newe India*, sigs. L5v–L6r.
125 Thevet, *New Found Worlde*, fol. 34–136.
126 Ibid., fol. 36.
127 Ibid., fol. 36.
128 Biographical information on Chilton taken from his own account. John Chilton, "A Notable Discourse of M. John Chilton, Touching the People, Maners, Mines, Cities, Riches, Forces, and Other Memorable Things of New Spaine, and Other Provinces in the West Indies," in *Principal Navigations*, 3:455–457.
129 Ibid., 3:456–461.
130 Ibid., 3:457.
131 Ibid.

132 Ibid., 3:458–460.
133 Ibid., 3:460.
134 Husband, *The Wild Man*, 3–6.
135 Settle, *A True Reporte*, title page.
136 Ibid., sigs. B6v–B7v.
137 Ibid., sigs. D1r–D1v.
138 Ibid., sig. D1v.
139 Ibid., sig. C3v.
140 Ibid., sigs. C1r–D8r.
141 Davies, "The Unlucky, the Bad and the Ugly," 69.
142 Arthur Barlowe, "The First Voyage Made to the Coasts of America, with Two Barks, Where in were Captaines M. Philip Amadas, and M. Arthur Barlowe," in *Principal Navigations*, 3:249.
143 Ibid.
144 Thomas Harriot, *A Briefe and True Report of the New Found Land of Virginia* (Frankfurt, 1590), 11. Subsequent references for this text will refer to this edition rather than the 1588 edition unless expressly stated.
145 Definition and etymology of the word 'savage' from Oxford English Dictionary, last accessed 8 July, 2016, www.oxforddictionaries.com/definition/english/savage. For more information on the connection between 'savagery' and 'wildness' see Sayre, *Les Sauvages Américains*, xv.
146 Harriot, *Briefe and True Report*, 25.
147 Ibid., 24.
148 Hulme, *Colonial Encounters*, 3.
149 Studies of how climate impacted early European colonisation in the Americas include Sam White, *A Cold Welcome: The Little Ice Age and Europe's Encounter with North America* (Cambridge MA: Harvard University Press, 2017); Karen Ordahl Kupperman, "The Puzzle of the American Climate in the Early Colonial Period," *The American Historical Review* 87, no. 5 (December, 1982): 1262-1289.
150 For a more detailed exposition of classical theories of climate see Lucian Boia, *The Weather in the Imagination*, trans. Roger Leverdier (London: Reaktion Books, 2005), 15–40.
151 Thomas Blundeville, *M. Blundevile his Exercises* (London, 1594), title page.
152 Ibid., fol. 155.
153 Ibid., fol. 193.
154 Ibid.
155 Martin Cortés, *The Arte of Navigation Conteyning a Compendious Description of the Sphere* (London, 1589), fol. 17–18.
156 Ibid., fol. 17.
157 Best, *A True Discourse*, sig. f4v.
158 This tension between expectation and reality in English perceptions of climate and its effect on colonial practice is also explored by Karen Kupperman for the early period of permanent English settlement in North America. See Kupperman, "Puzzle of the American Climate."

159 Best, *A True Discourse*, sigs. e3v–e4r.
160 Ibid., sig. e3v.
161 Cortés, *The Arte of Navigation*, fol. 18.
162 On other practical and political uses of climate theory in early modern Europe see Raphaël Morera, "Marshes as Microclimate: Governing with the Environment in Early Modern France," in *Governing the Environment in the Early Modern World: Theory and Practice*, eds. Sara Miglietti and John Morgan (London: Routledge, 2017), 95–125. On the rhetorical and metaphorical uses of theories of climate in early modern Europe see Richard Spavin, "Jean Bodin and the Idea of Anachronism," in *Governing the Environment in the Early Modern World: Theory and Practice*, eds. Sara Miglietti and John Morgan (London: Routledge, 2017), 67–94.
163 Best, *A True Discourse*, sig. a3r.
164 Thomas Churchyard, *A Prayse, and Reporte of Maister Martyne Forboishers Voyage to Meta Incognita* (London, 1578), sig. B3r.
165 Ibid.
166 Ibid., sigs. B3r–B3v and C7r.
167 Best, *A True Discourse*, sig. g2v.
168 Ibid., sigs. g3v–h2r.
169 Settle, *A True Reporte*.
170 Best, *A True Discourse*, sigs. h2v–h3r.
171 Ibid., sig. g3r.
172 Joep Leerssen, *National Thought in Europe: A Cultural History* (Amsterdam: Amsterdam University Press, 2006), 69.
173 Ibid., 2.
174 Mary Lindemann, *Medicine and Society in Early Modern Europe*, 2nd ed. (Cambridge: Cambridge University Press, 2010), 13.
175 Settle, A True *Reporte*, sig. A3r.
176 Ibid., sig. A3v.
177 Ibid., sig. A4r.
178 Peckham, *A True Reporte*, sig. B3v.
179 Ibid., sig. B4r.
180 Harriot, *Briefe and True Report*, 31.
181 Lindemann, *Medicine and Society*, 13.
182 Andrew Boorde, *A Compendyous Regyment or a Dyetary of Helth* (London, 1547), sig. A2v.
183 John Brereton, *A Briefe and True Relation of the Discouerie of the North Part of Virginia Being a Most Pleasant, Fruitfull and Commodious Soile* (London, 1602), 11.
184 Ibid., 15.
185 For an illuminating discussion of English fears of heat see Karen Ordahl Kupperman, "Fear of Hot Climates in the Anglo-American Colonial Experience," *The William and Mary Quarterly* 41, no. 2 (April, 1984), 213–240.
186 George Wateson, *The Cures of the Diseased, in Remote Regions* (London, 1598), sigs. B4r–C2r.

187 Ibid., sigs. C1v–C3r.
188 Kupperman, "Fear of Hot Climates," 218. For a further discussion of English attitudes towards heat and the tropics in the early modern period see Michael Hill, "Temperateness, Temperance, and the Tropics: Climate and Morality in the English Atlantic World, 1555–1705," PhD Thesis (Georgetown University, 2013).
189 Roger Barlow, *A Brief Summe of Geographie*, ed. E. G. R. Taylor (London: The Hakluyt Society, 1932), 180.

2

Commercialising America: Religion, trade, and the challenges of English colonialism

> *If hetherto in our owne discoveries we had not beene led with a preposterous desire of seeking rather gaine then Gods glorie, I assure my self that our labours had taken farre better effecte. But we forgotte, that Godlinesse is great riches, and that if we first seeke the kingdome of God, al other thinges will be given unto us.*[1]
>
> – Richard Hakluyt

The above quotation, taken from Richard Hakluyt's 1582 *Divers Voyages Touching the Discoverie of America*, illustrates a common anxiety felt by English explorers and advocates of overseas expansion in the 1580s: the fear that God had deserted them in their quest to explore and colonise the New World. This tension between the desire to seek wealth and riches in the New World and the need to advance the glory of God is something that was discussed by many writers commenting on English exploration and colonisation throughout the sixteenth century. The following pages explore this tension, identifying its roots in the 1550s, its reassessment in the 1570s, and its solidification in the 1580s. By tracing this process, it becomes clear that throughout the sixteenth century, ideas of religious evangelisation and commercialisation in the New World coexisted, but with shifting emphases. At times godly conquest was the most clearly articulated objective, while at others commercial gain was given priority by English explorers. By the end of the sixteenth century, however, the two had coalesced, ostensibly resolving the tension that had existed for the first century of English engagement with America. As Hakluyt suggested in 1582, the English need not compromise one for the other; with the glorification of God and the conversion of 'heathens', great riches would no doubt follow.

These changes in approach towards exploration and settlement in the Americas across the course of the sixteenth century were shaped by reciprocal influences from actual experience in the New World and the fluctuating religious and political landscape at home. In the 1550s, when the Catholic Mary I sat on the English throne, and when the royal consort was Philip II of Spain, English colonial schemes in America were presented as extensions of the already important work being undertaken by the Spanish in the region. English involvement in the New World would aid the Spanish objective of converting the 'heathen' of the Indies to Catholicism, bringing for the English, as it had done for the Spanish, the reward of material riches in return for their proselytising. The English approach to America in the 1550s, then, was shaped by the return of Catholicism to the realm under Mary I, a strong Anglo-Spanish political alliance, and the perceived success of Spanish imperialism in the New World.

With the accession of the Protestant Elizabeth I in 1558, and growing Anglo-Spanish hostility caused in part by political tensions in the Netherlands and subsequent trade embargos, the English attitude towards America and Spanish imperialism changed dramatically. It was no longer advocated that the English should imitate, and indeed bolster, the Spanish approach to colonisation. Instead, English calls for Catholic conquest were replaced with privateering and, at times, outright piracy in an attempt to wrestle the wealth of the New World from Spanish hands. At the same time, private English ventures in the Americas began to take off, with a number of expeditions taking place in the 1570s to search for a Northwest Passage to the riches of Asia and to attempt to plant an English colony at Newfoundland. These expeditions all ended in disaster, leading some key proponents of settlement in America, including Richard Hakluyt, to question the English approach to the lands across the Atlantic. While hostility with Spain had led to an English policy of seeking riches in the New World at the expense of their European rivals, the failure of many of these commercial ventures forced advocates of English involvement in America to rethink their methods.

By the 1580s, English commentators such as Richard Hakluyt and Edward Hayes were beginning to worry that God had deserted the English cause, basing these assertions on the disastrous nature of English projects in the New World throughout the 1560s and 1570s and the worsening economic and social conditions taking hold back home. This reading of English colonial and explorative failure, in which God's hand was ever present, is unsurprising given the fact that providentialism was part of mainstream religious culture in sixteenth-century England.[2] In order to win back God's favour, English writers, explorers, and future colonisers began once again in the 1580s to advocate a type of colonialism that had religion at its centre. Rather than seeking riches and material gain, advocates of overseas expansion now suggested that English colonialism should focus on converting Indigenous peoples and securing economic well-being for the people of England. These dual objectives led to the emergence of an embryonic English colonial policy in which anti-Spanish sentiment collided with the peculiarities of sixteenth-century English religious, political, and economic life. The changing English approach to America thus reflected a complex process that took into account both the harsh realities of English experience in the New World and the vacillating religious, political, and economic landscape of sixteenth-century English society.

The connection between commercialisation and religion in the English colonies of America has been fiercely debated among historians of the seventeenth century, but as of yet has received little detailed analysis for the earlier period of English involvement in the New World in the sixteenth century. Scholars working on the early English colonies of the seventeenth century have largely agreed that commercial incentives coexisted with religious motivations in the early decades of sustained English colonialism. According to Jack P. Greene, the initial phase of English colonisation across the Atlantic, which culminated in the establishment of the Jamestown colony in Virginia in 1607, was centred on commercial gain rather than religious expression.[3] Greene also argues, however, that this changed with the next wave of English migration to the New World, with the Plymouth colony, in particular, being more firmly religiously orientated due to its separatist puritan leaders.[4] Jamestown was built for commerce, Plymouth for religious expression and freedom. Karen Ordahl Kupperman also argues that the early English colonies were characterised by the blending of commercial incentives and pious intentions. Unlike Greene, Kupperman suggests that this coexistence can be seen *within* colonies, not just *between* them.[5] Even the staunchly puritan colony of Massachusetts Bay was not immune to economic considerations. The constriction of economic opportunity in England during the 1620s and 1630s, both for ordinary men and women and for university-trained men, pushed people toward emigration.[6] In the early English colonies, then, both economic and religious factors were high on the list of motivations for emigrants settling in the new colonies.

Both Greene's and Kupperman's interpretations are largely centred on the English experience after 1607 and set aside the fluctuating sixteenth-century approaches to English activity in the Americas. As this chapter illustrates, an analysis of this earlier period is critical for understanding the embedded nature of religious and economic motivations in English colonial practice in the New World. In the current historiography relating to the sixteenth-century context, however, economic motivation, rather than religious fervour, has often been considered the driving force behind early English exploration and settlement in the New World. According to Kenneth R. Andrews, John C. Appleby, and Carole Shammas, the main goal of early English activity in the New World was to procure wealth and valuable commodities for investors back home, whether through acts of piracy, privateering, and conquest, or through the establishment of English settlements and new trade links.[7] Andrews, in particular, argues that commercial incentives were integral to the development of the British Empire, both in the West and the East. In the Americas merchants dominated explorative projects, plunder became a 'commercialized business', and plans for colonisation increasingly became commercial in character.[8]

This focus on the economic incentives of early English projects in America, however, obscures the obvious religious motivations that men such as Hakluyt articulated in the sixteenth century. Although David Armitage has recently claimed that it is 'almost impossible' to discern any obvious Protestant contribution to the ideological origins of the British Empire, particularly in the work of Hakluyt, it is clear that towards the end of the sixteenth century religious language was increasingly used as the motivational ideology behind English colonialism, whether genuine or tinged by the conventions of rhetoric.[9] In direct contrast to Armitage, Nicholas Canny has analysed the religious credentials of Hakluyt, describing him as a propagandist for 'militant Protestantism'.[10] According to Canny, Hakluyt believed that England was 'duty-bound' to spread the word of God to the infidels of America, given that the English nation worshipped the one true church.[11] As Canny argues, then, English colonial thought in the late sixteenth century, as espoused by Richard Hakluyt, was centred on religion and in particular on the task of stabilising and spreading the Protestant faith. In a somewhat inverted analysis of the development of English colonialism proposed by Jack P. Greene, Canny suggests that material gain only became a priority for English colonisers in the late seventeenth century, instigating a new concept of Empire that measured success principally in material terms, attaching little importance to religion.[12]

In what follows, however, I will argue that these two positions were not mutually exclusive. Englishmen, including Hakluyt, recognised that material gain could be balanced with pious intentions, so long as the former was firmly defined as a result of the latter. Louis B. Wright was the first to propose that English colonialism in the New World should be interpreted as an alliance between piety and commerce. While contending that some early explorers' motivations can only be read, at best, as superficially religious, Wright nonetheless argues that religion was far more important to these earlier ventures than has previously been recognised.[13] Extending the work of Wright, Robert A. Williams has more recently argued that commercial incentives and religious motivations both played a central role in sixteenth-century English explorative and colonial discourse. As Williams contends, in the 1550s the work of Richard Eden had suggested that an individual could be 'a good merchant and a good Christian at the same time' and that commerce could be 'the emetic by which the Indians would gradually be purged of Satan's influence', an idea that, according to Williams, remained consistent throughout the sixteenth century.[14]

Although this colonial equation of religious reformation plus imperial revenue is helpful in explaining the way in which English plans for America developed in the sixteenth century, Williams's and Wright's assessments over-simplify the process by which Englishmen came to accept this approach. This over-simplification obscures the very real anxieties that English explorers and colonisers felt when attempting to reconcile their wish for trade and wealth accumulation with their Protestant spiritual duty of spreading God's word to 'the heathens' of America. They were able to do this but only by firmly couching the former in terms of the latter. By the end of the sixteenth century, English approaches to New World exploration and settlement would thus define commercial incentives and economic factors in terms of how they related to the glorification of God.

This apparent sixteenth-century belief that wealth accumulation should only ever be a by-product of piety has, of course, been explored in great detail by Max Weber in his influential work *The Protestant Ethic and the Spirit of Capitalism*. Introducing the notion of a 'Protestant ethic' that saw the amassing of wealth as acceptable when undertaken for the glorification of God, Weber suggested that this belief was particularly prevalent among Protestants of a puritanical persuasion due to their acceptance of the doctrine of predestination and their tendency to see God's hand at work in all aspects of life. Financial success, when not accompanied by idleness and the descent into luxury, was seen as a providential sign from God of a person's status as a member of the elect.[15] As has already been suggested though, belief in providentialism was part of mainstream English religious culture in the sixteenth century, and not merely the preserve of England's puritans.[16] The doctrine of predestination had also been enshrined in the Church of England with the adoption of the Thirty-Nine Articles of Religion in 1571.[17] It is likely, then, that the idea that commercial success could be a positive sign from God would have been shared by the majority of English Protestants, whether puritan or Church of England.

By the end of the sixteenth century, financial gain in the Americas would be seen as a reward from God, given to English Protestants in recognition of their pious intentions, trade with the New World would be seen as a necessary means to remove the English from the instability of intra-European commerce, and the development of overseas colonies would be explained as a charitable and godly way of relieving the miserable state of many Englishmen and women living in poverty back home. The process of constructing these ideas, however, was complex, being shaped by both experience in the New World and the fluctuating religious, political, and economic landscape of sixteenth-century England. The idea of merging religious intentions and commercial incentives had first been proposed by Richard Eden in the 1550s but due to its positive assessment of Spanish colonialism in the Americas, the emphasis began to shift. In the 1570s commercial gain became the most clearly articulated goal of English New World projects, with religious evangelisation becoming less of an explicitly expressed motivation. The failure of English ventures in the 1570s, however, provoked English explorers and writers to question their approach. As Richard Hakluyt had suggested in 1582, up until this point, English enterprises in the New World had focused far too much attention on commercial gain and had thus been deeply unsuccessful. This recognition of failure forced the English to reconsider their approaches to exploration and settlements and the role of religion within them. The idea that English overseas expansion should be first and foremost a religious enterprise, and that financial gain should represent a secondary consideration, would therefore re-emerge and solidify in the 1580s, having a profound effect on the course that English colonialism would take in subsequent decades.

Godly enterprises and Spanish successes

It was in the mid-sixteenth century that a colonial ideology, formed around religious considerations, was first articulated. Until this point, English interactions with America had been limited, with only sporadic publications appearing that made reference to the new discoveries in the West. Not only were these descriptions of America and her people extremely unsophisticated, the authors of these works made no attempt to promote English exploration in the region.[18] This, however, began to change in the 1550s, largely due to the efforts of one man: Richard Eden. Under the patronage of the Duke of Northumberland, a man who was keen to challenge Spain's global empire, Eden's first foray into the world of publishing came in 1553 with his partial translation of Sebastian Münster's *Cosmographia* under the English title *A Treatyse of the Newe India*.[19] It is clear from the outset of this text that Eden saw these new discoveries in religious as well as commercial terms, stating on the title page that enterprises in the New World not only allowed for the worldly obtainment of riches but also ensured that 'God is glorified, & the Christian fayth enlarged'.[20] Eden suggested, in his dedication to the Duke of Northumberland, John Dudley, that those travelling to new lands must keep God in mind and, until death, 'persist in a godly, honeste, & lawful purpose'.[21] In fact, according to Eden, those men who chose to explore the seas and new found lands for 'the Glorye of God & comoditie of our countrey' spent their time 'more honourably' than those who remained 'in soft beddes at home'.[22] To explore new lands was thus a religious endeavour; early modern explorers were tasked with spreading the word of God and, by extension, advancing the glory of God. In recognition of their piety, and as a sign of favour, God would then reward explorers, and indeed the English realm, with financial gain. Northumberland, as the protector to the devout Protestant Edward VI, and a committed Protestant himself, would have no doubt approved of this godly conception of an English Empire.[23] It is likely, therefore, that Eden's view of how English colonialism should proceed in America was coloured by the Protestantism of his patron rather than solely by his own personal convictions.[24]

In Eden's next text that dealt with the discovery of America he was to go even further in making the link between European religion and New World conquest. Although published just two years after his first work, by the time Eden's *The Decades of the Newe Worlde or West India* appeared, the political and religious landscape of England had changed dramatically. In July 1553, the devout Protestant Edward VI died, throwing the English monarchy into disarray. Earlier in the year Edward had taken the unusual step of naming his successor in his 'Devise for the Succession'.[25] Instead of passing the Crown to his Catholic half-sister, Mary, in the event of his own lack of issue, as had been the wish of his father Henry VIII, Edward named his cousin Lady Jane Grey, a committed Protestant, as heir to the English throne.[26] Ever the loyal subjects, Eden's family, including his father and uncle, supported Lady Jane's accession on Edward's death.[27] When Jane was deposed, found guilty of high treason, and eventually executed, Eden was faced with the difficult task of proving his loyalty to the new Catholic Queen Mary I. Nevertheless, Eden affirmed loyalty to the new sovereign and was able to prosper, with this loyalty being clearly expounded in the prefatory material of *The Decades*.[28] Undoubtedly still trying to prove his allegiance to Mary and her Spanish husband Philip, Eden constructed an image of the Spanish kings as pious, chosen by God, and even bordering on the divine. According to Eden, the 'kynges of Spayne of late dayes' are 'goddes made of men', comparable to those that Antiquity called heroes.[29] In Eden's opinion, moreover, the Spanish defeat of the Moors in 1492 and the recovery of Naples in 1503 was evidence that 'the nation of the Spanyardes had byn appoynted by god eyther to subdue the enemies of the fayth or to bringe theym to Christes religion'.[30] Within this narrative, the Spanish conquests in the New World were rendered as religious crusades ordained by God.

It was the Spanish king, Ferdinand, however, that Eden reserved special praise for, arguing that aside from Christ 'there never lyved man to whom god hath gyven greater benefites and shewed more favoure'.[31] Continuing his lavish praise of Ferdinand, Eden hyperbolically claimed that under Ferdinand God had 'saved not onely the bodies but also the soules of innumerable milliones of men' and in doing so 'planted a new Israell muche greater then that whiche Moises ledde throughe the red sea'.[32] It was thus religious conversion that Eden chose to focus on, rather than the commercial success of the Spanish enterprise. He admitted that there were riches to be had in the New World but it was the religious well-being of the Indigenous populations and the swelling of God's flock that should have been the true inspiration for global expansion. It was also within this framework of religious expansion and godly conquest that Eden critiqued the efforts of the English in the New World to date. Not only had England become 'decayed and impoverysshed', while Spain had become 'inryched', other Christians, like the English, had also shown 'negligence and slackenesse' in their task of building 'goddes lyvely temple'.[33] The Spanish had proven their commitment to God, and in return had been rewarded with unimaginable riches; the English, in comparison, had neglected their Christian duties leaving their society in a state of dearth and poverty. In Eden's opinion, then, England's economic and religious health depended on exploration and exploitation of the New World and its resources, and the successful conversion of those 'gentiles' who were not 'hytherto corrupted with any other false religion'.[34] With the word of God extolled to these 'heathen' populations, the English, like the Spanish, would then reap the economic rewards of God's favour.

There is, however, a subtle difference between Eden's first and second text regarding how this conversion and commercialisation should be achieved. In the *Treatyse of the Newe India*, Eden lamented the fact that the English had not capitalised on the explorations of John and Sebastian Cabot whose ventures had been sanctioned by King Henry VII, bemoaning how after these initial projects the English had chosen to abandon their claim to the New World.[35] His purpose for translating Münster's text, then, was to illustrate how would-be explorers should 'behave them selues & direct theyr viage to their most commoditie' and how they should persist in the face of adversity and failure.[36] In this text, English expansionism was to be solely for the benefit of the English nation, securing economic wealth and God's favour for the country. In *The Decades*, however, Eden linked English exploration to the wider expansionism of other European countries, particularly Spain. The imperative of European conquest in America, including the potential conquests of the English, was to ensure the saving of as many Indigenous souls as possible. However, Eden identified a principal problem with the process of converting the Indigenous populations to Christianity and cited it as a key motivation for the publication of his text, explaining the problem in the following way: 'the harvest is so great & the workemen so few'. If the enlarging of God's flock was to be achieved, more Christians needed to travel to the New World and begin proselytising. For Eden, the model of conversion to be followed by these Christians was that of the Spanish as they 'have shewed a good exemple to all Chrystian nations to folowe'.[37] As Eden continued, there was room enough in the Americas for all Christian nations to participate in this process; for the English 'there yet remayneth an other portion of that mayne lande reachynge towarde the northeast, thought to be as large as the other, and not yet knowen but only by the sea coastes, neyther inhabyted by any Christian men'.[38] It was in the northeast of America, in the region of Terra Florida, that the English would find their own 'abundaunce of golde' and do their duty to God by convincing the Indigenous population to embrace Christianity.[39] In the mid-1550s, then, Eden identified colonisation and exploration of the Americas as a duty for all of Christendom. Without the cooperation of all the Christian nations, the conversion of the 'gentiles' would not be possible and God's favour would not be maintained. In this interpretation of early English imperialism, religious incentives were at the fore, with the commercial gains to be reaped merely a reward for the explorers' piety.

Of course, this praise of Spanish achievements in the Americas and the unwillingness of Eden to challenge the Spanish Empire is unsurprising given the fact that in 1555 there was a Catholic monarch sitting on the English throne, whose consort was a Spanish king. Eden's flattery of the Spanish was, therefore, entirely appropriate and entirely expected, especially when considered in the context of Eden's rise to a prominent position within the treasury, secured no doubt through the support of Spanish nobles at court in 1555.[40] His decision to focus on the religious, rather than commercial, aspects of Spanish colonialism is, however, intriguing. Given the fact that the text is dedicated to Mary and Philip, it is possible that Eden's *Decades* was a piece of royally sanctioned pro-Catholic propaganda. After all, Mary had inherited a kingdom that was Reformed in nature and thus heretical in the eyes of the zealous queen.[41] The ferocity of the Marian persecutions, and the willingness of the Crown to revive medieval laws against heresy and execute those found guilty, was indicative of the English monarchy's concerted effort to secure Catholicism in England.[42] The multiple references to the 'monstrous' and 'deformed' minds of mid-century, ostensibly Reformed, English men and women, coupled with the unbridled praise of Spanish Catholicism, suggests an important function of Eden's text was to educate the English about their sinful living, force them to see the error of their ways, and convince them to return to the Catholic flock of their own volition.[43] It is of course possible that Eden was in fact expressing his own opinions about Catholicism and Spanish imperialism. This, however, is unlikely given the fact that Eden was accused of heresy towards the end of 1555, forcing him to leave his newly acquired office.[44] As early as the 1550s, then, exploration in America was impacting upon the religious debates taking place in Europe. In the case of England in 1555, the example of

America was being used to exemplify the pious, divinely ordained nature of the Spanish enterprise to convince lapsed English Catholics to return to the one true religion and do their duty to God by spreading his message to the 'heathen' peoples of the New World. America, and the Spanish involvement there, thus became symbolic of Christian piety properly expressed.

This pro-Spanish, pro-Catholic position, however, grew increasingly dangerous after the accession of Elizabeth I, as England became progressively religiously conformist, uniform, and Protestant, with the Church of England being established as the official faith of the realm. A variety of laws and statutes were introduced during Elizabeth's reign which punished lay Catholics for a variety of crimes, from not attending Church of England services, to harbouring Catholic priests and hearing masses, to actively educating their sons and daughters at Catholic schools, seminaries, and convents on the continent. Harsh anti-recusancy laws were introduced to erode English Catholicism and force outward conformity.[45] As the sixteenth century wore on, England became increasingly intolerant of openly practising Catholics; as John Coffey puts it, Elizabeth had had 'the good grace to conform under Mary, and she found it hard to understand why others would not do likewise under her'.[46] Religion was thus a highly contested issue in sixteenth-century England. In the mid-1550s, when England had returned to Catholicism under Mary, an English colonial identity emerged that was centred on religious motivations. It called for the emulation of Spanish imperialism that sought to convert the Indigenous population to Catholicism and reap the material rewards of God's divine favour. However, with increasingly hostile relations between Spain and England, and with the solidifying of the Church of England as the religion of the realm, this ideology would be fiercely challenged from the 1560s onwards.

English piracy, New World commodities, and the emergence of anti-Spanish sentiment

By the end of the 1560s it appears that Richard Eden's call to the English to emulate the Spanish Empire and convert the 'heathen' peoples of North America had fallen on deaf ears, a trend that would continue throughout the 1570s. The 1577 re-edition of Eden's translation of Martyr is indicative of how much the English attitude towards America had changed during the 1560s and 1570s.[47] This edition was, as the title page suggests, 'gathered in part' by Richard Eden, being now 'newly set in order, augmented, and finished by Richarde Willes'.[48] Willes, like Eden, appears to have led an ambiguous religious life. In the 1560s Willes had entered the Society of Jesus and began training for the Catholic priesthood. In the early 1570s

Willes abandoned his religious training and returned to England where he declared his loyalty to the Church of England and obtained the patronage of the firmly Protestant family of the Earl of Bedford, Francis Russell.[49] Given this change in religious outlook, and given the religious views of his patrons, it is unsurprising that the references to the success of Spanish missionary activity in the New World are gone from the address to the reader.[50] Rather than attempting to call the English to help support the Spanish programme of conversion in the New World, Willes, in his dedication to the Countess of Bedford, merely hoped that his patron would 'finde delight in reading over these relations, wherein so newe, so straunge, so divers, so many recreations and delightes of the mynd are expressed'.[51] Instead of attempting to promote an English colonialism that would emulate the Spanish, as Eden had done in 1555, Willes hoped to provide an entertaining text that would 'delight a mynde travelled in weighty matters, & weeried with great affayres'.[52] The religious nature of the Spanish conquest of America had thus been disconnected from Martyr's text by Willes, being replaced by a reading that saw the value of the text in its description of strange and unfamiliar sights.

The process by which religion became increasingly disentangled from English understandings of America, and the way in which the Spanish approach to the New World became unenviable, is a complex one. As has already been suggested, the growing intolerance towards Catholics in England made any positive assessment of the success of Spanish conversion in the Americas foolhardy and increasingly dangerous. It was not only, however, the solidifying of the Church of England that encouraged a less complimentary attitude towards Spain. A number of political and economic spats between England and Spain also helped stimulate this hardening attitude. The first of these came in 1563 with a trade embargo in Antwerp, caused in part by English piracy in the channel, but also by long-term disputes over duties and customs.[53] A severe outbreak of plague in London provided the regent of the Netherlands, the Duchess of Palma, with an excuse to enact the closure of trade that she had threatened for some time, resulting in the banning of the importation of English cloth and woollen goods, not only in Antwerp, but in all the dominions of the Spanish king. The shutting down of the cloth trade in Antwerp was particularly damaging for English merchants, given that woollen cloth was England's main export and Antwerp its largest market.[54] This tension between the two nations was, however, temporary as this embargo was later lifted and peaceful trade with Spain resumed once more. However, just two years later England and Spain were once again embroiled in hostility. As Jason Eldred has argued, the Dutch Revolt of 1566 'inescapably poisoned Anglo-Spanish relations', as Queen Elizabeth I supported the rebels in the hope of maintaining English national security.⁵⁵ While this development led to another trade embargo and undoubtedly alarmed merchants trading with Spain, it also gave other Englishmen the opportunity to retaliate against what they saw as a tyrannical and ungodly imperial Spain.⁵⁶ It is this group of men, with their virulent anti-Hispanicism and their aggressive approach to foreign policy with Spain, who Eldred has categorised as the 'martial maritime faction'.⁵⁷ This group argued that England's national interest was best served by hostility to Spain, suggesting that economic stability would come through aggressive expansion in the form of overseas settlement and the intrusion of the English into the 'lucrative Iberian trade routes to the Indies'.⁵⁸ Political tensions with Spain thus became the lens through which English exploration and action in the Americas was viewed. Gone was the adoration of the Spanish Empire and their conquest in America and gone were the religious justifications for English involvement in the New World; commercial gain was now the priority for English explorers and preferably at the expense of the Spanish.

One of the first men to tackle this new approach to the New World was John Hawkins. Hawkins had been trading in the Indies since the early 1560s, taking enslaved people from Africa to exchange for goods in the Caribbean. During these earlier slaving ventures Hawkins operated under a veil of legality, assuming that trade in this region was covered by the Anglo-Spanish commercial treaty of 1489. These voyages yielded Hawkins and his investors a handsome profit but they also increasingly incurred the anger of the Spanish, particularly as Anglo-Spanish relations deteriorated in the mid-1560s. After the completion of his second voyage in 1565, the king of Spain made his position in the Caribbean inescapably clear; the rival French colony in Florida was destroyed, Hawkins was forced by the Spanish ambassador to sign a bond promising not to trade with the Spanish in the West Indies, and thus Spanish hegemony in the Caribbean was restored.⁵⁹ However, this would not stop Hawkins pursuing a profit in the Indies. Hawkins's third slaving voyage of 1567, although ostensibly barred by the Privy Council to appease the Spanish, had the appearance of a 'national undertaking' and, more importantly, the support and indeed investment of the queen. Under the pretext that Hawkins's voyage would merely visit the African coast to search for an unclaimed gold mine, the Spanish ambassador was reassured that Hawkins would not break the bond that he had made after the second voyage.⁶⁰ Breaking these promises, however, Hawkins procured 500 men in Sierra Leone to sell into slavery and set sail for the West Indies. Hawkins described what happened in the Americas in a pamphlet published after his return home in 1569. His enterprise began well despite the fact that the king of Spain had commanded that the governors in the Indies should under no circumstances 'suffer anye trade' with him and his men.⁶¹ At the island of Margarita, off the Venezuelan coast, Hawkins and his men met with 'reasonable trade and courteous intertainemente', and although they encountered Spanish resistance at the town of Rio de la Hacha they managed to force their way into the town and obtain a 'secrete trade', thanks to the 'Spaniardes desire of Negrose' and to their 'frendship of the treasurer'.⁶² Hawkins was keen to point out that in all other places where he and his men had traded, 'the Spainiards inhabitaunts were glad of us and traded willingly'.⁶³ This point becomes important when considered in the context of what happened next, for Hawkins's voyage did not end in success but in outright catastrophe.

After failing to engage in trade at Cartagena, Hawkins decided it was time to return to England. An 'extreme storme', however, forced Hawkins to put in at San Juan de Ulúa in Mexico to repair his ships, take on water, and 'obtayne vittualles'.⁶⁴ This unplanned diversion ended badly as the Spanish 'had fornished them selves with a supplie of men to the nomber of. *1000*' from the mainland and proceeded to 'set uppon' the English from all sides.⁶⁵ Although many Englishmen were killed 'without mercye', the survivors were able to escape and eventually made it back to England with the majority of their treasure.⁶⁶ For Hawkins, the behaviour of the Spanish was unacceptable. On arrival home Hawkins even went as far as to open proceedings against the Spanish in the admiralty court, looking for compensation for the damage and losses incurred in Mexico.⁶⁷ Despite trading without the king's permission, Hawkins had categorised his dealings in the Caribbean as peaceful and mutually beneficial. The violent response of the Spanish would not be easily forgotten by Hawkins or indeed by the English more generally. With the Spanish illustrating just how far they would go in order to protect their New World possessions, a new phase of even more aggressive dealings by the English with the Spanish in the West Indies ensued.⁶⁸ Unwelcome and unauthorised, yet relatively peaceful, trade was now to be replaced with outright and aggressive piracy and plundering.

The epitome of this new and more aggressive approach was Francis Drake's circumnavigation of the world that was completed between 1577 and 1580. As well as being a triumph for early modern navigational and shipbuilding techniques, it was also a triumph for English piracy. From the account of the voyage published some years later in Richard Hakluyt's voluminous *Principal Navigations*, it is clear that English respect for Spanish possessions in the New World had entirely disappeared. While Hawkins had traded with the Spanish for the treasure he brought home, albeit secretly and illegally, Drake's approach was far more forceful, taking what he wanted and ransacking Spanish towns in the process. Throughout this narrative of the voyage there are multiple references to Drake's overt piracy. One of the greatest Spanish prizes taken by the English was the

Cacafuego, a Spanish ship that the English had followed from Lima to near the coast of Panama.[69] After entering the ship, Drake and his men 'found in her great riches, as jewels and precious stones, thirteene chests full of royals of plate, foure score pound weight of golde, and sixe and twentie tunne of silver'. This robbery continued on land in the town of Huatulco as the English 'ransaked the Towne', taking silver, gold, and other precious jewels from the inhabitants. According to the author of this account, this aggression towards the Spanish was Drake's revenge for the 'private injuries received from the Spaniards' and also for the Spanish 'contempts and indignities' towards the English nation and her majesty the queen.[70] Poor relations with Spain, and the perceived injustices dealt by the Spanish to the English, thus became justifications for piracy in the Americas. The English no longer wished to emulate the Spanish model of conquest and colonisation, but instead wished to take from the Spanish, by force, the treasures procured from their New World possessions. For Drake and Hawkins, the spiritual health of Indigenous communities seemed irrelevant to their enterprises. The purpose of their ventures was to acquire treasure, not to see the Indigenous inhabitants converted to Christianity. In fact, both accounts of these voyages had very little to say about the Indigenous populations of America in general, save for sporadic details about the nakedness and undoubted 'savagery' and 'ungodliness' of Indigenous people.[71] For Drake and Hawkins, then, the procurement of Spanish treasure was the principal motivation for travelling to the Americas. The idea that the spiritual health of the Indigenous inhabitants should be at the heart of English involvement in the New World had disappeared entirely. However, outside this circle of the 'martial maritime' elite, it appears that the model established by Richard Eden in the 1550s may not have died out completely.

The work of one author and translator that seems to challenge this notion of extreme Anglo-Spanish hostility in the late 1570s is that of Thomas Nicholls. He was responsible for bringing the events of the Spanish conquest of Mexico to an English audience in his 1578 translation of Francisco López de Gómara's *Historia General de Las Indias*, published under the English title, *The Pleasant Historie of the Conquest of the Weast India, Now Called New Spayne*.[72] In Nicholls's dedication to Francis Walsingham, a man who clearly saw Spain as a threat to English security, being as he was a principal member of the martial maritime faction, the ventures of Hernán Cortés in Mexico were described as 'valiant' and 'princely'.[73] Cortés was also cast by Nicholls as something of a religious crusader who had defeated the 'infidel' Aztecs and implanted Christianity in the recently conquered and renamed New Spain. In fact, the entire narrative of the conquest was summarised by Nicholls as a tale of religious success in which the 'ignorant *Indians*' were saved by the Spanish from 'worshipping Idolles', being given the knowledge of Jesus Christ and true Christian religion.[74]

It is difficult to determine why Nicholls may have had such a positive attitude towards the Spanish conquests in America and their religious successes, given what we know about Nicholls himself. From the scant biographical information we have on Nicholls, it would seem that he had little reason to praise the Spanish Crown and its achievements in the New World. He had, after all, been imprisoned in both the Spanish Canary Islands and in Spain for heresy.[75] After his acquittal for this second charge of heresy, Nicholls returned to England where he began translating works that would inform the Privy Council's strategy towards the military and financial strength of the Spanish monarchy.[76] However, there are several possible explanations for this surprisingly positive interpretation of the conquest of Mexico.

An important factor to consider is the reception of Gómara's original Spanish text in his home country. The conquest of Mexico represented a watershed moment in the cultural encounter between Spain and America, and provided an influx of New World gold into Europe. It was, however, not without its controversies. From the very start of his explorations of Mexico in 1518, Cortés had been acting in open rebellion, defying the authority of the governor of Cuba, Diego Velázquez de Cuéllar, who had instructed Cortés not to settle or conquer the lands that he discovered.[77] Therefore, although the conquest of Mexico represented a stunning success for the Spanish, the way that Cortés had achieved it increasingly drew criticism from the Crown. Gómara's account of Cortés's conquest of Mexico was first published in Zaragoza in 1552 and, despite being an immediate success, just a year after publication Charles V demanded that all copies of the book be seized. This censorship of Gómara occurred at a time when the Spanish Crown was attempting to diminish the power and influence of the *conquistadores* in New Spain. An intrinsic aspect of this campaign was to ban and seize texts that would support the *conquistadores*' claim for material compensation by praising their achievements.[78] Gómara's excessive praise of Cortés made his book one such text, and it remained banned in Spain until 1726.[79] The fact that the Spanish Crown condemned this book may have appealed to men hostile to Spain such as Francis Walsingham; Cortés may have been a Spaniard, but he was a Spaniard who had defied the authority of his superiors, and who continued to trouble imperial Spain well after the completion of the conquest. Indeed, the threat from Cortés to Spanish power in Mexico continued into the next generation when his son Martín attempted, unsuccessfully, to establish an independent Mexico in 1566.[80] Cortés and his conspiratorial heirs were thus considered traitors in Spain in the latter half of the sixteenth century. This goes some way to explaining why Nicholls, with the support of the vehemently anti-Spanish

Walsingham, was able to characterise Cortés as valiant and princely without compromising his loyalty to the queen. What it does not explain, however, is why Nicholls chose to frame the conquest as a predominantly religious event.

María Valencia Suárez has argued that this may be, in part, down to the source material that Nicholls chose to translate. Through her comparison of the English edition with its original Spanish, Suárez illustrates that Nicholls was heavily influenced by Gómara's mode of description and in particular his 'religious portrayal of the conquest' and his 'negative view of Aztec culture'.[81] Alongside this, Nicholls's own religious leanings can help explain his focus on the spiritual aspects of the conquest. Nicholls was clearly a very pious man, having endured two imprisonments for heresy abroad and having secured his induction as a rector at Widford on his return to England.[82] Nicholls was not only a religious man, but an apparently committed Calvinist. In fact, his extreme Calvinist preaching eventually led to his removal from Widford by the Bishop of Oxford in 1577.[83] It is clear from Nicholls's address to the reader that he was less than impressed by the religiosity of English society. According to Nicholls, the converted 'heathens' of Mexico were 'more devoute unto heavenly things' than the 'wretched Chrystians' of England, especially in 'Charitie, humilitie, and lively works of faith'.[84] Nicholls's decision to categorise the conquest of Mexico as a religious conquest can thus be read as a critique of English piety, rather than as a celebration of the success of Spanish conversion in the New World. For pious men such as Nicholls, then, religion was central to their understanding of European contact and conquest in the Americas, and yet on closer reading and contextualisation it is possible to deduce that this religious position was one of strictly Reformed Protestantism rather than one of pro-Hispanicism and pro-Catholicism. Nicholls's Reformed Protestantism, and his interpretation of Spanish imperialism, clashed with many other authors of the sixteenth century, reflecting the wide spectrum of English Protestant belief in Elizabethan England and the increasing puritan push for further religious reform.

It is clear, then, that different groups of people had varied approaches to how the English could and should be involved in New World projects. Men like Nicholls advocated a religious understanding of the encounter between Europe and America, but in general Englishmen moved towards a more commercial, anti-Spanish-centred ideology in the 1570s. This began with the trading of Hawkins and the piracy of Drake but continued with the independent English exploration of North America. In 1578 another book appeared on the booksellers' stalls of St. Paul's Churchyard, a book that took a very unambiguous approach to the record of the Spanish in the New World and towards English exploration in the region. The author of the text, George Best, had been a member of Martin Frobisher's crew during his three explorations of Meta Incognita in 1576, 1577, and 1578. Best had strong opinions about the way he thought English exploration in America should proceed, and it categorically did not involve emulating the Spanish model. Although not openly critical of the Spanish, it is clear that Best felt the English were more than capable of holding their own in the New World, even being 'greatly superior' in their 'hard adventures, and valiant resolutions' than their Spanish and Portuguese counterparts.[85] In fact, according to Best, 'by oure Englishmens industries, and these late voyages, the world is grown to a more fulnesse and perfection'. Thanks to the English the following had been achieved: 'Christs name spred: the Gospell preached: Infidels like to be converted to Christianitie, in places where before the name of God hath not once bin heard of'.[86] On closer reading, however, this celebration of the English evangelisation of the 'infidels' of America appears a little disingenuous, given the actual motives of Frobisher's exploration.

From the announcement on the text's title page it is clear that religious conversion of Indigenous people was not the principal motivation of the English ventures. Instead they were conducted 'for the finding of a passage to Cathaya, by the Northweast'.[87] The concept of a Northwest Passage to Asia, which could be accessed from the Arctic region of America, flourished in the 1560s and 1570s. For the proponents of this theory, most notably the promoter of grand schemes, Humphrey Gilbert, the scientist and mystic, John Dee, and the merchant and supporter of commercial ventures, Michael Lok, this new route would provide the English with a shorter and less dangerous journey than those undertaken by the Spanish and Portuguese in the southern oceans.[88] For the adventurers and promoters who subscribed to this theory, exploring America was merely a means of securing access to the wealth of the East. Frobisher's voyages, however, were entirely unsuccessful in this respect; the Northwest Passage remained hidden. Best's suggestion of the religious significance of Frobisher's voyages can thus be read as a narrative of consolation. The English explorers had not managed to achieve the stated objectives of their voyage but they had managed to implant the Christian faith in a land that had previously been devoid of true religious understanding.

Indeed, Best was not the only Englishman to categorise the exploration of Meta Incognita in religious terms. Thomas Churchyard, who also published his account of the third voyage in 1578, suggested that 'no further gaine then Goddes glorie were looked for' in the execution of this expedition.[89] In fact, he went even further than Best in establishing the venture's evangelical purpose; the preaching of Christianity to the Inuit was not merely a consolation, but a principal motivation. According to Churchyard, Frobisher, alongside his captains Fenton, York, and Best, hoped to 'spread Gods glorie farther then ever hath bin by our common knowledge understoode'. It was not just the personal drive of these men, however, that led them on their godly mission, but that of the entire English nation as being 'suche a christian sorte', it 'refuseth no hazarde nor daunger, to bryng Infidelles too the knowledge of the omnipotente God'.[90] In Churchyard's opinion, then, Frobisher's explorations of Meta Incognita were not undertaken to secure wealth and access to the East for the English, but to satisfy a godly mission for the entire nation.

There is also an entirely different interpretation of the exploration, an interpretation that is seen throughout the remainder of Churchyard's text and in surviving documents relating to the voyage. The main objectives of this final expedition were to mine for gold and colonise the region, not to proselytise the Christian faith and convert the 'infidel' Inuit. Exactly how these objectives were to be achieved was outlined in great detail by the royal commission that had been established to oversee the venture. Frobisher was to travel to the Countess of Warwick's Island, secure it against attacks from the Inuit, set his miners to work in search of gold, and to leave a group of men under the control of Edward Fenton to inhabit Meta Incognita.[91] Once again, the commercial aspects of Frobisher's explorations were at the fore. The remainder of Churchyard's text also unwittingly identified the economic motivations of the voyage, despite his initial insistence that the glory of God was the central concern of all those involved with the enterprise. For example, at no point in the rest of the book did Churchyard describe any encounter with the Inuit in which the word of God was preached. In fact, the majority of the encounters that Churchyard described are categorised by violence. The Inuit were clearly not happy with the arrival of the English as they 'tooke up' their arrows and 'most obstinatly shot those arrowes' at the English 'without regarde of their owne lives'.[92] These scuffles with the Inuit continued throughout the expedition, and eventually led the English to pack up their ships, conclude their business, and return home.[93] Although employing the language of religious conquest, both Best's and Churchyard's descriptions illustrate the centrality of commercial incentives in their voyages. The religious motivations that Best and Churchyard identified were retrospectively attached to their ventures in order to compensate for failing to achieve their intended aims. The voyages to Meta Incognita thus inverted the colonial ideology of the 1550s; commercialisation was the project's main objective while the spreading of God's word was a mere consolation prize.

English failure and God's disfavour

During the 1580s the tone of some English texts produced on the subject of exploration in the New World began to subtly change. After a number of bitterly disappointing voyages to America in the 1570s, Englishmen began to question their approach. Rather than the optimism of George Best, English explorers such as Dionyse Settle had been less than impressed with the harsh landscape of Meta Incognita. Settle was also a member of Frobisher's crew and published his account of the second voyage in 1577, a year before Best published his own account of the three Frobisher expeditions. Rather than reworking the narrative of the voyage as an example of English religious accomplishment in the New World as Best and Churchyard had done, Settle was willing to explain the failures of the expedition. As he frankly suggested, the lands that they had explored had 'nothing fitte, or profitable for the use of man'. The country was 'barren and unfertile', the people 'rude and of no capacitie to culture'.[94] The natural environment in general was extremely hostile; there was a 'great likelyhood of Earthquakes' and avalanches due to the 'huge and monstruous mounteynes'.[95] As Chapters 3 and 4 will demonstrate, Settle also used the appearance and diet of the Inuit to reinforce this negative interpretation of the region. On a slightly more positive note, Settle did suggest that the country might possess some useful commodities 'couched within the bowels of the earth', but as no extensive trial had yet been made, he preferred not to speculate further.[96]

It would seem that this negative assessment of the exploration did not go unnoticed by other members of the Frobisher expedition. Indeed, Best himself refers to texts such as Settle's in the dedication of his book to Christopher Hatton, an important English courtier who would go on to become the Lord Chancellor, stating that he had decided to publish his own 'true discourse' of the exploration as the 'common reporte' was 'vaine and uncertain', being as it was the product of 'sundrie mens fantasies'. These 'fantasies' and 'untruths', according to Best, had been spread abroad 'to the gret slaunder of this so honest and honorable an action'.[97] The fact that Settle's account had been published a year previous to Best's, and had been translated into French, Italian, German, and Latin, suggests that his narrative was part of this untrue 'common reporte' of which Best spoke.[98] This apparent English bad luck in the New World continued throughout the 1570s with Frobisher's next voyage to Meta Incognita also ending in failure. As Robert McGhee has argued, the failure of Frobisher's final voyage, despite the gloss provided by Best and Churchyard, was a bitter disappointment for the venture's investors, leading to much acrimony between themselves and the man ultimately responsible for how the voyage had proceeded, Martin Frobisher himself.[99]

This bitterness and pessimism towards English exploration in America was further compounded in the early 1580s by Humphrey Gilbert's untimely death at sea. Gilbert, as has already been suggested in Chapter 1, had been a keen advocate of English exploration in the New World, believing like

Frobisher in a Northwest Passage that would take them and their countrymen to the riches of the East. He was also, like many of his contemporaries who promoted English exploration and colonisation in the Americas, virulently anti-Spanish. In 1577 Gilbert famously presented Queen Elizabeth I with a proposal entitled *A Discourse How Her Majesty May Annoy the King of Spain*, suggesting that the English should complement Drake's raids on Spanish ships by attacking Spain's Atlantic fishing fleet.[100] Possibly in recognition of Gilbert's enthusiasm to extend English influence in the Americas and to temper Spanish power, in 1578 the queen awarded Gilbert letters patent to conduct a voyage of exploration to the New World, giving him the authority to 'discover, finde, search out, and view such remote heathen and barbarous lands, countreys, and territories not actually possessed by any Christian prince or people'.[101] In total, Gilbert conducted three expeditions to America. The first was inconsequential, being aborted early due to a shortage of supplies and fierce sea battles.[102] The second was more successful and brought back important information on the site that Gilbert hoped to realise his American colonisation scheme.[103] The third, however, undertaken in 1583, ended in disaster. The events of this final voyage were recorded by Edward Hayes, the captain and owner of one of the principal ships involved in the venture. Although probably written soon after his return to England in late 1583, Hayes's account was not published for the first time until 1589 when it appeared in Hakluyt's *Principal Navigations*. The voyage began well enough with the company of ships arriving successfully in the New World and Gilbert 'taking possession of those Countries', ostensibly without resistance. After securing possession, Gilbert went about obtaining money from his newly procured lands. Gilbert distributed these lands among his investors, crew, and the 'strangers' that he had encountered, all of whom 'did covenant to pay a certaine rent and service unto sir *Humfrey Gilbert*, his heires or assignes for ever'. Alongside this, Gilbert also enacted a tax upon every ship 'which did fish upon the coast adjoynin'.[104] Like those other English voyages before his own, Gilbert focused on acquiring monetary gain from the lands and peoples that he had explored and conquered. However, disaster struck as Gilbert and his men continued their explorations of the North American coast. After days of battling bad weather, and after losing one of their ships, *The Admiral*, it was decided that the expedition would head back to England.[105] The bad weather, however, continued and on Monday 9 September, Gilbert called out to Hayes on *The Golden Hind*, from his own sinking ship, 'we are as neere to heauen by sea as by land' before the ship was eventually 'devoured and swallowed up of the Sea'. After a fruitless search for survivors, Hayes and *The Golden Hind* headed home, with God's help, arriving in Falmouth on 22 September 1583.[106]

Rather than seeing Gilbert's death as a result of the bad weather and dangerous conditions inherent in early modern sea voyages, Hayes saw it as a providential warning from God. Although Hayes celebrated Gilbert's 'Christian pietie' and 'zeale', he also suggested that he had a tendency to ignore signs from God. His failure to listen to other men's opinions and find suitable land to settle on, 'pleased not God to prosper in his first and great preparation'. Rather than taking this initial failure as a sign from God, Gilbert, according to Hayes, threw himself in to another venture without proper organisation, 'presuming the cause pretended on Gods behalfe, would carie him to the desired ende'. As Hayes suggested, Gilbert was given no signs of encouragement from God to continue in his explorations; Gilbert was 'foyled in his first attempt, in a second should utterly be disgraced'.[107] In the end, 'it pleased the divine will to resume him [Gilbert] unto himselfe'.[108] Gilbert's explorations were ultimately unsuccessful because of his poor planning and his inability to recognise God's will.

Not only was Hayes critical of the Gilbert expeditions, he was also critical of the direction that all English exploration in America was taking. As he stated in the first sentence of his account, 'many voyages have bene pretended, yet hitherto never any thorowly accomplished by our nation'.[109] Hayes was clear about why he thought this was the case. Firstly, the English had not capitalised on the early expeditions of the Cabots; if they had done, Hayes believed that not only would 'her Maiesties territories and revenue' 'bene mightily inlarged and advanced', but also 'the seed of Christian religion' would have been 'sowed amongst those pagans'. Another reason for the ineffectuality of English expeditions in America was the apparent motivations of the explorers themselves who had shown that 'Gods cause hath not bene chiefly preferred by them'. Hayes called on future would-be explorers and colonisers to put aside 'ambition' and 'avarice' as these motives 'commeth not of God'. Without more pious intentions, English enterprises in the New World would never be successful, as explorers and colonisers would not enjoy the 'confidence of Gods protection and assistance'.[110] This increasingly providential view of English projects in America, in which establishing God's favour and reading divine signs were perceived to be critical to success, is unsurprising given the prevalence of providential thinking in sixteenth-century England. As Alexandra Walsham has convincingly argued, providentialism was not a 'marginal feature' of early modern English religious culture, but part of the mainstream, representing 'a cluster of presuppositions which enjoyed near universal acceptance'.[111] Ephemeral literature of the period was 'saturated' with references to divine providence, with such texts reaching a broad cross-section of English society.[112] The spread of providential news was encouraged by Protestant clergy who were anxious to undermine vestiges of the Old Faith, such as devotion to the saints, by emphasising God's omnipotence and providential power.[113] Within this context, then, Hayes's understanding of Gilbert's last voyage, and the reasons behind its failure, reflected the religious culture of sixteenth-century England in which providentialism was a key feature. The call to abandon worldly gain in preference of God's favour and spiritual enlightenment was thus a product of both negative English experiences in the New World and the religious culture of the period.

In fact, even before Gilbert's untimely death at sea advocates of the Newfoundland enterprise were already beginning to articulate their concerns about how the project was proceeding. In a letter written to Richard Hakluyt the elder in 1578, a letter that was eventually published in Richard Hakluyt the younger's *Principal Navigations*, the Bristol merchant Anthony Parkhurst, who had visited Newfoundland, lamented the fact that the men of sixteenth-century England could not 'suffer any thing (or at least few) to proceed and prosper that tendeth to the setting forth of Gods glory, and the amplifying of the Christian faith'.[114] Echoing the words of Richard Eden from decades earlier, Parkhurst complained that for the purpose of converting those Indigenous peoples currently in the 'captivitie of that spirituall *Pharao*, the devil', 'the labourers as yet are few, the harvest great'. Parkhurst encouraged Hakluyt to continue his work in bringing 'good and godly desires to some passe', believing him to be 'an instrument' of God that would 'moove men of power, to redeeme the people of *Newfoundland*'.[115]

Parkhurst's wish that something be done to change the direction and focus of English colonial projects was ostensibly fulfilled by Hakluyt's younger cousin of the same name. Like Parkhurst, Hakluyt the younger believed that English explorations in America had been too focused on the acquisition of treasure and commodities rather than on the saving of Indigenous souls. Expressing these concerns in print for the first time in 1582, Hakluyt suggested that had English explorers cared more about 'Gods glorie' than 'gaine', their projects would have had a 'farre better effecte', because as Hakluyt suggested, 'Godlinesse is great riches, and that if we first seeke the kingdome of God, al other things will be given unto us'.[116] By the early 1580s, then, a return to the colonial ideology that Richard Eden had proposed in the 1550s, in which the advancement of God's glory was the motive and economic gain the reward, had been set in motion. The way in which this model would be achieved, however, was significantly different to what Eden had suggested. Neither Hayes, Parkhurst, or Hakluyt, nor the Englishmen who agreed with their assessment of English exploration in America, encouraged the emulation of the Spanish Empire. Indeed, the ideology that would develop in England from the 1580s would position itself in staunch opposition to Spanish experiences and techniques in America, forging a discourse that was based on the peculiarities of both English religious life and society.

Godly enterprises and Spanish atrocities

In the early 1580s, English propagandists and promoters of colonial enterprises were fighting against a tide of English disillusionment. Up until this point, English exploration in America had achieved very little and increasingly this was being blamed upon the English focus on commercial gain at the expense of God's glorification. Once this uncomfortable fact had been articulated by the likes of Hakluyt and Hayes, other English colonisers and promoters could begin constructing an idealised, religiously inspired conquest and colonisation programme. One text that attempted to express coherently this new colonial message was George Peckham's *A True Reporte, of the Late Discoveries, and Possession, Taken in the Right of the Crowne of Englande*, published in London in 1583. Like Hayes, Peckham was close to the voyages of Humphrey Gilbert and wrote his book in response to Gilbert's last voyage. It is likely that Peckham composed this text almost immediately after the completion of Gilbert's third voyage as it appeared in 1583 and expressed uncertainty about Gilbert's fate; at the time of publication there was 'no certaine newes' as to what had become of Gilbert.[117] As Chapter 1 has suggested, it is also clear that Peckham published this text in a bid to encourage further investment in the project after Gilbert's death. Like Hayes, Peckham began to worry about the spiritual validity of Gilbert's venture, given what had happened during the final exploration. Peckham pondered whether or not this final voyage was 'as well pleasing to almightie God, as profitable to men?', 'as well gratefull to the Savages, as gainfull to the Christians'.[118] The rest of the book is dedicated to proving that English ventures in North America were indeed pleasing to God and beneficial to the Indigenous inhabitants. Not only was English colonialism 'commodious to the whole Realme' and 'profitable to the adventurers', it was also 'beneficial to the Savages' and, most importantly, 'a thing likewise tending to the honor and glory of almighty God'.[119]

Peckham was clearly echoing the sentiments of Hayes and Hakluyt, yet some historians have categorised his approach to the New World as something unique. In fact, Loren E. Pennington has argued that Peckham was the only commentator of the 1580s that attempted to fit the conversion of Indigenous people into a comprehensive theory of colonisation, with other Englishmen only following suit in the seventeenth century as a way of legitimising their claims to American lands.[120] As a Catholic nobleman, hoping to establish a refuge for other English Catholics in the New World, it is possible that Peckham's view on English colonialism in America may have been significantly different to those of his Protestant contemporaries.[121] In reality Peckham's faith was not an impediment to advancement. He was knighted in 1570, appointed sheriff of Buckinghamshire in 1572, and given a letter of recommendation by Francis Walsingham to aid his mission to secure investment for further exploration and settlement in the New World after the death of Gilbert. However, that is not to say that Peckham's Catholicism was left unchecked. He was imprisoned twice for offences relating to his religion and fell into debt due to the penalties incurred by his religious non-conformity. This did not appear to stop Peckham moving within the circles of the English Protestant elite, especially in the 1570s and 1580s. In fact, James McDermott has even argued that Peckham's plans for wide-scale Catholic emigration to America actually reflected a *de facto* recognition of the Acts of Supremacy (1559) and Uniformity (1559), thus illustrating Peckham's loyalty to the English Crown.[122] Peckham's loyalty to Elizabeth is clear throughout his treatise. He was convinced that Elizabeth held the rightful title over the lands of Newfoundland, virulently arguing that Elizabeth had more legitimacy than any Christian prince in the Indies.[123] Not only was Peckham loyal to his monarch, he also outwardly accepted that the principal faith of any New World colonies should be that of the Church of England, reiterating the laws established by Humphrey Gilbert that stated that 'religion publiquely exercised, should be such and none, other then is used in the Church of *England*'.[124]

It is also clear from a close reading of Peckham's text, alongside the views of Hayes, Parkhurst, and Hakluyt that have already been examined, that he was not the only Englishman that espoused a strong religious motivation for American enterprises. At the beginning of the book, before Peckham's main text begins, there are a number of endorsements for the tract from a variety of famous, well-connected explorers, adventurers, and courtiers. While some of these endorsements focused on the financial aspects of English activity in America, notably the one composed by Francis Drake, a number of others suggested that religious motivation should be at the front of any investor's mind.[125] William Pelham, the former Lord Justice of Ireland and an important diplomat to the Netherlands throughout the late sixteenth century, stated in his commendatory verses that he was sure that if the English motivation for expansion was virtuous, God's favour would be enjoyed by the English; 'For where the attempt, on vertue dooth depend: / No doubt but God, will blesse it in the ende'.[126] John Hawkins, the slave trader and man who was bent on turning a profit in the West Indies in the 1560s, had also, by the 1580s, incorporated religious motivations into his opinion on how enterprises in America should proceed. Under the English, for the first time 'the name of God shall founde, / Among a nation in whose eares the same did never sounde' and to those who bring glory to the name of God 'a private gaine shall bring'.[127] This connection between pleasing God and reaping financial reward in return is also clearly expressed by Captain John Chester who likely acted as a commander during Francis Drake's voyage that circumnavigated the world.[128] Chester believed that it was providence that the English should be successful in the New World, claiming that 'God hath left this honour unto us / The journey knowne, the passage quicklie runne, / The land full rich, the people easilie wunne. / Whose gaines shalbe the knowledge of our faith, / And ours such ritches as the country hath'.[129] In the 1580s, then, it was believed by a number of leading English explorers and their supporters that the successful spreading of God's word among the 'infidel' Indigenous population by the English, and the financial rewards that this would bring, was divinely ordained by God. Once this notion had been firmly established, the English could begin constructing how God's plan would be achieved in practice.

As well as promoting a religion-centred programme of English overseas exploration and settlement, Peckham's text also indicated the ways in which it could be achieved. This godly discourse not only extended to improving the religious lives of Indigenous Americans but also to rectifying the miserable state of many living in sixteenth-century England. As Peckham neatly summarised it, English settlement in North America should be 'principally undertaken for the enlargement of the christian fayth abroade, and the banishment of ydlenes at home'.[130] The spreading of God's word, then, collided with domestic economic necessity. Sixteenth-century England had witnessed huge population growth which had adversely affected prices. Employment opportunities and food supplies had not kept pace with these increases, leading to a peak in illegitimacy rates and levels of crime and vagrancy in the late sixteenth and early seventeenth centuries.[131] Alongside these domestic shortages and economic crises, the intensification of England's rivalry with Spain in the 1580s and the decline of traditional European markets for English products, encouraged England to look westwards for economic stability.[132] As Chapter 3 will explore in more detail, it was to be hoped, in particular, that America would become a thriving market for England's struggling cloth trade. These social uncertainties are clearly broached by Peckham and couched in terms of religious and providential thinking. Thanks to 'Gods especiall blessing', the many commodities and virtues of North America had been revealed. Thanks to 'the mighty assistaunce of the omnipotent God', 'all odious ydlenes' from England would be 'utterly banished', 'many poore and needy persons' would find relief, and 'the ignorant & barbarous Idolaters taught to knowe Christ.'[133] Idle children, for example, would be put to work to make 'a thousand kindes of trifeling thinges' as merchandise for the Americas.[134] Men would be employed in 'draging for Pearle, working for Mynes, and in matters of husbandry' as well as in 'fishing for Codde, Salmon and Herring'.[135] By stimulating trade with the 'savages' of America, who once having tasted English civility would become ripe consumers of English goods, 'all such Townes and Villages, as bothe have beene and nowe are utterlye decayed and ruinated' in England would be 'restored to theyr pristinate wealth and estate'.[136] In return for their trade and natural resources, the Indigenous population would be recompensed by being 'brought from falsehood to truth, from darknes to lyght, from the hieway of death, to the path of life, from superstitious idolatry, to sincere christianity'.[137] By revealing the lands of North America, God had bestowed his favour on the English, providing them with resources from America that would help banish poverty from the realm and a land in which the English idle poor could be put to good use. In return for God's good grace, the English would fulfil their pious duty by spreading the gospel to Indigenous 'heathens', raising them to civility and converting them to Christianity.

It was not just the Catholic Peckham, however, that presented English New World projects in this way. Christopher Carleill, in a short pamphlet aimed at inducing the Muscovy Company to invest in English enterprises in America, also illustrated the spiritual rewards that trade and settlement in the West would bring.[138] While it is clear that Carleill produced his text to illustrate the economic incentives of voyages to America, stating as he does that it was 'the Merchandizyng, whiche is the matter especially looked for', it is also evident that he believed the religious aspects of such enterprises were important draws for potential investors.[139] This consideration of the spiritual rewards of such enterprises may have been in part down to Carleill's association with Richard Hakluyt the younger, who had made his own printed plea for godly colonisation just a year earlier. As Rachel Lloyd has argued, although Hakluyt may have been one of the brains behind the text, Carleill was nonetheless able to transform Hakluyt's ideas into more practical terms.[140] In a similar fashion to Peckham, but in fact with a much more explicit religious message, Carleill explained to his readers that 'Christian charitie' 'perswade the furtherance' of English action in America. Not only would English trade and settlement in North America reduce 'the savage people, to Christianitie and civilitie', it would also help find employment for the great number of 'poore sorte of people', who were 'livyng altogether unprofitable, and often tymes to the great disquiet of the better sorte'.[141] Involvement in English New World projects, according to Carleill, did not merely reflect a sound monetary investment, then, but also a spiritual one. As well as reasserting the religious benefits of English engagement with America that had been identified in the same year by Peckham, Carleill also introduced another spiritual advantage that would be well received by the more 'godlie mynded' of his potential investors. Trade with the Americas would provide the unique advantage of sheltering merchants from 'Idolatrous Religion', allowing them a 'free libertie of conscience'. By trading in a land that was inhabited by an irreligious Indigenous population who could easily be converted to the form of Christianity most agreeable to the English, Carleill argued that those involved with the trade could avoid having profane religions 'enforced upon them', being instead able to practice the faith which was 'most agreable unto their parentes and Maisters'.[142] It is unclear from the context exactly which idolatrous religions Carleill was referring to, but it is likely to be either the religions of Muscovy and the Near East or the Roman Catholicism of some of England's nearer neighbours in Europe, given the extensive amount of English trade undertaken in these regions in the late sixteenth century.[143] Trading in regions with a different religion could be perilous, leading to imprisonment for heresy, or even worse, and as Carleill suggested, indoctrination into idolatry. Trading with the Indigenous peoples of the Americas, then, would not only open up a vast new market for English products and a new arena in which to source critical commodities for English import, it would also help protect the piety of those involved in such trade, insulating them from the dangers of idolatrous religions.

The idea that godly exploration and settlement in America was intimately tied to commercial gain and domestic economic stability, an idea which had been percolating among English advocates of New World colonialism since the 1580s, solidified at the turn of the century. Not only were Peckham's and Carleill's accounts reprinted in 1600 in Hakluyt's second and expanded edition of the *Principal Navigations* alongside Hayes's and Parkhurst's descriptions of Newfoundland, another tract also emerged in 1602 that synthesised the argument that had first been put forward in the early 1580s in which economic gain would follow godly settlement.[144] The pamphlet, although attributed to John Brereton, an explorer who made the first English attempt at settling the region which is now modern-day New England, was in fact a composite text that included a number of works that promoted the idea of English settlement in the New World.[145] Within these multiple works, written at different times but published together in 1602, many of the ideas that had first been introduced to English readers in the 1580s on the nature of English activity in the Americas were clearly rearticulated. Richard Hakluyt the elder composed a series of notes in 1585 outlining the many 'inducements' for planting the English in North America which were eventually printed posthumously in Brereton's text. Setting out the goals for English projects in America, Hakluyt argued, as his cousin had done in 1582, that 'the glory of God', achieved 'by planting of religion among those infidels', should be the principal motivation for English explorers and would-be colonisers.[146] In fact, Hakluyt helpfully listed and prioritised what the objectives of English activity in America should be: '1. To plant Christian religion. / 2. To trafficke. / 3. To conquer'.[147] Alongside reaffirming the ideas that had been put forward by his cousin in 1582, Hakluyt also argued, as Peckham and Carleill had done in 1583, that English settlement in America should provide an 'ample vent of the labour of our poore people at home'.[148] By engaging the poor in the production of merchandise to be sold to the Indigenous inhabitants of North America, the 'great reliefe' of England's poor and the 'woonderfull enriching' of the English realm would be achieved.[149] In another tract printed within Brereton's volume, Edward Hayes, the vocal critic of Gilbert's final voyage to Newfoundland, also reasserted these claims. As Hayes suggested, in sixteenth-century England there was a worrying surplus of people and a dearth of employment. This 'want' of jobs had led to the decay of English towns and ports and had caused 'the realme to swarme full with poore and idle people'. By stimulating new trade routes in the West through the exploitation of the diverse range of commodities found in North America, Hayes argued there would be an increase in the 'imploiment also of our [English] people and ships'.[150] Moreover, by settling in North America and by sourcing critical commodities from the region, such as fish oils, tar and pitch, timber, hemp, and flax, English merchants would ensure that other European nations in need of such products would trade directly with them. Once the lands of North America had been brought under the power of the English Crown, competing European countries would no longer be able to procure these commodities from the region without engaging in trade with the English. Instead, the English would reap the benefit of settlement by exchanging these essential products for luxury commodities from the Spanish and Portuguese such as wines, sweet oils, fruits, spices, sugars, silks, gold, and silver.[151] Continuing the providential framing of English overseas projects that he had begun in his account of Gilbert's last voyage, Hayes concluded that, in terms of settling North America, there was 'no nation of Christendom' 'so fit for this action as *England*'.[152]

At the same time that writers were exploring the various ways to banish idleness and poverty from England through trade and settlement in the New World, they were also considering the best way to approach the Christianisation of the Indigenous peoples of North America. Another critical aspect of this resurgent godly discourse, then, was the English approach to the spiritual health of Indigenous communities. English commentators addressed this issue in two distinct ways, firstly by criticising the Spanish approach to the conversion of Indigenous groups and secondly by suggesting a method that would see them reduced to civility and converted to Christianity through gentleness rather than force. Although English criticism of Spanish colonialism had been implicit in works produced from the late 1560s onwards, it was not until the 1580s, when relations between Spain and England were at an all-time low, that this criticism became more overt. As will be explored later, while the English planned to care and nurture the Indigenous groups they encountered, the Spanish, in contrast, were busy torturing and murdering, in huge numbers, the Indigenous communities of the New World that they had conquered. Arguably, this new highly critical interpretation of Spanish colonialism first emerged with the publication of the first English edition of Bartolomé de Las Casas's infamous tract *Brevísima Relación de la Destrucción de las Indias* in 1583. Under the English title *The Spanish Colonie*, the idea of the tyrannical, cruel, and ungodly *conquistador* burst its way into the English consciousness.[153] Originally published in Seville in 1542, Las Casas's text was written to convince the king of Spain to rethink the ways in which the Indigenous populations of America should be treated, encouraging him to abolish the *encomienda* system and introduce policies that would protect Indigenous people and curb the violence of the *conquistadores*.[154] Despite Las Casas's undoubted allegiance to the king, his assessment of those Spaniards conquering and colonising in the New World was damning. His account of Spanish atrocities in the New World thus became, as Lewis Hanke has argued, the 'choicest weapon of anti-Spanish propaganda' for Spain's political and religious enemies, with various foreign editions of the text being produced in the late sixteenth century.[155]

It is clear from the address to the reader from the 1583 edition that the purpose of the translation was to illustrate the cruelty and barbarity of the Spanish towards the 'poore reasonable creatures' of the Americas.[156] The preface of the text, presumably composed by the translator who only identified himself with the letters M. M. S., was dedicated to 'all the provinces of the Lowe countreys', highlighting once again how intra-European politics impacted upon English representations of the Americas in the late sixteenth century.[157] This nod towards the Netherlands in 1583 is unsurprising given the fact that a resurgent Dutch Revolt against Spanish rule had been raging for a number of years. Although Elizabeth I attempted to maintain a sense of neutrality to the fighting taking place in the Netherlands, at least until 1585 when the English position was re-examined in the light of the Prince of Orange's assassination, the Dutch Revolt nonetheless had a profound effect upon the English.[158] The history of the Dutch Revolt in England was largely written from the perspective of the Dutch rebels or by those who sympathised with their cause, thus demonising the Spanish and polluting still further the already tense relationship between England and Spain.[159] Within this context, then, the English edition of Las Casas's work, and its damning account of the atrocities committed by the Spanish in relation to the Indigenous inhabitants of the New World, reflected the growing criticism of Spanish colonialism in America and Spanish subjugation of the Netherlands. It was thus a reaction to the realities of the Spanish conquest in America and its perceived parallels with the violent dispute taking place back in Europe.

In the address to the reader, the Spanish were described as a most 'barbarous or cruell' nation, an unsurprising assessment given the entirely negative account of the Spanish conquest written by Las Casas.[160] According to Las Casas, the Spanish *conquistadores* had put 'to death unjustly and tyrannously more then twelve Millions of soules' in the Americas.[161] They 'roasted and broyled' Indigenous chiefs, they 'taught their houndes, fierce dogs, to teare them [Indigenous people] in peeces', and they took babies from their mothers, chopping them in 'small gobbettes, giving to every dog his livery or part there of'.[162] Las Casas also made it clear what had caused this despicable behaviour on the part of the Spanish; they destroyed an infinite number of Indigenous souls in order to 'gette golde, and to enriche them selves in a short tyme'.[163] The Spanish conquests in the Americas had thus illuminated for English readers what could happen if worldly gain was put before godly intentions, a point that was not lost on the writer of the address to the reader. As the author of the prefatory material explained, his motivation for translating Las Casas's text was to awaken the English 'out of their sleep' so they may begin to 'thinke upon Gods judgement: and refraine from their wickednes and vice'. The translator also encouraged his readers to 'consider with what enemie' they were to deal with, advocating that the English abandon their own 'quarrels, controversies, and partialities' in order to unite against the real enemy of Spain.[164] Not only did the publication of Las Casas's text encourage the English to heal the bitter divisions of their society, then, it also reinforced the notion that godly endeavour, rather than material gain, should be at the heart of overseas exploration.

This negative English assessment of Spanish colonialism in the Americas continued for the remainder of the sixteenth century, being explored by authors writing both directly and indirectly about European overseas projects. Walter Ralegh, although less concerned with the religious implications of Spanish colonialism, was nevertheless highly critical of the Spanish approach to the Indigenous inhabitants of the New World. In his account of his voyage to Guiana, published in 1596, Ralegh presented the Spanish as tyrannical and greedy, describing how they would sell Indigenous girls for a profit and satisfy their carnal lusts by taking 'both their wives and daughters daily', causing great enmity between themselves and the Indigenous population.[165] Others were more concerned with the spiritual tyranny of the Spanish *conquistadores*. The Archbishop of Canterbury, George Abbot, in his published dialogue with one Dr Hill over whether there was a need to uphold papistry in England, clearly articulated a hostile position towards Spain's evangelisation in the New World.[166] In contrast to Richard Eden, who had claimed in the 1550s that the Spanish had been responsible for the saving of millions of Indigenous souls, Abbot saw nothing commendable about the mass baptisms of Indigenous people by Spanish missionaries. In a sentence loaded with saracasm, Abbot replied to Hill's claim that the Catholic faith had been responsible for converting thousands in the West Indies to Christianity, by suggesting that the Spanish friars were indeed 'exceeding nimble in administring baptisme, to those who knewe very little'. Would not it have been better, so Abbot asked, to have preached the teachings of the Bible to the peoples of the Americas before 'the Sacrament had been imparted'?[167] In fact, instead of proselytising effectively and making sure that Indigenous people had a true understanding of the Christian faith, Abbot suggested that the Spanish chose to engage in ungodly and sinful activities, spending their time 'swearing, cursing & blaspheming God, in rapes & violent deflourings of the wives & daughters of the Americanes, & in al such incogitable & execrable vilainy, as if they had bin Divels and infernall spirites, let loose and sent from hell'.[168] Rather than being the saviours of Indigenous souls, then, the Spanish *conquistadores*, as both Las Casas and Ralegh had also suggested, were villainous, tyrannical, violent, and ungodly. Concluding his diatribe on Spanish evangelisation in the New World, Abbot stated that it was plain that 'dwellers in those parts of America which are said to be Christia[n], are few others but Spaniards'.[169]

This intensely critical reading of the Spanish approach to the Indigenous inhabitants of the New World and their conversion to Christianity contrasted starkly with English understandings of their own methods. As James Axtell has argued, merely desiring the conversion of Indigenous communities was 'insufficient' to accomplish the task.[170] Europeans realised that in order for Christianity to take hold, the Indigenous population had to be 'educable' and have the potential for civility. Without education and the raising to civilisation, the 'savages' of America would forever remain too degenerate for the Christian religion to flourish.[171] It was this process of civilising, followed by converting, that the English advocated in their own New World projects. A similar debate had, of course, taken place with regards to Spanish colonialism and yet, as we have seen above, it was the Spanish penchant for mass baptisms and violent coercion that became emblematic of Spanish missionary activity in the English imagination.[172] From the 1580s onwards, then, the English increasingly defined their methods in opposition to what they perceived the Spanish model to be, calling for a gentle and friendly approach to Indigenous people that would see them adopt English civility and, in turn, English Christianity.

In 1582 Richard Hakluyt the younger had distinguished between the Spanish approach and the English one directly. While the Spanish, and indeed Portuguese, merely *pretended* 'that they made their discoveries chiefly to convert Infidelles', their actual aim being to procure the 'goods and riches' of the New World, the English would instead, 'with great affection and zeale', *actually* reduce 'those gentile people to christianitie'.[173] Both George Peckham and Christopher Carleill agreed with Hakluyt that the Indigenous peoples of North America should be treated with affection by the English. Peckham suggested that the Christian settlers should 'endevour to take away such feare as may growe unto them [Indigenous people]' by engaging in 'quiet & peaceable conversation' and by 'letting them live in securitie'.[174] Likewise, Carleill advocated a policy that 'by gentle and familiar entreatyng' would encourage the Indigenous population to see what was 'better for them'. In approaching Indigenous communities with kindness and affection it was to be hoped that they would 'daiely by little & little, forsake their barbarous, and savage livyng, and grow to suche order and civilitie with us'.[175] Thomas Harriot, a principal participant in the first English attempt to settle Virginia, also agreed with this approach, arguing that by 'meanes of good government', and through 'friendships & love', the Virginia Algonquians would in 'short time be brought to civilitie, and the imbracing of true religion'.[176] This approach that saw the gentle entreating of Indigenous peoples to civility as a critical step towards conversion, would not only enable the English to distinguish themselves from the Spanish, but would also help them achieve their secondary colonial aim of establishing strong trade links with the Indigenous population. Both Peckham and Carleill suggested that the raising of the Indigenous community to civility would have the added advantage of creating a new set of consumers who would find English merchandise desirable; as Peckham put it, and as shall be explored in more detail in Chapter 3, once Indigenous people 'shall begin but a little to taste of civillitie' they would become a perfect 'vente for our English clothes'.[177] By introducing English standards of civility to the peoples of North America, then, not only would English settlers be able to convert these newly rational and civilised Indigenous peoples to Christianity, they would also be able to trade civilised English wares, such as clothing, with them. By the beginning of the seventeenth century, the English approach to the Indigenous inhabitants of America thus mirrored the English approach to colonisation more generally. While the spreading of God's word was the principal aim, trade and commerce remained a crucial, if ostensibly secondary, concern.

* * *

From the 1580s onwards, commercial incentives and religious imperatives collided in English approaches to trade and settlement in the Americas. Advocates of English settlement in the New World increasingly began to promote a type of colonialism which had godly endeavour at its heart. By revealing the lands of North America to the English, lands that were believed to be home to critical commodities needed in England and to an untapped market for English products, God had bestowed his divine favour upon England. In thanks for this sacred revelation, and with the hope of procuring more economic gains in the future, English commentators promoted an English approach to America which was first and foremost centred on spreading the word of God, bringing true Christianity to the 'godless' peoples of the New World. Through kindness and gentleness, the English, in their minds at least, would raise Indigenous people to civility, providing them with the necessary mental state to receive the word of God. By the end of the sixteenth century, then, the English approach to exploration and settlement was one in which God's good favour would inexorably lead to material and monetary gains. It was also one that was developed in opposition to that of the Spanish. While in English minds Spanish *conquistadores* raped and pillaged, using godliness as a disguise for greed, English explorers, merchants, and colonisers would forge friendly relations with Indigenous populations in order to create a suitable environment for both conversion and trade.

This approach to English projects in the New World was shaped by reciprocal influences from direct experience in America and from political, religious, and economic changes taking place back home. In the mid-1550s, when the Catholic Mary I still sat on the throne, a godly enterprise that emulated and bolstered the Spanish model of colonisation was advocated by Richard Eden. As Anglo-Spanish relations began to deteriorate, this religiously orientated approach was adapted into one in which commercial gain, preferably at the expense of the Spanish, took centre stage. As English explorers continued to fruitlessly search for riches in the Americas throughout the 1560s and 1570s, England continued to experience population growth, shortages of supplies, the contraction of traditional European markets, and an increase in poverty, vagrancy, and idleness. The disappointment and failure of English activity in America, coupled with the worsening economic and social conditions back home, forced English advocates of overseas expansion to consider that God may have abandoned the English cause. With this growing realisation, a new providential and godly approach to English projects was put into practice, seeking to rectify the perceived avarice and greed of the preceding decades. While trade and commerce remained critical aspects of these new explorative and colonial schemes, the profits to be had from the New World were now seen through the lens of Christian charity and morality and as evidence of God's increasing favour. The reality of life, both at home and in the embryonic English settlements in North America, dictated the English approach to the Americas, forcing commentators to confront the harsh realities of overseas exploration and the oscillating political and religious landscape of sixteenth-century England. As the final two chapters illustrate, at the same time that English writers were developing this godly theory of colonialism, they were also considering the ways in which the appearance and behaviour of the Indigenous inhabitants of the New World could provide information on the practicalities and necessities of English settlement in America.

Notes

1. Richard Hakluyt, *Divers Voyages Touching the Discoverie of America* (London, 1582), sig. ¶2v.
2. Alexandra Walsham, *Providence in Early Modern England* (Oxford: Oxford University Press, 1999), 2.
3. Greene, *Pursuits of Happiness*, 11.
4. Ibid., 19.
5. Kupperman, *Settling with the Indians*, 11–12.
6. Ibid., 12.
7. On early English privateering ventures see John C. Appleby, "War, Politics, and Colonization, 1558–1625," in *The Oxford History of the British Empire*, vol. 1: *The Origins of Empire: British Overseas Enterprise to the Close of the Seventeenth Century*, ed. Nicholas Canny (Oxford: Oxford University Press, 1998), 55–78; on early English attempts to extract wealth from Indigenous towns and cities see Carole Shammas, "English Commercial Development and American Colonization, 1560–1620," in *The Westward Enterprise: English Activities in Ireland, the Atlantic, and America, 1480–1650*, eds. K. R. Andrews, N. P. Canny and P. E. H. Hair (Liverpool: Liverpool University Press, 1978), 151–162; on the influence of trade and plunder on English overseas expansion see Kenneth R. Andrews, *Trade, Plunder and Settlement: Maritime Enterprise and the Genesis of the British Empire, 1480–1630* (Cambridge: Cambridge University Press, 1984).
8. Andrews, *Trade, Plunder and Settlement*, 1–22.
9. Armitage, *Ideological Origins*, 64.
10. Nicholas Canny, "The Origins of Empire: An Introduction," in *The Oxford History of the British Empire*, vol. 1: *The Origins of Empire: British Overseas Enterprise to the Close of the Seventeenth Century*, ed. Nicholas Canny (Oxford: Oxford University Press, 1998), 4.
11. Ibid., 4–5.
12. Ibid., 22.

13 Louis B. Wright, *Religion and Empire: The Alliance between Piety and Commerce in English Expansion, 1558–1625* (Chapel Hill: University of North Carolina Press, 1943), 3–56.
14 Robert A. Williams, Jr., *The American Indian in Western Legal Thought: The Discourses of Conquest* (New York and Oxford: Oxford University Press, 1990), 130.
15 Max Weber, *The Protestant Ethic and the Spirit of Capitalism*, trans. Talcott Parsons (London: George Allen & Unwin Ltd., 1930), 155–183. It is important to note here, however, that while it is clear that in the context of English encounters with America the accumulation of wealth was intimately tied to Protestant notions of piety, it is beyond the scope of this study to comment on Weber's wider thesis that connects the development of Western capitalism with the Protestant ethic.
16 Walsham, *Providence in Early Modern England*, 2.
17 "The Thirty-Nine Articles of Religion" (1571), Fordham University: Modern History Sourcebook, last accessed 16 November, 2016, http://sourcebooks.fordham.edu/mod/1571–39articles.asp.
18 Examples of these earlier works include: Anon., *Of the Newe La[n]des* (Antwerp, 1520); Rastell, *A New Interlude*. In fact, Richard Eden suggests that the poor and limited quality of the former text inspired him to produce his first work on the new lands, *A Treatyse of the Newe India*. He describes *Of the Newe La[n]des* in his work as 'a shiete of paper', unworthy of the title 'book'. Quotations from Sebastian Münster, *Treatyse of the Newe India*, sig. aa3r.
19 Andrew Hadfield, "Richard Eden," ODNB, last accessed 10 April, 2015, www.oxforddnb.com/view/article/8454.
20 Münster, *Treatyse of the Newe India*, title page.
21 Ibid., sig. aa4r.
22 Ibid.
23 Loades, "John Dudley."
24 For more on Eden's religious and political leanings and their connection to his writings on America see Barbara Fuchs, "Religion and National Distinction in the Early Modern Atlantic," in *Empires of God: Religious Encounters in the Early Modern Atlantic*, eds. Linda Gregerson and Susan Juster (Philadelphia: University of Pennsylvania Press, 2011), 58–69; Christopher Heaney, "Marrying Utopia: Mary and Philip, Richard Eden, and the English Alchemy of Spanish Peru," in *Entangled Empires: The Anglo-Iberian Atlantic, 1500–1830*, ed. Jorge Cañizares-Esguerra (Philadelphia: University of Pennsylvania Press, 2018), 85–104; Claire Jowitt, "'Monsters and Straunge Births': The Politics of Richard Eden. A Response to Andrew Hadfield," *Connotations* 6, no. 1 (January, 1996): 51–64; Hadfield, "Peter Martyr, Richard Eden," 1–22.
25 King Edward VI, "My Devise for the Succession, June, 1553," Luminarium Encyclopedia Project, last accessed 11 April, 2015, www.luminarium.org/encyclopedia/edward6devise.htm.
26 In 1544 Henry VIII had named his daughter Princess Mary as heir to the throne, followed by Princess Elizabeth, should Edward die without an heir.

Information taken from King Henry VIII, "The Third Act of Succession, 1544," Luminarium Encyclopedia Project, last accessed 11 April, 2016, www.luminarium.org/encyclopedia/actsuccession3.htm.
27 Hadfield, "Richard Eden."
28 Ibid.
29 Martyr, *Decades of the Newe Worlde*, sig. a2r.
30 Ibid., sig. a4v.
31 Ibid., sig. a3v.
32 Ibid., sigs. a3v–a4r.
33 Ibid., sigs. b3v–c3v.
34 Ibid., sig. c1v.
35 Münster, *Treatyse of the Newe India*, sigs. aa4r–aa4v.
36 Ibid., sigs. aa3v–aa4r.
37 Heaney and Fuchs have also examined the alignment between English and Spanish imperial goals in Eden's *Decades*. Fuchs, "Religion and National Distinction," 58–69; Heaney, "Marrying Utopia," 85–104.
38 Martyr, *Decades of the Newe World*, sig. c1r.
39 Ibid., sigs. c1r–c1v.
40 Hadfield, "Richard Eden." Claire Jowitt, however, has provided a different reading of the *Decades*, arguing that Eden's employment of tales of monsters and strange births in the text should be read as 'a carefully encoded critique of the uneasy English political situation of the 1550s.' Jowitt, "'Monsters and Straunge Births,'" 52.
41 John Coffey, *Persecution and Toleration in Protestant England, 1558–1689* (Harlow, UK and New York: Longman, 2000), 80.
42 Ibid., 80–81.
43 Martyr, *Decades of the Newe World*, sigs. b1v–b2r.
44 Hadfield, "Peter Martyr, Richard Eden and the New World," 14.
45 Arthur F. Marroti, "Alienating Catholics in Early Modern England: Recusant Women, Jesuits and Ideological Fantasies," in *Catholicism and Anti-Catholicism in Early Modern English Texts*, ed. Arthur F. Marroti (Basingstoke: Macmillan, 1999), 1–2. For a detailed discussion on outward conformity among English Catholics and the phenomenon of the 'church papist' see Alexandra Walsham, *Church Papists: Catholicism, Conformity and Confessional Polemic in Early Modern England* (Woodbridge: The Boydell Press, 1999).
46 Coffey, *Persecution and Toleration*, 81.
47 Peter Martyr, *The History of Travayle in the West and East Indies*, trans. Richard Eden and Richard Willes (London, 1577).
48 Ibid., title page.
49 Anthony Payne, "Richard Willes," ODNB, last accessed 12 August, 2016, www.oxforddnb.com/view/article/29444.
50 Martyr, *History of Travayle*, sigs. ❧3r–❧5v.
51 Ibid., sig. ❧2v.
52 Ibid.
53 Jason Eldred, "'The Just will Pay for the Sinners': English Merchants, the

Trade with Spain, and Elizabethan Foreign Policy, 1563–1585," *Journal for Early Modern Cultural Studies* 10, no. 1 (Spring/Summer 2010): 12.
54 Ibid., 13.
55 Ibid., 15.
56 Ibid., 11.
57 Ibid., 6. Some important members of this group included the Earl of Leicester, Francis Walsingham and Christopher Hatton.
58 Ibid., 9.
59 Basil Morgan, "John Hawkins," ODNB. Last accessed 29 May, 2015, www.oxforddnb.com/view/article/12672?docPos=1. For a contemporary account of the Spanish destruction of the French colony that was printed in English see Le Challeux, *True and Perfect Description*.
60 Morgan, "John Hawkins."
61 Hawkins, *A True Declaration*, sig. A4v.
62 Ibid., sigs. A4v–A5r.
63 Ibid., sig. A5v.
64 Ibid., sigs. A5v–A6v.
65 Ibid., sigs. B2r–B2v.
66 Ibid., sig. B3r.
67 Morgan, "John Hawkins."
68 Ibid.
69 Anon., "The Two Famous Voyages Happily Perfourmed Round About the World, by Sir Francis Drake, and M. Thomas Candish Esquire," in *Principal Navigations*, 3:735.
70 Ibid., 3:736.
71 Anon., "The Two Famous Voyages," 3:734; and Hawkins, *A True Declaration*, sig. B5r.
72 Francisco López de Gómara, *The Pleasant Historie of the Conquest of the Weast India, Now Called New Spayne*, trans. Thomas Nicholls (London, 1578).
73 Ibid., sigs. a2r–a4r.
74 Ibid., sigs. b1r–b1v.
75 R.C.D. Baldwin, "Thomas Nicholls," ODNB, last accessed 1 June, 2015, www.oxforddnb.com/view/article/20124?docPos=4.
76 Ibid.
77 Beatriz Pastor Bodmer, *The Armature of Conquest: Spanish Accounts of the Discovery of America, 1492–1589*, trans. Lydia Longstreth Hunt (Stanford, CA: Stanford University Press, 1992), 58–62.
78 Valencia Suárez, "Aztecs Through the Lens," 38.
79 Ibid., 39.
80 Ibid., 38–39.
81 Ibid., 40.
82 Baldwin, "Thomas Nicholls."
83 Ibid.
84 Gómara, *Pleasant Historie*, sigs. b1r–b1v.

85 Best, *A True Discourse*, sig. a4v.
86 Ibid., sigs. a4v–b1r.
87 Ibid., title page.
88 McGhee, *Arctic Voyages*, 13.
89 Churchyard, *A Prayse and Reporte*, sig. A7r.
90 Ibid., sig. A6v.
91 McGhee, *Arctic Voyages*, 99.
92 Churchyard, *A Prayse and Reporte*, sig. B8v.
93 Ibid., sig. C1r.
94 Settle, *A True Reporte*, sig. D1v.
95 Ibid., sigs. D1v–D2r.
96 Ibid., sig. D3r.
97 Best, *A True Discourse*, title page and sig. a3r.
98 McGhee, *Arctic Voyages*, 95.
99 Ibid., 142–149.
100 Williams, Jr., *American Indian in Western Legal Thought*, 154.
101 "The Letters Patents," 3:135.
102 Williams, Jr., *American Indian in Western Legal Thought*, 157.
103 Ibid., 158.
104 Edward Hayes, "A Report of the Voyage and Successe Thereof, Attempted in the Yeere of our Lord 1583 by Sir Humfrey Gilbert Knight," in *Principal Navigations*, 3:151.
105 Ibid., 3:156–157.
106 Ibid., 3:159.
107 Ibid., 3:160.
108 Ibid., 3:161.
109 Ibid., 3:143.
110 Ibid., 3:144.
111 Walsham, *Providence in Early Modern England*, 2.
112 Ibid., 33–38.
113 Ibid., 329.
114 Brief biographical information on Parkhurst taken from Olaf Uwe Janzen, "Review Article: Handcock, Marshall, and Breakwater Books," *Newfoundland and Labrador Studies* 7, no. 1 (January, 1991): 65. Quotation taken from Anthony Parkhurst, "A Letter Written to M. *Richard Hakluyt* of the middle Temple," in Hakluyt, *Principal Navigations*, 3:132.
115 Parkhurst, "A Letter Written to M. *Richard Hakluyt*," 3:132.
116 Hakluyt, *Divers Voyages*, sig. ¶2v.
117 Peckham, *A True Reporte*, sig. B3r.
118 Ibid., sig. B3v.
119 Ibid., sigs. C1r.–C1v.
120 Loren E. Pennington, "The Amerindian in English Promotional Literature, 1575–1625," in *The Westward Enterprise: English Activities in Ireland, the Atlantic, and America, 1480–1650*, eds. K. R. Andrews, N. P. Canny and P. E. H. Hair (Liverpool: Liverpool University Press, 1978), 87–88.

121 Alfred A. Cave, "Canaanites in a Promised Land: The American Indian and the Providential Theory of Empire," *American Indian Quarterly* 12, no. 4 (Autumn, 1988): 282.
122 James McDermott, "Sir George Peckham."
123 Peckham, *A True Reporte*, sigs. D4r.–E1r.
124 Ibid., sig. B2r.
125 The endorsement from Francis Drake is clearly focused on the pursuit of private gain, stating that 'If anie one there bee, that covettes such a trade: / Lo, here [in America] the plot for common weath, and private gaine is made'. Quotation taken from Peckham, *A True Reporte*, sig. *4v.
126 Peckham, *A True Reporte*, sig. *4r.
127 Ibid., sig. §1r.
128 In an anonymous account of Drake's voyage there is a brief reference to a fly boat of fifty tonnes that was commanded by John Chester. Given the fact that Drake himself also endorsed Peckham's text it seems possible that the John Chester mentioned in Peckham's text is the same John Chester that is referred to in the account; Anon., *The Voyages & Travels of that Renowned Captain, Sir Francis Drake, into the West-Indies* (London, 1652), 12.
129 Peckham, *A True Reporte*, sig. §2v.
130 Ibid., sig. H1v.
131 Steve Hindle, *The State and Social Change in Early Modern England, 1550–1640* (Basingstoke: Palgrave Macmillan, 2002), 38–53; Paul Slack, *The English Poor Law, 1531–1782* (Cambridge: Cambridge University Press, 1995), 3–4.
132 Appleby, "War, Politics, and Colonization," 58–59; Abbot, *Colonial Origins of the United States*, 13–15; Shammas, "English Commercial Development," 159–160.
133 Peckham, *A True Reporte*, sigs. G1r–H1v.
134 Ibid., sig. E2v.
135 Ibid., sig. E3r.
136 Ibid., sig. E2v.
137 Ibid., sig. F2v.
138 Rachel Lloyd has suggested that in the 1580s the Muscovy Company's trade with Russia came under increased pressure for a variety of reasons, causing the company to search for new trade markets. It was within this context that Carleill's text appeared. Lloyd, *Elizabethan Adventurer*, 63–64.
139 Carleill, *Breef and Sommarie Discourse*, sig. A2r.
140 Lloyd, *Elizabethan Adventurer*, 81.
141 Carleill, *Breef and Sommarie Discourse* sig. B1v.
142 Ibid., sig. A2r.
143 Robert Brenner has argued that trade with the Near East increased during Elizabeth's reign. He also argues, however, that trade with Catholic Europe was critical in the sixteenth century, with trade with Spain growing substantially in the 1570s and the chartering of the Venice Company in 1583; Robert Brenner, *Merchants and Revolution: Commercial Change, Political Conflict,*

and London's Overseas Traders, 1550–1653 (London and New York: Verso Books, 2003), 14–18.

144 George Peckham, "A True Report of the Late Discoveries, and Possession Taken in the Right of the Crowne of England," in *Principal Navigations*, 3:165–181; Christopher Carleill, "A Briefe and Summary Discourse upon the Intended Voyage to the Hithermost Parts of America," in *Principal Navigations*, 3:182–187.

145 Alongside Brereton's own account of his voyage to North Virginia, the pamphlet also included additional texts, one composed by Edward Hayes on the possible existence of the Northwest Passage to Asia, the published version of a text written by Richard Hakluyt the elder for the inducement of English settlement in Virginia, some brief extracts taken from René de Laudonnière's *L'histoire notable de la Floride* which had been translated into English by Richard Hakluyt the younger in 1587, a short extract taken from Thomas Harriot's account of Virginia published in 1588, 1590 and in 1600, and some very brief testimonies extracted from a variety of printed accounts of European exploration in North America, from Jacques Cartier to Fernando de Soto; Brereton, *A Briefe and True Relation*, 15–48.

146 Richard Hakluyt the elder, "Inducements to the Liking of the Voyage Intended Towards Virginia," in *A Briefe and True Relation of the Discouerie of the North Part of Virginia Being a Most Pleasant, Fruitfull and Commodious Soile*, ed. John Brereton (London, 1602), 25.

147 Ibid., 30.

148 Ibid., 29.

149 Ibid., 29–30.

150 Edward Hayes, "A Treatise, Conteining Important Inducements for the Planting in these Parts, and Finding a Passage that Way to the South Sea and China," in *A Briefe and True Relation of the Discouerie of the North Part of Virginia Being a Most Pleasant, Fruitfull and Commodious Soile*, ed. John Brereton (London, 1602), 17.

151 Ibid., 17–18.

152 Ibid., 19.

153 For many scholars, Las Casas's text represents the cornerstone of the development of the Black Legend in Europe. Coined in 1914 by the Spanish sociologist and historian Julián Juderías, 'the Black Legend' refers to a historical tradition that presents the character of the Spaniard as inherently cruel and intellectually redundant. Scholars that have examined Las Casas's text in relation to the development of the Black Legend include Valeri Afanasiev, "The Literary Heritage of Bartolomé de Las Casas," in *Bartolomé de Las Casas in History: Toward an Understanding of the Man and his Work*, eds. Juan Friede and Benjamin Keen (DeKalb: Northern Illinois University Press, 1971), 539–578; E. Shaskan Bumas, "The Cannibal Butcher Shop: Protestant Uses of Las Casas's Brevisima Relacion in Europe and the American Colonies," *Early American Literature* 35, no. 2 (2000): 107–136; Lewis Hanke, "Bartolomé de Las Casas and the Spanish Empire in America: Four Centuries of Misunderstanding,"

Proceedings of the American Philosophical Society 97, no. 1. (February, 1953): 26–30; William S. Maltby, *The Black Legend in England: The Development of Anti-Spanish Sentiment, 1558–1660* (Durham, NA: Duke University Press, 1971).

154 Lewis Hanke, *Bartolomé de Las Casas: An Interpretation of his Life and Writings* (The Hague: Martinus Nijhoff, 1951), 56–57.
155 Ibid., 57.
156 Bartolomé de Las Casas, *The Spanish Colonie*, trans. M. M. S. (London, 1583), sig. ¶3v.
157 Ibid., sig. ¶2v.
158 Maltby, *Black Legend*, 44–55.
159 Ibid., 44–47.
160 Las Casas, *Spanish Colonie*, sig. ¶2v.
161 Ibid., sig. A2v.
162 Ibid., sigs. A3v–F4v.
163 Ibid., sig. A2v.
164 Ibid., sig. ¶2v.
165 Ralegh, *The Discoverie*, 33–62.
166 George Abbot, *The Reasons Which Doctour Hill Hath Brought, for the Upholding of Papistry, which is Falselie Termed the Catholike Religion* (London, 1604).
167 Ibid., 135.
168 Ibid., 201.
169 Ibid., 202.
170 James Axtell, *The European and the Indian: Essays in the Ethnohistory of Colonial North America* (New York and Oxford: Oxford University Press, 1981), 43.
171 Ibid., 43–44.
172 Axtell, for example, makes no distinction between the approaches of different colonising nations, arguing that all European missionaries, whether Protestant or Catholic, recognised the need to civilise the 'savages' before converting them to Christianity. Axtell, *European and the Indian*, 44. Patricia Seed, in her analysis of Spanish missionary activity in Hispaniola, has argued that the mass baptisms practised by the Franciscans did not go unchallenged by other Spanish missionaries. In fact, and as Seed suggests, in Hispaniola, Dominicans wished to challenge the Franciscan monopoly on conversion by stimulating debates about the humanity of Indigenous people and the proper approach to Christian instruction. Patricia Seed, "'Are These Not Also Men?,'" 629–652.
173 Hakluyt, *Divers Voyages*, sigs. ¶1v–¶2v.
174 Peckham, *A True Reporte*, sig. C2v.
175 Carleill, *A Breef and Sommarie Discourse*, sig. A3r.
176 Harriot, *Briefe and True Report*, 25.
177 Peckham, *A True Reporte*, sig. E2r; Carleill, *A Breef and Sommarie Discourse*, sig. A3r.

3

Dressing America: Clothing, nakedness, and the foundations of civility

Apparel oft proclaims the man.[1]

– Hamlet, Act 1, Scene 3

The above quotation from Shakespeare's *Hamlet*, spoken by Polonius, reflects an integral aspect of early modern culture: the importance of clothing. Clothing could reflect a person's social and economic status, identify a person's occupation or religion, and illustrate their civility or barbarity; in short, clothing in the early modern period made the man, or indeed woman.[2] Early modern Europeans not only cared about what members of their own societies were wearing, but were also captivated by the clothing of people from far-flung parts of the world. The popularity of costume books in the sixteenth century, which visually represented the dress of foreign nations, illustrates this apparent fascination.[3] Unsurprisingly, then, when Europeans began to explore the new lands of America, the clothing, or indeed lack of clothing, of the Indigenous peoples they came across drew significant comment.

The following chapter examines the multi-faceted English understanding of both American clothing and nakedness, analysing the various ways that English explorers, writers, and translators described the appearances of the diverse groups of Indigenous people that they encountered. Descriptions of American clothing and nakedness in English print varied throughout the sixteenth century and performed a variety of functions, from shaping English approaches to trade and colonisation in the New World, to informing and framing moral and religious debates taking place back home, and reflecting shared European cultural values. The image of the naked 'Indian' was employed both positively and negatively, as was that of the clothed 'Indian'. Indigenous nakedness could be seen as indicative of impiety or as a sign of natural primitivism, while the simple clothing of other groups of Indigenous people could either be read as a refreshing alternative to the decadent clothing of early modern Europe or as yet more evidence for the savagery and barbarism of the New World. English interpretations of

Indigenous appearance, then, were used on the one hand to draw conclusions about the controllability of Indigenous populations and their potential to become consumers of English cloth, and on the other to inform debates taking place back home on a range of issues relating to decadence and impiety.

Those who have studied cultural encounters between Indigenous Americans and Europeans have only briefly assessed the meaning of Indigenous clothing, and more especially Indigenous nakedness, to European commentators, often categorising it as just one of a series of markers that Europeans used to denote Indigenous inferiority and savagery. The nakedness of Indigenous peoples, alongside their lack of material wealth, trade, and weaponry, became a clear marker of their lack of civilisation and the naked bodies of New World peoples became one of the many stereotypes of Indigenous shortcomings, alongside their sexual license, idolatry, and cannibalism. This resulted in the formation of a strongly pejorative image of Indigenous peoples.[4] This attitude towards the nakedness of non-Europeans was not specific to the sixteenth-century American context, however. Nakedness, and what it said about foreign 'others', became a stable feature of European colonial discourse, connoting the 'primitiveness' and 'savagery' of a wide-range of non-Europeans, from Africans, to the Aboriginal people of Australia, to the Indigenous communities of the Pacific Islands.[5] Whether in the Americas or in sub-Saharan Africa, nakedness, in the minds of Europeans, implied a social system in which hierarchy and delineated communal roles were entirely absent.[6] This negative attitude towards nakedness was commonplace in a diverse range of accounts of foreign 'others' during the Renaissance, and it continued to be prevalent in European colonial discourse beyond the early modern period. As Philippa Levine has illustrated in her study of nakedness in the Victorian colonial imagination, many of the assumptions that had been made about Indigenous Americans in the sixteenth century were still being employed to describe the colonised peoples of Asia, Africa, and Australasia in the nineteenth century. The nakedness of non-Western peoples continued to denote an inherent excessive sexuality and a lack of shame, social order, and civility in the European colonial imagination.[7]

English ideas relating to Indigenous nakedness and clothing were by no means static, however. English understandings of Indigenous clothing were in fact extremely dynamic in the sixteenth century, being moulded to meet the demands of both author and reader, and the requirements of both colonial activity in America and of a divisive and fractious society back home. Individual and national identity in early modern England was located in the clothing that one wore.[8] Due to its centrality in early modern identity formation, clothing could be at once stabilising and destabilising, both a means of conforming and transgressing. Clothing could not only fix one's identity, then, it could also transform it.[9] Because of its power in the formation of identity, however, clothing in early modern Europe was also highly regulated. Sixteenth-century England witnessed a burst of state legislation that attempted to regulate the clothing of the English population. The primary function of this type of sumptuary legislation was to control the luxuriousness of clothing and to maintain social distinctions. For example, purple silk and gold cloth were reserved only for the king and members of the Royal Family, and men beneath the rank of duke, earl, and marquis were not permitted to wear crimson, scarlet, or blue velvet, nor any clothing that had been embroidered.[10] Despite their limited success, sumptuary laws would continue to be introduced throughout the sixteenth century, reflecting the contemporary perception that clothing had the potential to be a tool of both social control and rebellion.[11] Identity could likewise be performed through the naked body as skin, like clothing, is an unstable surface that can be marked and ornamented in various ways, oscillating between signifying a natural state and cultural difference. While, for example, tattooed skin could represent a permanent cultural difference, the body paint used by various Indigenous groups reflected, as did clothing, a reversible alteration that could be replaced. Clothing and indeed the naked skin is thus 'an ambivalent surface upon which culture is endlessly performed'.[12]

The fluidity and ambiguity of clothing and bodily ornamentation as cultural markers is something that is clearly identifiable in English accounts of America written in the sixteenth and seventeenth centuries. Despite the obvious differences in appearance between the English and the Indigenous peoples of North America, English observers still believed that they saw a society that recognised the same kinds of gender distinctions and social hierarchies as their own. For example, the tattoos of the Virginia Algonquians, rather than reflecting alterity, could in fact be perceived of as signs of a social hierarchy that illustrated the Indigenous potential to receive English civility.[13] In a similar fashion, the way that the Algonquians wore their hair also seemed to confirm to the English that they, like the English themselves, delineated between genders and marked important life events through their appearance.[14] The men of Virginia, for example, were said to shave the hair on one side of their heads when coming of age. It was also possible to distinguish between maids and married women by their hairstyles. The primary purpose of many of these texts that described Indigenous appearance was to argue for English colonisation in America. Assessing the potential civility of the Algonquians through their clothing and bodily adornments, then, was an intrinsic aspect of this kind of English promotional literature from the late sixteenth century onwards. By identifying shared cultural priorities, an English society in America could be construed as being authorised by nature. English observers of America had convinced themselves that American society preserved all of the important social distinctions present in English society, making the possibility of recreating English society in the New World, in which the Algonquians would be raised to English standards of civility, all the more likely.[15]

While this type of cultural assimilation for promotional purposes is undoubtedly critical to our understanding of English perceptions of Indigenous appearance, ideas relating to Indigenous clothing and nakedness also served other important functions, from the utilitarian, to the moralistic and spiritual.[16] In what follows I establish the multi-faceted English understandings of Indigenous clothing, going beyond the positively constructed images of Indigenous dress and bodily adornment that served a particular promotional function from the late sixteenth century onwards. These representations of American appearance were variously influenced by what the Spanish, French, and Portuguese had experienced in the New World, by the practicalities and demands of early English colonisation in which securing private investment was critical, and by the moralistic and religious debates taking place back home that identified clothing as a tool of both social conformity and disruption.

Clothing, savagery, impiety, and sexuality

From the Indigenous communities of Central and South America, and indeed the Caribbean, to the inhabitants of the Far North and coastal areas of North America, portrayals of Indigenous peoples found in English print varied not only across the entire geography of the New World, but also across the regions controlled by competing colonial nations. What becomes obvious from a detailed analysis of early English Americana are the disparities between representations of Indigenous groups put forth in English promotional texts towards the end of the sixteenth century and those found in English translations of texts first produced in continental Europe. English understandings of Indigenous clothing were produced on a spectrum, with the 'naked', 'ungodly', and entirely 'savage' people of the Caribbean found at one end, and the 'primitive', 'innocent', and 'modest' peoples of Virginia found at the other. Conflicting images of Indigenous Americans thus coexisted in English print throughout the sixteenth century, highlighting the various concerns of those involved in bringing these images to an English readership.

In the early decades of the sixteenth century, in which English readers caught their first tentative glimpse of the new and exotic lands across the Atlantic, positive assessments of Indigenous appearance were far from coming to fruition. Instead, the earliest English texts dealing with the European encounter with America presented the clothing of these newly 'discovered' people as befitting their 'savage' and 'degenerate' state. The clothing, or more accurately lack of clothing, of these individuals could reflect their lack of civility and culture or their excessive idolatry and sexuality. Borrowing imagery from the Spanish, Portuguese, and French, the earliest printed accounts of America in England established a mostly pejorative representation of Indigenous peoples that confirmed their inherent 'savagery' and need for European civilisation and religion.

In one of the first English texts to explicitly reference the new land of America, published in 1520, the peoples of the New World were presented as lacking any real clothing. The anonymous author of this short, and it must be said hugely limited, description of America, described how the people of the region 'goeth all naked', save for their heads, necks, arms, knees, and feet which were covered with feathers.[17] The people of America, moreover, according to the author, 'lyven lyke bestes', had 'no kynge nor lorde nor theyr god', were 'dysposed to lecherdnes', and would commonly 'ete also on a nother'.[18] Signified by their lack of clothing, the Indigenous population also lacked religion, civility, sexual restraint, and basic humanity. The juxtaposition of a lack of clothing with an abhorrent lack of civility is also clearly identifiable in the image that accompanies this portion of the text. The woodcut, which is both included on the title page and as an insert to the text describing America, depicts two Indigenous people, naked save for the feathers that adorn their heads, necks, arms, groins, and legs. While the female figure serenely cares for and nurses her children in the foreground, a severed human head and leg dangle from a tree, while being roasted over a fire in the background (Figure 1). The cannibalism depicted in the image highlights the perceived depravity of American peoples, as does their obvious lack of appropriate clothing. In the earliest English printed image of Indigenous Americans, then, cannibalism and nakedness were both rendered emblematic of American savagery.[19]

The connection between clothing and Indigenous savagery continued throughout the 1550s with Richard Eden's translations of Peter Martyr's *Decades* (1555) and Sebastian Münster's *Cosmographia* (1553). Despite the occasional sympathetic interpretation of the Indigenous peoples of America, Martyr was obsessed by their nakedness.[20] Time and again, Martyr referred to the swarms of naked people that the Spanish *conquistadores* came across in the many 'naked nations' of the New World.[21] More than a mere bodily description, however, the nakedness of Indigenous groups, as described by Martyr, became indicative of their manner of living. In Cuba, the people were 'naked and contente with a lyttle', while in Darién the people were perceived to be 'pore naked wretches'.[22] In the mountains of Cibao

Figure 1 Unknown, woodcut, 'Feathered Native Americans', in Anonymous, *Of the Newe La[n]des and of ye People Founde by the Messengers of the Kynge of Porty[n]gale* (Antwerp, 1520).

the people lived 'in nakedness, and rude simplicitie', while the man-eating *canibales* were believed to be nothing more than 'naked Barbarians'.[23] The nakedness of Indigenous people, in the European mind, was thus symptomatic of their savage living. Even when Indigenous communities managed to illustrate some level of civility and education, Martyr appeared surprised. In skirmishes with the Spanish, some Indigenous people, 'althowgh they bee naked', were able to overcome their aggressors.[24] Other Indigenous Americans, despite being naked, were also able to appreciate the superiority of some European tools; as Martyr explained, 'even these naked men doo perceive that an axe is necesarye for a thousande uses'.[25] Nakedness, then, became synonymous with savagery in the European imagination, being used to connote a variety of traits from barbarity and rude simplicity, to poverty and material destitution.[26]

The nakedness of Indigenous Americans could also point towards other behavioural shortcomings, most notably sexual promiscuity and a lack of shame. According to Münster, Amerigo Vespucci came across a 'nacion of naked people' who 'goe all as naked as they came forth of their mothers wombe'.[27] Despite willingly submitting to the Spanish, these naked 'Indians' were nonetheless regarded as entirely savage, living in many ways 'fylthy and withoute shame', especially in regards to marriage practices; these naked people observed 'no lawfull conjunccion of mariage', with every man having 'as many women as him listeth', leaving them again 'at his pleasure'.[28] In Münster's retelling of Vespucci's encounter with this naked nation, a lack of clothing was once again an implicit cause of Indigenous licentiousness and brazenness. This uncomfortable relationship with nakedness had begun at the very beginning of human history with the fall of man in the Garden of Eden. The story of Adam and Eve would have been one that almost all Christian Europeans were familiar with in the early modern period.[29] In the story of their fall from grace, nakedness was central, with the shame associated with it becoming a 'prerequisite for Christian salvation'. Those who displayed their nakedness with no shame, moreover, were identified as people whose souls were in danger.[30] As well as reflecting a lack of shame, voluntary nakedness was also connected to sexual promiscuity in Christian doctrine. The Bible clearly links the sin of adultery with nakedness, with multiple references to both appearing in the book of Leviticus.[31] For Europeans well aware of the sin of adultery, the nakedness of the Indigenous populations of America became emblematic of their loose sexual morals. Indeed, biblical scholars such as Jon Levenson have suggested that 'to uncover nakedness' was actually euphemistic for sexual intercourse, thus illustrating the strong connection between nakedness and sexuality in Christian tradition.[32] The licentious lives of the naked nation that Vespucci had come across, coupled with their lack of shame for their 'filthy' manner of living, was thus unsurprising given their nakedness. The Bible had taught early modern Europeans that living nakedly was a sin and was reflective of a promiscuous and ungodly lifestyle.

The ungodly nakedness of the peoples of America remained a constant image in English print throughout the sixteenth century, appearing in various texts, both directly and indirectly related to the European conquests of the New World. In 1568 an English edition of André Thevet's account of the New World appeared in London.[33] Thevet had been given the position of chaplain for a French voyage to Brazil in 1555, returning to France just ten weeks after the beginning of the expedition due to illness.

Upon his return, Thevet wrote an account of his experiences that was printed in Paris in 1557 under the title *Les Singularitez de la France Antarctique*.[34] Thomas Hacket's English translation of Thevet's text was dedicated to Henry Sidney, the Lord Deputy of Ireland at the time.[35] Thevet's various descriptions of the 'wild', 'savage' peoples of America would no doubt have been recognisable to Sidney, who, at around the same time, was dealing with the expanding power of the O'Neill chief Shane, causing increased animosity between the English and the Irish.[36] In his text, Thevet divided the New World roughly into three parts: America, from Argentina to the Amazon; Peru, from the Amazon to Florida; and Canada, from Florida and Mexico northwards.[37] Thevet's opinions on different groups within these three regions could vary wildly and it was the peoples of America that were awarded the most damning of descriptions, particularly in relation to their lack of clothing and 'ungodly' behaviour. Thevet explained to his readers how the people of America were far more intolerable than the 'savages' of the East. Whereas the peoples of the East Indies covered their private parts, those of America lived 'all naked even as they come out of their mothers wombe, as well men as women without any shame'. Responding to debates that were taking place back in Europe, Thevet condemned those who argued that Europeans 'ought to goe naked as *Adam* and *Eve*' had in the Garden of Eden, explaining how nakedness was not found to be 'Gods commaundement'. Those in Europe who had chosen to live naked 'as these *Americans* of which we speake', were, in Thevet's opinion, heretics.[38] Expanding his denunciation of nakedness still further, Thevet argued that not even the pagan Romans 'remained naked', even though they were 'very straunge in their livings'.[39] Thevet neatly summed up the savagery of the Americans, claiming them to be 'a marvellous strange wild and brutish people, without faith, without Lawe, without Religion, and without any civilite: but living like brute beasts, as nature hath brought them out, eating herbes and rootes, being always naked'.[40]

English writers of the sixteenth century largely agreed with Thevet's religiously motivated understanding of nakedness. The theologian and later Bishop of Worcester, Gervase Babington, for example, explained in his published notes on the book of Genesis in 1592 that the 'beginning of apparell' came from the beginning of sin, with nakedness only being appropriate in 'the life to come, when nakednesse shall shame us no more'.[41] Henry Smith, a Church of England clergyman, agreed, arguing in his 1593 book of sermons that nakedness was indicative of sin, as sin is 'no shrowder but a stripper'.[42] The English published works of Reformed Protestants such as John Calvin made the same point. In Calvin's commentary on Genesis, published in England in 1578, nakedness was once again something to be ashamed of, for as Calvin suggested, it reflected 'the fowlnesse of the vice' by which Adam and Eve defiled themselves.[43] Whether Catholic, Church of England, or Calvinist, then, it appears that nakedness was almost universally considered a sin within Western Christendom as it reflected the shame bestowed upon humankind by God, and resulted in ungodly and lustful behaviour. By living nakedly and crucially without shame, Indigenous peoples, in the minds of Christians, were not only leaving themselves vulnerable to licentious behaviour, they were also illustrating their failure to acknowledge the fault of original sin.

The resilience of the image of the naked and ungodly Indigenous American, among writers of varying religious persuasions, is therefore unsurprising given the shared religious teachings on nakedness of the period. Even as more positive assessments of the peoples of North America were appearing in English print, as we shall see later, the naked and ungodly American remained a potent force. In 1604, the king of England himself employed this image. James I of England and VI of Scotland, in a short treatise denouncing the use of American tobacco, invoked the image of naked, ungodly Indigenous people to illustrate the corrupting force of the New World herb. As James argued, if Englishmen were to imitate Indigenous peoples by smoking tobacco, why should they not also imitate them 'in walking naked as they doe' or by 'denie[ing] God and adore[ing] the Devill as they doe'.[44] By referencing nakedness and ungodliness together, the former became an indicator of the latter. Throughout the sixteenth century the nakedness of the Indigenous peoples of America was used by various European commentators, whether writing directly about New World discoveries, or about the corrupting potential of New World products, to illustrate the savagery, ungodliness, and licentiousness of the Americas. The Bible taught Europeans to be shameful of nakedness and to wear clothes in remembrance of man's sinful nature. The fact that Indigenous people appeared to live naked without any shame highlighted to Europeans just how far removed from God's word they really were, exemplifying the need for education in civility and true religion.

European superiority and charity

The impious and naked American was not the only prevalent image of Indigenous people to emerge in English print in the sixteenth century. Europeans were keen to illustrate their superiority in relation to the peoples of the New World, with the outrageous clothing, or indeed lack of clothing, of the inhabitants of America providing ample evidence for this. Not all the peoples of the New World seemed to wear their nakedness without shame, however, leading some Europeans to conclude that they were open to the possibility of being raised to European standards of civility. The inadequacy of Indigenous dress, in contrast to the luxurious clothing of the visiting Europeans, not only illustrated their lower level of civility and religiosity, but also the means by which Europeans could begin to take control. Clothing the Indigenous population thus became a tool with which to wield colonial mastery, exemplifying European beliefs in their own superiority and charitable good will, and the perceived Indigenous urge to become more like Europeans.

In Eden's 1555 work, which included an abridged version of Gonzalo Fernández de Oviedo's history of the Indies and a number of other texts alongside Martyr's *Decades*, it is clear that not all Indigenous peoples seemed to be happy to go unclothed. As Martyr explained, many of the Indigenous people that the Spanish had come across in the New World were naked, 'savynge that theyr pryvies partes were covered with breeches of gossampine cotton'.[45] Similarly, Oviedo suggested that the people of Hispaniola, although going 'naked as they were borne', would wear 'on the partes which may not with honestie bee seene' 'a certeyne leafe as brode as a mans hande'.[46] To be naked, then, in the early modern European mind at least, did not necessarily mean being entirely without any form of clothing or covering. Indeed, English writers of the late sixteenth and early seventeenth centuries often tied the term 'naked' to simplicity in clothing.[47] While in the context of English colonisation this simplicity could be rendered as a positive exemplification of modesty, in earlier accounts of America, written by continental Europeans and Englishmen who did not necessarily have a stake in English colonial projects, this kind of frugality was not described in positive terms.

What these earlier descriptions have in common is the fact that Indigenous people were perceived to have an implicit sense of their own savagery, as evidenced through their attitude towards clothing. Just as Martyr and Oviedo suggested, they felt shame at their nakedness and attempted to cover it to the best of their abilities. Thevet, like Oviedo, suggested that some Indigenous groups attempted to maintain their modesty by hiding 'their privie partes with leaves'.[48] These attempts at covering the shame of nakedness with leaves is particularly interesting, given its parallels with the story of man's fall taken from the book of Genesis. As Chapter 3 tells us, once Adam and Eve had eaten from the tree of knowledge, their eyes were opened and they perceived their nakedness for the first time. In order to cover their shame, they sewed together fig leaves and made aprons for themselves. God, on learning of their sin, punished Eve by bringing her sorrow in child birth and subordination to her husband, and Adam by forcing him to toil and labour for his food. God then made for Adam and Eve garments made of skin, thus clothing them for the first time. The sorry tale ended with humankind's banishment from Paradise.⁴⁹ The fig leaves that Adam and Eve used to cover their modesty were thus inappropriate and unsuitable, being replaced with proper garments by God. The attempts of the Indigenous people of the New World to hide their shameful nakedness with leaves were likewise considered feeble and insufficient. In fact, according to Thevet, only the peoples of Canada managed to achieve any form of appropriate clothing; after Adam and Eve's sin, 'God gave them garments of lether to cover their nakednesse, as the *Canadians* use at this day'.⁵⁰ As Thevet suggested, the Canadians had 'much more civilite than the inhabitants of *America*' as they, unlike their neighbours to the south, knew how to 'cover and cloth themselves in beastes skins'.⁵¹ This decidedly more positive description of the people of Canada is unsurprising, given the fact that French efforts in the Americas were largely centred on this region. Indigenous clothing could undoubtedly exhibit savagery, but it could equally delineate potential for civility.

The attempts of Indigenous people to cover their perceived shame was not, however, the only way in which they indicated that they were aware of the importance of clothing to the visiting Europeans. According to those writing about America, including English authors, the Indigenous peoples of America had a tendency to steal clothes. Thevet recorded how, despite their nakedness, the 'Indians' appeared to be 'very desirous of gownes, shirts, hats, and other clothing'.⁵² In fact, if they came across a stranger or a Christian they would 'rifle him' of his 'garments', leaving behind any gold or silver as they had 'not the knowledge nor use therof'.⁵³ From Thevet's story it would appear that European clothing, in the eyes of Indigenous people, was far more precious than gold or silver. In a specific English example of clothing theft taking place in the Americas, both Job Hortop and Miles Philips described an encounter they had had in the wilderness of Mexico. Both men had been members of John Hawkins's privateering venture in the Caribbean in 1568. The two Englishmen, along with another ninety four members of the crew, were abandoned on the shores of Mexico when provisions became critically low among the fleet.⁵⁴ On their second day on land, the Englishmen came across a group of Indigenous people in a field. Speaking in Spanish, the 'Captaine of the Indians' willed the Englishmen to give them some of their clothes and shirts, which the Englishmen duly agreed to. The 'Indians', however, were not satisfied and demanded that the English explorers give them all of their clothes. The explorers refused, a skirmish ensued, and eventually the English retreated.⁵⁵ Sometime later, five members of the English company went to search for 'reliefe'. They were captured by the 'Indians' and 'stript as naked as ever they were borne'. Later still, the entire company of the English, while marching 'betwixt two groves' were once again set upon by the 'Indians' who robbed them of all of their clothes, leaving them stark naked.[56] Miles Philips, who had also written an account of the many miseries endured by the Englishmen who had been abandoned in Spanish America, corroborated Hortop's story, save for one minor adjustment. According to Philips, the English were indeed set upon by the Indigenous population who took from them 'any coloured clothes', choosing not to meddle with those men 'apparelled in blacke'. Having stripped the men who had been unlucky enough to be wearing coloured clothes 'starke naked', the 'Indians' then went on their way.[57] What these stories of clothing theft suggest is that European garments ostensibly became sought-after items among the Indigenous peoples of America.

This revelation that Indigenous groups coveted European clothing would not have come as a particular surprise to the English men and women who would have read the works of Thevet, Hortop, and Philips, given the prevalence of clothing theft in early modern English society. In early modern England there was a strong connection between crime and consumerism, with one of the most obvious examples of this being the theft of clothing.[58] Stealing clothing, which was a particularly sought-after commodity in the early modern period, reflected the new popular ambitions and aspirations of the period.[59] By stealing the clothes of people higher up the social scale, the thieving poor or disloyal servants could feed their desire for luxury. This 'involuntary and illegal redistribution' of fashionable clothing through the social hierarchy extended the volume of attire available to the public and fuelled a growing consumerism that perceived clothing as a desirable and marketable commodity.[60] When early modern English men and women read tales of Indigenous Americans stealing European clothes, it is entirely possible that they interpreted these actions as a sign of Indigenous aspiration. Like the poor of England wishing to improve themselves through the acquisition of refined clothing, the Indigenous peoples of America could have been equally illustrating their desire for European civility through their illicit procurement of cultured European attire.

It is likely, of course, that Indigenous people had their own motives for stealing the clothes of the interloping Europeans. By taking European clothing, items that were obviously of huge cultural importance, Indigenous groups may have been expressing their own defiant resistance rather than a desire for civility. Whatever the true motivations behind clothing theft were, it is all too obvious that in European minds clothing was intimately connected to civility. Whether the Indigenous population stole colonisers' clothes in an attempt to gain this civility or not, it is apparent that Europeans quickly identified clothing as a tool that could be used to control Indigenous populations and construct a civilised American society. From the outset of European contact with America, clothing became symbolic of European civility and superiority. A common technique used by Europeans, particularly the Spanish, to establish their authority and superiority in the New World, was to use Indigenous women as emissaries. They would take an unclothed Indigenous woman, give her gifts and clothe her, and return her to her people as a symbol of Spanish generosity and civility.[61] English texts produced in the sixteenth century recounted tales such as this. For example, both Münster and Richard Eden, in his preface to Martyr's work, told the story of Columbus taking an Indigenous woman whom he 'commanded to be gorgeously decked after the maner of our [European] women, and with many rewardes to be sent agayne to theyr owne companye'.[62]

Martyr clearly articulated what he thought the purpose of such actions was. When describing another similar instance of the Spanish clothing of Indigenous people, Martyr explained how an Indigenous king's son was apparelled 'gorgiously' by the Spanish and then sent back to his father in order to 'persuade hym of the puissaunce, munificence, liberalitie, humanitie, and clemencie' of the visiting Europeans.[63] The giving of clothes was thus meant to signify to Indigenous communities a number of important European traits, from wealth and dominance, to Christian humility and charity. Clothing Indigenous peoples was not only considered a way of indicating European superiority, but also as a remedy for both material and spiritual poverty. In the sixteenth century, naked could also literally mean poverty-stricken, suggesting that the clothing of Indigenous people by Europeans may have represented an act of Christian charity towards a poorer and more destitute people.[64] In the case of Columbus, the man who began the trend of clothing Indigenous people in luxurious European garments, the charitable aspects of such acts should not be underestimated. The religious zeal of Columbus was made legendary in contemporary accounts. Columbus was well-known for his connections with monks and friars, particularly the Franciscans, with his staunchest supporters to be found in mendicant Franciscan religious circles.[65] Contemporary accounts also suggested that Columbus dressed simply, in the manner of a Franciscan monk.[66] This connection with the Franciscans would therefore suggest that ideas relating to poverty and charity would have been particularly meaningful for Columbus, given the order's rejection of material wealth and dedication to charitable and social acts.[67] This, combined with the fact that almsgiving remained an important way to achieve salvation in the late medieval Catholic Church, indicates that Columbus's personal piety and achievement of grace would have been intimately bound up with the way in which he dealt with the 'pore naked wretches' of the New World.[68] By clothing the 'poor', 'naked' people of America, men like Columbus could simultaneously illustrate European civility and wealth and ensure their own spiritual health through the alleviation of perceived Indigenous poverty.

In the most famous example of the English gifting of clothes in the Americas, Francis Drake and his men claimed that the Indigenous population of modern-day California, a region named by the English Nova Albion, were so pleased with English clothing that they mistook the Englishmen for gods. According to an account written by an anonymous author that was printed in the third volume of Richard Hakluyt's *Principal Navigations* in 1600, when the people of North America came to the English 'they greatly wondered' at the things they brought.[69] Drake 'curtesously intreated them [Indigenous people], and liberally bestowed on them necessarie things to cover their nakednesse, whereupon they supposed us [the English] to be gods'.[70] As Joan Pong Linton has argued, in this account of European apotheosis clothing is the 'crucial semiotic identifying Englishmen with gods', with the cloth in this case being directly responsible for this supposed Indigenous misconception.[71] This tale once again has striking parallels with the one told in Genesis. Just as the Christian God bestowed clothing upon Adam and Eve to help them cover their shame, so too did the supposed English gods with the Indigenous community.[72] The fact that the Indigenous population had clearly been mistaken, as the author is clear to point out, in fact validated the colonists' desire to be viewed as gods without them having to confront the blasphemous implications of such a desire.[73] For Englishmen such as Drake, the nakedness of the Indigenous community they had encountered, and their mistake that the Englishmen were gods, was reflective of their spiritual poverty. By clothing the peoples of California, the English not only imposed their own sense of religiously inspired shame onto Indigenous people, but also invented for themselves a mission of saving souls.[74] Just as Martyr had suggested that the Spanish clothing of Indigenous people indicated much more than a mere attempt to illustrate European superiority, so too did the author who depicted Drake's story. Drake did not bestow clothing on Indigenous peoples as a way of emphasising English wealth and power, but as a way of exhibiting English 'naturall and accustomed humanitie'.[75] The act of providing appropriate clothing to Indigenous groups was thus an act of Christian charity, an act that would help Indigenous peoples recognise their own shame and place them on a path towards Christian enlightenment and salvation.

Whether these charitable acts were successful or not, and indeed sincere or not, these anecdotes illustrate that the gifting of clothing as a form of charity was well established and was something that seems to have been prevalent in both Catholic and non-Catholic societies in the early modern period.[76] Christian citizens were more likely to give alms when faced with people dressed in rags or even with nudity, as this meagre or nonexistent clothing was symbolic of acute poverty in Christian theology.[77] The giving of clothing to the poor was also popular in pre-Reformation and post-Reformation religious communities in rural England, especially among pious women. Clothing given as charity was a visual reminder of the generosity of the benefactor. Europeans who gave the gift of clothing to Indigenous people were thus simultaneously doing their duty as good Christians and exerting their power and wealth visually and materially over the bodies of the Indigenous communities of the Americas.[78] The clothing of Indigenous people by Europeans was thus an act of religious, economic, cultural, and political dominance.

In the early decades of the sixteenth century a number of representations of Indigenous appearance emerged in English print. From the brazen, naked, and ungodly 'Indian', to the shamefaced, scantily clad individual who desired European clothes, the dress of Indigenous peoples became a device for assessing perceived levels of savagery and for concocting methods of European control. By framing their colonial exploits in religious terms, Europeans involved in the exploration and exploitation of America could legitimise their ventures, proving that they held the spiritual health of the Indigenous population to be just as important as the riches that could be derived from the New World. The nakedness of New World peoples identified their desperate need for Christian conversion, while their apparent desire for clothes established a viable method for achieving this. By clothing the 'ungodly' peoples of America, Europeans, in their own eyes at least, forced Indigenous peoples to confront their own savagery and ungodliness, and to accept the superiority of both European culture and religion. Clothing, in the American context, was thus symbolic of both civility and proper piety. By compelling Indigenous people to wear 'appropriate' clothing, European explorers and colonisers could also compel them to accept true religion and Old World notions of civility. These images would remain influential in English Americana throughout the sixteenth century, being adopted by English authors to illustrate the 'savagery' of some American peoples, to comment on the use of New World commodities, to reflect the perceived difficulties and abnormalities of some English encounters with Indigenous peoples, and to bolster shared European cultural values that taught that nakedness was inherently sinful and shameful. Despite the continued utilisation of the image of the ungodly, naked 'Indian' among some Englishmen, both directly and indirectly involved in overseas exploration, another more potent image was to emerge from the 1570s onwards in which English colonial aims and ventures vigorously collided with ideas relating to clothing.

Clothing, climate, and consumerism

In the 1570s the English began their first proper foray into colonial projects in the New World. With this new focus on establishing English settlements in America came new interpretations of Indigenous appearance that could help bolster and validate English colonial plans. While the Spanish had been preoccupied with the religious implications of Indigenous appearance, using their lack of clothing to indicate their ungodliness and need for Catholicism, English explorers and colonisers began to develop their own more worldly and utilitarian views of Indigenous dress. This difference in focus is unsurprising, given the very different models of overseas expansion employed by the two competing nations. While Spanish conquest and colonisation was a state-run and state-funded programme in which Spanish claims to the New World were dependent on the conversion of the Indigenous population to Catholicism, English ventures were largely reliant on private investors, meaning that the commercial viability of each English project was of critical importance.

In the late 1570s, when commercial incentive was the principal concern of those exploring the New World, English explorers writing about their experiences in the Far North used Indigenous clothing to validate their opinions on the viability of successful English settlement in the region. As Chapter 1 suggested, for early English explorers of the New World, proving that America enjoyed habitable climates was paramount, with this being particularly true for those involved in the explorations of the Far North. George Best, in particular, had done his utmost to try and prove that the lands of Meta Incognita enjoyed a temperate and hospitable climate, arguing that in the Far North 'the Sommers are warme & fruitful, & the Winters nights under the pole, are tollerable to living creatures'.[79] Unfortunately, Dionyse Settle, a fellow member of Frobisher's second voyage to Meta Incognita in 1577, undermined Best's arguments in a variety of ways, including through his description of the 'inappropriate' clothes of the Inuit.

Like many European commentators before him, Settle appeared thoroughly unimpressed by Indigenous clothing. While the Inuit did not go about naked like many of the Indigenous peoples encountered by Europeans in the warmer, southerly regions of America, their appearance still reflected their 'savage' character. In contrast to Thevet, who had seen the leather clothing of the peoples of Canada as a positive sign, Settle identified the beast-skin clothing of the Inuit as yet another indication of the desolate, barbaric, and impoverished nature of the region. Settle described the Inuit appearance as thoroughly beastly. Not only did they use beast-skin to clothe themselves, they also created bodily adornments that rendered their appearance even more feral and animal-like. The Inuit clothed themselves 'in the skinnes of such beastes as they kill, sewed together with the sinewes of them'.[80] As well as using fibrous tissue, rather than thread, to sew together their garments, they also used 'a bone within their hose' 'in place of garters' to stop their clothes from falling 'downe about their feete' and fashioned 'tailes' for their apparel which they gave to each other as tokens of friendship.[81] By utilising base materials that had not gone through sophisticated processes of manufacture to make their clothes, and by including bestial tails in their attire, the Inuit, in Settle's opinion, were illustrating their savage manner of living.[82] In fact, Settle concluded that the Inuit of Meta Incognita were entirely 'rude' with absolutely 'no capacitie to culture'.[83]

For Settle, the clothing of the Inuit also reflected their poverty. As Settle claimed, 'all their riches' were the beasts, fowls, and flesh they killed and used for 'both meate, drinke, apparel, houses, bedding, hose, shooes, thred, [and] saile for their boates'.[84] For early modern Europeans, clothes were regarded as the most visible marks of high living.[85] Conversely, then, the Inuit inability to differentiate the materials they used for clothing and, for example, housing, was a visible mark of their low living. This is also reminiscent of descriptions of the clothing of the early modern European poor. In the case of the very poor, clothing was often no more than a piece of canvas, a material usually associated with ships' sails.[86] The poor of Europe, therefore, used whatever materials they could access to make their clothing. It is likely, then, that Englishmen such as Settle would see the Inuit use of materials for various purposes as a marker of their poverty rather than as a sign of resourcefulness. In fact, this poverty in clothing echoed Settle's wider description of the region. The Inuit had to use whatever materials they could source in a variety of ways as the region was essentially 'barren and unfertile'.[87] Not only did the clothing of the Inuit reflect the destitution and savagery of the region, it also, in Settle's opinion, was more than likely completely ineffective for the harsh climate of the region. Their apparel, so Settle concluded, was 'of no such force to withstand the extremitie of colde, that the countrie seemeth to be infected with all'. If not even the Inuit could protect themselves from the cold, what chance did the English have? Despite the perceived technological, and indeed cultural, superiority of the English, Settle believed that the climate was so intolerable that it seemed unlikely that the English would be able to withstand the cold either.[88] The clothing of the Inuit confirmed Settle's assumption that the region was populated with rude and savage peoples and home to an inhospitable, even uninhabitable, climate. Inuit apparel, alongside the many other disappointments noted by Settle, suggested that settlement in the region was not viable. It was too cold for the English to survive, and even if they did manage to withstand the harsh climate, the landscape offered the explorers little of any commercial worth.

Conversely, George Best utilised ideas relating to Indigenous clothing to make the exact opposite claims to Settle. Best began his quest to prove the habitability and temperance of Meta Incognita by exploring the many falsehoods of classical understandings of the hot, torrid zone and contemporary misunderstandings relating to Indigenous nakedness. According to Best, some ignorant people claimed that the middle, torrid zone of the earth was 'extreme hote, bycause the people of that Countrie can live withoute clothing'. Best, on the other hand, argued that, in fact, the Indigenous use of clothing illustrated that the West Indies enjoyed a climate that fluctuated between hot and cool. As Best suggested, the Spanish had found that in this region of America Indigenous people were 'often forced to provide themselves clothing' due to the cold weather – something they would not otherwise do as wearing clothes was a 'griefe and trouble' for them. This was especially true in the winter months when 'with their heate, there is colde intermingled'. Alongside this, Best also suggested that the wearing of 'many cloths', as was the common practice of those living in England during the winter, was 'a remedy against extremetie, & argueth not the goodnesse of that habitation'.[89] In Best's interpretation, then, clothing was a necessity born from colder climates, rather than an indication of the 'goodnesse' of a particular region. In fact, the wearing of clothes, whether in England or in the West Indies, was an indication of temperate climes, rather than extreme ones; just as the weather in England fluctuated between warm and cool throughout the seasons, so too did the weather of the equatorial region of America.

The seasonality of America, and how it was reflected in the Indigenous use of clothing, was also critical to Best's arguments about the climate of the Far North. In the introductory remarks to a chapter of the book entitled 'of the temperature of colde Regions all the Sommer long, and also howe in Winter the same is habitable', Best promised to keep his arguments 'very shorte bicause the same reasons serve for this purpose, which were alleaged before in the proving the middle Zone to be temperate'.[90] Just as the climate of the middle zone ranged between hot and cold, so too did that of the Far North. Just as the temperature varied between summer and winter in the West Indies, so too did the temperature of Meta Incognita.[91] Presumably, then, just as the nakedness of Indigenous groups of the equatorial region did not indicate a land of extreme heat, the leather and fur clothing of the Inuit did not point to a climate that was too cold to endure. For Best, the clothing of the Indigenous inhabitants of America was evidence of the temperateness of the climates of both the middle and the northern zones of the earth. In proving that the Far North enjoyed habitable, temperate climes, especially during the summer months, Best also proved, in his mind at least, that English settlement in the region was possible and even desirable. Both Best and Settle had used the appearance of Indigenous peoples, and especially their clothing, to articulate their differing views on the Meta Incognita project. For Settle, the beastly and ineffective clothing of the Inuit reflected the savage, desolate, and impoverished nature of the region, while for Best, the fact that Indigenous people, who preferred to go naked, occasionally wore clothes to protect themselves from the cold was evidence of a continent that experienced fluctuating temperatures that made all regions of the Americas habitable and temperate.

This suggestion that Indigenous communities did in fact require more appropriate clothing may have also pricked the interest of some of England's struggling cloth merchants, as another feature of early English colonial discourse was the assertion that the Indigenous peoples of North America would become great consumers of English clothes. Throughout the sixteenth century, English exports of cloth had been contracting, with the trade experiencing a slow but significant decline in the latter half of the century.[92] The cloth trade in Antwerp, England's most significant market, had been negatively affected throughout the sixteenth century, with trade embargos being placed on England due to English piracy in the Caribbean, ongoing disputes over the payment of duties, and, later, English support of Dutch rebels during the revolt against Spain.[93] These disruptions were compounded by disputes taking place between the Merchant Adventurers, a group whose main business was the export of undressed cloth to Europe and the Levant, and the Clothworkers of London, a confederation of clothiers and tradesmen in various finishing crafts.[94] From the 1570s onwards, the Clothworkers of London were essentially shut out of European markets altogether by rival monopolistic parties, leading to a turn westward for new markets for dressed English cloth.[95] This new focus on American markets may have also been influenced by Richard Hakluyt's dealings with the company. As well as being a vigorous supporter and promoter of English settlement in the New World, for nearly ten years he was also a pensioner of the Clothworkers' Company.[96] Hakluyt, and indeed the other Englishmen associated with New World projects, appeared to welcome the Clothworkers' increasing attention towards long-range trades, making it an integral aspect of their promotional writing on potential English settlements in North America.

George Peckham, a key protagonist in the English attempt to colonise Newfoundland in the late 1570s, made his distaste for the Merchant Adventurers' tendency to export undressed cloth to short-range markets all too obvious. As he suggested, multiple towns and villages throughout England were now 'utterlye decayed and ruinated' due to the simple fact that the poor people of England were not being put to work finishing cloth 'by reason of the transportation of rawe wooll of these late dayes, more excessively then in tymes past'.[97] Luckily, Peckham, alongside many of the other men involved in early English colonial projects in the Americas, had a plan to rectify this, which centred on the scantily-dressed, if not fully naked, peoples of the New World. According to Peckham, it was 'wel known that all Savages', once they had begun 'but a little to taste civilitie', would 'take mavailous delight in any garment be it never so simple'. As Peckham also claimed, Englishmen who had experience in the more southerly parts of America had confirmed that the people of those regions were 'easily reduced to civilitie bothe in manners and garments', suggesting that the same could be hoped for the Indigenous people of Newfoundland.[98] Just like the Spanish and French explorers before him, Peckham also subscribed wholeheartedly to the notion that Indigenous groups desired European clothing. Peckham viewed this desire as an economic opportunity that was advantageous for both English workers and merchants, and Indigenous peoples. The Indigenous population would be reduced to civility, while the poor clothworkers of England would be put to work, producing garments that could be traded for critical commodities, such as pitch, tar, hemp, flax, gold, silver, copper, timber, and furs.[99] The clothing of Indigenous people was thus believed to be the gateway to a new and lucrative trading network that had the potential to enrich the realm, increase England's dominions, and reduce domestic unemployment and idleness.[100]

The notion that the Indigenous people of North America were likely to become great consumers of English cloth was reasserted time and again by authors promoting English overseas expansion in America in the late sixteenth and early seventeenth centuries. Christopher Carleill, the stepson of Francis Walsingham and, just like his stepfather, a keen promoter of English voyages to the New World, similarly used the idea of Indigenous consumerism to entice merchants of the Muscovy Company to invest in his project to settle and trade in North America.[101] Like Peckham, Carleill also believed that trading clothing with the Indigenous population was key to the success of English trade in the region. As he suggested, if the project prospered 'there muste of necessitie fall out, a verie liberall utteraunce of our Englishe Clothes, into a maine Countrey, described to be bigger then all *Europe*'.[102] Not only would English settlement in North America provide a new market for the struggling cloth trade, it would also be a market much greater in size than that of Europe. Edward Hayes, who had been a member of Gilbert's final disastrous voyage to Newfoundland in 1583, was once again busy promoting English settlement in the New World at the beginning of the seventeenth century. Hayes also believed that trade with Indigenous communities was critical to the success of any English project in the Americas. Once again, clothing was regarded as the principal English commodity that would be desired by Indigenous peoples. While the Indigenous population would provide the English with a 'staple of all vendible commodities of the world', the English, in return, would 'vent a very great quantitie of our English cloth into all the cold regions of America'.[103] Similar proposals were made for the Virginia enterprises of the 1580s. Richard Hakluyt the elder, in his inducements for planting an English settlement in Virginia which were written in 1585 but not published until 1602, argued that the region would provide 'an ample vent in time to come of the Woollen clothes of England'. Like Peckham, Hakluyt claimed that trading clothes with Indigenous communities would revitalise the cloth industry, aiding 'the maintenance of our [English] poore, that els sterve or become burdensome to the realme'.[104] Aside from confirming that English colonisation in the New World would help stimulate the English cloth trade, promoters of the Virginia enterprise from the 1580s onwards went even further to harness Indigenous appearance to promote their project back home, using the modesty and simplicity of Algonquian dress to illustrate their potential for civility and the ease with which colonial control could be established. By employing contemporary English views on appropriate appearance, English writers assessed the civility of the Virginia Algonquians, concluding that although in some respects their appearance pointed towards a certain level of savagery, in other ways it also highlighted their natural modesty and thirst for civility.

Modesty, simplicity, and the foundations of civility

In the latter half of the sixteenth century English advocates of overseas settlement were increasingly defining their own projects in opposition to Spanish methods, both implicitly and explicitly. This differentiation in approach is clearly identifiable in English attitudes towards Indigenous dress and partial nudity. While those writing about the Spanish conquests in America viewed the simplicity, or indeed absence, of Indigenous clothing as an indication of American spiritual and material poverty, for those Englishmen writing about Virginia from the 1580s onwards the basic clothing of the Algonquians was more positively construed as illustrating an appropriate level of modesty and a promising foundation on which to build English civility. Nowhere is this clearer than in the engravings that accompanied the 1590 edition of Thomas Harriot's *Briefe and True Report*.

First published in 1588, Harriot's *Briefe and True Report* was most likely written in response to John White's voyage of 1587 to Virginia that found the English settlement deserted, with the garrison that had been left behind in 1586 to protect the English claim to the region nowhere to be seen.[105] Harriot's text went through a second edition in 1590, with the Virginia colony's poor fortunes once again likely motivating its publication. Once White had found the colony completely deserted, he, and the new colonists that had accompanied him, set about establishing a new colony on Roanoke Island. After a number of terrifying skirmishes with the Indigenous population, White, who had been made governor, was persuaded to leave the colony in order to procure help and further supplies from England. Plans to send a relief fleet to the colony were met with a series of delays, caused in large part by the sequestering of all English ships to fight the Anglo-Spanish war that was instigated by the Armada of 1588. White was unable to mount a voyage to Virginia until 1590, when he gained passage upon a privateering venture that agreed to put in at Roanoke on the return voyage from the Caribbean. White found the colony deserted with absolutely no trace of the 115 colonists that had been left behind.[106] While the re-edition of Harriot's text was conceived before White's discovery of August 1590, it is still likely that the text was produced in order to drum up support for a venture that looked to be faltering.[107] As the colonists had not been heard of since White's departure in 1587, it is possible that Harriot's text was reproduced in 1590 in part, at least, to remind English men and women of the colony and its likely success. The promotional nature of the text no doubt took on a new sense of urgency once White had discovered that the colonists were missing and the English settlement completely deserted. Within this context, English perceptions of the appearance of Indigenous people became a critical tool for reasserting the viability and favourability of the English venture in Virginia.

The 1590 edition of Harriot's text was an elaborate affair. Not only was it printed in folio, it was also accompanied by an exquisite set of engravings created by the printer of the book, Theodore de Bry. These engravings were based on watercolours that had been produced by John White, the future governor of the Roanoke colony, during his time in Virginia in 1585 and 1586. The watercolours depicted the people of the region and many aspects of their daily lives, from their burial rituals and religious dances, to their fishing techniques and methods of cooking.[108] Both White's original watercolours and de Bry's subsequent engravings have been the subject of a large amount of scholarly interest, not only in terms of their artistic value but also in terms of what they can tell us about early English encounters with the people of North America. Opinion is somewhat divided over whether or not either set of images are ethnographically accurate. As Stephanie Pratt has suggested, scholars have tended to make a clear distinction between White's watercolours and de Bry's engravings, arguing that in the former, 'authentic American Indian content' can be found while in de Bry's images the subjects are 'derivative, manipulated and manipulative, ideologically suspect and Europeanized'.[109] More recently, historians have begun to move away from this absolute distinction, exploring the ways in which both sets of images have been manipulated by their creators. White's watercolours were not immune to the artistic conventions of the period, with Mannerist forms, and books of habits and customs influencing his depictions of the Virginia Algonquians.[110] In the de Bry engravings, these artistic manipulations become even more pronounced. The conventions of copper engraving explain the heightened 'classicizing proportions' of de Bry's engravings, while the images themselves appear to convey a stronger visual message of the Algonquians' capacity for civilisation, a theme that is central to Harriot's entire text.[111] In their engraved form, White's images take on a more conspicuous promotional quality, reaffirming Harriot's arguments that English colonialism in the region would proceed with ease. The de Bry engravings are further manipulated through the structuring and sequencing of this visual material. De Bry's engravings incorporated the Algonquians into a clear scheme of European history and ethnography. The images of the Indigenous people of Virginia are placed between those depicting Adam and Eve in the Garden of Eden and those depicting the ancient inhabitants of the British Isles. By sequencing the engravings in this way, the Algonquians were framed genealogically by Adam and Eve and anthropologically by the ancient Picts and Britons. The Algonquians are thus deprived of any sense of their own history; there are no 'in times past' for the Indigenous peoples of Virginia beyond the original moment of first contact with the English.[112]

These subtle manipulations of White's images are unsurprising given the objectives of de Bry's edition of Harriot's account. Richard Hakluyt, the avid promoter of English settlement in North America, was heavily involved with the edition's conception and production, convincing de Bry to produce a text that not only disseminated the Tudor claim to Virginia throughout Europe, but also promoted the region's abundance, fertility, and gentle people.[113] While Harriot's original publication of 1588 had prioritised descriptions of the many commodities of the region over a detailed account of the peoples of Virginia, the supplementary visual material included in the 1590 edition effectively equalised this previous imbalance.[114] De Bry's decision to include engravings of White's images of the Algonquians, rather than those that depicted the flora and fauna of the region, highlights what he considered the most important aspects of Harriot's account to be.[115] It is possible that de Bry rejected White's botanical and zoological images solely for financial reasons, instead providing his engravings of Algonquians with backgrounds that emphasised the region's fertile environment as a compromise.[116] Whatever the motivation behind this exclusion, it is clear that the visual material included in the 1590 edition served a particular promotional function that emphasised Harriot's assertion that English settlement in the region would prevail thanks to a temperate and abundant environment, and a gentle and industrious Indigenous population. Although undoubtedly accurately depicting aspects of Indigenous life, these illustrations should nonetheless be viewed as functional, representational and, like Harriot's text, promotional.[117]

De Bry's engravings, in conjunction with English textual descriptions of the Algonquian population, when viewed through the lens of contemporary understandings of appropriate appearance and dress, present a clear rhetorical message. The Algonquians, while currently savage and vastly inferior to the English, possessed a natural sense of modesty and shame, and a promising capacity for civilisation and assimilation into English culture. Through their appearance, the Algonquians were rendered simultaneously 'savage' and 'civilised'. The 'superior' English would nurture these seeds of civility, using the Algonquians' inherent pliable and impressionable nature, which were symptoms of their simple and savage form of living, to exert complete colonial and cultural control.

The first thing to note is that in the de Bry engravings, and indeed in White's original watercolours, the nudity of the Algonquians of Roanoke is presented as a pleasing sign of simplicity rather than as one of perversity. In contrast to other visual images of Indigenous people produced in the sixteenth century, the nakedness of the Algonquians is not represented alongside instances of inhuman, abhorrent Indigenous behaviour such as cannibalism. Instead, the partially nude people of Virginia partake in normal, everyday activities; they craft their boats, they fish, the children play with toys (Figures 2–4).

As well as not engaging in the perverse behaviour often associated with nakedness in the early modern European mind, the poses and gestures of the Algonquians in de Bry's engravings also reflect a more positive English attitude towards their appearance. The use of the 'Renaissance elbow' in the depiction of an Algonquian chief served to establish similarity between the Indigenous North Americans and the colonising English. This pose, which depicts the subject with one hand placed on the hip, was considered one of arrogance, afforded only to those men who could 'command respect'.[118] This pose also signified someone fit and active in European iconography, and thus amounted to an 'idealization and Europeanization' of the original Algonquian sitter.[119] By recreating this pose in the portrait of the chief, White and de Bry were emphasising the subject's power and dominance, awarding him a degree of English respect and esteem (Figure 5). The women of Virginia are likewise depicted respectfully, despite their obvious nudity. In one illustration, a young woman from Secotan wears an apron that covers both her front and behind from her midriff to her thigh. She places her arms across her chest to cover her breasts (Figure 6). The caption helpfully interprets this gesture for the viewer; she did this in 'token of maydenlike modestye'.[120] The young woman was thus depicted as recognising the need

Figure 2 Theodore de Bry, copper engraving, 'The Manner of Makinge Their Boates', in Thomas Harriot, *A Briefe and True Report of the New Found Land of Virginia* (Frankfurt, 1590).

for modesty. Unlike Spanish tales of shameless naked South Americans, the English showed that Indigenous North Americans wore their partial nakedness with shame. The perceived modesty of Algonquian women was also broached by James Rosier in his account of his travels to the north of Virginia in 1605. When the English arrived on the New England shore, the Indigenous women retreated to the woods, leading Rosier to speculate that the reason for this shyness was their 'owne naturall modestie'.[121]

This modest posture could also have been used to identify the woman in question as high-born, for European portraiture often depicted women of status with their arms 'self-enclosing' in this manner.[122] The high status of the young woman was corroborated in the caption which claimed she was a virgin of 'good parentage'.[123] The chief and young woman were shown to exhibit normative early modern European gender roles – the chief through his apparent power and dominance, the young woman through her natural modesty. These images also suggest that English observers such as White saw distinct social hierarchies in the communities that they encountered in North America.[124] By illustrating the fact that it was possible to differentiate between various strata of Algonquian society, de Bry and White imbued the Indigenous population with a degree of civility that would in

Figure 3 Theodore de Bry, copper engraving, 'Their Manner of Fishynge in Virginia', in Thomas Harriot, *A Briefe and True Report of the New Found Land of Virginia* (Frankfurt, 1590).

turn convince potential investors that the recreation of English society in America was entirely possible.

Not only did these images of ostensibly civilised Algonquians contrast heavily with the other depictions of Indigenous peoples explored in the first half of this chapter, they also diverged with other illustrations included in the de Bry edition of Harriot. Alongside de Bry's positive rendering of the

Figure 4 Theodore de Bry, copper engraving, 'A Chieff Ladye of Pomeiooc', in Thomas Harriot, *A Briefe and True Report of the New Found Land of Virginia* (Frankfurt, 1590).

Algonquians, a number of other images illustrating the ancient peoples of the British Isles also appeared. Gone are the allusions to female modesty and male dominance, and to harmless behaviour and civil living. The people of ancient Britain, as depicted by both de Bry and White, were illustrative of utter savagery. The females fail to cover their breasts out of modesty, instead opening up their largely naked bodies to the viewer (Figures 7 and 8). In fact, in the image of a young daughter of the Picts, the Renaissance elbow, a gesture normally associated with authoritative and dominant males, is reproduced, thus inverting and transgressing normative European gender traits; it was the female Pict, rather than her male counterpart, who was awarded this iconic posture of aggression and authority (Figure 8). While the Algonquians were depicted engaging in everyday activities, the Picts were exclusively shown participating in, or preparing for, violent action. Both the men and women carry terrifying swords and spears, while in the image of a male Pict the subject clutches the severed head of his enemy by the hair (Figures 7, 8, and 9).

It is clear why these images of the ancient Picts were included alongside those of the Algonquians. As the writer of the introduction to the Pict images stated, they were there to illustrate that 'the Inhabitants of the great

Dressing America 139

Figure 5 Theodore de Bry, copper engraving, 'A Weroan or Great Lorde of Virginia', in Thomas Harriot, *A Briefe and True Report of the New Found Land of Virginia* (Frankfurt, 1590).

Bretannie have been in times past as sauvage as those of Virginia'.[125] As the caption to the first image of a male Pict explained, their savagery was evidenced by their long, unruly hair, the painting of 'sum feere full and monstreus face' upon their bellies, and the fact that after overcoming their enemies 'they did never felle to carye a we their heads with them'.[126] The message here is inescapable; just as the ancient, savage tribes of England were civilised by the Roman Empire, the Virginia Algonquians could also be tamed and brought to culture by the civilised Englishmen of the sixteenth century.

Yet the appearance of the Algonquians was rendered far more civilised than that of the Picts by both de Bry and White. The Algonquians engaged in civilised activities, they covered their private parts with simple clothes, and they arranged their society into a clearly defined hierarchy. This implicit suggestion that the Indigenous population of Virginia were a step further along the path to civility than the Picts of ancient Britain, served a useful rhetorical function. It illustrated, as had much of Harriot's text pertaining to the Indigenous population, the ease with which English colonial control could be achieved in the region.[127] While the Romans had had their work cut out with the savage and brutal Picts, the English subjugation of

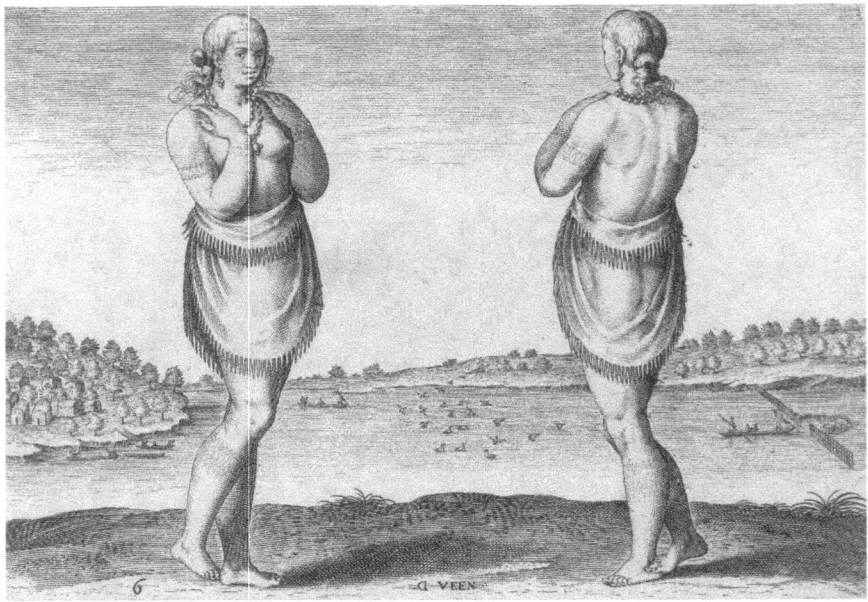

Figure 6 Theodore de Bry, copper engraving, 'A Younge Gentill Woeman Doughter of Secota', in Thomas Harriot, *A Briefe and True Report of the New Found Land of Virginia* (Frankfurt, 1590).

Virginia would be a far simpler affair thanks to the Algonquians' obvious desire for civility.

Having said all this, the images also attest to the savage traits that the Algonquians were believed to possess but, once again, this fact was rendered useful for the English colonial strategy in the region. The blending of the Algonquians' potential civility with their current savagery was critical to the English validation of their colonial project. It was crucial that proponents of colonisation in Virginia were able to illustrate that the Indigenous population needed, and indeed wanted, access to English civility and religion. The savage aspects of both de Bry's illustrations and written accounts of the people of Virginia should therefore not be underestimated. It is obvious from the illustrations that the garments of the Algonquians were not particularly sophisticated, especially in comparison to the, at times, ostentatious clothing of the early modern English. The Algonquians were depicted wearing simple deer skin aprons, tied about their waist, their backs and behinds often remaining exposed. Even the high-born chiefs and ladies of the region wore these simple garments, being represented in much the same fashion as those engaged in laborious activities such as crafting boats and fishing (Figures 2–6). Indigenous clothing, as depicted by de Bry, was thus not used as a tool

Figure 7 Theodore de Bry, copper engraving, 'The True Picture of a Women Picte', in Thomas Harriot, *A Briefe and True Report of the New Found Land of Virginia* (Frankfurt, 1590).

Figure 8 Theodore de Bry, copper engraving, 'The True Picture of a Yonge Dowgter of the Pictes', in Thomas Harriot, *A Briefe and True Report of the New Found Land of Virginia* (Frankfurt, 1590).

Figure 9 Theodore de Bry, copper engraving, 'The True Picture of One Picte', in Thomas Harriot, *A Briefe and True Report of the New Found Land of Virginia* (Frankfurt, 1590).

with which to distinguish between peoples of different social statuses, a fact that contrasted heavily with common English practice.[128]

Sixteenth-century England witnessed a flurry of state proclamations and legislation designed to regulate clothing. The primary function of this extensive sumptuary legislation was to maintain social ranks and make sure people did not dress above their station.[129] Sumptuary laws regulated what colours, fabrics, and adornments a person could wear, and in doing so defined difference between certain groups and 'conferred the distinction of high status'.[130] Dress, in short, was a carefully controlled symbolic system which marked out, if the rules were followed, a person's economic and social status.[131] These rules and expectations, when applied to the Indigenous peoples of North America, confirmed that the structure of their society was far more underdeveloped than that of England. The fact that the Algonquians did not seem to distinguish between social rank through their clothing was indicative, in the English mind, of a primitive social system.

That does not necessarily mean, however, that this perceived primitivism was always viewed negatively. At the same time that men such as Harriot were busy exploring the lands of North America, English society was embroiled in fierce debates over religious reformation and moral decay. People of a puritan persuasion, famously described by Patrick Collinson as the 'hotter' sort of Protestant, increasingly used clothing as evidence for society's descent into immorality and as proof that further religious reform was needed.[132] One such godly commentator, Philip Stubbes, was highly concerned with the effect that fashionable apparel was having on English society. In his extremely popular pamphlet of 1583, *The Anatomie of Abuses*, Stubbes explained to his many readers that 'the greatest abuse, which (.) offendeth god moste' 'is the execrable sinne of Pride, and excesse in apparell'.[133] Apparel, so Stubbes's argument went, was 'given us of god to cover our shame' and 'to put us in mind of our frailties, imperfections and sin'.[134] Because clothing was symbolic of the sinfulness of man, Stubbes argued that it should be like that of Adam and Eve 'in Godly simplicitie and Christian sobrietie'. By clothing themselves simply and modestly, the godly of England would simultaneously 'please God a great deale the more' and 'avoyd many scandals & offences which grow daily by our excessive ryot'.[135] Stubbes also suggested that pride in apparel was a particular sin of the English. In his diatribe against the excesses of the people of 'Ailgna', which is of course an anagram of 'Anglia', Stubbes argued that pride in apparel had 'infected and poysoned' no other country as much.[136] While the people of Ailgna clothed themselves in 'unhandsame, brutish and monstrouse' clothing, the 'savage' peoples of lands such as Brazil had little esteem for fine garments, preferring instead to either 'go cleane naked' or clothe themselves modestly and simply in 'Beasts skinnes' or whatever else they had to hand.[137] Sumptuous clothing, then, in the opinion of Stubbes, was considered monstrous and unnatural, while the simple beast-skin clothing of Indigenous peoples was deemed more appropriate and in keeping with godly simplicity and natural modesty.

It was not just godly commentators who used the simpler, primitive dress of Indigenous groups to address the perceived degradation of sixteenth-century English society. The celebration of Indigenous primitivism was also informed by the re-emergence of stoic understandings of nature among humanist thinkers. Both Harriot and de Bry participated in this humanist culture that expressed nostalgia for the virtues of primitive forms of living.[138] The relatively primitive lifestyle of the Algonquians became a reminder of what was lost through the process of civilisation; Indigenous people were perceived to be happy, healthy, and uncorrupted, living in a state of nature in which worldly goods such as luxurious clothing were unnecessary. This notion of the healthy, uncorrupted 'savage' is reinforced through the classicised figures of de Bry's engravings, which depict the Algonquians as muscular and statuesque, and by textual descriptions of the Indigenous people of North American that highlight their robust, active bodies and gentle, loving condition. John Brereton, who explored the northerly region of Virginia in 1602, claimed that the Indigenous inhabitants were 'of a perfect constitution of body', being 'active, strong, healthfull, and very wittie'.[139] Alongside their healthy bodies, the people of Virginia were also portrayed as living in a state of natural serenity. As Arthur Barlowe, one of the first Englishmen to explore Virginia, put it, the people of the region were 'most gentle, loving, and faithfull, voide of all guile and treason, and such as live after the maner of the golden age'.[140] However, this did not mean that these writers and commentators rejected civilisation. On the contrary, what this celebration of the primitive reflected was the fact that the transition from barbarism to civility was not one of absolute gains but one of 'tragic loss in the context of obvious gains' that were impossible to renounce.[141] These ideas relating to primitivism, modesty, and godly simplicity thus helped define English reactions to the peoples of North America. By invoking the image of the savage and the primitive, promoters of English voyages in the Americas could validate the need for English colonisation. The English would eradicate the less desirable aspects of Indigenous living, while nurturing those that displayed a commitment to achieving civility on the part of Indigenous peoples. English notions of civilised and modest appearance shaped English responses to North America, allowing for the development of a rhetorical message that presented the Indigenous population as savage but ready to accept English civilisation and religion.

* * *

Representations of Indigenous appearance in sixteenth-century English print were varied and, at times, contradictory. In the early decades of the sixteenth century, English readers were reliant on continental European ideas of America, gaining their first glimpse of Indigenous people through translations of key texts that recounted the tales of Spanish, Portuguese, and French exploits in the region. It was from these texts that the image of the ungodly, naked, brazen, and perverse 'Indian' first made its appearance, being shaped by shared European beliefs on the sinfulness of nakedness and by English authorial agendas that wished to utilise Indigenous appearance to denounce other aspects of Indigenous behaviour, such as the smoking of tobacco, and to highlight the difficulties faced while traveling through 'savage' and 'exotic' lands.

At the same time, however, many of these early texts also introduced the notion that Indigenous populations could be controlled and manipulated through clothing, something that would become key to English colonial aspirations from the 1570s onwards. The Spanish, and indeed some early English explorers such as Francis Drake, had illustrated the perceived power of clothing in a colonial context. Accounts of clothing theft, coupled with the extravagant European gifting of clothes to the Indigenous population, highlighted, in European minds at least, the Indigenous desire for civility. By displaying European wealth and Christian charity through this act of gift giving, colonisers and explorers could exert their power both visually and materially over Indigenous bodies, using clothing as a tool of both colonial mastery and justification.

As the English embarked on their own programme of exploration and colonisation in the New World, they too used beliefs surrounding clothing and appearance to validate and justify their colonial projects, both intellectually and commercially. In the explorations of the Far North in the 1570s, Best and Settle used the attire of Indigenous peoples to comment on the climate and habitability of Meta Incognita in an attempt to bolster, or indeed, debunk arguments surrounding the most suitable regions of the New World for English settlement. In the early 1580s, when English focus shifted further southwards and securing private investment became critical to colonial success, English advocates of overseas settlement and Anglo-American trade such as Peckham, Carleill, Hayes, and Hakluyt began to suggest that English clothing could be the key to successful trade in North America. Like Spanish and French commentators before them, they too believed that the peoples of the New World desired European clothing. Instead of using this idea as a means to exert overt colonial control, however, these English writers used it to convince embittered English cloth merchants to invest in their projects. In return for their money, investors would receive a vast array of vital commodities and a significant new market for their own wares.

As the English moved still further southwards in the mid-1580s to explore and colonise Virginia, Indigenous appearance and clothing was once again critical to the articulation of their colonial plans. Basing their beliefs on common English assumptions surrounding clothing and on contemporary debates about appropriate dress and lifestyle, those involved in the Virginia enterprise highlighted the potential of the Algonquians to receive English civility through their appearance. By emphasising this potential, alongside traits that pointed towards a current level of primitivism and savagery, the appearance of the Virginia Algonquians would illustrate to readers and potential investors back home the ease with which English society could be recreated in North America. Indigenous clothing and appearance were thus rendered crucial to English colonial success, becoming a practical tool that had the potential to enrich investors and allow colonisers to incorporate Indigenous peoples into their colonial plans. Throughout the sixteenth century a number of images of Indigenous Americans coexisted in English print. These representations were employed for a number of reasons: to bolster shared European assumptions about the sinful nature of nakedness, to explain the perceived negative aspects of Indigenous culture and society, to emphasise the dangers inherent in international travel, and, most crucially, to justify and validate colonial projects.

Notes

1 William Shakespeare, *Hamlet* (Act 1, Scene 3), Open Source Shakespeare, last accessed 12 March, 2014, www.opensourceshakespeare.org.
2 Susan Vincent, *Dressing the Elite: Clothes in Early Modern England* (Oxford: Berg, 2003), 1–6; Carole Collier Frick, *Dressing Renaissance Florence: Families, Fortunes, and Fine Clothing* (Baltimore, MD and London: Johns Hopkins University Press, 2005), 179–180. Other studies that have analysed the connection between clothing and identity in early modern Europe include Ulinka Rublack, *Dressing Up: Cultural Identity in Renaissance Europe* (Oxford: Oxford University Press, 2010); Carlo Marco Belfanti and Fabio Giusberti, "Clothing and Social Inequality in Early Modern Europe: Introductory Remarks," *Continuity and Change* 15, no. 3 (December, 2000): 359–365; Jean E. Howard, "Crossdressing, the Theatre, and Gender Struggles in Early Modern England," *Shakespeare Quarterly* 99, no. 4 (Winter, 1988): 418–440.
3 Michael Gaudio has explored the popularity of costume books in the sixteenth century, as has Kim Sloane. Both place the work of John White within this tradition, illustrating a clear link between this tradition and English representations of Indigenous people. Michael Gaudio, "The Truth in Clothing: The Costume Studies of John White and Lucas de Heere," in *European Visions:*

American Voices, ed. Kim Sloan (London: British Museum Press, 2009), 24–32; Kim Sloan, "Catalogue: John White's Watercolours," in *A New World: England's First View of America*, ed. Kim Sloan (Chapel Hill: University of North Carolina Press, 2007), 147–151.

4 Bodmer, *Armature of Conquest*, 32–33; Pagden, *Fall of Natural Man*, 52–53; Alden T. Vaughan, "People of Wonder: England Encounters the New World's Natives," in *New World of Wonders: European Images of the Americas, 1492–1700*, ed. Rachel Doggett (Seattle and London: University of Washington Press, 1992), 15–16.

5 Philippa Levine, "States of Undress: Nakedness and the Colonial Imagination," *Victorian Studies* 50, no. 2 (Winter, 2008): 189–190.

6 Jill Burke, "Nakedness and Other Peoples: Rethinking the Italian Renaissance Nude," *Art History* 36, no. 4 (September, 2013): 724–726.

7 Levine, "States of Undress," 191–197.

8 Gaudio, "Truth in Clothing," 26.

9 Ibid., 29. Jean E. Howard has made a similar argument in her discussion of crossdressing in Elizabethan England. As Howard argues, dress became a primary site where 'a struggle over the mutability of the social order was conducted', with crossdressing being just one manifestation of this struggle. Howard, "Crossdressing," 422.

10 Alan Hunt, "The Governance of Consumption: Sumptuary Laws and Shifting Forms of Regulation," *Economy and Society* 25, no. 3 (August, 1996): 410–413.

11 Wilfrid Hooper, "The Tudor Sumptuary Laws," *The English Historical Review* 30, no. 119 (July, 1915): 433–448.

12 Gaudio, "Truth in Clothing," 30–31. Quotation from 31.

13 Karen Ordahl Kupperman, "Presentment of Civility: English Reading of American Self-Presentation in the Early Years of Colonization," *The William and Mary Quarterly* 54, no. 1 (January, 1997): 218.

14 For detailed analyses of the various cultural meanings of hairstyles and hair accessories in early modern Europe see Will Fisher, "The Renaissance Beard: Masculinity in Early Modern England," *Renaissance Quarterly* 54, no. 1 (Spring, 2001): 155–187; Evelyn Welch, "Art on the Edge: Hair and Hands in Renaissance Italy," *Renaissance Studies* 23, no. 3 (June, 2009): 241–268.

15 Kupperman, "Presentment of Civility," 205–228.

16 Kupperman briefly refers to some of these other English perceptions of Indigenous appearance but does not explore them in detail. For example, Kupperman references the fact that some English observers believed the simplicity of Indigenous dress reflected the innocence of Indigenous people and was, therefore, a virtue. Kupperman also briefly alludes to the fact that social distinctions in clothing were particularly important to the English as there was a perception that their own society was breaking down, with gender and social distinctions being elided. This chapter will explore the origins and manifestations of both of these ideas in the sixteenth century in more detail. Kupperman, "Presentment of Civility," 194–203.

17 Anon., *Of the Newe La[n]des*, sig. A1r.
18 Ibid., sigs. A1r–A1v.
19 This image is consistent with the types of early sixteenth-century images identified by Alden Vaughan in which naked bodies and cannibalism, alongside common ownership, sexual licence, frequent warfare and idolatry, were common themes; Vaughan, "People of Wonder," 15. Susi Colin has also explored the use of these behavioural traits in early sixteenth-century images of Indigenous people, arguing that these early depictions were largely based around the European pictorial tradition of the wild man; Susi Colin, "The Wild Man and the Indian in Early 16th Century Book Illustration," in *Indians & Europe: An Interdisciplinary Collection of Essays*, ed. Christian F. Feest (Lincoln, NE and London: University of Nebraska Press, 1999), 5–36. For more on early images of America and the modification of traditional European imagery see William C. Sturtevant, "The Sources for European Imagery of Native Americans," in *New World of Wonders: European Images of the Americas, 1492–1700*, ed. Rachel Doggett (Seattle and London: University of Washington Press, 1992), 25–33; William C. Sturtevant, "First Visual Images of Native Americans," in *First Images of America: The Impact of the New World on the Old*, ed. Fredi Chiappelli (Berkeley and London: University of California Press, 1976), 417–454.
20 Vaughan, "People of Wonder," 16.
21 For just a small number of references that Martyr makes to naked peoples and naked nations see Martyr, *Decades of the Newe Worlde*, fols. 47, 51, 52, 67, 73, 78 and 87.
22 Ibid., fols. 49 and 68.
23 Ibid., fols. 20 and 114.
24 Ibid., fol. 48.
25 Ibid., fol. 100.
26 Karen Kupperman has defined the complex meaning of the word 'naked' in early English travel literature thus: 'naked as a description seemed automatically to go with the word savage'. It is my contention that rather than just being used alongside the word 'savage', the word 'naked' in fact became a synonym for the word 'savage'; Kupperman, "The Presentment of Civility," 201.
27 Münster, *Treatyse of the Newe India*, sig. K7r.
28 Ibid., sigs. K7r–K8r.
29 For the importance of the story of Adam and Eve in early modern England see Philip C. Almond, *Adam & Eve in Seventeenth-Century Thought* (Cambridge: Cambridge University Press, 1999).
30 Levine, "States of Undress," 191.
31 Leviticus 20, The Official King James Bible Online, last accessed 19 November, 2013, www.kingjamesbibleonline.org/; Leviticus 20, The Latin Vulgate Bible, Last accessed 8 September, 2016, www.latinvulgate.com/lv/verse.aspx?t=0&b=3&c=20; Anon. *Holy Byble*, The First Part (London, 1576), fol. 60.
32 Jon D. Levenson, "Genesis: Introduction and Annotations," in *The Jewish Study Bible*, eds. Adele Berlin and Marc Zvi Brettler (Oxford: Oxford

University Press, 2004), 26. For a detailed analysis of the connections between Christianity and sexuality in the early modern world see Merry E. Wiesner-Hanks, *Christianity and Sexuality in the Early Modern World: Regulating Desire, Reforming Practice* (London: Routledge, 2000).
33 Thevet, *New Found Worlde*.
34 Roger Schlesinger and Arthur P. Stabler, "Introduction," in *André Thevet's North America: A Sixteenth-Century View*, eds. Roger Schlesinger and Arthur P. Stabler (Kingston, Ontario and Montreal: McGill-Queen's University Press, 1986), xx–xxi.
35 Thevet, *New Found Worlde*, sigs. *2r–*3v.
36 E. W. Lynam, "Sir Henry Sidney," *Studies: An Irish Quarterly Review* 2, no. 7 (September, 1913): 188.
37 Thevet, *New Found Worlde*, fols. 106–107.
38 Ibid., fol. 45.
39 Ibid., fols. 45–46.
40 Ibid., fol. 36.
41 Gervase Babington, *Certaine Plaine, Briefe, and Comfortable Notes Upon Everie Chapter of Genesis* (London, 1592), fols. 14–22.
42 Henry Smith, *The Sermons of Master Henry Smith* (London, 1593), 598.
43 John Calvin, *A Commentarie of John Calvin Upon the First Booke of Moses Called Genesis*, trans. Thomas Tymme (London, 1578), 79–102.
44 James I, *A Counterblaste to Tobacco* (London, 1604), sigs. B1v–B2r.
45 Martyr, *Decades of the Newe Worlde*, fol. 23.
46 Ibid., fol. 213.
47 Kupperman, "The Presentment of Civility," 200.
48 Thevet, *New Found Worlde*, fol. 45.
49 Genesis 3, King James Bible; Genesis 3, Vulgate Bible; Anon., *Holy Byble*, The First Part, fol. 3.
50 Thevet, *New Found Worlde*, fol. 45.
51 Ibid., fol. 127.
52 Ibid., fol. 45.
53 Ibid., fol. 46.
54 Job Hortop, *The Travailes of an English Man Containing his Sundrie Calalmities* (London, 1591), 5–18; Miles Philips, "A Discourse Written by One *Miles Philips* Englishman," in *Principal Navigations*, 3:469–474.
55 Hortop, *Travailes of an English Man*, 18–19.
56 Ibid., 19.
57 Philips, "A Discourse Written by One *Miles Philips*," 3:474.
58 Beverly Lemire, "The Theft of Clothes and Popular Consumerism in Early Modern England," *Journal of Social History* 24, no. 2 (Winter, 1990): 255.
59 Ibid., 257.
60 Ibid., 258.
61 Jennifer L. Morgan, "'Some Could Suckle over their Shoulder': Male Travelers, Female Bodies and the Gendering of Racial Ideology, 1500–1770," *The William and Mary Quarterly* 54, no. 1 (January, 1997): 172.

62 Quotation taken from: Münster, *Treatyse of Newe India*, sig. H2r. The same story from Martyr reads: the Spanish 'tooke onely one woman, whom they brought to the shyppes: where fyllinge her with meate and wyne, and apparelinge her, they let her departe to her company'; Martyr, *Decades of the Newe Worlde*, fol. 2.
63 Martyr, *Decades of the Newe Worlde*, fol. 93.
64 Levine, "States of Undress," 194.
65 Leonard I. Sweet, "Christopher Columbus and the Millennial Vision of the New World," *The Catholic Historical Review* 72, no. 3 (July, 1986): 378.
66 Paul M. Lester, "Looks Are Deceiving: The Portraits of Christopher Columbus," *Visual Anthropology* 5, nos. 3–4 (1993): 214.
67 Lee Palmer Wandel, "The Poverty of Christ," in *The Reformation of Charity: The Secular and the Religious in Early Modern Poor Relief*, ed. Thomas Max Safley (Leiden: Brill, 2003), 15–29.
68 Sigrun Kahl, "The Religious Roots of Modern Poverty Policy: Catholic, Lutheran, and Reformed Protestant Traditions Compared," *European Journal of Sociology* 46, no. 1 (2005): 95–96; Brian Pullman, "Catholics and the Poor in Early Modern Europe," *Transactions of the Royal Historical Society* 26 (December, 1976): 15–34. The phrase 'pore naked wretches' comes from Martyr's description of the people of Darién. Martyr, *Decades of the Newe Worlde*, fol. 68.
69 Anon., "The Course Which Sir *Francis Drake* Held from the Haven of *Guatulco* in the South Sea on the Backe Side of *Nueva Espanna*, to the Northwest of *California*," in *Principal Navigations*, 3:440.
70 Ibid., 3:440–441.
71 Joan Pong Linton, *The Romance of the New World: Gender and the Literary Formations of English Colonialism* (Cambridge: Cambridge University Press, 1998), 78.
72 Ibid., 79.
73 As the author suggested, the Indigenous population would 'not be perswaded' that the Englishmen were not gods which implies that the English explorers did at least attempt to dispel their mistake. It is not clear, however, what methods they actually employed. Anon., "The Course Which Sir *Francis Drake* Held," 3:441; Linton, *Romance of the New World*, 79.
74 Linton, *Romance of the New World*, 79.
75 Anon., "The Course Which Sir *Francis Drake* Held," 3:440.
76 On gifting in early modern Europe see Ilana Krausman Ben-Amos, *The Culture of Giving: Informal Support and Gift-Exchange in Early Modern England* (Cambridge: Cambridge University Press, 2008); Felicity Heal, *The Power of Gifts: Gift-Exchange in Early Modern England* (Oxford: Oxford University Press, 2014); Linda Levy Peck, *Court Patronage and Corruption in Early Stuart England* (London: Routledge, 2004); Natalie Zemon Davis, *The Gift in Sixteenth-Century France* (Oxford: Oxford University Press, 2000).
77 Robert Jütte, *Poverty and Deviance in Early Modern Europe* (Cambridge: Cambridge University Press, 1994), 80.

78 Dolly Mackinnon, "'Charity is worth it when it looks that good': Rural Women and Bequests of Clothing in Early Modern England," in *Women, Identities, and Communities in Early Modern Europe*, eds. Susan Broomhall and Stephanie Tarbin (Aldershot: Ashgate, 2008), 79–89.
79 Best, *A True Discourse*, sig. h2r.
80 Settle, *A True Reporte*, sig. C6r.
81 Ibid., sigs. C6r–C6v.
82 For more detail on European artisanal practice and luxury textile production see Amelia Peck, ed., *Interwoven Globe: The World Textile Trade, 1500–1800* (New Haven, CT: Yale University Press, 2013); Beverly Lemire, *Global Trade and the Transformation of Consumer Cultures: The Material World Remade, c. 1500–1820* (Cambridge: Cambridge University Press, 2017).
83 Settle, *A True Reporte*, sig. D1v.
84 Ibid., sig. C6v.
85 Belfanti and Giusberti, "Clothing and Social Inequality," 359.
86 Jütte, *Poverty and Deviance*, 78.
87 Settle, *A True Reporte*, sig. D1v.
88 Ibid., sig. C8r.
89 Best, *A True Discourse*, sig. f2v.
90 Ibid., sigs. g2v–g3v.
91 Ibid., sigs. g2v–h2r.
92 Appleby, "War, Politics, and Colonization," 56.
93 Eldred, "The Just Will Pay for the Sinners," 12–16.
94 G. D. Ramsay, "Clothworkers, Merchants Adventurers and Richard Hakluyt," *English Historical Review* 92, no. 364 (July, 1977): 504–510; Linton, *Romance of the New World*, 62.
95 Linton, *Romance of the New World*, 64.
96 Ramsay, "Clothworkers, Merchants Adventurers," 504.
97 Peckham, *A True Reporte*, sig. E2v.
98 Ibid., sig. E2r.
99 Ibid., sigs. E1v–F1v.
100 Ibid., sigs. E1v–E2v.
101 Lloyd, *Elizabethan Adventurer*, xi.
102 Carleill, *A Breef and Sommarie Discourse*, sig. A3r.
103 Brereton, *A Briefe and True Relation*, 18.
104 Ibid., 25.
105 Harriot himself referred to some of the negative opinions about Virginia circulating in England at the time, arguing that the publication of his book would dispel them. Harriot, *A Briefe and True Report*, 5–6.
106 Quinn, *England and the Discovery of America*, 298–300 and 437–440.
107 As Michiel van Groesen has argued, de Bry's project began in England in the late 1580s when he met Richard Hakluyt who convinced him to publish Harriot's book; Michiel van Groesen, *The Representations of the Overseas World in the De Bry Collection of Voyages, 1590–1634* (Leiden and Boston: Brill, 2008), 112.

108 Sloan, "John White's Watercolours," 107–132.
109 Stephanie Pratt, "Truth and Artifice in the Visualization of Native Peoples: From the Time of John White to the Beginning of the 18th Century," in *European Visions: American Voices*, ed. Kim Sloan (London: British Museum Press, 2009), 35.
110 Pratt, "Truth and Artifice," 34–35; Joan-Pau Rubiés, "Texts, Images, and the Perception of 'Savages' in Early Modern Europe: What We Can Learn from White and Harriot," in *European Visions: American Voices*, ed. Kim Sloan (London: British Museum Press, 2009), 129; Gaudio, "Truth in Clothing," 24–25. Joyce Chaplin has argued that aside from incorporating artistic conventions of the period, White's watercolours were, in their content, highly propagandistic, being intended to publicise the English outpost at Roanoke; Joyce Chaplin, "Roanoke 'Counterfeited According to the Truth'," in *A New World: England's First View of America*, ed. Kim Sloan (Chapel Hill: University of North Carolina Press, 2007), 51–61.
111 Rubiés, "Texts, Images," 127–129. For a more detailed examination of how the tools and techniques of copperplate engraving shaped European responses to Indigenous peoples see Michael Gaudio, *Engraving the Savage: The New World and Techniques of Civilization* (Minneapolis: University of Minnesota Press, 2008).
112 Pratt, "Truth and Artifice," 35–36.
113 van Groesen, *Representations of the Overseas World*, 43, 112, and 173.
114 The 1588 edition dedicates twenty five pages to commodities and just eleven to the manners and nature of the Indigenous inhabitants; Thomas Harriot, *A Briefe and True Report of the New Found Land of Virginia* (London, 1588). For commodities see sigs. B1r–E1v and for people sigs. E1v–F2v.
115 van Groesen, *Representations of the Overseas World*, 128–146.
116 Ibid., 147.
117 My analysis of the de Bry engravings therefore follows an approach similar to that of Pratt and Chaplin.
118 Kupperman, "Presentment of Civility," 210.
119 Pratt, "Truth and Artifice," 35.
120 Harriot, *Briefe and True Report*, pl. VI.
121 James Rosier, *A True Relation of the Most Prosperous Voyage Made this Present Yeere 1605* (London, 1605), sig. C2r.
122 Sloan, "John White's Watercolours," 130.
123 Harriot, *Briefe and True Report*, pl. VI.
124 This point has also been explored in great detail by Karen Kupperman; "Presentment of Civility," 196–218.
125 Harriot, *Briefe and True Report*, title page to images of the ancient Britons from the appendix to the illustrations of the Indians.
126 Ibid., pl. I.
127 Ibid., 24–33.
128 Although clothing did not seem to help distinguish between lords and commoners, the clothing of the religious men of Virginia did seem to be more

distinctive. A religious man of Secotan, for example, is depicted as wearing a cloak of hare skin rather than the deer skin aprons shown in a majority of the other images; "On the Religeous Men in the Towne of Secota," by de Bry, pl. V in Harriot, *Briefe and True Report*. As Karen Kupperman has suggested, the Virginians did appear to differentiate social status through appearance, but via body art, tattoos, and hairstyles rather than clothing; Kupperman, "The Presentment of Civility," 206–218.

129 Hooper, "Tudor Sumptuary Laws," 433–449.
130 Howard, "Crossdressing," 421; quotation from Vincent, *Dressing the Elite*, 124.
131 Howard, "Crossdressing," 422.
132 Patrick Collinson, *The Elizabethan Puritan Movement* (London: Cape, 1967), 26–27.
133 The pamphlet was an immediate success, going through four editions in twelve years; Roze Hentschell, "Moralizing Apparel in Early Modern London: Popular Literature, Sermons, and Sartorial Display," *Journal of Medieval and Early Modern Studies* 39, no. 3 (Fall, 2009): 575. Quotation taken from Philip Stubbes, *The Anatomie of Abuses* (London, 1583), sig. B5v.
134 Stubbes, *Anatomie*, sigs. C4r–C4v.
135 Ibid., sigs. C5v–C6r.
136 Ibid., sig. B8r.
137 Ibid., sigs. B8v–C1r.
138 Rubiés, "Texts, Images," 127–128.
139 Brereton, *A Briefe and True Relation*, 11.
140 Barlowe, "The First Voyage," 3:249.
141 Rubiés, "Texts, Images," 128.

4

Eating America:
Bodily discourse in the early English colonial imagination

> *The holsomnesse and temperature of this Climat, doth not onely argue this people to be answerable to this description, but also of a perfect constitution of body, active, strong, healthfull, and very wittie, as the sundry toies of theirs cunningly wrought, may easily witnes. For the agréeing of this Climat with us (I speake of my selfe, & so I may justly do for the rest of our company) that we found our health & strength all the while we remained there, so to renew and increase.*[1]
>
> – John Brereton

This quotation, taken from John Brereton's exceedingly favourable 1602 account of northern Virginia, illustrates the centrality of European understandings of the body, and their relationship to environment, in early English exploration and colonisation. Brereton commented on the natural constitution of the Indigenous population but also suggested what effect the new American environment would have on English bodies. Rather than impacting negatively on the English explorers' constitutions, the wholesome and temperate climate of Virginia in fact made English bodies stronger and healthier. Two different forces are at play in descriptions such as this; on the one hand, Brereton's words reflect the dominance of humoralism, and more specifically geohumoralism, in English understandings of New World peoples, and on the other they highlight the ways in which both Indigenous and English bodies were used for rhetorical purposes to explain the perceived successes, and indeed failures, of English colonial projects.[2] This chapter examines these European bodily constructions and assesses how New World environments, climates, and, in particular, food were believed to impact them. In doing so, this chapter will demonstrate that European understandings of the body, and especially the ways in which the body was believed to interact with different environments and their produce, were central to early English approaches to New World exploration and settlement.

Although the role of food and diet in the English colonial experience of the seventeenth century has been well documented by historians, the ways in which food, diet, and understandings of the body relate to English explorations and attempts at settlement in the sixteenth century has been less clearly defined.[3] The sixteenth century saw the development of a clear, if not always consistent, bodily discourse that reflected colonial disappointment and failure in the 1560s and 1570s, and then conversely, colonial confidence and optimism from the 1580s onwards. In the 1580s English explorers and colonists grew more optimistic, believing that they had finally found a region and Indigenous population of the Americas that could be moulded and shaped in a way that would ensure English colonial success. Understandings of the body, when placed in a colonial context, mirrored the changing attitudes of English men and women towards the American environment, which in turn reflected alternating English colonial and explorative fortunes throughout the sixteenth and early seventeenth centuries.

By 1602, when Brereton's narrative was published, a bodily discourse that lauded the American environment as healthy and wholesome for both Indigenous and English bodies was well established. American food was abundant and appropriate for the English complexion, and the Indigenous peoples were healthy and had the potential for civility. This positive assessment of Indigenous bodies, and the effects of the local environment on English bodies, had not always been the case, however. In the early decades of exploration in the New World, concerns surrounding English bodies and their ability to cope in a vastly new environment superseded any considerations of what Indigenous bodies could tell English explorers about the new lands. In the 1560s, when English activity in the Americas was largely confined to piracy and privateering in the Caribbean, the ability of English sailors to secure and preserve provisions, and thus maintain bodily health, was a central concern. In these early years of English encounters with the Americas, depleted victuals, the eating of inappropriate food, and corporeal corruption became emblematic of troublesome, arduous, and unsuccessful voyages.

The three voyages of Martin Frobisher to the Far North of the American continent, undertaken in the late 1570s, represented the first systematic English attempt at exploration, exploitation, and settlement in the New World. With this push for greater English involvement in New World projects came fresh concerns relating to the body and how it might react to unfamiliar climates and diets. While the privateers of the 1560s had largely ignored the Indigenous populations, for Frobisher and his men the bodies of the supposedly deformed Inuit, and their apparently atrocious diets and poor gastronomical techniques, exemplified the detrimental effects that environment and food could have on Indigenous and English bodies alike. The inability to source appropriate food would leave the bodies of the

English severely weakened, if not irrevocably altered, making permanent English settlement an impossibility.

This negativity and anxiety surrounding the consumption of inappropriate food and its effect on the body, in the context of European encounters with the New World, has been explored in great detail by a number of scholars.[4] Focusing specifically on Spanish attitudes towards New World foods, Rebecca Earle has suggested that for Spanish *conquistadores*, diet was one of the principal factors that helped create the 'bodily differences' that underpinned the categories of 'Spaniard' and 'Indian'.[5] The differing diets of Spaniard and 'Indian' not only served to explain bodily difference, but also encouraged the belief that in order for the *conquistadores* and colonists to maintain their natural temperaments while in the Americas, the restoration of a healthy and civilised Spanish diet was critical.[6] In the early modern period it was believed that a person's natural humoral complexion was affected by external forces such as diet. Changing your diet could lead to an imbalance of humours, which in turn could cause illness. More worryingly from the Spanish perspective, if the explorers could not access Spanish food there was a real fear that sooner or later they would permanently alter their humoral complexion and 'turn into Indians'.[7]

The fear of 'indianisation' was also felt keenly by the English, particularly in relation to the consumption of certain American goods such as tobacco. The incorporation of tobacco into early modern European markets was by no means a simple process, as the herb arrived in Europe with considerable 'cultural baggage' from America.[8] Many Indigenous groups regarded the herb as a gift from powerful deities who would respond when humans smoked or burned it. This ritualistic use of tobacco was observed by many European explorers in the sixteenth century, thus connecting the plant with the worship of false gods and devils in disguise in European imaginations.[9] Although some physicians and botanists praised what they deemed to be the various curative powers of tobacco, others, including James I, felt that by imitating the Indigenous cultural practice of smoking, Englishmen and women risked 'Indianising' their bodies, implicating themselves in the devilish rituals associated with the Indigenous use of tobacco.[10]

This was not an anxiety felt only by the English at home in response to the influx of new and potentially dangerous American products. For those men and women making the voyage to the colonies of the New World in the seventeenth century, the fear of American foods was often far greater. They too worried about 'going native', fearing that consuming Indigenous products such as maize would strip away their very Englishness.[11] In fact, Trudy Eden goes as far as to suggest that the Starving Time of 1609 to 1610, in which the majority of English colonists at Jamestown died from starvation, was in part the result of this fear.[12] Although Michael A. LaCombe has disagreed with this argument, suggesting instead that in early America 'hunger regularly trumped fears of hybridity', he agrees with Eden that early English colonists feared the effects of foreign environments and diets on their bodies.[13] English colonists circumvented this fear in much the same way as Earle suggests the Spanish did; through the introduction of English staples to the American colonies.[14]

In the late sixteenth century, however, the English response to Indigenous bodies, environments, and diets was one of confidence and optimism. The negative attitude towards Indigenous products in the seventeenth century was by no means a constant from the time of the first encounter between the English and Indigenous peoples of the Americas. English attitudes towards Indigenous bodies and diets were in no way static in the sixteenth century. Just as early modern bodies themselves were flexible and porous, responding to external forces and environmental changes, so too was English bodily discourse, mirroring the changes, adaptations, and frustrations of English explorers and colonists in the Americas.[15] From the 1580s onwards, the English became more confident in their colonial exploits and, crucially, more confident in the regions of America that they explored.

While the lack of appropriate Indigenous food sources had made English settlement in the Far North unviable, the abundance and sophistication of the Algonquian diet convinced English explorers that their attempts at colonisation in this region would be far more successful. If scarcity, perversity, and unwholesomeness were the defining features of the Meta Incognita environment that Frobisher and his men had explored in the 1570s, Virginian foodstuffs were conversely characterised by plenty, familiarity, and delectability. It was not just the ample provisions of the Virginian environment that were met with enthusiasm. The Indigenous people themselves, and the way they looked and behaved, also instilled an optimistic belief among the English that they could be brought easily to civility and thus subservience to the English Crown. Unlike the Inuit of Meta Incognita, the Virginia Algonquians had food preparation techniques that mirrored those used in England, suggesting to colonists that they had a seed of civility that could be nurtured. Alongside this, and as expressed by Brereton in the quotation at the beginning of this chapter, the Algonquians, thanks to their abundant diet and temperate climate, were robust and healthy. The strong, active bodies of the Indigenous population suggested that English bodies would not be weakened through exposure to Indigenous foods and unfamiliar climates. The bodies of the Algonquians were thus used by English explorers and writers to allay the concerns of those who feared the effects of unfamiliar environments on their bodies, and to validate their colonial enterprises by highlighting the ways in which the Indigenous population could be incorporated into them.

Indigenous bodies, whether perceived as pure, debauched, or uncivil, narrated the English colonial experience in the sixteenth and early seventeenth centuries. An analysis of the specificities of English perceptions of balanced, unbalanced, and corrupted bodies, and their development throughout the later sixteenth century, makes it clear that corporeality was vital to the formation and dissemination of English ideas about the Americas and the potential for English colonies in the region to be successful. Eating and the effect of food on the body became, when placed in an American context, indicative of successful and profitable ventures or unsuccessful and troublesome ones. In the early decades of English exploration in the Americas, in which hostile relations with the Spanish, inhospitable climates, and inappropriate food hampered efforts, Indigenous bodies reflected the disappointment of explorers and colonisers and were used to justify the abandonment of certain projects. By the end of the century, however, the perception of Indigenous bodies as healthy, productive, and robust, and the belief that English bodies would fare equally well in the temperate climes of North America was well established, reflecting the optimism of a variety of early English explorers and proto-colonialists and their attempts to instil this sense of optimism in their readers and investors back home. Perceptions of the body were integral to the encounter between England and America, allowing for the defence of failed attempts at settlement, the celebration of English colonial projects as providential and ordained by God, and for the establishment of a colonial ideology that had notions about food, the environment, and the body at its centre.

Humoralism and the early modern body

In the sixteenth century, the body was governed by a set of principles that presented it as flexible, porous, and deeply connected to external forces. In particular, it was humoral theory that helped early modern Europeans make best sense of their bodies and the diseases that affected them. Developed by classical writers, most notably Hippocrates and Galen, humoral theory posited that the human body was ruled by four bodily fluids, known as humours. The balance of these humours – blood, phlegm, black bile, and yellow bile – were thought to directly influence a person's health and temperament. When the humours remained balanced and in equilibrium, the body remained temperate and healthy. However, when a person's humours became unbalanced through the excess or deficiency of one or more humours, the body became diseased and unhealthy.[16]

The body's humoral balance was believed to be affected by exposure to what was known as the six non-natural things, listed by the sixteenth-century physician Thomas Elyot as 'ayre', 'meate and drynke', 'slepe and watche', 'mevyng and rest', 'emptynesse and repletion', and 'affections of the mynd'.[17] Each of these external forces could affect the level of any one humour in the body. The moderate use of the six non-naturals was therefore seen as the most reliable method for preserving bodily health.[18] Healthcare in sixteenth-century Europe was thus based around long-term prevention rather than short-term curative treatment.[19] Maintaining a healthy body may have been more difficult than it seems, however, as each individual was believed to have their own 'naturalle complexion' that determined the levels of each humour in their bodies.[20] Sanguine men were believed to have a hot and moist complexion, their bodies governed by the humour of blood. Those of a phlegmatic disposition were believed to have a cold and moist complexion that was caused by an abundance of phlegm. Choleric people were hot and dry, their bodies ruled by yellow bile, while melancholic bodies were cold and dry, being more active in black bile.[21] Because each individual had their own specific humoral make-up, the way in which they engaged with the six non-naturals and maintained a healthy body was also specific and highly individualised. Given this deeply personal and precarious understanding of how to maintain bodily health, it is unsurprising that the body, when placed in the context of international travel, took on an even greater significance.

In the early modern period, individuals were encouraged to establish a good regimen, namely the rules to be followed in order to maintain a healthy body, particularly in relation to the six non-naturals.[22] These health regimens, as well as being based on classical medical discourse, were underpinned by Christian principles of sobriety and moderation.[23] For each specific humoral complexion – sanguine, phlegmatic, choleric, or melancholic – the rules were different. In order to help early modern Europeans traverse the difficult path towards bodily, and indeed spiritual health, regimens became extremely popular. The fact that such texts were increasingly published in the vernacular in cheap octavo or quarto format suggests that a good proportion of the literate population took an active interest in nutrition and medical theory.[24] In these handbooks, authors set out exactly how to avoid humoral imbalance through a detailed discussion of the six non-naturals and their effects on bodies of different complexions.

The advice for maintaining a good diet was complex and tailored to particular humoral complexions, relative states of health, and environmental considerations. One general rule surrounding food for people of all complexions, however, related to quantity. Moderation in food and drink was seen to be key to maintaining good health and humoral balance.[25] As we shall see, in Virginia the Algonquians' moderation in eating was identified as a positive attribute, illustrating their relative self-restraint compared to elite members of English society.²⁶ The fact that their bodies remained healthy and active despite their moderation served to reinforce the arguments of both physicians and clergymen that over-eating and gluttony were vices that corrupted the body.

Alongside the quantity of food eaten, the type of food eaten was also of critical importance. In general, people were advised to eat foods that matched the qualities of their complexions.²⁷ As the physician Thomas Elyot suggested in his discussion on the quality of different foods, 'qualitie is in the complexion'. Each complexion, 'temperate & untemperate is conserved in his state, by that which is lyke therto in fourme and degree'.²⁸ Following this logic, Elyot advised that 'to them whose naturall complexion is moyste, ought to be gyven meates that be moste [moist] in vertue or power' while those whose complexion is dry 'ought to be gyven meates drye in vertue or power'.²⁹ By eating foods that possessed similar 'complexions', a person could maintain the balance of their humours. However, in cases 'whiche excedeth moche in dystemperaunce', the opposite advice was given.³⁰ In order to restore balance to a 'distemperate' body, it was advised that a person follow the principle of *contraria contrariis curantur:* conditions are cured by their opposite.³¹ The sixteenth-century English physician William Bullein, for example, advised that when a person was sick they 'must have meate, contrarie to their complexion'; those that are cold 'must have hote meate' while those 'that be drie, must have moyst thinges'.³² The logic here was that different foods, and their inherent qualities, could counter-balance excessive humours. For example, if a person was suffering from an excess of phlegm which was both moist and cold, a physician would prescribe a food with the opposite composition, such as hot, dry pepper. The heat in the pepper was thought to help dry and heat the body internally and thus banish any excess phlegm. In the sixteenth century, then, it was not only imperative that a person knew their own humoral complexion but that they also knew the complexions of various foods.

This complex assessment of the elemental qualities of food would prove problematic in the context of English travel to America. With unfamiliar foods came the potential for unfamiliar side effects. The question of how English bodies would react to new, previously unknown foods in America became a central feature of both English travel writing and colonial rhetoric in the sixteenth century. While the region of the Far North lacked many of the key components needed to maintain a good diet and thus a healthy body, the food of Virginia, although different to that found in England, could provide many of the constituent parts of the traditional English diet such as bread, meat, and ample beer. Maintaining a temperate body through diet thus went hand in hand with creating successful, permanent English settlements in the New World.

Humoralism as a general theory was largely accepted by most Europeans in the sixteenth century, but it also incorporated regional specificities. Despite the general principles of the theory being the same throughout Europe, writers of the sixteenth century also believed that different regions of the world had different natural complexions. The English, as northern Europeans, were often characterised by their continental neighbours as being temperamentally inferior. As the French philosopher Jean Bodin argued in the late sixteenth century, the people of the North were 'sanguin and warlike', and did nothing but 'laugh and leape in their fooleries'.[33] The naturally choleric French, on the other hand, were described by Bodin as 'active and prompt', showing 'diligence and quicknesse in all their actions'.[34] Pierre Charron, the French theologian and philosopher, was equally disparaging about the Northern temperament. Unlike Bodin, however, Charron suggested that Northerners were 'of a phlegmatick and sanguine temperature'.[35] Whether sanguine or phlegmatic, the Northern temperament was not to be envied as it made men 'cruell and inhumane', 'stupid', 'inconstant', 'little religious', and 'want of judgement, whereby like beasts, they know not how to conteine and governe themselues'. In contrast, the inhabitants of the middle, temperate region of the world, which unsurprisingly included France, were considered to enjoy more temperate, balanced complexions. These 'midlers' were, according to Charron, 'sanguin and cholericke' which made them 'ingenious', 'wise', and 'temperate in all those things as neuters'.[36] These positive attributes, and the temperateness they generated, led Charron to conclude that those who inhabited the middle, temperate zone of the earth were, in fact, 'perfect men'.[37] The English in their relatively cold, wet, northern climate were ascribed distemperate complexions of either extreme sanguine or phlegmatic composition by continental writers such as Bodin and Charron, and were thus vulnerable to the various diseases and illnesses that were thought to spring from unbalanced humours.

The goal of many early modern Europeans was to maintain a temperate and healthy body. For the English, with their naturally distemperate northern bodies, this goal seemed particularly difficult to achieve. Whether naturally temperate or distemperate, eating, and indeed regulating the body more generally, was a hazardous affair. The equilibrium of their bodies and humours could be disrupted by unfamiliar air, unfamiliar foods, and changes in the environment. It was within this framework of bodily discourse that travel came to be seen as either damaging or curative. For those whose bodies enjoyed relative temperance, like early modern Mediterraneans, travelling to a new and unfamiliar environment could be treacherous, while for those who had unenviable intemperate complexions, like the early modern English, travel could be seen as a treatment that would actually aid their pursuit of bodily temperance. While unfamiliar and exotic foods could damage European bodies by unbalancing the humours, the new environments of America could also provide an array of health benefits due to the temperate climate and the abundance of natural and miraculous remedies. Food and other environmental produce, and their effects on the body, were thus central to early modern understandings of health and character. Unsurprisingly, then, food and eating played a significant role in early modern colonial discourse. For the English in particular, America's food, diet, and gastronomy, along with its ability to produce temperate, healthy bodies, became a barometer by which to measure colonial success and failure.

Depleted victuals and troublesome voyages

In the mid-sixteenth century, English involvement in the New World was largely confined to raids on Spanish ships and port towns in the Caribbean. As Anglo-Spanish hostility at home intensified, so too did English piracy and privateering. Unsurprisingly, the Spanish-American towns and ports that the English attempted to raid were often inhospitable, with Spanish governors refusing to openly trade with the marauding visitors. Within this context of hostility and conflict, the maintenance of appropriate and plentiful provisions became central to successful privateering ventures. Nowhere is this clearer than in the writings of those involved in John Hawkins's raids on the Caribbean in the 1560s. These accounts highlight the centrality of food in the early English encounter with America, reflect the disastrous effects that eating a poor diet could have on the body, and illustrate the myriad difficulties faced by European explorers in the sixteenth century.

In 1567 John Hawkins and his men set sail for a third privateering voyage to the New World. Hawkins's previous two expeditions had caused much animosity between the English and the Spanish. As outlined in Chapter 2, the first voyage of 1562 resulted in a ban on English ships trading in the West Indies, while after the second in 1564 Hawkins was forced to sign a bond promising not to trade with the Spanish in the Caribbean. By 1567 the attitude of the Spanish towards Hawkins and his crew was so inimical that a fiction was created to explain the impending English voyage; the ships were bound for the coast of Africa to extract reparations for previous injury and to investigate vague claims of an extensive gold mine that was surrounded by rich and fertile lands. With this illusion apparently fooling the Spanish ambassador to England, Diego Guzmán de Silva, Hawkins and his fleet set sail from Plymouth in October 1567.[38]

In Hawkins's own account of the expedition, published after his return home in 1569, it is clear that the voyage was anything but straightforward.

Despite the king of Spain commanding the governors of the Indies 'by no meanes to suffer anye trade' with the English, Hawkins and his men did manage some 'reasonable trade and courteous intertainemente' with the Spanish at Margarita.[39] This, however, was where their luck ran out. After being refused trade and water at Rio de la Hacha, the English attacked the town, taking it by force so that trade could take place.[40] Hawkins decided against landing at Cartagena, a heavily fortified port on the Caribbean coast, choosing instead to return home.[41] Appalling weather, however, battered Hawkins's ship, forcing him to put in at the port of San Juan de Ulúa to make vital repairs and to obtain victuals.[42] After securing entry into the port, Hawkins became suspicious of Spanish intentions, suspecting a 'great number of men to be hid in a great ship of 900 tonnes' that was moored next to the English ship, *The Minion*.[43] Hawkins's suspicions proved accurate as the English were 'set uppon' from all sides by 300 Spaniards.[44] After hours of fighting, Hawkins and his surviving crew managed to escape in *The Minion*, yet 'having a great number of men and lytell victuals' their 'hope of life waxed lesse & lesse'.[45]

After two weeks at sea, 'honger inforced' the crew to seek land. The situation became so desperate that 'hides weare thoughte verire good meate, ratts, cattes, mise and dogges none escaped that might bee gotten'. Foods that would have normally been deemed inappropriate for the European diet increasingly became a 'great pris' and thought 'verie proffitable'.[46] After more fruitless searches for victuals and a 'haven of relife', some of Hawkins's men 'being forced with honger desired to bee sett a land'.[47] Ninety six members of the crew were deserted somewhere in the Gulf of Mexico and left to fend for themselves.[48] Hawkins and the rest of the crew continued their tortuous journey home. During the lengthy Atlantic crossing, many more of the crew perished being 'oppressed with Famine'.[49] Eventually the fleet arrived in Vigo, Spain but this was not the end of their misery. After so long without appropriate and nourishing food, still more men succumbed to disease due to the 'excesse of freshe meate' that they consumed at Vigo, a great number of them dying from their illnesses.[50]

The experiences of Hawkins and his men illustrate just how vulnerable bodies were to changes in diet. It was not only starvation that decimated the crew, but also over-zealous eating after a prolonged period without food. The equilibrium of the crew's bodies had been disturbed by the interruption of normal eating patterns. This disruption had forced the fleet to put in at San Juan de Ulúa to obtain victuals, which had led to the English retreat and the onset of starvation. Food, therefore, or more accurately the lack of it, had proven to be the downfall of the expedition. Without enough provisions, and without the knowledge or means to secure food from the American environment or the Spanish colonies, voyages such as Hawkins's could end in complete disaster. The expedition had shown that maintaining victuals could be extremely difficult, especially when dealing with the hostile Spanish. It had also illustrated the centrality of food in English voyages to the New World, demonstrating how hunger and poor diet could decimate a crew and devastate an expedition. It had highlighted how a lack of basic sustenance could foil the plans of even the most experienced sailor such as Hawkins. And yet, the publication of Hawkins's narrative was not the end of the story. The fate of those sailors who had been left in Mexico would exemplify how a lack of food could transform the fortunes of explorers and force them to confront the realities of the American environment.

In 1591, some twenty-three years after those ninety-six men were left in the Gulf of Mexico, an account of their experience was published in London. Composed by Job Hortop, powder-maker and gunner for *The Jesus* on Hawkins's third voyage, the narrative documents the 'sundrie calalmities' endured by Hortop and the other men in the intervening years between when they were set ashore and when they managed to return to England.[51] Like Hawkins, Hortop referenced the desperate food situation that the crew faced after their retreat from San Juan de Ulúa. He too explained how 'victuals were so scarse' that he and the other surviving members of the crew were 'driven to eat hides, cats, rats, parrats, munkies, and dogges'. After mutiny broke out among the crew 'for want of victuals', Hortop and a number of other men decided to take their chances in the unfamiliar lands of Mexico, preferring to be 'on the shoare to shift for themselves amongst the enemies, than to sterve on shippe-boord'.[52] Not only had depleted victuals led to the abandonment of the expedition, it had also caused mutiny and the splintering of the crew, an action that would have considerable consequences for those men who chose to remain in the Americas.

Hortop and the other men began making their way towards the Pánuco River, walking day and night for seven days, 'feeding on nothing but roots, and Guiavos [guavas], a fruite like figges'.[53] On being captured by two Spanish horsemen on the banks of the Pánuco, the English explorers were transported to the town where they were able to gain sustenance from other native foods. As well as eating guavas, Hortop also tried a number of other unfamiliar foods, from manatees that apparently tasted 'not much unlike to bacon', to avocados which were described by Hortop as 'an excellent good fruite'.[54] Engaging with the American environment and experimenting with Indigenous foods was crucial for Hortop's survival. Not only was he willing to try these unfamiliar foods, he found them to be tasty and comparable to foods back home. While many of his fellow crew members had succumbed to starvation on the voyage home, Hortop and the other men who had remained in the Americas survived through consuming native produce.

English readers had already been reminded of the plight faced by these men in 1589 when Richard Hakluyt published, in his *Principal Navigations*, another account written by a member of Hawkins's crew who had stayed behind in America. Like Hortop, Miles Philips had spent many years trying to get back to England, eventually returning to his native country in 1582.[55] In Philips's account, as in Hortop's, the search for food was a prominent theme. His account of the crew's quest to find food is far more detailed than Hortop's, describing the varied reactions of English bodies to American foods, and noting the fatal effects of restored diet and nutritional rehabilitation on severely malnourished and starved bodies. Immediately after coming ashore, Philips and the other men managed to find fresh water but some 'drunke so much' that they 'almost cast themselves away', while others ended up 'cruelly swollen' from ingesting too much. Alongside this excessive consumption of water, the English explorers also ate a fruit that they found on the land called a *Capule* [a type of black cherry]. Rather than providing nourishment to the starved adventurers, the fruit made them 'very ill', leaving them 'both feeble, faint and weake'.[56] Their first foray into native foods had thus not been a success, the cherries damaging their already weakened bodies. Philips also made reference to eating guavas as Hortop had done, but unlike Hortop, Philips explained the effect that the unfamiliar fruit had on the Englishmen's bodies. The fruit made the bodies of the men 'so sore', creating a pain that could not be eased for the space of ten or twelve days.[57]

Not all American food made the English explorers sick, however. On being captured by the Spanish on the Pánuco River, the men were given loaves of bread 'made of that countrey wheat, which the Spaniards call *Maiz*'. According to Philips, the bread was 'very sweet and pleasant' for he and the other men had 'not eaten any in a long time before', but as he went on to ask, 'what is it that hunger doth not make to have a savory and a delicate taste?' Subsequent experiences of eating maize were not so pleasant. Having been imprisoned in a small house 'much like a hogstie', the Englishmen were given sodden maize to eat, a food which the Spanish 'feede their hogs'. Although not deadly, this unprocessed version of maize was only suitable for animal consumption.[58] After surviving this 'miserable state' the men were released to be transported to Mexico City.[59] On the way they stopped at the town of Santa Maria where a house of 'white friers' [Carmelites] fed them with 'hote meat, as mutton and broth'. Unfortunately, the men could not control themselves, feeding 'very greedily of the meat', causing them 'to fall sicke of hote burning agues'.[60] As Thomas Elyot had suggested in his popular health regimen of 1539, 'contynuall gourmandyse' was the 'greatest ennemy to helth'.[61] For those who had been starved, like Philips and the other Englishmen, excessive eating would therefore have been even more dangerous. Starvation was thus not the only problem that the remainder of Hawkins's crew faced. They also had to deal with the dangers of eating after a period of deprivation as this could be equally damaging to their carefully balanced and vulnerable English bodies.

Having managed to avert starvation, Hortop and Philips were nonetheless unable to return to England for a number of years. They were imprisoned then forced to work in the Spanish monasteries and galleys, only making it home by convincing captains of English ships to allow them aboard.[62] The 'sundry great troubles and miseries' endured by these men stemmed from the English inability to preserve and obtain provisions.[63] The experiences of Hawkins, Hortop, and Philips had highlighted how food could be the key to explorative and privateering success or failure. Hunger had forced Hortop and Philips to engage with native foods and Indigenous environments for survival. It had led to their imprisonment, forced labour, and extended displacement abroad. By 1600, when both Hortop's and Philips's narratives appeared together in Hakluyt's second edition of the *Principal Navigations*, English explorers had learned how critical provisions were to the success of overseas voyages. The reappearance of both Hortop and Philips in England served as an excellent reminder for what could go wrong if food became scarce during international travel, reaffirming the belief that diet, and the English ability to source appropriate food, was critical in the colonial decision-making process. Another set of expeditions in the 1570s, before the tales of Hortop's and Philips's calamitous experiences were published, once again illustrated the detrimental effect that a lack of provisions and a hostile environment could have on English overseas projects.

Indigenous diets, bodies, and early English colonial failure

By the 1570s English readers had a basic understanding of how food and diet impacted European voyages of discovery. John Hawkins's account of his third voyage of 1567 had highlighted how expeditions could end in disaster if provisions became depleted and could not be replenished. Although Hawkins barely mentioned the Indigenous environment of the lands to which he and his men travelled, nor the dining practices of the region's inhabitants, English readers had been exposed to ideas about American food from translations of key histories documenting the Spanish and Portuguese explorations and conquests in the Americas. In both Richard Eden's translated versions of Peter Martyr's *Decades* (1555) and Sebastian Münster's *Cosmographia* (1553), American food played a crucial role in disseminating the idea of a new world different to anything Europeans had experienced before. The exoticisation of Indigenous food by Martyr and Münster was very much in keeping with the overall messages of their texts; America was a fundamentally new world in which strange and marvellous peoples and products could be found. Both Martyr and Münster commented on the radical strangeness of American food and Indigenous diets. According to Münster, the American diet was filled with innumerable fruits 'utterlye unlyke' any found in Europe.[64] Elaborating on this claim, and giving English readers a greater insight into the American diet, Martyr explained that in the Americas all the 'accustomed foode' of the Spanish such as 'wyne, oyle, flesshe, butter, chiese, and milke' were 'lackynge'.[65] Instead, the inhabitants of the New World subsisted on a diet filled with strange and unknown fruits and roots, and exotic, and somewhat peculiar meats. The people of the Caribbean ate '*Guannaba* [guanábana or soursop]', a fruit 'unknowen' to the Spanish but 'sumwhat lyke vnto a quynse'.[66] Instead of making bread from wheat, which was the traditional European method, Indigenous peoples made their bread from roots such as '*Maizium, Iucca, and Ages*'.[67] Even the meat of the Indigenous diet was unfamiliar, being largely centred around fish and in some cases 'serpentes they caule *Iuannas* [iguanas]' which, according to Martyr, were 'lyke vnto Crocodiles'.[68] In an endeavour to categorise these new fruits, roots, and sources of meat, Martyr attempted to assimilate them into Old World frameworks of understanding; although the guanábana was a fruit unknown to the Spanish, and although Europeans did not eat serpents such as iguanas, they became somewhat comprehensible to readers in Europe through their comparison to quinces and crocodiles. And yet, despite a narrative that highlighted the pronounced differences between Indigenous and European food, Martyr did not seem to find these divergences particularly alarming.

The food was undoubtedly different, but not necessarily unappetising or dangerous.[69] In fact, Martyr claimed that the king of Spain himself was partial to some of the newly discovered American foodstuffs, declaring that the king had eaten of a 'frute browght from those landes, beinge full of scales with keyes much lyke a pine apple in forme and coloure, but in tendernes equal to melopepones, and in taste excedyng al garden frutes'.[70] It was not only American fruits that proved delectable to Spanish taste buds. Even the strange crocodile-like iguanas were confirmed to be particularly agreeable to the European explorers. Despite none of the men at first wishing to 'adventure to taste of them by reason of theyr horrible deformitie', a lieutenant, having been 'entysed by the pleasantnes of the [Indigenous] kynges syster, determined to taste of the serpentes', followed quickly by the rest of his men who were 'behynde hym in greedines'.[71] According to the men who had tried the serpent, the flesh was of a delicious 'sweetenes', being a 'more pleasaunte taste' than either pheasant or partridge.[72]

This openness to trying Indigenous food, however, did not last for long. Throughout the early modern period disrupting customary eating habits was understood to be medically dangerous. The sudden change in dietary traditions could provoke the humours and result in ill health, a worry that Europeans took with them during their explorations of the Americas.[73] The Spanish began to pine for their Old World foods, complaining that they fell ill when they did not eat familiar foods and could only be healed through the restoration of their normal diets.[74] This more negative opinion of Indigenous food is also found in Martyr's writings. As he worked his way through the first decades of discovery, the attitude towards Indigenous food became more negative. The *conquistadores*, so Martyr argued, were unable 'to abyde suche calamities as to lyue onely contented with the breade of those regions, and wylde herbes without salte' as their 'stomakes had byn vsed to good meates'.[75] Columbus, in an attempt to avoid mutiny, even returned to Spain 'for vitailes, as wheat, wyne, oyle, and such other which the Spanyardes are accustomed to eate, bycause they coulde not yet well agree with such meates as they fownde in the Ilandes'.[76] By the mid-sixteenth century, then, an ambiguous template for attitudes towards Indigenous food had been established in the English imagination. On the one hand, some of the newly discovered foodstuffs were highly delectable, and yet on the other they were perceived to do harm to the European constitution, unbalancing temperate complexions and leading to inevitable bodily disease.

This knowledge about Indigenous foods, and the uncertain attitude it provoked, combined with the conviction that plentiful provisions were needed for voyages to be successful, impacted significantly on the Martin Frobisher voyages of the 1570s. From the published narratives of the second voyage of 1577 in particular, it would seem that English attitudes towards Indigenous foods and eating habits were confused and even contradictory. George Best's account of the voyage which was published in 1578 draws an especially conflicted picture of the American diet, focusing on both the fantasy and reality of New World food. This divergence between fantasy and reality is clearly seen in the front matter to Best's text. On the book's contents page, Best laid out the topics to be discussed. The eighth section of the text dealt with how 'pleasaunt and profitable' new discoveries were, both for experiencing 'different manners and fashions of diverse nations' and for discovering 'straunge trees, fruite, foules, and beastes, the infinite treasure of Pearle, Gold and Silver'. From this list it would seem to the reader that Best was presenting the lands he had explored as abundant in both precious metals and exotic foods. Yet at the same time, Best's summary of his text also introduced a far more negative perception of the American environment and sources of food. In the listing of a section on the perils of attempting new discoveries, Best highlighted a number of dangers that would-be explorers should watch out for. They should be wary of 'theeves and robbers', the 'dangerousness of Seas', and the 'feare of hidden rockes'. They should also expect to be confronted by 'unaccustomed Elementes and ayres' and 'straunge and unsavery meats'.[77] On the one hand, then, Best presented America as a land that was undoubtedly exotic and with impressive natural resources, while on the other claiming it to be a treacherous environment in which unaccustomed airs and unsavoury meats could do damage to explorers' bodies. From a close reading of the rest of Best's text, it becomes clear that the author is torn between the fantasy of the American environment and the disappointing reality of the desolate landscape and resources of Meta Incognita.

In his preface, Best introduced the topic of American food, describing it in glowing, almost fantastical terms. In the Americas there could be found 'al kind of spices, and delectable fruites, both for delicacie, & health' in 'such aboundance, as hitherto they haue bene thought to haue bene bred no where else, but there'.[78] Plants such as 'Radishe, Lettuce, Colewortes, Borage, and suche like' were 'greater, more saverie and delectable in taste' than those found in England. Aside from the plants of the New World being more delicious and plentiful than those in England, the harvests in America were also quicker and more numerous than those back home. In the New World, wheat would be 'ripe the fourth Moneth after the séede is sowne', while 'Beanes, Pease, &c. are there ripe twice a yeare'.[79] The apparent bounty of American crops, alongside the abundance of precious metals in the region, led Best to conclude that 'no where else but vnder the Equinoctiall, or not farre from thence, is the earthlye Paradise, and the only place of perfection in this world'.[80] Best recognised, however, that conditions in the Far North may prove less favourable, given the very different environment. Nonetheless, exploring the more 'intemperate places' of the world was framed by Best as a virtuous mission, for as he suggested, 'the adventure the more hard the more honorable'.[81] Despite this admission that the lands to the north might not offer the same environmental rewards that the Spanish had enjoyed close to the equator, Best still optimistically believed that as the classical geographers had been so wrong about the habitability of the torrid zone, they might have likewise over-exaggerated the harshness of the earth's frigid zones and their inability to provide abundant crops. As Chapter 1 has suggested, Best saw the idea of temperate climates as relative; a man born in Morocco, if brought to England in his normal hot weather attire, would 'judge this Region presently not to be habitable' as he was used to a warm climate.[82] Likewise, Best hoped that as the English were used to cold climates, they would find the frozen lands of Meta Incognita more temperate and habitable than the classical writers of the Mediterranean had thought possible.

Throughout the rest of the text, however, Best's picture of the American environment, in which the soil was always fruitful and the crops always plentiful, delectable, and healthy, was systematically eroded by the reality of the harsh, forbidding landscape of the Far North. Rather than finding abundance and plenty, Best and his fellow explorers found only want. They discovered, to their horror, that the Inuit were not in the least bit discerning when it came to what they ate. Unlike the English, who were advised to meticulously consider how food might affect their health, the Inuit would, according to English observers, 'eate rawe fleshe and fishe, and refuse no meate, howsoever it be stincking'.[83] As medical handbooks of the time argued, consuming both raw and spoiled meat could be detrimental to a person's health. From antiquity onwards there was a strong connection between rotten and spoiled food, infected air, and evil diseases in the European imagination. These 'miasmas' or bad airs were believed to arise from processes of organic decomposition that would infect the air. Once inhaled, this infected air would inevitably lead to infected bodies. Because infected air was linked to stinking organic matter, it was rightly believed that consuming rotten food could lead to infection.[84] The stinking meat of the Inuit would undoubtedly, therefore, have produced bad airs that could have infiltrated and infected English bodies.

The eating of raw food was also particularly perilous for early modern Europeans. As Thomas Elyot advised his readers in 1539, eating raw fruits and herbs for complexions other than extreme choleric engendered 'thynne watry bloudde' and 'sondry diseases'.[85] Andrew Boorde, in his 1587 *Breviarie of Health*, even equated the eating of raw foods with perverse appetites, explaining how an unnatural appetite could be defined by the 'desyre to eate rawe & unlawfull thinges'.[86] In fact, the eating of raw flesh was considered so abnormal by English standards that Best even suggested that, based on the dining habits that he had witnessed, the Inuit of Meta Incognita were 'ravenous, bloudye, and Man eating people'.[87] Best made no suggestion that he had actually witnessed or seen direct evidence of Inuit cannibalism, and yet, when discussing the fate of some Englishmen left behind on the previous voyage to the region, he concluded that due to the Inuits' 'bloudy disposition, in eating anye kinde of rawe fleshe or carr[.]e[.], howsoever stincking, it is to be thoughte, that they had s[l]aine and devoured oure men'.[88]

This is an assertion also made by another member of the Frobisher voyage, Dionyse Settle. He likewise found the Inuit 'rather *Anthropophagi*, or devourers of mans fleshe', given that there was 'no flesh or fishe, which they finde dead (smell it never so filthily) but they will eate it, as they finde it'.[89] David Quinn and William C. Sturtevant have also argued that there was a strong connection between eating raw and spoiled meat and cannibalistic tendencies in the early modern English imagination.[90] They suggest that it is possible that this notion was derived from a passage from John Mandeville's *Travels*, a copy of which was known to have been purchased for the Frobisher voyages. This edition of Mandeville described 'a great yle' off the coast of Asia in which the people 'eat no bread but flesh raw, and they drink milke, & they have no houses, & they eat gladiyer fleshe of men then other'.[91] Best also claimed that the Inuit fed their 'sucking children' with raw meat, the mothers, in an animal-like manner, chewing the raw flesh in their own mouths before feeding it to their babies.[92] Settle also suggested that the Inuit were particularly animalistic in their feeding habits, neither using 'table, stoole, or table cloth for comelinesse'. Instead, 'when they are imbrued with bloud, knuckle deepe', they 'use their tongues as apt instruments' to lick themselves clean, making sure 'to loose none of their victuals'.[93] This type of behaviour would have undoubtedly been considered uncivilised and even savage by early modern European standards. Erasmus, the influential Renaissance humanist, explained, in a handbook aimed at children, how one should behave when eating. In an attempt to teach children how to become civilised and courteous adults, Erasmus explained that it was 'an uncivill thing' to lick one's fingers or to 'wipe them upon' one's clothes while eating.[94] Erasmus warned his readers that 'to gnawe bones doth pertaine to dogges', while 'to licke the dishe with thy tong' 'doeth pertain to cattes, and not to men'.[95] The Inuit, then, who would take care to devour every morsel of food using their mouths and fingers as tools, were perceived as beast-like, highlighting to English observers their inherent incivility and savagery.

According to both Best and Settle, though, this appalling beast-like diet was the product of necessity rather than choice. Despite his attempts at optimism in the prefatory material, Best concluded that the lands he and his fellow voyagers had explored were, in reality, barren, the earth yielding 'no graine or fruite of sustenaunce for man'.[96] Given the desolate nature of the landscape, it was unsurprising that the Inuit would eat almost anything. Settle also felt that the inappropriate diet of the Indigenous population was born from desperation rather than gastronomical taste. He explained to his readers that when food became scarce in the region, the Inuit would, 'for lacke of other victuals', slay their own work animals, in this case dogs, and use their flesh for sustenance.[97] Making much the same observations as Best, Settle described how the people of the region ate 'their meate all rawe, both fleshe, fishe, and foule' and, 'for necessities sake', they ate 'such grasse as the countrie yeeldeth', 'not deintily, or salletwise', and 'without either salt, oyles, or washing, like brutish beasts devoure the same'.[98]

These descriptions of dietary desperation, of which the practice of cannibalism was the ultimate expression, differ markedly from other European accounts of American anthropophagi. Rather than representing the hopelessness of Indigenous populations to source appropriate food, cannibalism was seen by many European writers to reflect the innate savagery of American peoples; they did not devour man's flesh because they had to, but because they wanted to. According to André Thevet the *canibales*, whom Columbus had first come across, ate 'humayne flesh, as we [Europeans] do biefe or mutton', having 'thereunto more appetite and delight'.[99] This was an opinion shared by Sebastian Münster, who suggested that the *canibales* treated prisoners of war like livestock, feeding them 'untyll they be very fat, as we [Europeans] are wont to doe with capons or hennes' before killing them, pulling out their guts, and eating the flesh 'freshe and newe'.[100] Not only did the *canibales* prepare men to be eaten, they also, as Münster explained, preserved human flesh for consumption later, 'poudering the residue with salte, or keping it in a certayne pickle as we [Europeans] do iegottes or sansages'.[101] The *canibales* chose to engage in cannibalism, treating human flesh in much the same way as any other kind of meat and utilising sophisticated methods to preserve it. The Inuit whom the English had encountered, on the other hand, were forced to eat inappropriate food, from raw and spoiled meat, to work animals and human flesh, due to the harsh, barren environment in which they lived.

English distaste for the Inuit diet, as described by Best and Settle, eventually came to reflect English disappointment with the region more generally. Those who had set out alongside Frobisher had hoped not only to find a Northwest Passage to Asia but also to explore a region of the Americas that they believed rich in natural resources, especially gold. In reality, the English explorers found neither; the Northwest Passage remained elusive, the gold of Meta Incognita stayed undiscovered, and the belief that the climate to the north would suit the hardy English was left in tatters.

The English explorations of Meta Incognita, moreover, had proven to them just how detrimental the environment was in shaping bodies. Not only did the lands of Baffin Island fail to produce the types of food necessary to maintain a temperate complexion, the Inuit themselves illustrated how the body could be irrevocably changed by a consistently bad diet. When invited to partake in English food, food that the explorers considered more wholesome and healthy, the Inuit body reacted badly. According to Settle, the English had to source local food for their captives as they were unable to digest the meat that the explorers had brought with them from England.[102] The fate of the Inuit who the explorers had captured and taken back to England also reflected how vulnerable their bodies were to changes in diet. Despite continuing to eat the raw meat and fish they were used to alongside the more common roasted and boiled meat of the English, the two Inuit captives, Kalicho and Arnaq, quickly succumbed to the unfamiliar environment of England, probably contracting one of the many Old World diseases to which they had no tolerance.[103] They had arrived in England at the end of September 1577 and by mid-November they were both dead, with their physician Dr Dodding diagnosing 'an Anglophobia' as the possible cause of death.[104]

Not only was the environment and diet of the English inappropriate, and indeed dangerous, for the perceived debased complexions of the Inuit, it was also clear that the English were not willing to defile their own bodies by partaking of typical Inuit fare. The English ensured that they would not have to survive on the corrupted and uncivilised foods of the Inuit by embarking on their voyage with plenty of healthy and appropriate victuals from England. As Best pointed out to his readers, the expedition of 1577 had enough victuals 'for twelve monethes provision'.[105] This dietary tactic for avoiding Indigenous food by bringing sufficient provisions from England did not always go to plan however. Despite the confirmation that the lands of Meta Incognita held little potential and that the hostile environment could have disastrous effects on English bodies, Frobisher and Best made one last voyage to the region in 1578. In Best's account of this third and final voyage, an account that was published alongside his description of the second voyage, the importance of English provisions to the success of the venture was all too clear. As Best recorded, the voyage was hampered by appalling weather and by hostility from the Inuit who were no doubt still reeling from the confrontations of the previous summer.[106] The expedition's fleet had become separated and the bark *Dennis* had been sunk. After managing to eventually reconvene on Kodlunarn Island, then known to the English as the Countess of Warwick's Island, the explorers assessed their situation and discovered that the fleet was in 'want of drinke and fuel'.[107] It was the loss of a substantial amount of the fleet's provisions of beer that ultimately led to the abandonment of the project and the hasty retreat home.

Beer was considered an essential form of nutrition for the early modern English.[108] Alcoholic beverages, just like foodstuffs such as bread and meat, were believed to provide nourishment to the body and keep the humours in balance. For northern Europeans, like the early modern English, the beverage of choice was typically ale or beer.[109] Three of Frobisher's ships that had been lost during the torturous journey had carried eighty four tonnes of beer meant for the group of men tasked with establishing a colony in the region. When it was discovered that the expedition had only twenty four tonnes of beer remaining, Captain Edward Fenton, who was to lead the wintering party, declared that these depleted provisions were insufficient to sustain the proposed colony throughout the winter. Most probably to the relief of those men who had been assigned to remain in Meta Incognita, Frobisher decided to abandon the planned colony, with the last of the English fleet sailing away from the Countess of Warwick's Island on 1 September 1578.[110] The English experience in Meta Incognita had thus highlighted how important food was to colonial success. The inappropriate and scarce food of the region, coupled with the difficulty of retaining victuals during challenging and unpredictable voyages, had made settlement in the Far North a near impossibility. It had taught the English just how detrimental food and environment was to their bodies and had illustrated the difficulty of maintaining health and temperance during international travel to unknown regions of the world.

Temperate climes and the French model for success?

After the disastrous decade of the 1570s, English explorers, commentators, and pro-colonists began to regroup and assess exactly what had gone wrong in the Meta Incognita voyages. A key text in this process of reassessment came in the form of an English translation of an Italian version of a French text, documenting the expeditions of Jacques Cartier to New France, modern-day Canada, in the 1530s. Published in 1580, this book set out exactly how the English could learn from the French experience in Canada and how they could rectify the mistakes that had been made in the Frobisher voyages.[111] Cartier's expeditions were by no means a complete success, failing as they did to establish a permanent French colony in the region. They did, however, illustrate the importance of the American environment for explorative and colonial survival. Cartier's experience, and apparent accidental stay in the region throughout the winter of 1535 to 1536, had highlighted that native food could sustain European bodies, decreasing the need for extensive provisions and allaying fears that American food would damage and alter European complexions. The lessons learned from the French experience in New France would significantly influence the English approach to the Virginian landscape and its peoples in subsequent years, encouraging explorers to engage with the Indigenous environment and diet, and brave staying in the region for an extended period of time.

In the preface to the English edition of Cartier's travel accounts, written by the translator, John Florio, the failure of the Frobisher voyages is tackled head on. Florio admitted that the English had 'not had as yet suche successe as was wished' in their exploration of the Americas. He argued, however, that the English should persist in these attempts and not become 'slower in this enterprice'. He identified a number of factors that led to the failure of these voyages, citing insufficient victuals as a primary determinant; if Frobisher's 'store of victualles had been sufficient', the English could 'have stayed al the Winter in those colder Countries'. He also implied, however, that the English should look for more temperate regions to settle, arguing that Cartier was able to remain 'a whole Winter contrary to hys determination when he set out of Fraunce' in Canada due to the country's 'more temperate clime'.[112] Florio was clear about why he chose to translate this particular text, explaining the 'use' of it to his readers. Cartier had shown that the 'Northwest partes of *America*' were 'no lesse fruitful and pleasant in al respects than is *England, Fraunce*, or *Germany*'; the Indigenous people, although 'simple and rude in manners', were by nature 'gentle and tractable, and most apt to receive the Christian Religion'; and 'the commodities of the Countrey' were 'not inferiour to the Marchandize of *Moscovy, Danske*, or many other frequented trade'.[113] Florio hoped that this positive assessment of the region discovered by Cartier would encourage Englishmen to explore the northern parts of America for themselves, inducing them 'not onley to fall to some traffique wyth the Inhabitants, but also to plant a Colonie in some convenient place'.[114] For Florio, then, the Cartier voyages illustrated the success that could be had in temperate regions: food for potential colonists was plentiful, the soil was fruitful and ripe for cultivation, commodities and merchandise were abundant, and the Indigenous people, like the environment, were temperate and tractable.

The rest of the text appeared to confirm Florio's arguments, highlighting time and again the abundance of the environment and the ability of Europeans to survive in the region. In Canada, Cartier found 'divers' sorts of venison, a river with 'the plentifullest of Fish that ever hath of any man bin seene or heard of'.[115] It also seemed that much of the land was suitable for arable farming. Cartier found land that was 'smooth, and leavel' and 'small Peason as thicke as if they had bin sown & plowed'.[116] The land was obviously very fertile, with Cartier even claiming that Brion Island had 'the best soyle that ever we saw'.[117] Throughout his voyage, Cartier saw a diverse array of plants flourishing, from gooseberries, strawberries, and blackberries to wild corn, parsley, nuts, and beans.[118] There were also 'many meadowes full of grasse' and 'Lakes wher gret plenty of Salmons be'.[119] The fact that the Iroquoians had techniques for cooking and preserving food was also a positive sign. Unlike their purportedly uncouth neighbours to the north in Baffin Island, the Iroquoians 'bake their Bread' on 'hote stone'.[120] They also prepared 'sundrye sortes of Pottage' with corn, peas, musk, and great cucumbers and preserved food by drying fish and damsons in the summer sun and placing them in 'certayne Vessels' to be kept for winter.[121]

The local environment even provided a natural remedy for a cruel disease that swept through both the Indigenous and European communities in the winter of 1535 to 1536.[122] Plant physiologist Don Durzan, through a consideration of the symptoms described by Cartier, has identified this disease as scurvy.[123] The outbreak started in December among the local Iroquoians and quickly spread to the ships of the French explorers. By mid-February, eight Frenchmen were already dead, with another fifty gravely ill, thought to be 'past al hope of recoverie'.[124] In a desperate attempt to identify the disease and 'save and preserve the reste of the company', an autopsy was even performed on one Philip Rougemont. His body was ripped open; inside his lungs were 'blacke and mortified', 'rotten bloud' surrounded his heart, and his spleen had perished and was 'rough as if it had bin rubbed against a stone'.[125] Despite these gruesome discoveries, Cartier and his men were none the wiser, becoming so 'greeved with that sicknesse' that they 'lost all hope ever to see *France* agayne'.

Just when all hope looked to be lost, God sent Cartier and his men 'the knowledge and remedie' of the disease that had stubbornly continued to afflict the French travellers.[126] Having ventured ashore, Cartier came across an Iroquoian man who twelve days previously had been so sick that 'all his sinowes shruncke together, hys teeth spoyled, his gummes rotten, and stinking'. Just twelve days later this man was now 'whole and sound', having somehow managed to heal himself. When asked how he had been cured, the man responded by saying that he had taken the juice and sap of the leaves of a certain tree, claiming it to be 'a singular remedie agaynst that disease'.[127] After taking the sap for themselves the afflicted Frenchmen found themselves 'delyvered of that sickenesse'. Not only did this natural medicine appear to cure scurvy, it also seemed to have a curative effect on other diseases, so much so that 'there were some hadde beene diseased and troubled wyth the French Pockes foure or five yeares, and wyth thys drinke were cleane healed'. Cartier was so impressed with the results that he even stated that 'if all the Phisitions of *Mountpelier*, and of *Louaine*, hadde beene there wyth all the drugges of *Alexandria*, they woulde not have done so muche in one yeare, as that tree dydde in six dayes'.[128]

Cartier's voyage to the northern regions of America had illustrated a number of issues that would be central to the Virginia enterprise in the 1580s. Cartier's experiences had shown that surviving on Indigenous foods was possible and that consuming them did not drastically alter European complexions. Cartier and his men had also shown this region of the Americas to be particularly temperate, abundant, and fertile, thus encouraging English explorers to focus their attention further south than they had done in the 1570s. Not only had the French voyages highlighted the European ability to survive prolonged periods of settlement in the Americas, they had also suggested that the region was home to a number of untapped, miraculous resources, such as the sap of the tree that appeared to cure scurvy and syphilis. Not only was the American environment safe for European bodies, it might even be good for them, a suggestion that was to be employed by English writers themselves in their descriptions of both the

Virginian and New England landscapes. As the 1580s wore on, the English would become increasingly positive about their overseas exploits, with bodily discourse becoming central to the articulation of this new-found confidence.

Bodily discourse and colonial confidence

In 1578 Elizabeth I awarded letters patent for the exploration and colonisation of the Americas to Humphrey Gilbert, whose ruthless campaigns in Ireland had won him considerable favour at court.[129] Gilbert was given the authority 'to discover, finde, search out, and view such remote heathen and barbarous lands, countreys and territories not actually possessed of any Christian prince or people', and to 'inhabite or remaine there'.[130] In effect, this restricted Gilbert's exploration to the regions of North America that were outside the control of Spain to the south and outside the sporadic interest of the French to the north. After mustering enough investment, Gilbert set sail for the Americas, taking possession of Newfoundland for the English in 1583. On this occasion, no attempt was made to establish a settlement in the region and after a few weeks Gilbert and his crew departed.[131] As Chapter 2 has established, this was to be Gilbert's last adventure; on the journey home his fleet ran into bad weather with his ship eventually being 'devoured and swallowed up of the Sea'.[132] On Gilbert's death, Walter Ralegh, his half-brother, inherited the patent and directed his attention to a more southerly colonial site, Virginia.[133]

Ralegh wished to capitalise on the patents as quickly as possible, so he immediately began arranging an expedition to North America. In 1584 Philip Amadas and Arthur Barlowe set out with their crew to assess the lands of Virginia. Amadas was an official member of Ralegh's household, and possibly learned navigational techniques from Thomas Harriot, who would also become a central figure in English projects in America. Barlowe, while not a member of the household, had likely become a servant of Ralegh's in as early as 1580, while both men were in Ireland.[134] Barlowe's account of the voyage was originally sent to Ralegh as a report and only published in 1589 in Hakluyt's first edition of the *Principal Navigations*.[135] In stark contrast to the English assessment of Meta Incognita, Barlowe's description of Virginia brimmed with praise for the region and optimism for future English colonial ventures. A large part of Barlowe's commendation was focused on the abundance of the environment and on the temperate, tractable nature of the Indigenous population. In many ways, Barlowe's account of Virginia directly echoed the positive aspects of Cartier's description of New France.

The expedition set sail on 27 April 1584, reaching the Americas in June of the same year. On sailing northwards from Florida to the intended destination of Virginia in July, Barlowe noted the sweetness of the air, stating that it was 'so sweet, and so strong a smel, as if we had bene in the midst of some delicate garden abounding with all kinde of odoriferous flowers'.[136] This was a good start because, as the physicians of the era taught, good air was central to good health.[137] Following the sweet smells that filled their nostrils, Barlowe and the rest of the crew made their way to the coast, eventually finding a haven in which to drop anchor. After taking possession of the region for the queen, Barlowe began to survey the land.[138] He was not disappointed. He found an abundance of grapes, growing both on the sand and on the 'green soile on the hils', the like of which, he claimed, could not be found anywhere else in the world. Moving further inland, abundance and plenty continued to define the Virginian landscape; Barlowe saw 'goodly woodes fall of Deere, Conies, Hares, and Fowle, even in the middest of Summer in incredible abundance'. Unlike the 'barren and fruitles' woods of Bohemia and Muscovy, those of Virginia were home to 'the highest and reddest Cedars of the world', not to mention an array of 'Pynes, Cypres, [and] Sassaphras'.[139] Throughout his time in Virginia, Barlowe and the other English explorers were sent by the Roanoke king's brother 'bucks, conies, hares, fish the best of the world', 'divers kindes of fruites, melons, walnuts, cucumbers, gourdes, pease, and divers rootes, and fruites very excellent good'.[140] In sharp contrast to Meta Incognita, the Virginian landscape provided the explorers with an abundance of delectable foods.

While Hortop and Philips had found that Indigenous Mexican foods could have terrible effects on English bodies, causing weakness and severe sickness, this did not seem to be the case with the food of Virginia. At no point in his narrative did Barlowe mention sickness among his men or indeed the local population. In fact, he made a point to explain that this lack of ill health could be down to the bounty of the Virginian environment, describing how the Algonquians had access to a variety of 'wholesome, and medicinable hearbes and trees'.[141] In many ways, Barlowe identified similarities between the English and the Algonquians. The abundant environment of Virginia included many components familiar to the English diet, from fowl and game, to fruits and vegetables.[142] In fact, more than just providing some of the key elements of a typical English diet, the Virginian environment was home to an array of foods normally associated with an elite diet. Melons and cucumbers did not grow in common gardens, and nor did sturgeon, venison and domestic fowl find their way onto the plates of English commoners. By illustrating the luxury of the Virginian environment Barlowe promised 'self-improvement' to people that did not consume these foods regularly.[143]

Barlowe's account also implied that Algonquian bodies were not all that different to English ones. While the Inuit had become sick from eating the rich foods of the English, the Algonquians appeared to have no such problem. When visiting the English ships, an Algonquian man was invited to dine with the foreign visitors. Being made to taste the wine and meat of the English, the local man declared he liked it 'very wel'. Later in the voyage, after friendly relations had been established with the Indigenous population, the king's brother, Granganimo, was also invited aboard the visitors' ships to partake in English fare. He too ate English meat and bread, and drank wine brought from Europe and 'liked exceedingly thereof'.[144] Not only was the Algonquian diet safe for English bodies, the English diet was also said to be safe for Indigenous bodies.

As well as describing the Algonquians as physically analogous with the English, Barlowe also portrayed them as socially similar, particularly in terms of their approach to preparing food. In a lengthy passage, Barlowe explained how he and the other English explorers were treated by Granganimo's wife, recounting the many attributes that she shared with the ideal English woman: she 'was very well favoured, of meane stature and very bashfull', and 'tooke great paines to see all things ordered in the best maner shee could, making great haste to dresse some meate for us [the English] to eate'.[145] On the departure of the English, Granganimo's wife even gave to them 'supper halfe dressed, pottes and all' to be taken back to the ships.[146] This description of female deportment closely echoed what early modern conduct books had to say about the role of women in English society. Edmund Tilney, probably best known today as Master of the Revels to Elizabeth I, wrote a short treatise, published in 1568, explaining a woman's duties in marriage. One character, Lady Julia, outlined the proper duties of a wife. She should be 'shamefast' as this 'is the onely defence that nature hath given to women' to 'keepe their reputation' and 'preserve their chastity'.[147] She 'ought not to commaund the man, but to be always obedient', be skilful 'in dressing of meate', and maintain 'honestie of behaviour, and talke'.[148] In appearing bashful and providing the English explorers with well-dressed meat, Granganimo's wife was illustrating the Algonquians' capability to live according to English conceptions of civility. The expression of this civility came in the context of food, something that was to be an important theme in other English descriptions of Virginia.

Alongside this abundance of wholesome local produce and similar etiquette towards food preparation, Barlowe also explained to his readers that the Virginian landscape had the potential to provide plentiful supplies of English crops through the establishment of arable farming. Just as Jacques Cartier had found the soil of Canada very fertile, Barlowe too discovered a land where the 'soil is the most plentifull, sweete, frutifull and wholesome of all the worlde'.[149] Although Barlowe identified a number of products that grew naturally in the Virginian environment, he also emphasised the fact that the Algonquians farmed their land. As George Best had suggested in his discussion of the equatorial region of America, the lands were so fertile that crops could be harvested multiple times a year.[150] Barlowe claimed that this was also possible in Virginia. He recounted the process by which the Algonquians grew corn, stating that it 'groweth three times in five moneths'. While some varieties of peas grew naturally in the wilderness, others were cultivated in Algonquian gardens. The Algonquians did practice a type of farming, but Barlowe made it inescapably clear that compared to English processes, Indigenous agriculture was much easier.[151]

While the English struggled with adverse weather conditions and failed harvests at home, the Algonquians merely had to 'cast the corne into the ground, breaking a little of the soft [t]urfe with a wodden mattock, or pick eare' to produce excellent results.[152] According to Barlowe, it was not just American corn that fared well in the fertile soil of Virginia. Crops that were familiar to the English also seemed to thrive in the North American environment. Given the importance of custom in early modern European dietary practices, the fact that native English crops seemed to fare well in the American environment was a good sign that English settlement in the region would first be possible, and second successful. The Algonquians already grew 'both wheat and oates' and the English explorers 'prooved the soile' themselves, sowing 'some of oure [English] Pease in the ground'. Within ten days the English crop had apparently grown 'fourteene ynches high', proving the fertility of the soil and the ease of cultivation.[153] The Virginian landscape offered English explorers and settlers two advantages: it naturally provided suitable food for the English in abundance, and it afforded colonists the opportunity to cultivate their own produce, thus ensuring the survival of the English in America.

These themes of abundance, fertility, physical similarity, and bodily health were also employed by other authors writing about their experiences in Virginia. Even before the return of Barlowe and Amadas, plans were already being made in England for a second voyage to the region, of which the establishment of a permanent settlement was a key objective. On his return to England, Barlowe's account of his time in Virginia was circulated in manuscript form, most likely in an attempt to secure further investment for the second expedition.[154] Shortly after Barlowe's successful return home, Ralegh was knighted by Queen Elizabeth I on 6 January 1585, inscribing on his seal, 'Lord and Governor of Virginia'. He managed to secure the queen's support for the second voyage, being supplied with a ship and possibly money from the Crown.[155] In April 1585 a second fleet set sail from Plymouth for Virginia, this time under the command of Ralegh's distant relative Richard Grenville. Accompanying Grenville was Colonel Ralph Lane, who was to serve as the colony's governor, and Thomas Harriot, a member of Ralegh's household.[156]

The failure of this attempt at settling at Roanoke Island is well known. Food shortages and the non-arrival of supplies from England led to the desertion of the colony and the return home of the English settlers with Francis Drake's West Indian fleet in June 1586.[157] On first glance, then, it would seem that this English attempt at settling in Virginia had gone much the same way as the attempts of the 1570s in Meta Incognita; the lack of appropriate food and a scarcity of English supplies had once again led to the abandonment of an English attempt at colonisation. A close analysis of the texts relating to this second voyage, however, paints a more complex picture. Harriot, in particular, retained in his 1588 narrative of the voyage the same sense of optimism and confidence in the project that had exuded from Barlowe's account of the 1584 reconnaissance voyage. Once again, specific foodstuffs, dietary habits, and dining practices were at the centre of this colonial confidence.

Having matriculated at Oxford in 1577, Harriot quickly became known for being a skilled maker of mathematical and navigational instruments. Undoubtedly compelled by his interest in establishing English colonies in the Americas, Ralegh employed the gifted Harriot to teach him and his circle of sea captains the science of navigation.[158] Harriot, by all accounts, was an enthusiastic supporter of Ralegh's attempts to plant the English in America. Before his departure with the 1585 voyage, he learned the Indigenous language of Virginia from the two Algonquians whom Barlowe and Amadas had brought to England in 1584, producing a phonetic language to represent Carolina Algonquian.[159] After his return home to England, Harriot composed a 'report' of the voyage which was first published in 1588 and gave a glowing account of his time in Virginia.[160]

From the preface to this work it is clear that Harriot's positive interpretation of the voyage was not shared by all of his fellow explorers. According to Harriot, one of the principal reasons for publishing his account was to set the record straight and refute the 'divers and variable reportes' of the voyage that were both 'slaunderous and shamefull'.[161] Having been an important member of the voyage, Harriot had 'seene and knowne more then the ordinarie', giving him the authority to prove to his readers 'howe injuriously' the voyage had been 'slaundered' by those of the company who had 'maliciously not onelie spoken ill of their Governours; but for their sakes slaundered the countrie it selfe'.[162] Harriot hoped to reassert confidence in the Virginia project and provide evidence that English colonisation in the region was sustainable. Through the consistent representation of the Virginian environment as abundant, fertile, and possessing the ability to produce temperate, healthy bodies, Harriot was, in many ways, able to achieve these aims. Food and diet thus became key rhetorical tools for bolstering and reinforcing confidence in a colonial project that seemed to be stalling.

Harriot began his report by listing the various 'Marchantable Commodities' that the Virginian environment could offer the colonists, from flax, hemp, pitch, and tar to copper, iron, and pearls.[163] It was not just, however, the profitable commodities of the region that interested Harriot; he also wished to highlight how the country could sustain English bodies, making permanent settlement in Virginia entirely feasible. In a large section of the text dedicated to this very argument, Harriot set out the various 'commodities as Virginia is knowne to yeelde for victuall and sustenance of mans life'.[164] Like Barlowe, Harriot found Virginia to be home to foods that were comparable to those of an English diet. Using the Carolina Algonquian words, Harriot identified a number of foodstuffs that, despite being undoubtedly different and unique to the region, would still be familiar to his English readers. There were 'okindgier' which were 'like to the Beanes in England'. There were 'wickonzowr', called by the English 'peaze', which were 'in goodnesse of tast [...] far better than our English peaze'.[165] There were familiar sources of meat, such as deer and conies, and 'good bread' could be made from native roots such as 'cocushaw' and maize, while the region's 'hops' and 'mault' could be used to brew those staples of the English diet, 'good ale' and 'good Beere'.[166]

Despite this air of familiarity, Harriot also stressed the differences of the Virginian environment, describing a range of exotic foods and commodities that were relatively unknown in 1580s England. While travellers such as Hortop and Philips had found some of the New World's exotic foods highly dangerous, Harriot discovered that the unfamiliar produce of Virginia was easy to cultivate, harmless, and even invigorating. In particular, he reserved his praise for two commodities that would become central to English colonialism in the Americas: maize and tobacco. As the staple food of many Indigenous communities across the American continent, maize was not only integral to Indigenous survival but also became increasingly indispensable to English settlers. As English settlement became more permanent in North America, colonisers were forced out of necessity to try the American corn, despite their apparent concerns that it would not provide sufficient nourishment for their northerly European bodies.[167] Harriot, on the other hand, espoused what he perceived to be the many virtues of maize, from its taste to its easy cultivation. As has already been suggested, Miles Philips had found during his imprisonment in New Spain that maize was often only good enough for pigs. Harriot, in contrast, found that the Algonquians of Roanoke used maize to 'maketh a very good bread', a crucial constituent of the English diet.[168] Harriot also found that maize was extremely versatile, being used in 'manifold waies' for victuals.[169] Not only could it taste good and be used to produce an array of dishes, its cultivation was also effortless.

In much the same way as Barlowe had done, Harriot explained in great detail the processes needed to raise an abundant crop of maize. Compared to the cultivation of English 'corn', such as rye and wheat, that of Virginia required 'small labour and paines' from farmers.[170] Unlike in England, the Algonquians never enriched the ground 'with mucke, dounge or any other thing' and nor did the ground require ploughing or digging as was the case in England. Instead, using wooden instruments that were comparable to hoes and mattocks, the Algonquians prepared their land for sowing by merely breaking 'the upper part of the ground to rayse up the weedes, grasse, & old stubbes of corne stalkes with their rootes'.[171]

Alongside requiring little preparation, the cultivation of maize in Virginia also led to bumper crops. Harriot, however, did not just *suggest* that maize could be produced in abundance with ease; he attempted to *prove* just how fertile the Virginian soil was by conducting his own scientific trials. In these experiments Harriot illustrated how an English acre in Virginia yielded a crop of American corn, beans, and peas, of 200 London bushels, while in England only forty bushels of wheat would be yielded from the same acreage. According to this rate that Harriot had 'made proofe of', he concluded that with 'lesse then foure and twentie houres labour' the Virginian soil could yield 'victuall in a large proportion for a twelve moneth'.[172] By proving that an abundance of food could be produced with very little effort, Harriot was showing his readers, a large number of whom were probably potential investors, that English settlement in Virginia was viable.[173] The land was home to a variety of foods, both familiar and exotic, and the soil was fertile enough to easily sustain an English colonial population.

Harriot did more than just portray the Virginian land as abundant and fertile, however. He also attempted to allay many of the fears that English men and women back home might have regarding the Indigenous diet and its effects on English bodies, which would in turn bolster the appeal of English emigration to Virginia. While Barlowe had indicated that, in the short-term at least, Virginian food did not appear to have a detrimental effect on the English complexion, Harriot, having spent an extended period of time in the region, was better placed to highlight the long-term effects of these foods on settlers' bodies. As Harriot explained, save for twenty days of the expedition, which represented a fraction of the ten-month stay, the English explorers 'lived only by drinking water and by the victual of the countrey'.[174] Harriot went on to say that due to much of the Indigenous food being 'very strange' to the English, it 'might have been thought to have altered our [English] temperatures in such sort as to have brought us into some grievous and dangerous diseases'.[175] And yet, as Harriot informed his readers, only four of the 108 members of the company died all that year, three of whom had already been feeble, weak, and sickly.[176] In fact, the men that knew these sickly members of the crew well 'marveyled that they lived so long'.[177] For these three infirm adventurers who had travelled alongside Harriot, exposure to Virginian food had prolonged their lives rather than hastening their deaths.

There was another Indigenous product that may have contributed to preserving the health of the English colonisers, one which even seemed to have some miraculous properties. Just as Cartier had found a tree in Canada that could apparently cure the specific ills of his men, Harriot also came across a native plant that appeared to cure some of the most common illnesses of early modern England. This miraculous herb was tobacco. Called in Carolina Algonquian *Uppowóc*, tobacco had first come to the attention of English readers with Richard Eden's 1555 translation of Peter Martyr's *Decades*.[178] In the early decades of the sixteenth century, the European attitude towards tobacco was ambivalent. On the one hand, European commentators were quick to emphasise tobacco's use in 'diabolical' Indigenous rituals, but on the other balanced this negative opinion with the belief that the herb had significant medicinal potential.[179] Peter Mancall has identified a key European text that attempted to perpetuate a positive interpretation of tobacco's use, praising its virtues and spreading this message as widely as possible: Nicholas Monardes's medical history of the Western Hemisphere.[180] Translated into English in 1577, Monardes's text set out a dizzying array of tobacco's 'greate vertues', from curing 'griefes' of the head, stomach, and breast, to alleviating tooth ache, rheumatism, kidney stones, bad breath, and chilblains.[181]

Harriot was influenced by Monardes's text, citing it in his own work in relation to sassafras and cassia bark.[182] Aside from these two explicit references, Harriot's description of tobacco also echoed that of Monardes. According to Harriot, tobacco could 'purgeth superfluous fleame & other grosse humors', opening 'all the pores & passages of the body', thus preserving 'the body from obstructions'.[183] For the cold, wet, phlegmatic complexion of the northerly English, smoking hot, dry tobacco seemed to represent one way of achieving a more temperate, balanced body. Indeed, through the continual use of tobacco, Harriot suggested, English bodies were 'notably preserved in health', and free from the 'greevous diseases wherewithall wee in England are oftentimes afflicted'.[184] Not only would tobacco become an important cash crop, sustaining the English colonies and boosting the economy back home, it increasingly became seen as a panacea throughout much of Europe.[185] Harriot, therefore, introduced to his readers a crop that not only could become a commodity, but also would lead the English on a path to temperance and bodily health. Tobacco had been transformed from a plant that provoked fear and revulsion among Europeans due to its connection with Indigenous religious rituals, to one that was considered a cure-all for early modern European ills.

In a concerted effort to build confidence and optimism in the project back home, Harriot also considered how Indigenous attitudes towards food could help validate the English colonial project. In the 1590 edition of the report, which included de Bry's engravings of the local people, the Algonquians' capacity for civility is portrayed through the lens of their eating habits. As Janet Whatley has argued in her study of Jean de Léry's account of his time living among the Tupi in Brazil, 'civility itself is structured in alimentary terms'.[186] This, it would appear, was no different for Harriot. But unlike Léry, who found his own notions of civility stretched to breaking point due to famine, quarrels over the Eucharist, and the fact that the Tupi practised cannibalism, Harriot saw Algonquian alimentary processes as an indication of their potential to achieve English civility.[187]

Indigenous techniques of food preparation, in particular, allowed for a degree of comparison between the English and the Algonquians of Roanoke. While the Inuit ate their food raw, the Algonquians used cooking techniques that would have been recognisable to Harriot's readers. They broiled, roasted, and boiled their fish, taking 'great heede that they bee not burntt'.[188] They cooked stews 'like a galliemaufrye', meaning a medley or hodgepodge, similar to the pottages that the physician Andrew Boorde claimed were used more by the English than the rest of Christendom.[189] These images and descriptions were, however, not merely an attempt by Harriot and de Bry to appropriate Algonquians into a framework of European civility. In much the same way that Indigenous nakedness was used to point to a type of primitivism that could easily be replaced with civility, as outlined in Chapter 3, these images of Algonquian food preparation also reflected a social structure that, while undoubtedly primitive by European standards, seemed to offer promising foundations for the building of English civility. Although they cooked their food, they did so outside, contrasting sharply with how cooking took place in England. Whether in the well-equipped and large kitchens of royalty and the nobility, or over the fire in the main room of the humble houses of those at the lower end of the social spectrum, cooking in 'civilised' England took place indoors.[190] The image of the broiling fish therefore reflects a curious, and potentially purposeful, mix of the primitive and the civilised, a mix that was indicative of the English understanding of Indigenous peoples in the early decades of English contact and colonisation (Figure 10). This perception is also reflected in the image of the Algonquian pottage. In their earthen pots,

Figure 10 Theodore de Bry, copper engraving, 'The Browyllinge of their Fishe over the Flame', in Thomas Harriot, *A Briefe and True Report of the New Found Land of Virginia* (Frankfurt, 1590).

the Algonquians stewed unfamiliar local produce such as maize, once again building an outdoor fire for the cooking (Figure 11). Men and women also seemed to share some aspects of the food preparation process, contrasting with how cooking took place in most English homes.

The prolific writer Gervase Markham suggested in his popular book, *Countrey Contentments, or The English Huswife*, that the most important aspect of being an English housewife was the acquisition of 'a perfect skill and knowledge in Cookery'. This skill was so important that without it, a woman would only be fulfilling half her marriage vows as 'she may love and obey, but shee cannot serve and keepe him with that true dutie which is ever expected'.[191] These clear gender divisions in food preparation appear to be somewhat blurred in the de Bry engravings, once again highlighting the current 'incivility' of the Algonquians. It was the men who broiled the fish, and while the women tended to the stew, the men stoked and maintained the fire (Figures 10–11).

This blending of current primitivism with potential future civility is also illustrated in English descriptions and depictions of Indigenous eating habits and table manners. Once again, elements of seemingly appropriate English manners are displayed alongside more crude and underdeveloped Algonquian habits. In early modern England, table manners were of the utmost importance, principally among the elite and socially aspirational.

Figure 11 Theodore de Bry, copper engraving, 'Their Seetheynge of their Meate in Earthen Pottes', in Thomas Harriot, *A Briefe and True Report of the New Found Land of Virginia* (Frankfurt, 1590).

Handbooks for children emphasised the necessity of good table manners. Children, in order to grow into civil adults, were encouraged to respect their elders at table and to eat with grace, modesty, and cleanliness.[192] One aspect of this inclination towards cleanliness was the use of tablecloths that would be made from coarse to very fine linen depending on the household.[193] One author of a handbook aimed at children, Francis Segar, highlighted the importance of the tablecloth, warning children that 'Disshes with measure thou oughtest to fyll / Els mayste thou happen thy service to spyll / On theyr [the children's parents] apparel Or els on the cloth / whiche for to does wolde move them [parents] to wroth'.[194]

Like the English, the Algonquians also seemed to appreciate the necessity of dining upon a cloth. They would 'lay a matt made of bents on the grownde and sett their meate on the mids therof'.[195] Despite this, they lacked the most important element of the English, and indeed European, dining experience: the table. Sitting outside on the ground, their legs splayed open, would have undoubtedly been considered uncouth by English standards (Figure 12).

In one important respect, however, Harriot presented the eating habits of the Algonquian population as superior to those of the English. In the caption that accompanied the image of the man and woman eating

Eating America 189

Figure 12 Theodore de Bry, copper engraving, 'Their Sitting at Meate', in Thomas Harriot, *A Briefe and True Report of the New Found Land of Virginia* (Frankfurt, 1590).

(Figure 12), Harriot was keen to emphasise the Algonquian propensity for moderation. According to Harriot, the Algonquians were 'verye sober in their eatinge, and trinkinge, and consequentlye verye longe lived because they doe not oppress nature'.[196] In the humoralist thinking of early modern Europe, moderation in food and drink was seen to be key to maintaining good health and humoral balance. The sixteenth-century physician William Bullein provided his readers with a medical explanation for why eating excessive amounts was likely to cause sickness. Eating too much, especially of varied types of food, inhibited digestion bringing 'much paine to the stomack' and engendering 'many diseases'.[197] Another physician, Thomas Elyot, went as far as to suggest that 'sondry meates, beynge dyvers in substance and qualitie, eaten at one meale, is the greatest ennemy to helth'. Not only was eating various types of food detrimental to a person's health due to the different lengths of time it took each food to be digested, Elyot considered it a particular vice and abuse of the English who engaged in 'the contynuall gourmandyse & dayely fedynge on sondry meates', proving that 'the spirite of gluttony' was 'triumphynge' in the realm.[198] The Algonquians, by moderating what they ate, preserved their health, living longer and more in accordance with nature. Over-eating, however, was more than just a cause of ill health, it was also an expression of incivility and, in extreme cases, outright debauchery. According to Erasmus, children must avoid putting 'so muche in their mouthes that theyr chekes be blowne up and swell on every side like beastes' as this was a sure sign of gluttony and, indeed, incivility.[199]

The pamphleteer Philip Stubbes, however, went much further in his diatribe against what he perceived to be the various vices of the English. Avoiding greediness was not just a question of courtesy but one of piety. In his popular and often reprinted pamphlet of 1583, *The Anatomie of Abuses*, Stubbes lists the sin of gluttony alongside those of 'drunkennesse, thiefte, murther, swearing' and 'whoredom'.[200] As he suggested, 'the rich glutton in the Gospel, for his riotous feastings & proposterous living was condemned to the fire of hel'.[201] Stubbes was a fervent Protestant and instrumental in reformist debates surrounding the incomplete nature of the English Reformation.[202] Just as debates surrounding decadent clothing were used to argue for greater religious reform, so too were arguments that stated an English propensity for excess and the deadly sin of gluttony.[203] Not only were the Algonquians illustrating dietary restraint for the purposes of maintaining good health, then, they were also highlighting their purity and innocence. Within this context, these debates surrounding religious reform were being played out in early English accounts of America. By portraying Algonquians as moderate eaters, entirely disengaged from the sin of gluttony, writers such as Harriot helped shape debates back home about the form that religious settlement should take. English religion should be void of excess, decadence, and luxury, with the 'savage', yet simple, Algonquians illustrating the possibilities and advantages of living a pure, natural, and innocent life.

Harriot had thus established a clear picture of the Virginian environment and its inhabitants. It was a land of abundance and fertility, where familiar and exotic crops could be found in equal measure. It was a region of the world that would suit the temperaments of the early modern English body, providing ample appropriate nutrition and miracle herbs such as tobacco that could cure stubborn English ailments. Harriot had shown that English bodies in Virginia could survive and even thrive, encouragement indeed for readers back home who were thinking about making the voyage to the new lands. The Algonquians of Roanoke, through their cooking and eating habits, had also proven themselves capable of receiving English civility. They cooked their food, sat together to dine, and exhibited alimentary moderation – encouraging signs that raising them to civility would be a straightforward, even effortless task. This colonial narrative of abundance, health, and ease was summed up by Harriot in his concluding passage: in Virginia the air was 'temperate and holsome, the soyle so fertile' and for future settlers the land promised 'victuals that is excellent good and plentie enough'.[204]

* * *

In 1602 John Brereton published his account of his voyage to the north part of Virginia, a region that is known today as New England. In this text, the success of Harriot's rhetoric, articulated for the first time over a decade earlier, is obvious. Like Harriot, Brereton found the New England environment full of fare, from 'Cranes, Hernshawes, Bitters, Geese, Mallards, Teales and other Fowles', to 'great store of Pease' and 'an abundance of Strawberies & other berries'.[205] Like Harriot, Brereton and his fellow explorers undertook agricultural trials that produced stunning results, sowing 'Wheat, Barley, Oats, and Pease, which in fourteene daies were sprung up nine inches and more'.[206] Like Harriot, Brereton found a climate of extraordinary 'holsomnesse and temperature' in which he found his English body 'much fatter and in better health' than when he left England, with no hint of any disease nor sickness.[207] Like Harriot, Brereton found the Indigenous population 'exceeding courteous, gentle of disposition, and well conditioned, excelling all others'.[208] It is extraordinary that a text running to just fourteen pages in quarto format could include so many of the rhetorical elements that had first been seen in Barlowe's and Harriot's work.

By the beginning of the seventeenth century, and despite the clear failings of the early Roanoke colony, the idea of Virginia as the perfect region for English colonisation was entrenched, being articulated through a bodily discourse that had food, diet, and dining at its core. This type of discourse had first been utilised in the 1560s as a way of explaining colonial and explorative failure. This negative attitude towards the American environment, and its effects on both English and Indigenous bodies, continued into the 1570s with the exploration of Meta Incognita, where the lack of appropriate food and the supposedly bestial dining practices of the Inuit contributed significantly to the abandonment of the project. Whether employed positively or negatively, then, food, dining, and bodily health became barometers through which sixteenth-century English explorers and colonists measured the success of their projects. In Meta Incognita bodily discourse confirmed English suspicions that settlement was impossible, while in Virginia it became a rhetorical device used to instil optimism and colonial confidence at home. By the end of the sixteenth century, with the abandonment of colonial projects in the Far North and a new focus on building English settlements in the more temperate region of Virginia, Harriot's positive understanding of the body and the American environment triumphed, leaving behind the negativity of the 1560s and 1570s.

The victory of Harriot's rhetoric of abundance, temperance, and health, alongside an apparent English amnesia on the failure of the Roanoke colony, would, however, have a detrimental effect on English colonialism well into the seventeenth century. In the early years of the Jamestown colony, a settlement that had arguably been built on the rhetoric of the Roanoke years, food, and the colonisers' ability to source it, played a critical role. In the winter of 1609, following an uncharacteristically dry spell, the colonists found themselves facing famine. During this period, now known as 'the Starving Time', the majority of the settlers succumbed to starvation, being forced to eat unsavoury foods, even boiling and eating their shoes and other leather goods.[209] The experiences of the Jamestown colonists during the winter of 1609–1610 illustrates how fragile the positive rhetoric of bodily discourse was, but it also highlights how food and its centrality to health remained at the heart of the English colonial experience in America.

Notes

1 Brereton, *A Briefe and True Relation*, 11.
2 The term 'geohumoralism' is used by Mary Floyd-Wilson to describe regionally framed humoralism, i.e. a theory that attempted to explain climatic extremes and their relation to bodily difference; Mary Floyd-Wilson, *English Ethnicity and Race in Early Modern Drama* (Cambridge: Cambridge University Press, 2003), 1–2.
3 For scholarship on food and diet in colonial America see Robert, Appelbaum, "Hunger in Early Virginia: Indians and English Facing Off Over Excess, Want, and Need," in *Envisioning an English Empire: Jamestown and the Making of the North Atlantic World*, eds. Robert Appelbaum and John Wood Sweet (Philadelphia: University of Pennsylvania Press, 2005), 195–216; Alfred Crosby, *The Columbian Exchange: Biological and Cultural Consequences of 1492* (Westport, CT: Greenwood Press, 1972); Rebeccae Earle, *The Body of the Conquistador: Food, Race and the Colonial Experience in Spanish America, 1492–1700* (Cambridge: Cambridge University Press, 2012); Trudy Eden, *The Early American Table: Food and Society in the New World* (DeKalb: Northern Illinois University Press, 2008); Jess Edwards, "'Plain Wilderness' and 'Goodly Corn Fields': Representing Land Use in Early Virginia," in *Envisioning an English Empire: Jamestown and the Making of the North Atlantic World*, eds. Robert Appelbaum and John Wood Sweet (Philadelphia: University of Pennsylvania Press, 2005), 217–235; Rachel Herrmann, "The 'Tragicall Historie': Cannibalism and Abundance in Colonial Jamestown," *The William and Mary Quarterly* 68, no. 1 (January, 2011): 47–74; Michael A. LaCombe, *Political Gastronomy: Food and Authority in the English Atlantic World* (Philadelphia: University of Pennsylvania Press, 2012); Luis Millones Figueroa,

"The Staff of Life: Wheat and 'Indian Bread' in the New World," *Colonial Latin American Review* 19, no. 2 (2010): 301–22; Enrique Rodríguez-Alegría, "Eating Like an Indian: Negotiating Social Relations in the Spanish Colonies," *Current Anthropology* 46, no. 4 (August/October, 2005): 551–573; Janet Whatley, "Food and the Limits of Civility: The Testimony of Jean de Léry," *Sixteenth-Century Journal* 15, no. 4 (Winter, 1984): 387–400.

4 Earle, *Body of the Conquistador*; Craig Rustici, "Tobacco, Union, and the Indianized English," in *Indography: Writing the "Indian" in Early Modern England*, ed. Jonathan Gil Harris (New York and Basingstoke: Palgrave Macmillan, 2012); Trudy Eden, "Food, Assimilation, and the Malleability of the Human Body in Early Virginia," in *A Centre of Wonders: The Body in Early America*, eds. Janet Moore Lindman and Michele Lise Tarter (Ithaca, NY and London: Cornell University Press, 2001); LaCombe, *Political Gastronomy*.
5 Earle, *Body of the Conquistador*, 2.
6 Ibid., 54.
7 Ibid., 47.
8 Peter C. Mancall, "Tales Tobacco Told in Sixteenth Century Europe," *Environmental History* 9, no. 4 (October, 2004): 649.
9 Ibid., 651–652. This complex European relationship with tobacco has also been explored in greater detail in Marcy Norton, *Sacred Gifts, Profane Pleasures: A History of Tobacco and Chocolate in the Atlantic World* (Ithaca, NY and London: Cornell University Press, 2008); Rustici, "Tobacco, Union, and the Indianized English"; Kristen G. Brookes, "Inhaling the Alien: Race and Tobacco in Early Modern England," in *Global Traffic: Discourses and Practices of Trade in English Literature and Culture from 1550–1700*, eds. Barbara Sebek and Stephen Deng (New York: Palgrave Macmillan, 2008), 157–178; Tanya Pollard, "The Pleasures and Perils of Smoking in Early Modern England," in *Smoke: A Global History of Smoking*, eds. Sander L. Gilman and Xun Zhou (London: Reaktion Books Ltd., 2004), 38–45.
10 Rustici, "Tobacco, Union, and the Indianized English," 118–123.
11 Eden, "Food, Assimilation, and the Malleability," 30.
12 Ibid., 38. For a detailed analysis of the Starving Time and its impact upon both colonial measures relating to food and the mythology of Jamestown see Herrmann, "The 'Tragicall Historie'".
13 LaCombe, *Political Gastronomy*, 51.
14 Ibid., 49 and 62; A similar point has been made by Joyce Chaplin. Chaplin argues that by cultivating English crops in the new American environment, English colonists were able to maintain a 'corporeal link' with England and prevent degradation into outright 'Indian' savagery; Chaplin, *Subject Matter*, 211–212.
15 For a detailed discussion of the porous early modern body see Ulinka Rublack, "Fluxes: The Early Modern Body and the Emotions," trans. Pamela Selwyn, *History Workshop Journal* 53, no. 1 (Spring, 2002): 1–16.
16 For scholarship on the humoral system see Lindemann, *Medicine and Society*, 13; Ken Albala, *Eating Right in the Renaissance* (Berkeley: University of

California Press, 2002); Heikki Mikkeli, *Hygiene in the Early Modern Medical Tradition* (Helsinki: Academia Scientiarum Fennica, 1999); Klaus Bergdolt, *Wellbeing: A Cultural History of Healthy Living*, trans. Jane Dewhurst (Cambridge: Polity Press, 2008); David Gentilcore, *Food and Health in Early Modern Europe: Diet, Medicine and Society, 1450–1800* (New York: Bloomsbury, 2016); Steven Shapin, "You Are What You Eat: Historical Changes in Ideas About Food and Identity," *Historical Research* 87, no. 237 (August, 2014): 377–392.

17 Thomas Elyot, *The Castel of Helth* (London, 1539), fol. 1.
18 Lindemann, *Medicine and Society*, 14.
19 On preventative healthcare during the Renaissance see Sandra Cavallo and Tessa Storey, *Healthy Living in Late Renaissance Italy* (Oxford: Oxford University Press, 2013).
20 Elyot, *Castel of Helth*, fol. 18.
21 Boorde, *A Compendyous Regyment*, sigs. H2r–H3r.
22 Lindemann, *Medicine and Society*, 23.
23 Gentilcore, *Food and Health*, 95–114.
24 Ken Albala, *Food in Early Modern Europe* (Westport, CT: Greenwood Press, 2003), 216.
25 William Bullein, *The Government of Health* (London, 1595), fol. 26.
26 Viktoria von Hoffmann, *From Gluttony to Enlightenment: The World of Taste in Early Modern Europe* (Chicago: University of Illinois Press, 2016); Robert Appelbaum, *Aguecheek's Beef, Belch's Hiccup, and Other Gastronomic Interjections: Literature, Culture, and Food Among the Early Moderns* (Chicago: University of Chicago Press, 2006), 240–245.
27 Earle, *Body of the Conquistador*, 28; Albala, *Food in Early Modern Europe*, 215.
28 Elyot, *Castel of Helth*, fol. 17.
29 Ibid., fol. 18.
30 Ibid., fol. 17.
31 Earle, *Body of the Conquistador*, 28.
32 Bullein, *Government of Health*, fol. 28.
33 Jean Bodin, *The Six Bookes of a Common-weale* (London, 1606), 556 and 562.
34 Ibid., 553–554.
35 Pierre Charron, *Of Wisdome Three Bookes Written in French by Peter Charro[n]* (London, 1608), 167.
36 Ibid., 164–167.
37 Ibid., 167.
38 Morgan, "Sir John Hawkins."
39 Hawkins, *A True Declaration*, sig. A4v.
40 Ibid., sigs. A4v–A5v.
41 Ibid., sig. A5v.
42 Ibid., sigs. A6r–A6v.
43 Ibid., sig. B2v.

44 Ibid., sig. B3r.
45 Ibid., sig. B5r.
46 Ibid., sig. B5v. For more on European conceptions of inappropriate and taboo foods see Piero Camporesi, *Bread of Dreams: Food and Fantasy in Early Modern Europe*, trans. David Gentilcore (Chicago: University of Chicago Press, 1989).
47 Hawkins, *A True Declaration*, sig. B6r.
48 Hortop, *Travailes of an English Man*, 17.
49 Hawkins, *A True Declaration*, sig. B6v.
50 Ibid., sig. B7r.
51 Hortop, *Travailes of an English Man*, title page.
52 Ibid., 17.
53 Ibid., 20.
54 Ibid., 20–21.
55 Philips, "A Discourse Written by One *Miles Philips*," 3:469.
56 Ibid., 3:474.
57 Ibid., 3:477.
58 The belief that maize was only suitable for animal consumption was also referred to in herbals of the early modern period. For example, John Gerard, in a highly popular book, argued that 'we [i.e. the English] may easily judge that it nourisheth but little and is of hard and evil digestion, a more convenient food for swine than for men'. Information from John Gerard, *The Herball or Generall Historie of Plantes* (London, 1633), 3.
59 Philips, "A Discourse Written by One *Miles Philips*," 3:476.
60 Ibid., 3:477.
61 Elyot, *Castel of Helth*, fol. 45.
62 Philips, "A Discourse Written by One *Miles Philips*," 3:481–487; Hortop, *Travailes of an English Man*, 29–30.
63 This quotation is taken from Philips, "A Discourse Written by One *Miles Philips*," 3:487.
64 Münster, *Treatyse of the Newe India*, sig. L1v.
65 Martyr, *Decades of the Newe Worlde*, fols. 105–110.
66 Ibid., fol. 45.
67 Ibid., fol. 17.
68 Ibid., fol. 25.
69 Europeans had, of course, been open to trying foods from different regions of the world for centuries. The process of naturalisation was, however, often gradual and limited to foodstuffs that did not represent a significant component of the European diet or came with perceived medicinal benefits (e.g. spices). For more on the late medieval spice trade and its relevance to European diets see Paul Freedman, "Spices and Late-Medieval European Ideas of Scarcity and Value," *Speculum* 80, no. 4 (October, 2005): 1209–227; Elaine Leong, "Making Medicines in the Early Modern Household," *Bulletin of the History of Medicine* 82, no. 1 (Spring, 2008): 145–68; Jack Turner, *Spice: The History of a Temptation* (London: Harper Perennial, 2005); Anne C. McCants, "Exotic Goods, Popular Consumption, and the Standard of Living: Thinking about

Globalization in the Early Modern World," *Journal of World History* 18, no. 4 (December, 2007): 433–462.
70 Martyr, *Decades of the Newe Worlde*, fol. 81.
71 Ibid., fol. 25.
72 Ibid., fols. 25–26.
73 For the importance of custom and tradition for early modern European diets see Steven Shapin, "Why was 'Custom a Second Nature' in Early Modern Medicine?" *Bulletin of the History of Medicine* 93, no. 1 (Spring, 2019): 1–26.
74 Earle, *Body of the Conquistador*, 47.
75 Martyr, *Decades of the Newe Worlde*, fol. 99.
76 Ibid., fol. 18.
77 Best, *A True Discourse*, sig. A1v.
78 Ibid., sig. e3v.
79 Ibid., sig. e3r.
80 Ibid., sig. e3v.
81 Ibid., sig. a3v.
82 Ibid., sigs. g2v–g3r.
83 Ibid., sig. N3v.
84 Michael Stolberg, *Experiencing Illness and the Sick Body in Early Modern Europe*, trans. Leonhard Unglaub and Logan Kennedy (Basingstoke: Palgrave Macmillan, 2011), 116.
85 Elyot, *Castel of Helth*, fol. 17.
86 Andrew Boorde, *The Breviarie of Health* (London, 1587), fol. 17.
87 Best, *A True Discourse*, sig. H2r.
88 Ibid., sig. C4v.
89 Settle, *A True Reporte*, sig. D1r.
90 Sturtevant and Quinn, "This New Prey," 77–80.
91 Ibid., 115.
92 Best, *A True Discourse*, sig. O1r.
93 Settle, *A True Reporte*, sig. C5v.
94 Desiderius Erasmus, *The Civilitie of Childehode*, second edition, trans. Thomas Paynell (London, 1560), sig. D1r.
95 Ibid., D2r.
96 Best, *A True Discourse*, sig. O1r.
97 Settle, *A True Reporte*, sig. C6r.
98 Ibid., sig. C5v.
99 Thevet, *The New Found Worlde*, fol. 98.
100 Münster, *Treatyse of the Newe India*, sig. G6v.
101 Ibid., It is possible that 'iegottes or sansages' refer to faggots and sausages.
102 Settle, *A True Reporte*, sig. C4r.
103 Sturtevant and Quinn, "This New Prey", 80–84.
104 Ibid., 84.
105 Best, *A True Discourse*, sig. h3v.
106 Ibid., sigs. F1r–O2v.

107 Ibid., sig. K3r.
108 For the nutritional importance of beer see Gentilcore, *Food and Health*, 156–168.
109 Wine was typically considered more nourishing than beer but as wine was expensive to import, most early modern English men and women relied on beer or ale as their principal form of liquid nourishment. See Gentilcore, *Food and Health*, 156.
110 McGhee, *Arctic Voyages*, 125–134.
111 Cartier, *Shorte and Briefe Narration*.
112 Ibid., sig. B2v.
113 Ibid., sig. B1r.
114 Ibid., sig. B1v.
115 Ibid., 63.
116 Ibid., 18.
117 Ibid., 10.
118 Ibid., 10–21.
119 Ibid., 18.
120 Ibid., 50.
121 Ibid., 20 and 50–51.
122 For scholarship on the medicalisation of American commodities see Antonio Barrera, "Local Herbs, Global Medicine, Commerce, Knowledge, and Commodities in Spanish America," in *Merchants and Marvels: Commerce, Science and Art in Early Modern Europe*, eds. Pamela Smith and Paula Findlen (London: Routledge, 2002), 163–181; Harold J. Cook, *Matters of Exchange: Commerce, Medicine, and Science in the Dutch Golden Age* (New Haven, CT: Yale University Press, 2007); Karen Reeds, "Don't Eat, Don't Touch: Roanoke Colonists, Natural Knowledge, and Dangerous Plants of North America," in *European Visions: American Voices*, ed. Kim Sloan (London: British Museum, 2009), 51–57.
123 Don J. Durzan, "Arginine, Scurvy and Cartier's 'Tree of Life'," *Journal of Ethnobiology and Ethnomedicine* 5, no. 5 (February, 2009): 1–3.
124 Cartier, *Shorte and Briefe Narration*, 94–95.
125 Ibid., 65.
126 Ibid., 66.
127 Ibid., 67.
128 Ibid., 68.
129 David B. Quinn, "Introduction," in *The Voyages and Colonising Enterprises of Sir Humphrey Gilbert*, vol. 1, ed. David B. Quinn (London: Routledge, 2010), 1–104.
130 "The Letters Patents," 3:135.
131 Rapple, "Humphrey Gilbert."
132 Hayes, "Report of the Voyage and Successe Thereof," 3:159.
133 Miller, *Invested with Meaning*, 7.
134 Quinn, *Set Fair for Roanoke*, 21–22.
135 This text was first published in 1589 in Hakluyt's first edition of the *Principal*

Navigations and then reprinted in a second edition in 1598–1600. Quotations and information for this text are taken from the second edition.
136 Barlowe, "The First Voyage," 3:246.
137 Boorde, *A Compendyous Regyment*, sigs. A2v–A3r.
138 For more information on European notions of possession see Patricia Seed, *Ceremonies of Possession in Europe's Conquest of the New World, 1492–1640* (Cambridge: Cambridge University Press, 1995).
139 Barlowe, "The First Voyage," 3:246.
140 Ibid., 3:248.
141 Ibid., 3:249.
142 Ibid., 3:248.
143 Eden, "Food, Assimilation," 34.
144 Barlowe, "The First Voyage," 3:247.
145 Ibid., 3:247 and 249.
146 Ibid., 3:249.
147 Edmund Tilney, *A Brief and Pleasant Discourse of Duties in Mariage* (London, 1568), sig. D7v.
148 Ibid., sigs. E2r–E4v.
149 Barlowe, "The First Voyage," 3:248.
150 Best, *A True Discourse*, sig. c3r.
151 Barlowe, "The First Voyage," 3:248.
152 Ibid., For scholarship relating to climate and its impact on food production in early modern Europe see Wolfgang Behringer, *A Cultural History of Climate* (London: Polity Press, 2009); Brian Fagan, *The Little Ice Age: How Climate Made History* (New York: Basic Books, 2000); Emmanuel Le Roy Ladurie, *Times of Feast Times of Famine: A History of Climate since the Year 1000*, trans. Barbara Bray (New York: Doubleday, 1971); Geoffrey Parker, *Global Crisis: War, Climate Change and Catastrophe in the Seventeenth Century* (New Haven, CT: Yale University Press, 2013); John Walter and Roger Schofield, eds., *Famine, Disease and the Social Order in Early Modern Society* (Cambridge: Cambridge University Press, 1989).
153 Barlowe, "The First Voyage," 3:248.
154 Michael G. Moran, *Inventing Virginia: Sir Walter Raleigh and the Rhetoric of Colonization, 1584–1590* (New York: Peter Lang, 2007), 34–61.
155 Quinn, *Raleigh and the British Empire*, 63–64.
156 Moran, *Inventing Virginia*, 61–97.
157 Quinn, *England and the Discovery of America*, 283.
158 Robert Fox, "The Many Worlds of Thomas Harriot," in *Thomas Harriot and His World: Mathematics, Exploration, and Natural Philosophy in Early Modern England*, ed. Robert Fox (Farnham: Ashgate, 2012), 2.
159 Karen Ordahl Kupperman, "Roanoke's Achievement," in *European Visions: American Voices*, ed. Kim Sloan (London: British Museum Press, 2009), 3–12, at 5.
160 Another edition of Harriot's text was published in 1590, with a third edition being included in Hakluyt's *Principal Navigations*. To avoid

confusion, citations for the text refer to the 1590 edition unless expressly stated.
161 Harriot, *A Briefe and True Report*, 5.
162 Ibid., 5–6.
163 Ibid., 7–11.
164 Ibid., 13.
165 Ibid., 14.
166 Ibid., 14–19.
167 LaCombe, *Political Gastronomy*, 60.
168 Harriot, *Briefe and True Report*, 13.
169 Ibid., 15.
170 In the early modern period 'corn' was a generic term used to denote any type of cereal. In an English context, the word 'corn' most likely referred to wheat. When Harriot used the word 'corn' he differentiated between 'our' corn (presumably wheat) and the corn of 'that countrey', referring to the maize of Virginia. For more information on the word 'corn' see Duccio Bonavia, *Maize: Origin, Domestication, and its Role in the Development of Culture*, trans. Javier Flores Espinoza (Cambridge: Cambridge University Press, 2013), 18; For an example of Harriot's use of the word 'corn' and for quotation see Harriot, *Briefe and True Report*, 15.
171 Harriot, *Briefe and True Report*, 14.
172 Ibid., 15.
173 For scholarship on how English projects were promoted through print see Borge, *A New World*; Chaplin, "Roanoke 'Counterfeited According to the Truth'," 51–64; Fuller, *Voyages of Print*; Mary C. Fuller, *Remembering the Early Modern Voyage: English Narratives in the Age of European Expansion* (London: Palgrave, 2008); Linton, *Romance of the New World*; Miller, *Invested with Meaning*; Moran, *Inventing Virginia*; Pennington, "The Amerindian in English Promotional Literature, 1575–1625," 175–194.
174 This expedition to Virginia, according to the account of the colony's governor, Ralph Lane, lasted from 17 August 1585 until 18 June 1586. Information taken from Ralph Lane, "An Account of the Particularities of the Imployments of the English Men Left in Virginia by Sir Richard Greenevill," in *Principal Navigations*, 3:255; Quotation taken from Harriot, *Briefe and True Report*, 31.
175 Harriot, *Briefe and True Report*, 31.
176 Ibid., 32.
177 Ibid., 32.
178 Mancall, "Tales Tobacco Told," 657.
179 Ibid., 651.
180 Ibid., 656.
181 Nicholas Monardes, *Joyfull Newes out of the Newe Founde Worlde* (London, 1577), fols. 35–37.
182 Stephen Clucas, "Thomas Harriot's *A Briefe and True Report*: Knowledge-Making and the Roanoke Voyage," in *European Visions: American Voices*,

ed. Kim Sloan (London: British Museum Press, 2009), 17–23, at 19; Harriot, *Briefe and True Report*, 9 and 23.
183 Harriot, *Briefe and True Report*, 16.
184 Ibid., 16.
185 Mancall, "Tales Tobacco Told," 670. Somewhat ironically Harriot died of nose cancer in 1621, quite probably from his own tobacco use. See Mancall, "Tales Tobacco Told," 665.
186 Whatley, "Food and the Limits of Civility," 387. Jean de Léry was a French Calvinist explorer who travelled to Brazil in 1556 in order to establish the first Protestant mission in the New World. His account of his voyage appeared in print in 1578 and became one of the most detailed and engaging French reports of the early years of European contact with America. Information from Janet Whatley, "Introduction," in *History of a Voyage to the Land of Brazil*, ed. and trans. Janet Whatley (Berkeley and London: University of California Press, 1990), xv–xviii.
187 Whatley, "Food and the Limits," 387–388.
188 Harriot, *Briefe and True Report*, pl. XIIII.
189 Ibid., pl. XV; Boorde, *A Compendyous Regyment*, sig. E1r.
190 Alison Sim, *Food & Feast in Tudor England* (Stroud: The History Press, 2005), 16. For more detailed analysis of the materiality of early modern kitchens see Sara Pennell, "Getting down from the table: Early modern foodways and material culture," in *The Routledge Handbook of Material Culture in Early Modern Europe*, eds. Catherine Richardson, Tara Hamling and David Gaimster (London and New York: Routledge, 2017), 185–195; Sara Pennell, *The Birth of the English Kitchen, 1600–1850* (London: Bloomsbury, 2016).
191 Gervase Markham, *Countrey Contentments, or The English Huswife* (London, 1623), 57. The popularity of the book is attested to by the fact that it went through nine printings between 1615 and 1683. This information is derived from a search of the English Short Title Catalogue, last accessed 27 November, 2016, http://estc.bl.uk/F/RMULVCU3VFBJEG7BKDH2R97KUB735H6CDS AHJCGY3851DGR51I-15264?func=short-sub.
192 Francis Segar, *The Schoole of Vertue and Booke of Good Nourture for Chyldren*, Second Edition (London, 1557), sigs. B1r–B6v.
193 Sim, *Food & Feast*, 106.
194 Segar, *Schoole of Vertue*, sig. B2r.
195 Harriot, *Briefe and True Report*, pl. XVI.
196 Ibid.
197 Bullein, *Government of Health*, fols. 25–26.
198 Elyot, *Castel of Helth*, fol. 45.
199 Erasmus, *Civilitie of Childehode*, sig. D2v.
200 Stubbes, *Anatomie of Abuses*, sig. M7r.
201 Ibid., sig. I2r.
202 Alexandra Walsham, "Philip Stubbes," ODNB, last accessed 18 June, 2016, www.oxforddnb.com/view/article/26737.
203 For more on the role played by food in early modern confessional identity

see Christopher Kissane, *Food, Religion and Communities in Early Modern Europe* (London: Bloomsbury, 2018); Andrew Morrall, "Protestant Pots: Morality and Social Ritual in the Early Modern Home," *Journal of Design History* 15, no. 4 (2002): 263–273.
204 Harriot, *Briefe and True Report*, 32.
205 Brereton, *Briefe and True Relation*, 5–6.
206 Ibid., 6.
207 Ibid., 11.
208 Ibid., 10.
209 LaCombe, *Political Gastronomy*, 52–53.

Conclusions

In 1612 the Virginia Company, in a bid to drum up financial support for the struggling Jamestown colony that had been blighted since its establishment by failed harvests and hostility from the Powhatan, launched a lottery. In order to illustrate the benefits of playing the lottery Robert Johnson, a principal member of the Virginia Company, wrote a brief history of the colony.[1] Despite the earlier setbacks, Johnson argued that in terms of useful commodities and profitable trade 'no Countrie under heaven' could go beyond Virginia. Johnson bolstered this assertion, which seemed to fly in the face of English experience in the region, by referring to the 'sundrie discourses' that proved Virginia was a land of abundance and rich commodities.[2] Johnson, relying on the rhetoric of the earliest English voyagers to Virginia, including Arthur Barlowe and Thomas Harriot, constructed a positive image of the region and colony that would convince English men and women to play the newly established lottery.

Johnson's use of earlier, positive descriptions of Virginia to encourage the playing of the lottery demonstrates the continued dynamic of adaptation and retention in English approaches to the New World that this book has traced. On the one hand, Johnson's pamphlet shows that English colonial decisions were still being shaped by changing social and economic conditions both in the New World and in England. The emergence of colonial lotteries was part of a larger consumer revolution taking place back in Europe and a consequence of the need to raise revenues to ensure the survival of the fledgling English settlements.[3] On the other hand, the rhetoric employed by Johnson to convince people to play the lottery indicates that his views of Virginia were indebted to older, entrenched, and widely publicised descriptions of the region. Johnson's publication is thus emblematic of an English approach to exploration and colonisation that was a century in the making. This approach was characterised by dynamism and adaptation, and was shaped by changing social, economic, and cultural conditions both at home and in the New World.

This adaptive approach to New World projects, which continued to be employed in the seventeenth century, was the result of decades of translating and transforming images of America that first came from continental Europe; of utilising and adapting intellectual and cultural frameworks of understanding to explain the existence of this new and shockingly different world; of experiencing and responding to both English colonial failure and success; and of incorporating the peoples and environments of America into the mental world of early modern England in an attempt to persuade English men and women to make the difficult decision to cross the Atlantic in search of a new life. It was in the sixteenth century that the English first came to understand and define the new lands across the Atlantic and how they came to craft their own approach to exploration and colonisation that would challenge their rivals and restore the English realm to economic and political health. The sixteenth-century English encounter with America, although at times sporadic and limited to a small group of interested parties, was foundational, establishing and defining the multiplicity of approaches to English overseas expansion that would continue to characterise English New World projects in the seventeenth century.

It was in the sixteenth century that important debates surrounding colonial legitimacy, the function of English colonies, and the practicalities of settlement in the new and exotic lands of the New World first came to the fore. Theories on American origins that were first developed in the sixteenth century became crucial tools of colonial legitimisation, proving Elizabeth I's lawful title to the lands of North America through her genealogical connection with the Welsh Prince Madoc and being used as evidence for the existence of a Northwest Passage to Asia that could be secured by the English. The appearance of Indigenous peoples, particularly in the regions of Newfoundland and Virginia, also validated English enterprises. By proving, in their own minds at least, that the Indigenous population had the potential, and indeed desire, to receive English civility and religion, commentators and advocates of overseas expansion attempted to convince their readers that English settlement in America was both necessary for the spiritual health of Indigenous communities and desirable for those back home that wished to recreate English society in the lands of North America.

It was also in the sixteenth century that ideas about what exactly English colonies in the New World should look like were first articulated. The development of an approach to exploration and colonisation in which godliness and material gain became intertwined objectives was the result of a decades-long process of exploration followed by assessment and adaptation. This mixture of godly settlement and material exploitation would continue to characterise the early English colonies in North America, whether in Virginia, Plymouth, or Massachusetts Bay, shaping both the economic and cultural life of these early settlements.[4] The practicalities of English settlement in the New World also drew much comment from those writing about America in the sixteenth century. English interest in the American environment and American peoples was by no means purely academic. These early observations of the American landscape helped construct rhetorical strategies that would have far-reaching consequences, confirming that English settlement was not possible in the far north of Meta Incognita and establishing the belief that the more southerly regions of North America were home to an abundant and fertile environment that would easily support English colonies. A crucial aspect of this strategy was establishing whether or not English bodies could survive in the foreign lands of America. In the explorations of Meta Incognita in the 1570s, the dietary practices of the Inuit had illustrated just how difficult English settlement in this region would be: the Inuit ate raw and spoiled meat, foods that sixteenth-century English men and women considered deeply unhealthy and corporeally corrupting, while the local environment provided little sustenance for visiting explorers, and provisions from England were difficult to maintain in the face of hostile seas and even more hostile local inhabitants. With the growing acceptance that successful English settlement in the Far North was unlikely, those Englishmen wishing to establish colonies in the New World largely abandoned their plans of finding a Northwest Passage to Asia, instead turning their focus to the more southerly regions of North America where they hoped prosperous trading links with Indigenous peoples could be created. With this new focus came a newly found optimism towards the American environment. Instead of finding dearth and want, as had been the case in Meta Incognita, explorers involved in the early Virginia project found a land that they believed to be abundant and filled with suitable foods that would complement the natural English constitution. This discourse of abundance became highly pervasive and undoubtedly contributed to the continuing English efforts to plant a colony in Virginia after the failure at Roanoke. The English belief in American abundance would go on to have a detrimental impact on the early English colonies of North America, where food was often scarce and difficult to source. The colonists of Jamestown had been convinced by the writers of the 1580s that sourcing appropriate food in Virginia was simple and required little effort, a belief that would lead the colony to the brink of starvation in 1609 and to a re-evaluation of their understanding of abundance.[5] Sixteenth-century English portrayals of the American environment and its perceived effects on both English and Indigenous bodies thus played a significant role in dictating which regions of the New World were suitable for English settlement, advocating the abandonment of colonial plans in the Far North and the concentration of colonial effort further south, thus cementing English patterns of colonisation in the Americas for decades to come.

As well as establishing the centrality of the sixteenth century in the development of English approaches to New World exploration and settlement, this book has also examined the complex process by which these approaches were created. By challenging the often-stated assertion that English understandings of America were in some way static, or even non-existent, during the majority of the sixteenth century, it is now clear that English beliefs about America, and indeed the English approach to exploration and colonisation in the region, were highly volatile and changeable, being determined by an ever-fluctuating set of factors.[6] Early English representations of America were a complex composite of various cultural influences, both consciously and unconsciously employed. English understandings of bodily health, the dispersal of humankind, the history of the British Isles, correct religious observation, and contemporary worries about moral decay, the rise of luxury, and economic decline were all assembled and redeployed in the context of English activity in the Americas. Those men who attempted to make sense of the new and unknown American environment employed a diverse set of cultural tools and materials that were available to them in the sixteenth century. These cultural instruments allowed English commentators to variously explain the existence of the Indigenous peoples of the Americas in a way that was beneficial to their colonial objectives, to confirm that the lands of North America would not have a detrimental effect on English bodies, both in terms of climate and diet, and to make claims about the potential civility of Indigenous communities based on their behaviour and appearance. Early English understandings of the New World were, therefore, very much a product of sixteenth-century English culture. The portrayals of America found in English print, and their subsequent use in the formation of English plans for overseas expansion, not only reflected the ways in which English commentators understood exotic 'others' but also how they understood themselves and their own society.

The early English encounter with America was dynamic and flexible. As the cultural apparatus of the sixteenth-century English changed, so too did their understandings of America. This changing cultural equipment was shaped by events taking place in both England and the regions of America that the English set out to explore. The English move towards Protestantism and the establishment of the Church of England unsurprisingly affected the English view of America. In the early 1550s, when the Protestant Edward VI sat on the throne, Richard Eden advocated a godly approach to colonialism in the Americas that looked towards Spain for ideas on how this could be implemented, but without suggesting direct emulation and alliance with their Catholic rival. On the accession of Mary I, this attitude shifted. With the return of Catholicism to the realm and with the marriage of the queen to Philip II of Spain, Eden began to suggest instead that the English should seek to emulate and work alongside the Spanish in America, focusing their attention on the regions of the new continent that were not of interest to the increasingly powerful Imperial Spain. In the 1560s and 1570s, when English involvement in the Americas was largely characterised by failure and disappointment, English writers began to rethink their approach, worrying that God had deserted them. This providential understanding of English colonialism encouraged those men who were interested in establishing permanent English overseas settlements to put godliness at the heart of their programmes, arguing that great riches would undoubtedly follow thanks to God's good favour. Changing domestic religious concerns thus collided with English experience in America, being incorporated into English understandings of the New World and early English plans for colonisation. Domestic economic concerns also permeated English accounts of America. The idea that the naked peoples of America would become consumers of English cloth, a trade that had been dwindling from the 1560s onwards, became particularly potent. By identifying what they perceived to be an Indigenous desire for English civility, English colonisers connected their observations of Indigenous peoples with the economic distress taking hold back home. Likewise, the belief that the Virginian environment could sustain a large English population was used to convince people to make the journey across the Atlantic, promising a better life than the one endured back in England, where failed harvests and scarce food supplies were a common occurrence.

Early English portrayals of the New World were also indebted to ideas and images of America from continental European texts and to influences from British history, medieval ethnography, and classical geography. Accounts of the New World that appeared in English print, therefore, were highly attuned to a wider European context of exploration and colonisation. By selectively appropriating and manipulating continental European images of America, alongside classical and medieval theories that attempted to explain the existence of foreign peoples and environments, English writers transformed these images in order to meet the demands of their own projects. Ideas relating to human diversity, monstrosity, and climate that were first articulated in an American context by Spanish and French explorers in the early decades of the sixteenth century, were appropriated and remodelled by the English to help validate their burgeoning colonial programmes. Just as continental European writers had found these ideas useful for framing their colonial projects, so too did the English. The theory that America was Atlantis, while used by the Spanish as a means of bolstering their American conversion project, was employed by English writers to validate their beliefs in the existence of a Northwest Passage to Asia. While the unravelling of classical climate theory by early explorers in America could be used to comment on the incomplete nature of early modern European knowledge and the errors of classical geographers, English explorers used this change in understanding to manipulate ideas about climate in an attempt to prove the habitability of the Far North. Continuing the French and Spanish trend of portraying Indigenous people as wild and savage, an idea that was undoubtedly influenced by classical and medieval ethnography, those writing about English exploits in America moulded this image into a range of useful, multi-functional forms, both positive and negative. While continental European images of America undoubtedly circulated in sixteenth-century England, then, they were often transformed and adapted to meet the specific needs and objectives of an emerging English colonial discourse.

The influence of other competing colonial nations on English ideas about America could also be far more divisive, leading to complete divergences rather than selective appropriations. Nowhere is this more clearly evident than in the deteriorating relationship between England and Spain in the late sixteenth century. As Anglo-Spanish hostility grew with the accession of Elizabeth I, Spanish colonialism increasingly became a target of English jealousy and outright criticism. The English began to define their colonial programme in opposition to that of the Spanish model, both implicitly and explicitly, highlighting how they, unlike the Spanish, could conquer through kindness, maintain control of Indigenous populations, and bring about their true conversion to Christianity. English writers, in texts both directly and indirectly related to European overseas projects, critiqued the Spanish approach to colonisation, claiming that the Spanish *conquistadores'* only motive for conquest was the gaining of Indigenous treasure. While the Spanish, in the minds of the sixteenth-century English at least, tortured and murdered huge numbers of Indigenous people in pursuit of this impious and avaricious goal, English advocates of overseas expansion put forward their own vision for the New World in which securing control of Indigenous groups would be achieved through kindness rather than cruelty. While the Spanish undertook conquest and colonisation in a bid to enrich themselves monetarily, the English increasingly claimed that spiritual enrichment was their only colonial objective.

The story of early English exploration and settlement in America is thus undoubtedly one that must be read within an international framework. The history of the British Empire is not one of exceptionalism and national independence, but one of heated rivalry and, at times, cultural interdependence. English ideas about America that shaped a range of explorative and colonial enterprises, were the product of a century-long engagement with the colonial methods of other nations, the transference and adaptation of ideas and theories first proposed in continental Europe, and the concerted

English effort to carve out an approach to overseas settlement that was substantially different to that of their European rivals. This resulted in a set of English images of America that both converged with and diverged from those created by other colonising European nations. English explorers and colonisers appropriated images of America that they found helpful for achieving their own colonial ambitions, while simultaneously creating their own images that allowed for the condemnation of the Spanish approach and the celebration of their own.

This book, although uncovering the rich variety of cultural forces that impacted upon the early English approach to America, has not assessed how this process continued into the later period of English colonialism in North America, nor how it developed in other colonial contexts such as Ireland, the Caribbean, India, Africa, and Australasia. With many historical debates now focused on an extra-European world, and on the multitude of cultural encounters between varied historical actors, there remain numerous avenues of research in which to explore the issues that this book has raised. From examining the cultural connections between English portrayals of the East and the West, to analysing the interplay between New World reality and Old World rhetoric during the period of sustained English colonialism in America from 1607 onwards, a number of important avenues for future research remain open, areas that will further enrich our understanding of the often complex, diverse, and fluctuating ways that the English, and later British, responded to cultural encounters with foreign peoples and foreign environments, and constructed theories of colonialism and imperialism. What remains unescapably clear, however, is that the origins of the British Empire were neither exceptional nor particularly calculated. They were the result of numerous explorative failures, the consequence of adaptations of other more successful colonial models, and the product of a messy trial-and-error approach to overseas expansion.

Notes

1 Robert C. Johnson, "The Lotteries of the Virginia Company, 1612–1621," *The Virginia Magazine of History and Biography* 74, no. 3 (July, 1966): 259–267.
2 Robert Johnson, *The New Life of Virginea* (London, 1612), sigs. G3r–G3v.
3 For more on the colonial lotteries see Neal E. Millikan, *Lotteries in Colonial America* (London: Routledge, 2011).
4 Scholars who have analysed the competing and complementary aspects of this discourse in the context of the seventeenth-century English colonies include Greene, *Pursuits of Happiness;* Kupperman, *Settling with the Indians;* Wright, *Religion and Empire.*

5 Herrmann, "The 'Tragicall Historie'," 49–72.
6 Joyce Chaplin has suggested that the period from 1500 to 1585 represented a distinct phase of English colonisation, allowing for little discussion of change across the sixteenth century. Chaplin, *Subject Matter*, 16–21. Mary Fuller has argued that between 1576 and 1624 English accounts of America were characterised by a rhetorical strategy that attempted to recuperate failure. This analysis therefore fails to examine the many differences between accounts written about Meta Incognita and Virginia. Fuller, *Voyages in Print*. Other scholars have neglected the sixteenth century English approach to America or begun their analysis in the 1580s with the Roanoke voyages. For this scholarship see the Introduction, 21–23.

Bibliography

Printed sources first published before 1607

Abbot, George. *The Reasons Which Doctour Hill Hath Brought, for the Upholding of Papistry, which is Falselie Termed the Catholike Religion*. London, 1604.
Abbot, George. *A Briefe Description of the Whole Worlde*. London, 1599.
Acosta, José de Acosta. *The Naturall and Morall Historie of the East and West Indies*. London, 1604.
Anon. *Of the Newe La[n]des and of ye People Founde by the Messengers of the Kynge of Porty[n]gale*. Antwerp, 1520.
Anon. *The Deceyte of Women*. London, 1557.
Anon. *Holy Byble*. London, 1576.
Anon. "The Course Which Sir *Francis Drake* Held from the Haven of *Guatulco* in the South Sea on the Backe Side of *Nueva Espanna*, to the Northwest of *California*." In *The Principal Navigations, Voyages, Traffiques and Discoveries of the English Nation*, vol. 3, edited by Richard Hakluyt, 440–442. London, 1598–1600.
Anon. "The Letters Patents Graunted by her Majestie to Sir Humfrey Gilbert Knight, for the Inhabiting and Planting of our People in America." In *The Principal Navigations, Voyages, Traffiques and Discoveries of the English Nation*, vol. 3, edited by Richard Hakluyt, 135–137. London, 1598–1600.
Anon. "The Two Famous Voyages Happily Perfourmed Round About the World, by Sir Francis Drake, and M. Thomas Candish Esquire." In *The Principal Navigations, Voyages, Traffiques and Discoveries of the English Nation*, vol. 3, edited by Richard Hakluyt, 731–742. London, 1598–1600.
Babington, Gervase. *Certaine Plaine, Briefe, and Comfortable Notes Upon Everie Chapter of Genesis*. London, 1592.
Barlowe, Arthur. "The First Voyage Made to the Coasts of America, with Two Barks, Where in were Captaines M. Philip Amadas, and M. Arthur Barlowe." In *The Principal Navigations, Voyages, Traffiques and Discoveries of the English Nation*, vol. 3, edited by Richard Hakluyt, 246–251. London, 1598–1600.
Best, George. *A True Discourse of the Late Voyages of Discoverie, for the Finding of a Passage to Cathaya*. London, 1578.
Bigges, Walter. *A Summarie and True Discourse of Sir Frances Drakes West Indian Voyage*. London, 1589.
Blundeville, Thomas. *M. Blundevile his Exercises*. London, 1594.
Boazio, Baptista. *The Famouse West Indian Voyadge Made by the Englishe Fleete*. London, 1589.

Bodin, Jean. *The Six Bookes of a Common-weale*. Translated by Richard Knolles. London, 1606.
Boorde, Andrew. *A Compendyous Regyment or a Dyetary of Helth*. London, 1547.
Boorde, Andrew. *The Breviarie of Health*. London, 1587.
Bourne, William. *A Booke Called the Treasure for Traveilers*. London, 1578.
Brereton, John. *A Briefe and True Relation of the Discoverie of the North Part of Virginia Being a Most Pleasant, Fruitfull and Commodious Soile*. London, 1602.
Bullein, William. *A Dialogue Bothe Pleasaunte and Pietifull*. London, 1564.
Bullein, William. *The Government of Health*. London, 1595.
Calvin, John. *A Commentarie of John Calvin Upon the First Booke of Moses Called Genesis*. Translated by Thomas Tymme. London, 1578.
Carleill, Christopher. *A Breef and Sommarie Discourse Upon the Entended Voyage to the Hethermoste Partes of America*. London, 1583.
Carleill, Christopher. "A Briefe and Summary Discourse upon the Intended Voyage to the Hithermost Parts of America." In *The Principal Navigations, Voyages, Traffiques and Discoveries of the English Nation*, vol. 3, edited by Richard Hakluyt, 182–187. London, 1598–1600.
Cartier, Jacques. *A Shorte and Briefe Narration of the Two Navigations and Discoveries to the Northweast Partes called Newe Fraunce*. Translated by John Florio. London, 1580.
Chilton, John. "A Notable Discourse of M. John Chilton, Touching the People, Maners, Mines, Cities, Riches, Forces, and Other Memorable Things of New Spaine, and Other Provinces in the West Indies." In *The Principal Navigations, Voyages, Traffiques and Discoveries of the English Nation*, vol. 3, edited by Richard Hakluyt, 455–462. London, 1598–1600.
Churchyard, Thomas. *A Prayse, and Reporte of Maister Martyne Forboishers Voyage to Meta Incognita*. London, 1578.
Chute, Anthony. *Tabacco*. London, 1595.
Cleaver, Robert. *A Godlie Forme of Householde*. London, 1598.
Cooper, Thomas. *A Briefe Exposition of Such Chapters of the Olde Testament*. London, 1573.
Cortés, Martín. *The Arte of Navigation Conteyning a Compendious Description of the Sphere*. Translated by Richard Eden. London, 1561.
Crowley, Robert. *The Voyce of the Laste Trumpet Blowen*. London, 1549.
Cuningham, William. *The Cosmographical Glasse*. London, 1559.
Ellis, Thomas. *A True Report of the Third and Last Voyage into Meta Incognita*. London, 1578.
Elyot, Thomas. *The Castel of Helth*. London, 1539.
Erasmus, Desiderius. *The Civilitie of Childehode*, second edition. Translated by Thomas Paynell. London, 1560.
Fernández de Enciso, Martín. *A Briefe Description of the Portes, Creekes, Bayes, and Havens, of the Weast India*. Translated by John Frampton. London, 1578.
Galvão, António. *The Discoveries of the World from their First Originall unto the Yeere of our Lord 1555*. Translated by Richard Hakluyt. London, 1601.
Gerard, John. *The Herball or Generall Historie of Plantes*. London, 1633.
Gilbert, Humphrey. *A Discourse of a Discoverie for a New Passage to Cataia*. London, 1576.

González de Mendoza, Juan. *New Mexico Otherwise, The Voiage of Anthony of Espeio.* Translated by Francesco Avanzi. London, 1587.
Gosson, Stephen. *Playes Confuted in Five Actions.* London, 1582.
Greepe, Thomas. *The True and Perfecte Newes of the Woorthy and Valiaunt Exploytes, Performed and Doone by that Valiant Knight Syr Frauncis Drake.* London, 1587.
Hakluyt, Richard, ed. *Divers Voyages Touching the Discoverie of America.* London, 1582.
Hakluyt, Richard, ed. *The Principal Navigations, Voyages, Traffiques and Discoveries of the English Nation.* London, 1589.
Hakluyt, Richard, ed. *The Principal Navigations, Voyages, Traffiques and Discoveries of the English Nation.* London, 1598-1600.
Hakluyt the elder, Richard. "Inducements to the Liking of the Voyage Intended Towards Virginia." In *A Briefe and True Relation of the Discoverie of the North Part of Virginia Being a Most Pleasant, Fruitfull and Commodious Soile,* edited by John Brereton, 25-36. London, 1602.
Harriot, Thomas. *A Briefe and True Report of the New Found Land of Virginia.* London, 1588.
Harriot, Thomas. *A Briefe and True Report of the New Found Land of Virginia.* Frankfurt, 1590.
Hawkins, John. *A True Declaration of the Troublesome Voyadge of M. John Haukins to the Parties of Guynea and the West Indies.* London, 1569.
Hayes, Edward. "A Report of the Voyage and Successe Thereof, Attempted in the Yeere of our Lord 1583 by Sir Humfrey Gilbert Knight." In *The Principal Navigations, Voyages, Traffiques and Discoveries of the English Nation,* vol. 3, edited by Richard Hakluyt, 143-161. London, 1598-1600.
Hayes, Edward. "A Treatise, Conteining Important Inducements for the Planting in these Parts, and Finding a Passage that Way to the South Sea and China." In *A Briefe and True Relation of the Discoverie of the North Part of Virginia Being a Most Pleasant, Fruitfull and Commodious Soile,* edited by John Brereton, 15-24. London, 1602.
Hortop, Job. *The Rare Travailes of Job Hortop.* London, 1591.
Hortop, Job. *The Travailes of an English Man Containing his Sundrie Calalmities.* London, 1591.
Huygen van Linschoten, Jan. *Itinerario, Voyage ofte Schipvaert / van Jan Huygen van Linschoten naer Dost ofte Portugaels Indien.* Amsterdam, 1596.
Huygen van Linschoten, Jan. *John Huighen van Linschoten. His Discours of Voyages Into ye Easte & West Indies.* Translated by William Phillip. London, 1598.
James I, King of England. *A Counterblaste to Tobacco.* London, 1604.
Keymis, Lawrence. *A Relation of the Second Voyage to Guiana.* London, 1596.
Lane, Ralph. "An Account of the Particularities of the Imployments of the English Men Left in Virginia by Sir Richard Greenevill." In *The Principal Navigations, Voyages, Traffiques and Discoveries of the English Nation,* vol. 3, edited by Richard Hakluyt, 255-260. London, 1598-1600.
Las Casas, Bartolomé de. *Brevissima Relacion de la Destruycion de las Indias.* Seville, 1552.
Las Casas, Bartolomé de. *The Spanish Colonie.* Translated by M. M. S. London, 1583.

Laudonnière, René Goulaine de. *L'histoire Notable de la Floride*. Paris, 1586.
Laudonnière, René Goulaine de. *A Notable Historie Containing Foure Voyages Made by Certayne French Captaynes unto Florida*. Translated by Richard Hakluyt. London, 1587.
Le Challeux, Nicolas. *A True and Perfect Description, of the Last Voyage or Navigation, Attempted by Capitaine John Rybaut*. London, 1566.
López de Gómara, Francisco. *La Historia General de las Indias*. Antwerp, 1554.
López de Gómara, Francisco. *The Pleasant Historie of the Conquest of the Weast India, Now Called New Spayne*. Translated by Thomas Nicholls. London, 1578.
Martyr, Peter. *The Decades of the Newe Worlde or West India*. Translated by Richard Eden. London, 1555.
Martyr, Peter. *The History of Travayle in the West and East Indies*. Translated by Richard Eden and Richard Willes. London, 1577.
Monardes, Nicholas. *Joyfull Newes out of the Newe Founde Worlde*. Translated by John Frampton. London, 1577.
Montaigne, Michel de. *The Essayes or Morall, Politike and Millitarie Discourses of Lo: Michaell de Montaigne*. Translated by John Florio. London, 1603.
More, Thomas. *A Fruteful, and Pleasaunt Worke of the Beste State of a Publyque Weale, and of the Newe Yle Called Utopia*. London, 1551.
Münster, Sebastian. *A Treatyse of the Newe India With Other New Founde Landes and Islandes*. Translated by Richard Eden. London, 1553.
Nicholl, John. *An Houre Glasse of Indian Newes*. London, 1607.
Ortelius, Abraham. *An Epitome of Ortelius his Theater of the World*. London, 1601.
Parkhurst, Anthony. "A Letter Written to M. *Richard Hakluyt* of the middle Temple, Conteining a Report of the True State and Commodities of Newfoundland." In *The Principal Navigations, Voyages, Traffiques and Discoveries of the English Nation*, vol. 3, edited by Richard Hakluyt, 132–134. London, 1598–1600.
Peckham, George. *A True Reporte, of the Late Discoveries, and Possession, Taken in the Right of the Crowne of Englande*. London, 1583.
Peckham, George. "A True Report of the Late Discoveries, and Possession Taken in the Right of the Crowne of England." In *The Principal Navigations, Voyages, Traffiques and Discoveries of the English Nation*, vol. 3, edited by Richard Hakluyt, 165–181. London, 1598–1600.
Philips, Miles. "A Discourse Written by One *Miles Philips* Englishman, One of the Company Put on Shoare Northward of Panuco, in the West Indies by M. John Hawkins 1568." In *The Principal Navigations, Voyages, Traffiques and Discoveries of the English Nation*, vol. 3, edited by Richard Hakluyt, 469–487. London, 1598–1600.
Powell, David. *The Historie of Cambria, Now Called Wales*. London, 1584.
Powell, David. "The Most Ancient Discovery of the West Indies by Madoc the Sonne of Owen Guyneth Prince of North-Wales, in the Yeere 1170." In *The Principal Navigations, Voyages, Traffiques and Discoveries of the English Nation*, vol. 3, edited by Richard Hakluyt, 1. London, 1598–1600.
Ralegh, Walter. *The Discoverie of the Large, Rich, and Bewtiful Empire of Guiana*. London, 1596.
Rastell, John. *A New Interlude and a Mery, of the Nature of the iiij Elements*. London, 1520.

Ribault, Jean. *The Whole and True Discoverye of Terra Florida*. Translated by Thomas Hacket. London, 1563.
Rosier, James. *A True Relation of the Most Prosperous Voyage Made this Present Yeere 1605*. London, 1605.
Seall, Robert. *A Commendation of the Adventerus Viage of the Wurthy Captain M. Thomas Stutely Esquyer and Others, Towards the Land Called Terra Florida*. London, 1563.
Segar, Francis. *The Schoole of Vertue and Booke of Good Nourture for Chyldren*, second edition. London, 1557.
Settle, Dionyse. *A True Reporte of the Laste Voyage into the West and Northwest Regions, &c. 1577*. London, 1577.
Shakespeare, William. *The Tragicall Historie of Hamlet Prince of Denmarke*. London, 1603.
Smith, Henry. *The Sermons of Master Henry Smith*. London, 1593.
Stubbes, Philip. *The Anatomie of Abuses*. London, 1583.
Thevet, André. *Les Singularitez de la France Antactique*. Paris, 1558.
Thevet, André. *The New Found Worlde, or Antarktike*. Translated by Thomas Hacket. London, 1568.
Tilney, Edmund. *A Brief and Pleasant Discourse of Duties in Mariage*. London, 1568.
Topsell, Edward. *Times Lamentation: or an Exposition on the Prophet Joel*. London, 1599.
Wateson, George. *The Cures of the Diseased, in Remote Regions*. London, 1598.
Zárate, Agustín de. *Historia del Descubrimiento y Conquista del Peru*. Antwerp, 1555.
Zárate, Agustín de. *The Strange and Delectable History of the Discoverie and Conquest of Peru*. London, 1581.

Primary sources published after 1607

Anon. *The Voyages & Travels of that Renowned Captain, Sir Francis Drake, into the West-Indies*. London, 1652.
Barlow, Roger. *A Brief Summe of Geographie*. Edited by E.G.R. Taylor. London: The Hakluyt Society, 1932.
Charron, Pierre. *Of Wisdome Three Bookes Written in French by Peter Charro[n]*. Translated by Samson Lennard. London, 1608.
Columbus, Christopher. "A Letter Written by Don Christopher Columbus, Viceroy and Admiral of the Indies, to the Most Christian and Mighty Sovereigns, the King and Queen of Spain." In *Select Letters of Christopher Columbus, With Other Original Documents Relating to the Four Voyages to the New World*, edited and translated by R. H. Major esq., 169–203. London: The Hakluyt Society, 1847.
Columbus, Christopher. *The Journal of Christopher Columbus*. Translated by Cecil Jane. London: Anthony Blond & the Orion Press, 1960.
Dee, John. "Unto your Majesties Tytle Royall to these Forene Regions & Ilandes." In *John Dee: The Limits of the British Empire*, edited by Ken MacMillan and Jennifer Abeles, 43–50. Westport, CT and London: Praeger, 2004.
Johnson, Robert. *The New Life of Virginea*. London, 1612.
Llywd, Humphrey. *Cronica Walliae*, edited by Ieuan M. Williams. Cardiff: University of Wales Press, 2002.
Markham, Gervase. *Countrey Contentments, or The English Huswife*. London, 1623.

de Oviedo, Gonzalo Fernández. *Historia General y Natural de las Indias*, edited by José Amador de los Rios. Madrid: La Real Academia de la Historia, 1851.
Smith, John. *The Generall Historie of Virginia*. London, 1624.

Secondary sources

Abbot, W. W. *The Colonial Origins of the United States, 1607–1763*. New York: Wiley, 1975.
Afanasiev, Valeri. "The Literary Heritage of Bartolomé de Las Casas." In *Bartolomé de Las Casas in History: Toward an Understanding of the Man and his Work*, edited by Juan Friede and Benjamin Keen, 539–578. DeKalb: Northern Illinois University Press, 1971.
Albala, Ken. *Eating Right in the Renaissance*. Berkeley: University of California Press, 2002.
Albala, Ken. *Food in Early Modern Europe*. Westport, CT: Greenwood Press, 2003.
Almond, Philip C. *Adam & Eve in Seventeenth-Century Thought*. Cambridge: Cambridge University Press, 1999.
Andrews, Kenneth R. *Trade, Plunder and Settlement: Maritime Enterprise and the Genesis of the British Empire, 1480–1630*. Cambridge: Cambridge University Press, 1984.
Appelbaum, Robert. "Hunger in Early Virginia: Indians and English Facing Off Over Excess, Want, and Need." In *Envisioning an English Empire: Jamestown and the Making of the North Atlantic World*, edited by Robert Appelbaum and John Wood Sweet, 195–216. Philadelphia: University of Pennsylvania Press, 2005.
Appelbaum, Robert. *Aguecheek's Beef, Belch's Hiccup, and Other Gastronomic Interjections: Literature, Culture, and Food Among the Early Moderns*. Chicago: University of Chicago Press, 2006.
Appleby, John C. "War, Politics, and Colonization, 1558–1625." In *The Oxford History of the British Empire*, vol. 1: *The Origins of Empire: British Overseas Enterprise to the Close of the Seventeenth Century*, edited by Nicholas Canny, 55–78. Oxford: Oxford University Press, 1998.
Appleby, Joyce et al., eds. *The American Vision*. New York: McGraw Hill Education, 2001.
Armitage, David. *The Ideological Origins of the British Empire*. Cambridge: Cambridge University Press, 2000.
Armitage, David and Jo Guldi, *The History Manifesto*. Cambridge: Cambridge University Press, 2014.
Armitage, David and Michael J. Braddick, eds. *The British Atlantic World, 1500–1800*. Basingstoke: Palgrave Macmillan, 2009.
Armstrong, Catherine. "Representations of American 'Place' and 'Potential' in English Travel Literature, 1607–1660." PhD dissertation, University of Warwick, 2004.
Armstrong, Catherine. *Writing North America in the Seventeenth Century: English Representations in Print and Manuscript*. Farnham: Ashgate, 2007.
Axtell, James. *The European and the Indian: Essays in the Ethnohistory of Colonial North America*. New York and Oxford: Oxford University Press, 1981.
Baker, Ted and Reed E. Nelson. "Creating Something from Nothing: Resource Construction through Entrepreneurial Bricolage." *Administrative Science Quarterly* 50, no. 3 (September, 2005): 329–366.

Barrera, Antonio. "Local Herbs, Global Medicine, Commerce, Knowledge, and Commodities in Spanish America." In *Merchants and Marvels: Commerce, Science and Art in Early Modern Europe*, edited by Pamela Smith and Paula Findlen, 163–181. London: Routledge, 2002.

Bartlett, Robert. "Medieval and Modern Concepts of Race and Ethnicity." *Journal of Medieval and Early Modern Studies* 31, no. 1 (Winter, 2001): 39–56.

Behringer, Wolfgang. *A Cultural History of Climate*. London: Polity Press, 2009.

Beier, A. L. *The Problem of the Poor in Tudor and Stuart England*. London: Methuen, 1983.

Belfanti, Carlo Marco and Fabio Giusberti. "Clothing and Social Inequality in Early Modern Europe: Introductory Remarks." *Continuity and Change* 15, no. 3 (December, 2000): 359–365.

Ben-Amos, Ilana Krausman. *The Culture of Giving: Informal Support and Gift-Exchange in Early Modern England*. Cambridge: Cambridge University Press, 2008.

Bennett, H. S. *English Books and Readers, 1558–1603*, vol. 2. Cambridge: Cambridge University Press, 1965.

Bergdolt, Klaus. *Wellbeing: A Cultural History of Healthy Living*. Translated by Jane Dewhurst. Cambridge: Polity Press, 2008.

Berkhofer Jr., Robert F. *The White Man's Indian: Images of the American Indian from Columbus to the Present*. New York: Knopf, 1978.

Bernhard Jackson, Gabriele. "Topical Ideology: Witches, Amazons, and Shakespeare's Joan of Arc." *English Literary Renaissance* 18, no. 1 (December, 1988): 40–65.

Bernheimer, Richard. *Wild Men in the Middle Ages: A Study in Art, Sentiment, and Demonology*. Cambridge, MA: Harvard University Press, 1952.

Bildhauer, Bettina and Robert Mills, eds. *The Monstrous Middle Ages*. Toronto: University of Toronto Press, 2003.

Billings, Warren M. *Jamestown and The Founding of the Nation*. Gettysburg, PA: Thomas Publications, 1990.

Boia, Lucian. *The Weather in the Imagination*. Translated by Roger Leverdier. London: Reaktion Books, 2005.

Bolaños, Álvaro Félix. "The Historian and the Hesperides: Gonzalo Fernández de Oviedo and the Limitations of Imitation." *Bulletin of Hispanic Studies* 72, no. 3 (1995): 273–287.

Bonavia, Duccio. *Maize: Origin, Domestication, and its Role in the Development of Culture*. Translated by Javier Flores Espinoza. Cambridge: Cambridge University Press, 2013.

Borge, Francisco J. *A New World for a New Nation: The Promotion of America in Early Modern England*. Oxford: Peter Lang, 2007.

Bovey, Alixe. *Monsters & Grotesques in Medieval Manuscripts*. Toronto: University of Toronto Press, 2002.

Boyer, Paul S. et al., eds. *The Enduring Vision: A History of the American People*. Boston, MA and New York: Houghton Mifflin Company, 2006.

Braddick, Michael J. *State Formation in Early Modern England, c. 1550–1700*. Cambridge: Cambridge University Press, 2000.

Braham, Persephone. "The Monstrous Caribbean." In *The Ashgate Research Companion to Monsters and the Monstrous*, edited by Asa Mittman and Peter J. Dendle, 17–47. Farnham: Ashgate, 2012.

Breitenberg, Mark. *Anxious Masculinity in Early Modern England*. Cambridge: Cambridge University Press, 1996.
Brennan, Michael G. "The Literature of Travel." In *The Cambridge History of the Book in Britain, 1557–1695*, vol. 4, edited by John Barnard and D. F. McKenzie, 246–273. Cambridge: Cambridge University Press, 2014.
Brenner, Robert. *Merchants and Revolution: Commercial Change, Political Conflict, and London's Overseas Traders, 1550–1653*. London and New York: Verso Books, 2003.
Brookes, Kristen G. "Inhaling the Alien: Race and Tobacco in Early Modern England." In *Global Traffic: Discourses and Practices of Trade in English Literature and Culture from 1550–1700*, edited by Barbara Sebek and Stephen Deng, 157–178. New York: Palgrave Macmillan, 2008.
Bryson, Anna. *From Courtesy to Civility: Changing Codes of Conduct in Early Modern England*. Oxford: Oxford University Press, 1998.
Bucher, Bernadette. *Icon and Conquest: A Structural Analysis of the Illustrations of de Bry's Great Voyages*. Translated by Basia Miller Gulati. Chicago and London: University of Chicago Press, 1981.
Bumas, E. Shaskan. "The Cannibal Butcher Shop: Protestant Uses of Las Casas's Brevisima Relacion in Europe and the American Colonies." *Early American Literature* 35, no. 2 (2000): 107–136.
Burke, Jill. "Nakedness and Other Peoples: Rethinking the Italian Renaissance Nude." *Art History* 36, no. 4 (September, 2013): 714–739.
Burton, Jonathan. "Western Encounters with Sex and Bodies in Non-European Cultures, 1500–1750." In *The Routledge History of Sex and the Body, 1500 to the Present*, edited by Sarah Toulalan and Kate Fisher, 495–510. London and New York: Routledge, 2013.
Bushnell, Rebecca W. *A Culture of Teaching: Early Modern Humanism in Theory and Practice*. Ithaca, NY and London: Cornell University Press, 1996.
Byrd Simpson, Lesley. "Introduction." In *Cortés: The Life of the Conqueror by His Secretary Francisco López de Gómara*, edited and translated by Lesley Byrd Simpson, xv–xxvi. Berkeley and London: University of California Press, 1964.
Camargo, Martin. "The Book of John Mandeville and the Geography of Identity." In *Marvels, Monsters, and Miracles: Studies in the Medieval and Early Modern Imaginations*, edited by Timothy S. Jones and David A. Sprunger, 67–84. Kalamazoo, MI: Medieval Institute Publications, 2002.
Campbell, Mary B. *The Witness and the Other World: Exotic European Travel Writing, 400–1600*. Ithaca, NY and London: Cornell University Press, 1988.
Campbell, Mary B. *Wonder & Science: Imagining Worlds in Early Modern Europe*. Ithaca, NY and London: Cornell University Press, 1999.
Camporesi, Piero. *Bread of Dreams: Food and Fantasy in Early Modern Europe*. Translated by David Gentilcore. Chicago: University of Chicago Press, 1989.
Cañizares-Esguerra, Jorge. *Puritan Conquistadors: Iberianizing the Atlantic, 1550–1700*. Stanford: Stanford University Press, 2006.
Cañizares-Esguerra, Jorge. "Entangled Histories: Borderland Historiographies in New Clothes?" *The American Historical Review* 112, no. 3 (June, 2007): 787–799.
Cañizares-Esguerra, Jorge. "Introduction." In *Entangled Empires: The Anglo-Iberian Atlantic, 1500–1830*, edited by Jorge Cañizares-Esguerra, 1–15. Philadelphia: University of Pennsylvania Press, 2018.

Canny, Nicholas. *The Elizabethan Conquest of Ireland: A Pattern Established, 1565–76*. New York: Barnes and Noble, 1976.
Canny, Nicholas. *Kingdom and Colony: Ireland in the Atlantic World, 1560–1800*. Baltimore, MD and London: Johns Hopkins University Press, 1988.
Canny, Nicholas. "The Origins of Empire: an Introduction." In *The Oxford History of the British Empire*, vol. 1: *The Origins of Empire: British Overseas Enterprise to the Close of the Seventeenth Century*, edited by Nicholas Canny, 1–33. Oxford: Oxford University Press, 1998.
Carney, Judith A. and Richard Nicholas Rosomoff. *In the Shadow of Slavery: Africa's Botanical Legacy in the Atlantic World*. Berkeley: University of California Press, 2009.
Cavallo, Sandra and Tessa Storey. *Healthy Living in Late Renaissance Italy*. Oxford: Oxford University Press, 2013.
Cave, Alfred A. "Canaanites in a Promised Land: the American Indian and the Providential Theory of Empire." *American Indian Quarterly* 12, no. 4 (Autumn, 1998): 277–297.
Cervantes, Fernando. *The Devil in the New World: The Impact of Diabolism in New Spain*. New Haven, CT and London: Yale University Press, 1994.
Chaplin, Joyce E. *Subject Matter: Technology, the Body, and Science on the Anglo-American Frontier, 1500–1676*. Cambridge, MA and London: Harvard University Press, 2001.
Chaplin, Joyce E. "Roanoke 'Counterfeited According to the Truth.'" In *A New World: England's First View of America*, edited by Kim Sloan, 51–64. Chapel Hill: The University of North Carolina Press, 2007.
Chartier, Roger. *The Author's Hand and the Printer's Mind*. Translated by Lydia G. Cochrane. Cambridge: Polity Press, 2014.
Chiappelli, Fredi, ed. *First Images of America: The Impact of the New World on the Old*, vol. 1. Berkeley and London: University of California Press, 1976.
Clendinnen, Inga. "'Fierce and Unnatural Cruelty': Cortés and the Conquest of Mexico." In *New World Encounters*, edited by Stephen Greenblatt, 12–47. Berkeley: University of California Press, 1993.
Clendinnen, Inga. *Ambivalent Conquests: Maya and Spaniard in Yucatan, 1517–1570*. Cambridge and New York: Cambridge University Press, 2003.
Clucas, Stephen. "Thomas Harriot's *A Briefe and True Report*: Knowledge-Making and the Roanoke Voyage." In *European Visions: American Voices*, edited by Kim Sloan, 17–23. London: British Museum Press, 2009.
Coffey, John. *Persecution and Toleration in Protestant England, 1558–1689*. Harlow, UK and New York: Longman, 2000.
Cogley, Richard W. "John Eliot and the Origins of the American Indians." *Early American Literature* 21, no. 3 (Winter, 1986/87): 210–225.
Cogley, Richard W. "'Some Other Kinde of Being and Condition': the Controversy in Mid-Seventeenth-Century England over the Peopling of Ancient America." *Journal of the History of Ideas* 68, no. 1 (January, 2007): 35–56.
Cohen, Jeffrey Jerome. *Of Giants: Sex, Monsters and the Middle Ages*. Minneapolis: University of Minnesota Press, 1999.
Colin, Susi. "The Wild Man and the Indian in Early 16th Century Book Illustration." In *Indians & Europe: An Interdisciplinary Collection of Essays*, edited by Christian F. Feest, 5–36. Lincoln, Nebraska and London: University of Nebraska Press, 1999.

Collinson, Patrick. *The Elizabethan Puritan Movement*. London: Cape, 1967.
Cook, Harold J. "Ancient Wisdom, the Golden Age, and Atlantis: The New World in Sixteenth-Century Cosmography." *Terrae Incognitae* 10, no. 1 (1978): 25–43.
Cook, Harold J. *Matters of Exchange: Commerce, Medicine, and Science in the Dutch Golden Age*. New Haven, CT: Yale University Press, 2007.
Cronon, William. *Changes in the Land: Indians, Colonists, and the Ecology of New England*. New York: Hill and Wang, 2003.
Crosby, Alfred. *The Columbian Exchange: Biological and Cultural Consequences of 1492*. Westport, CT: Greenwood Press, 1972.
Danton, Robert. *The Great Cat Massacre: And Other Episodes in French Cultural History*. New York: Basic Books, 1984.
Danzer, Gerald A. et al., eds. *The Americans: Reconstruction to the 21st Century*. Sacramento, CA: McDougal Littell, 2006.
Daston, Lorraine and Katharine Park. *Wonders and the Order of Nature, 1150–1750*. New York: Zone Books, 1998.
Davies, Surekha. "The Unlucky, the Bad and the Ugly: Categories of Monstrosity from the Renaissance to the Enlightenment." In *The Ashgate Research Companion to Monsters and the Monstrous*, edited by Asa Mittman and Peter J. Dendle, 49–75. Farnham: Ashgate, 2012.
Davies, Surekha. *Renaissance Ethnography and the Invention of the Human*. Cambridge: Cambridge University Press, 2016.
Delumeau, Jean. *History of Paradise: The Garden of Eden in Myth & Tradition*. Translated by Matthew O'Connell. Urbana and Chicago: University of Illinois Press, 2000.
Dodds Pennock, Caroline. *Bonds of Blood: Gender, Lifecycle, and Sacrifice in Aztec Culture*. Basingstoke: Palgrave Macmillan, 2008.
Doran, Susan. "The Queen." In *The Elizabethan World*, edited by Susan Doran and Norman Jones, 35–58. London and New York: Routledge, 2011.
Douglas, Mary. *Purity and Danger: An Analysis of Concepts of Pollution and Taboo*. London and New York: Routledge, 2002.
Durzan, Don J. "Arginine, Scurvy and Cartier's 'Tree of Life'." *Journal of Ethnobiology and Ethnomedicine* 5, no. 5 (February, 2009).
DuVal, Kathleen. "Indian Intermarriage and Métissage in Colonial Louisiana." *William and Mary Quarterly* 65, no. 2 (April 2008): 267–304.
Earle, Rebecca. *The Body of the Conquistador: Food, Race and the Colonial Experience in Spanish America, 1492–1700*. Cambridge: Cambridge University Press, 2012.
Eden, Trudy. "Food, Assimilation, and the Malleability of the Human Body in Early Virginia." In *A Centre of Wonders: The Body in Early America*, edited by Janet Moore Lindman and Michele Lise Tarter, 29–42. Ithaca, NY and London: Cornell University Press, 2001.
Eden, Trudy. *The Early American Table: Food and Society in the New World*. DeKalb: Northern Illinois University Press, 2008.
Edwards, Jess. "'Plain Wilderness' and 'Goodly Corn Fields': Representing Land Use in Early Virginia." in *Envisioning an English Empire: Jamestown and the Making of the North Atlantic World*, edited by Robert Appelbaum and John Wood Sweet, 217–235. Philadelphia: University of Pennsylvania Press, 2005.

Eldred, Jason. "'The Just will Pay for the Sinners': English Merchants, the Trade with Spain, and Elizabethan Foreign Policy, 1563–1585." *Journal for Early Modern Cultural Studies* 10, no. 1 (Spring / Summer, 2010): 5–28.
Eley, Geoff. *A Crooked Line: From Cultural History to the History of Society*. Ann Arbor: University of Michigan Press, 2005.
Elliott, J. H. *The Old World and the New: 1492–1650*. Cambridge: Cambridge University Press, 1970.
Elliott, J. H. *Empires of the Atlantic World: Britain and Spain in America, 1492–1830*. New Haven, CT and London: Yale University Press, 2006.
Ewen, Misha Odessa. "'To a Foundation of a Common-Wealth': English Society and the Colonisation of Virginia, c. 1607–1642." PhD Thesis, University College London, 2017.
Fagan, Brian. *The Little Ice Age: How Climate Made History*. New York: Basic Books, 2000.
Fisher, Will. "The Renaissance Beard: Masculinity in Early Modern England." *Renaissance Quarterly* 54, no. 1 (Spring, 2001): 155–187.
Fitzmaurice, Andrew. *Humanism and America: An Intellectual History of English Colonisation, 1500–1625*. Cambridge: Cambridge University Press, 2003.
Floyd-Wilson, Mary. *English Ethnicity and Race in Early Modern Drama*. Cambridge: Cambridge University Press, 2003.
Fox, Robert. "The Many Worlds of Thomas Harriot." In *Thomas Harriot and His World: Mathematics, Exploration, and Natural Philosophy in Early Modern England*, edited by Robert Fox, 1–10. Farnham: Ashgate, 2012.
Foyster, Elizabeth A. *Manhood in Early Modern England: Honour, Sex and Marriage*. London and New York: Longman, 1999.
Frank, Andrew K. and A. Glenn Crothers, eds. *Borderland Narratives: Negotiation and Accommodation in North America's Contested Spaces, 1500–1850*. Gainesville: University Press of Florida, 2017.
Franklin, Caroline. "The Welsh American Dream: Iolo Morganwg, Robert Southey and the Madoc Legend." In *English Romanticism and the Celtic World*, edited by Gerard Carruthers and Alan Rawes, 69–84. Cambridge: Cambridge University Press, 2003.
Freedman, Paul. "Spices and Late-Medieval European Ideas of Scarcity and Value." *Speculum* 80, no. 4 (October, 2005): 1209–227.
Frick, Carole Collier. *Dressing Renaissance Florence: Families, Fortunes, and Fine Clothing*. Baltimore, MD and London: Johns Hopkins University Press, 2005.
Friedman, John Block. *The Monstrous Races in Medieval Art and Thought*. Syracuse, NY: Syracuse University Press, 2000.
Fuchs, Barbara. "Religion and National Distinction in the Early Modern Atlantic." In *Empires of God: Religious Encounters in the Early Modern Atlantic*, edited by Linda Gregerson and Susan Juster, 58–69. Philadelphia: University of Pennsylvania Press, 2011.
Fuller, Mary C. *Voyages in Print: English Travel to America, 1576–1624*. Cambridge: Cambridge University Press, 1995.
Fuller, Mary C. *Remembering the Early Modern Voyage: English Narratives in the Age of European Expansion*. London: Palgrave, 2008.
Gallagher, Catherine and Stephen Greenblatt. *Practicing New Historicism*. Chicago and London: University of Chicago Press, 2000.

Games, Alison. *The Web of Empire: English Cosmopolitans in an Age of Expansion, 1560–1660*. Oxford: Oxford University Press, 2008.
Gardina Pestana, Carla. *Protestant Empire: Religion and the Making of the British Atlantic World*. Philadelphia: University of Pennsylvania Press, 2009.
Gaskill, Malcolm. *Between Two Worlds: How the English Became Americans*. Oxford: Oxford University Press, 2014.
Gaudio, Michael. *Engraving the Savage: The New World and Techniques of Civilization*. Minneapolis: University of Minnesota Press, 2008.
Gaudio, Michael. "The Truth in Clothing: The Costume Studies of John White and Lucas de Heere." In *European Visions: American Voices*, edited by Kim Sloan, 24–32. London: British Museum Press, 2009.
Geertz, Clifford. *The Interpretation of Cultures: Selected Essays*. New York: Basic Books, 1973.
Genette, Gérard. *Palimpsests: Literature in the Second Degree*. Translated by Channa Newman and Claude Doubinsky. Lincoln and London: University of Nebraska Press, 1997.
Gentilcore, David. *Food and Health in Early Modern Europe: Diet, Medicine and Society, 1450–1800*. New York: Bloomsbury, 2016.
Gerbi, Antonello. *Nature in the New World: From Christopher Columbus to Gonzalo Fernández de Oviedo*. Translated Jeremy Moyle. Pittsburgh, PA: University of Pittsburgh, 2010.
Ginzburg, Carlo. *The Cheese and the Worms: The Cosmos of a Sixteenth-Century Miller*. Baltimore, MD: Johns Hopkins University Press, 1980.
Gould, Eliga H. "Entangled Atlantic Histories: a Response from the Anglo-American Periphery." *The American Historical Review* 112, no. 5 (December, 2007): 1415–1422.
Grafton, Anthony. *New Worlds, Ancient Texts: The Power of Tradition and the Shock of Discovery*. Cambridge, MA and London: Harvard University Press, 1992.
Grafton, Anthony and Lisa Jardine. *From Humanism to the Humanities: Education and the Liberal Arts in Fifteenth- and Sixteenth-Century Europe*. Cambridge, MA: Harvard University Press, 1986.
Greenblatt, Stephen. *Marvellous Possessions: The Wonder of the New World*. Oxford: Clarendon, 1991.
Greene, Jack P. *Pursuits of Happiness: The Social Development of Early Modern British Colonies and the Formation of American Colonies*. Chapel Hill and London: University of North Carolina Press, 1988.
Greene, Jack P. and Philip D. Morgan, eds. *Atlantic History: A Critical Appraisal*. Oxford: Oxford University Press, 2009.
van Groesen, Michiel. *The Representations of the Overseas World in the De Bry Collection of Voyages, 1590–1634*. Leiden and Boston: Brill, 2008.
Gutiérrez, Ramon A. *When Jesus Came, the Corn Mothers Went Away: Marriage, Sexuality, and Power in New Mexico, 1500–1846*. Stanford: Stanford University Press, 1991.
Hadfield, Andrew. "Peter Martyr, Richard Eden and the New World: Reading, Experience and Translation." *Connotations* 5, no. 1 (1995/96): 1–22.
Hadfield, Andrew. "Irish Colonies and the Americas." In *Envisioning an English Empire: Jamestown and the Making of the North Atlantic World*, edited by Robert Appelbaum and John Wood Sweet, 172–191. Philadelphia: University of Pennsylvania Press, 2005.

Hadfield, Andrew. *Literature Travel and Colonial Writing in the English Renaissance*. Oxford: Oxford University Press, 2007.
Hall, Kim F. *Things of Darkness: Economies of Race and Gender in Early Modern England*. Ithaca, NY: Cornell University Press, 1995.
Hämäläinen, Pekka and Samuel Truett. "On Borderlands," *Journal of American History* 98, no. 2 (September, 2011): 338–361.
Hanke, Lewis. *Bartolomé de Las Casas: An Interpretation of his Life and Writings*. The Hague: Martinus Nijhoff, 1951.
Hanke, Lewis. "Bartolomé de Las Casas and the Spanish Empire in America: Four Centuries of Misunderstanding." *Proceedings of the American Philosophical Society* 97, no. 1 (February, 1953): 26–30.
Harris, Jonathan Gil. "Sick Ethnography: Recording the Indian and the Ill English Body." In *Indography: Writing the "Indian" in Early Modern England*, edited by Jonathan Gil Harris, 133–147. Basingstoke: Palgrave Macmillan, 2012.
Hart, Jonathan. *Representing the New World: The English and French Uses of the Example of Spain*. Basingstoke: Palgrave, 2001.
Hartog, Francois. *Mirror of Herodotus: The Representation of the Other in the Writing of History*. Translated by Janet Lloyd. Berkeley: University of California Press, 1988.
Haskell, Alexander B. *For God, King, and People: Forging Commonwealth Bonds in Renaissance Virginia*. Chapel Hill: University of North Carolina Press, 2017.
Heal, Felicity. *The Power of Gifts: Gift-Exchange in Early Modern England*. Oxford: Oxford University Press, 2014.
Healy, Margaret. *Fictions of Disease in Early Modern England: Bodies, Plagues and Politics*. New York: Palgrave, 2001.
Heaney, Christopher. "Marrying Utopia: Mary and Philip, Richard Eden, and the English Alchemy of Spanish Peru." In *Entangled Empires: The Anglo-Iberian Atlantic, 1500–1830*, edited by Jorge Cañizares-Esguerra, 85–104. Philadelphia: University of Pennsylvania Press, 2018.
Helgerson, Richard. *Forms of Nationhood: The Elizabethan Writing of England*. Chicago: University of Chicago Press, 1992.
Hentschell, Roze. "Moralizing Apparel in Early Modern London: Popular Literature, Sermons, and Sartorial Display." *Journal of Medieval and Early Modern Studies* 39, no. 3 (Fall, 2009): 571–595.
Herrmann, Rachel. "The 'Tragicall Historie': Cannibalism and Abundance in Colonial Jamestown." *The William and Mary Quarterly* 68, no. 1 (January, 2011): 47–74.
Higgins, Iain Macleod. *Writing East: The "Travels" of Sir John Mandeville*. Philadelphia: University of Pennsylvania Press, 1997.
Hill, Michael. "Temperateness, Temperance, and the Tropics: Climate and Morality in the English Atlantic World, 1555–1705." PhD dissertation, Georgetown University, 2013.
Hindle, Steve. *The State and Social Change in Early Modern England, 1550–1640*. Basingstoke: Palgrave Macmillan, 2002.
Hodgen, Margaret. *Early Anthropology in the 16th and 17th Centuries*. Philadelphia: University of Pennsylvania Press, 1964.
von Hoffmann, Viktoria. *From Gluttony to Enlightenment: The World of Taste in Early Modern Europe*. Chicago: University of Illinois Press, 2016.

Hooper, Wilfrid. "The Tudor Sumptuary Laws." *The English Historical Review* 30, no. 119 (July, 1915): 433–449.
Hotchkiss, Valerie and Fred C. Robinson. *English in Print from Caxton to Shakespeare to Milton*. Urbana and Chicago: University of Illinois Press, 2008.
Householder, Michael. *Inventing Americans in the Age of Discovery: Narratives of Encounter*. Farnham: Ashgate, 2011.
Howard, Jean E. "Crossdressing, the Theatre, and Gender Struggle in Early Modern England." *Shakespeare Quarterly* 99, no. 4 (Winter, 1988): 418–440.
Huddleston, Lee Eldridge. *Origins of the American Indians: European Concepts, 1492–1729*. Austin: University of Texas Press, 1967.
Hull, Suzanne W. *Chaste, Silent and Obedient: English Books for Women, 1475–1640*. San Marino: Huntington Library Press, 1982.
Hulme, Peter. *Colonial Encounters: Europe and the Native Caribbean, 1492–1797*. London and New York: Routledge, 1992.
Hulton, P. H. *America 1585: The Complete Drawings of John White*. Chapel Hill: University of North Carolina Press, 1984.
Hunt, Alan. *Governance of the Consuming Passions: A History of Sumptuary Law*. Basingstoke: Macmillan Press, 1996.
Hunt, Alan. "The Governance of Consumption: Sumptuary Laws and Shifting Forms of Regulation." *Economy and Society* 25, no. 3 (August, 1996): 410–427.
Husband, Timothy. *The Wild Man: Medieval Myth and Symbolism*. New York: The Metropolitan Museum of Art, 1980.
Iyengar, Sujata. *Shades of Difference: Mythologies of Skin Color in Early Modern England*. Philadelphia: University of Pennsylvania Press, 2005.
Janzen, Olaf Uwe. "Review Article: Handcock, Marshall, and Breakwater Books." *Newfoundland and Labrador Studies* 7, no. 1 (January, 1991): 65–77.
Johnson, Christopher. "*Bricoleur* and *Bricolage:* From Metaphor to Universal Concept." *Paragraph* 35, no. 3 (November, 2012): 355–372.
Johnson, Robert C. "The Lotteries of the Virginia Company, 1612–1621." *The Virginia Magazine of History and Biography* 74, no. 3 (July, 1966): 259–292.
Jowitt, Claire. "'Monsters and Straunge Births': The Politics of Richard Eden. A Response to Andrew Hadfield." *Connotations* 6, no. 1 (January, 1996): 51–64.
Jütte, Robert. *Poverty and Deviance in Early Modern Europe*. Cambridge: Cambridge University Press, 1994.
Kahl, Sigrun. "The Religious Roots of Modern Poverty Policy: Catholic, Lutheran, and Reformed Protestant Traditions Compared." *European Journal of Sociology* 46, no. 1 (2005): 91–126.
Kelsey, Harry. *Sir John Hawkins: Queen Elizabeth's Slave Trader*. New Haven, CT and London: Yale University Press, 2003.
King, John N. "Queen Elizabeth I: Representations of the Virgin Queen." *Renaissance Quarterly* 43, no. 1 (Spring, 1990): 30–74.
Kissane, Christopher. *Food, Religion and Communities in Early Modern Europe*. London: Bloomsbury, 2018.
Knapp, Jeffrey. *An Empire Nowhere: England, America, and Literature from Utopia to The Tempest*. Berkeley: University of California Press, 1992.
Knepper, Wendy. "Colonization, Creolization, and Globalization: The Art and Ruses of *Bricolage*." *Small Axe A Caribbean Journal of Criticism* 21, no. 3 (October, 2006): 70–86.

Kuhlemann, Ute. "Between Reproduction, Invention and Propaganda: Theodor de Bry's Engravings After John White's Watercolours." In *A New World: England's First View of America*, edited by Kim Sloan, 79–92. Chapel Hill: University of North Carolina Press, 2007.

Kupperman, Karen Ordahl. *Settling with the Indians: The Meetings of English and Indian Cultures in America, 1580–1640*. London: Dent, 1980.

Kupperman, Karen Ordahl. "The Puzzle of the American Climate in the Early Colonial Period." *The American Historical Review* 87, no. 5 (December, 1982): 1262–1289.

Kupperman, Karen Ordahl. "Fear of Hot Climates in the Anglo-American Colonial Experience." *The William and Mary Quarterly* 41, no. 2 (April, 1984): 213–240.

Kupperman, Karen Ordahl. "Presentment of Civility: English Reading of American Self-Presentation in the Early Years of Colonization." *The William and Mary Quarterly* 54, no. 1 (January, 1997): 193–228.

Kupperman, Karen Ordahl. *Indians and English: Facing Off in Early America*. Ithaca, NY and London: Cornell University Press, 2000.

Kupperman, Karen Ordahl. *The Jamestown Project*. Cambridge, MA: Harvard University Press, 2007.

Kupperman, Karen Ordahl. "Roanoke's Achievement." In *European Visions: American Voices*, edited by Kim Sloan, 3–12. London: British Museum Press, 2009.

LaCombe, Michael A. *Political Gastronomy: Food and Authority in the English Atlantic World*. Philadelphia: University of Pennsylvania Press, 2012.

Lazzarini, Elena. "Wonderful Creatures: Early Modern Perceptions of Deformed Bodies." *Oxford Art Journal* 34, no. 3 (October, 2011): 415–431.

Le Roy Ladurie, Emmanuel. *Times of Feast Times of Famine: A History of Climate since the year 1000*. Translated by Barbara Bray. New York: Doubleday, 1971.

Leerssen, Joep. *National Thought in Europe: A Cultural History*. Amsterdam: Amsterdam University Press, 2006.

Lemire, Beverly. "The Theft of Clothes and Popular Consumerism in Early Modern England." *Journal of Social History* 24, no. 2 (Winter, 1990): 255–276.

Lemire, Beverly. *Global Trade and the Transformation of Consumer Cultures: The Material World Remade, c. 1500–1820*. Cambridge: Cambridge University Press, 2017.

Leong, Elaine. "Making Medicines in the Early Modern Household." *Bulletin of the History of Medicine* 82, no. 1 (Spring, 2008): 145–68.

Lester, Paul M. "Looks Are Deceiving: The Portraits of Christopher Columbus." *Visual Anthropology* 5, no. 3–4 (1993): 211–227.

Levenson, Jon D. "Genesis: Introduction and Annotations." In *The Jewish Study Bible*, edited by Adele Berlin and Marc Zvi Brettler, 8–101. Oxford: Oxford University Press, 2004.

Levin, Carole. "Introduction." In *Ambiguous Realities: Women in the Middle Ages and Renaissance*, edited by Carole Levin and Jeanie Watson, 14–21. Detroit, MI: Wayne State University Press, 1987.

Levin, Carole. *The Heart and Stomach of a King: Elizabeth I and the Politics of Sex and Power*. Philadelphia: University of Pennsylvania Press, 1994.

Levine, Philippa. "States of Undress: Nakedness and the Colonial Imagination." *Victorian Studies* 50, no. 2 (Winter, 2008): 189–219.

Lévi-Strauss, Claude. *The Savage Mind*. Chicago: University of Chicago Press, 1966.

Lévi-Strauss, Claude. *The Raw and the Cooked: Introduction to a Science of Mythology.* Translated by John and Doreen Weightman. London: Cape, 1970.
Lévi-Strauss, Claude. *The Origin of Table Manners.* Translated by John and Doreen Weightman. Chicago: University of Chicago Press, 1978.
Levy Peck, Linda. *Court Patronage and Corruption in Early Stuart England.* London: Routledge, 2004.
Lim, Walter S. H. *The Arts of Empire: The Poetics of Colonialism from Ralegh to Milton.* Newark and London: University of Delaware Press and Associated University Presses, 1998.
Lindemann, Mary. *Medicine and Society in Early Modern Europe, 2nd Edition.* Cambridge: Cambridge University Press, 2010.
Linton, Joan Pong. *The Romance of the New World: Gender and the Literary Formations of English Colonialism.* Cambridge: Cambridge University Press, 1998.
Llewelyn Price, Merrall. *Consuming Passions: The Uses of Cannibalism in Late Medieval and Early Modern Europe.* New York and London: Routledge, 2003.
Lloyd, Rachel. *Elizabethan Adventurer: A Life of Captain Christopher Carleill.* London: Hamish Hamilton Ltd., 1974.
Lynam, E. W. "Sir Henry Sidney." *Studies: An Irish Quarterly Review* 2, no. 7 (September, 1913): 185–203.
MacCaffrey, W. T. *Elizabeth I: War and Politics, 1588–1603.* Princeton, NJ: Princeton University Press, 1992.
McCants, Anne C. "Exotic Goods, Popular Consumption, and the Standard of Living: Thinking about Globalization in the Early Modern World." *Journal of World History* 18, no. 4 (December, 2007): 433–462.
MacCormack, Sabine. *Religion in the Andes: Vision and Imagination in Early Colonial Peru.* Princeton, NJ: Princeton University Press, 1991.
McDermott, James. *Martin Frobisher: Elizabethan Privateer.* New Haven, CT and London: Yale University Press, 2001.
McDermott, James, ed. *The Third Voyage of Martin Frobisher to Baffin Island, 1578.* London: The Hakluyt Society, 2001.
McGhee, Robert. *The Arctic Voyages of Martin Frobisher: An Elizabethan Adventure.* London: British Museum Press, 2001.
Mackenthun, Gesa. *Metaphors of Dispossession: American Beginnings and the Translation of Empire, 1492–1637.* Norman, Oklahoma and London: University of Oklahoma Press, 1997.
Mackinnon, Dolly. "'Charity is worth it when it looks that good': Rural Women and Bequests of Clothing in Early Modern England." In *Women, Identities, and Communities in Early Modern Europe*, edited by Susan Broomhall and Stephanie Tarbin, 79–93. Aldershot: Ashgate, 2008.
McLean, Matthew. *The Cosmographia of Sebastian Münster: Describing the World in the Reformation.* Aldershot: Ashgate, 2007.
MacMillan, Ken. *Sovereignty and Possession in the English New World: The Legal Foundations of Empire, 1576–1640.* Cambridge: Cambridge University Press, 2006.
McRae, Andrew. *God Speed the Plough: The Representation of Agrarian England, 1500–1660.* Cambridge: Cambridge University Press, 1996.

Magasich-Airola, Jorge and Jean-Marc de Beer. *America Magica: When Renaissance Europe Thought it had Conquered Paradise*, 2nd edition. Translated by Monica Sandor. London and New York: Anthem Press, 2007.

Maltby, William S. *The Black Legend in England: The Development of Anti-Spanish Sentiment, 1558–1660*. Durham, NC: Duke University Press, 1971.

Mancall, Peter C. "Tales Tobacco Told in Sixteenth Century Europe." *Environmental History* 9, no. 4 (October, 2004): 648–678.

Mancall, Peter C. *Hakluyt's Promise: An Elizabethan's Obsession for an English America*. New Haven, CT and London: Yale University Press, 2007.

Mancall, Peter C. and James H. Merrell, eds. *American Encounters: Natives and Newcomers from European Contact to Indian Removal, 1500–1850*. New York: Routledge, 2007.

Marroti, Arthur F. "Alienating Catholics in Early Modern England: Recusant Women, Jesuits and Ideological Fantasies." In *Catholicism and Anti-Catholicism in Early Modern English Texts*, edited by Arthur F. Marroti, 1–34. Basingstoke: Macmillan, 1999.

Martínez, María Elena. *Genealogical Fictions: Limpieza de Sangre, Religion, and Gender in Colonial Mexico*. Stanford: Stanford University Press, 2008.

Mason, Peter. *Deconstructing America: Representations of the Other*. London: Routledge, 1990.

Mellor, Philip A. and Chris Shilling. *Re-forming the Body: Religion, Community and Modernity*. London: SAGE, 1997.

Mennell, Stephen. *All Manners of Food: Eating and Taste in England and France from the Middle Ages to the Present*, 2nd edition. Urbana and Chicago: University of Illinois Press, 1996.

Mikkeli, Heikki. *Hygiene in the Early Modern Medical Tradition*. Helsinki: Academia Scientiarum Fennica, 1999.

Miller, Shannon. *Invested With Meaning: The Raleigh Circle in the New World*. Philadelphia: University of Pennsylvania Press, 1998.

Millikan, Neal E. *Lotteries in Colonial America*. London: Routledge, 2011.

Millones Figueroa, Luis. "The Staff of Life: Wheat and 'Indian Bread' in the New World." *Colonial Latin American Review* 19, no. 2 (2010): 301–22.

Mittman, Asa. *Maps and Monsters in Medieval England*. New York: Routledge, 2006.

Montaño, John Patrick. *The Roots of English Colonialism in Ireland*. Cambridge: Cambridge University Press, 2016.

Montrose, Louis. "'Shaping Fantasies': Figurations of Gender and Power in Elizabethan Culture." *Representations* 2 (Spring, 1983): 61–94.

Montrose, Louis. "The Work of Gender in the Discourse of Discovery." In *New World Encounters*, edited by Stephen Greenblatt, 177–217. Berkeley: University of California Press, 1993.

Moore Lindman, Janet and Michele Lise Tarter. "'The Earthly Frame, a Minute Fabrick, a Centre of Wonders': An Introduction to Bodies in Early America." In *A Centre of Wonders: The Body in Early America*, edited by Janet Moore Lindman and Michele Lise Tarter, 1–9. Ithaca, NY and London: Cornell University Press, 2001.

Moran, Michael G. *Inventing Virginia: Sir Walter Raleigh and the Rhetoric of Colonization, 1584–1590*. New York: Peter Lang, 2007.

Morera, Raphaël. "Marshes as Microclimate: Governing with the Environment in Early Modern France." In *Governing the Environment in the Early Modern World: Theory and Practice*, edited by Sara Miglietti and John Morgan, 95–125. London: Routledge, 2017.
Morgan, Jennifer L. "'Some Could Suckle over their Shoulder': Male Travelers, Female Bodies and the Gendering of Racial Ideology, 1500–1770." *The William and Mary Quarterly* 54, no. 1 (January, 1997): 167–192.
Morrall, Andrew. "Protestant Pots: Morality and Social Ritual in the Early Modern Home." *Journal of Design History* 15, no. 4 (2002): 263–273.
Newton, Hannah. *The Sick Child in Early Modern England, 1580–1720*. Oxford: Oxford University Press, 2012.
Noll, Mark A. *The Old Religion in a New World: The History of North American Christianity*. Grand Rapids, MI and Cambridge: Willian B. Eerdmans Publishing Company, 2002.
Norton, Marcy. *Sacred Gifts, Profane Pleasures: A History of Tobacco and Chocolate in the Atlantic World*. Ithaca, NY and London: Cornell University Press, 2008.
Nugent, Elizabeth M., ed. *The Thought & Culture of the English Renaissance: An Anthology of Tudor Prose, 1481–1555*, vol. 2. The Hague: Martinus Nijhoff, 1969.
O'Brien, Jean. *Dispossession by Degrees: Indian Land and Identity in Natick, Massachusetts, 1650–1790*. Cambridge: Cambridge University Press, 1997.
O'Gorman, Edmundo. *The Invention of America*. Bloomington: Indiana University Press, 1961.
Oswald, Dana. "Monstrous Gender: Geographies of Ambiguity." In *The Ashgate Research Companion to Monsters and the Monstrous*, edited by Asa Mittman and Peter J. Dendle, 343–363. Farnham: Ashgate, 2012.
Pagden, Anthony. *The Fall of Natural Man: The American Indian and the Origins if Comparative Ethnology*. Cambridge: Cambridge University Press, 1982.
Pagden, Anthony. *European Encounters with the New World*. New Haven, CT and London: Yale University Press, 1993.
Pagden, Anthony. *Lords of All the World: Ideologies of Empires in Spain, Britain and France, c. 1500–c. 1800*. New Haven, CT and London: Yale University Press, 1995.
Palmer, Patricia. *Language and Conquest in Early Modern Ireland: English Renaissance Literature and Elizabethan Imperial Expansion*. Cambridge: Cambridge University Press, 2001.
Parker, Geoffrey. *Global Crisis: War, Climate Change and Catastrophe in the Seventeenth Century*. New Haven, CT: Yale University Press, 2013.
Parker, John. "Religion and the Virginia Colony, 1609–10." In *The Westward Enterprise: English Activities in Ireland, the Atlantic, and America, 1480–1650*, edited by K. R. Andrews, N. P. Canny and P. E. H. Hair, 245–270. Liverpool: Liverpool University Press, 1978.
Pastor Bodmer, Beatriz. *The Armature of Conquest: Spanish Accounts of the Discovery of America*. Translated by Lydia Longstreth Hunt. Stanford, CA: Stanford University Press, 1992.
Peck, Amelia, ed. *Interwoven Globe: The World Textile Trade, 1500–1800*. New Haven, CT: Yale University Press, 2013.

Pennell, Sara. *The Birth of the English Kitchen, 1600–1850*. London: Bloomsbury, 2016.
Pennell, Sara. "Getting down from the table: Early modern foodways and material culture." In *The Routledge Handbook of Material Culture in Early Modern Europe*, edited by Catherine Richardson, Tara Hamling and David Gaimster, 185–195. London and New York: Routledge, 2017.
Pennington, Loren E. "The Amerindian in English Promotional Literature, 1575–1625." In *The Westward Enterprise: English Activities in Ireland, the Atlantic, and America, 1480–1650*, edited by K. R. Andrews, N. P. Canny and P. E. H. Hair, 175–194. Liverpool: Liverpool University Press, 1978.
Pennycock, Alastair. *English and the Discourses of Colonialism*. London: Routledge, 1998.
Pollard, Tanya. "The Pleasures and Perils of Smoking in Early Modern England." In *Smoke: A Global History of Smoking*, edited by Sander L. Gilman and Xun Zhou, 38–45. London: Reaktion Books Ltd., 2004.
Ponterotto, Joseph G. "Brief Note on the Origins, Evolution, and Meaning of the Qualitative Research Concept 'Thick Description'." *The Qualitative Report* 11, no. 3 (September, 2006): 538–549.
Popkin, Richard H. "The Rise and Fall of the Jewish Indian Theory." In *Menasseh ben Israel and his World*, edited by Henry Méchoulan and Richard H. Popkin, 63–82. Leiden: Brill, 1989.
Pratt, Stephanie. "Truth and Artifice in the Visualization of Native Peoples: From the Time of John White to the Beginning of the 18th Century." In *European Visions: American Voices*, edited by Kim Sloan, 33–40. London: British Museum Press, 2009.
Pullman, Brian. "Catholics and the Poor in Early Modern Europe." *Transactions of the Royal Historical Society* 26 (December, 1976): 15–34.
Quinn, David B. *Raleigh and the British Empire*. London: Hodder and Stoughton, 1947.
Quinn, David B. *The Roanoke Voyages, 1584–90*. London: The Hakluyt Society, 1955.
Quinn, David B. *England and the Discovery of America, 1481–1620*. London: Allen & Unwin, 1974.
Quinn, David B., ed. *The Hakluyt Handbook*, vols. I and II. London: The Hakluyt Society, 1974.
Quinn, David B. *Set Fair for Roanoke: Voyages and Colonies, 1584–1606*. Chapel Hill and London: University of North Carolina Press, 1985.
Raman, Shankar. *Framing "India": The Colonial Imaginary in Early Modern Culture*. Stanford, CA: Stanford University Press, 2002.
Ramey, Lynn. "Monstrous Alterity in Early Modern Travel Accounts: Lessons from the Ambiguous Medieval Discourse on Humanness." *L'Esprit Créateur* 48, no. 1 (Spring, 2008): 81–95.
Ramsay, G. D. "Clothworkers, Merchants Adventurers and Richard Hakluyt." *English Historical Review* 92, no. 364 (July, 1977): 504–521.
Reeds, Karen. "Don't Eat, Don't Touch: Roanoke Colonists, Natural Knowledge, and Dangerous Plants of North America." In *European Visions: American Voices*, edited by Kim Sloan, 51–57. London: British Museum Press, 2009.
Richter, Daniel K. *Facing East from Indian Country: A Native History of Early America*. Cambridge, MA: Harvard University Press, 2001.

Riello, Giorgio and Prasannan Parthasarathi, eds. *The Spinning World: A Global History of Cotton Textiles, 1200–1850.* Oxford and New York: Oxford University Press, 2009.

Robe, Stanley L. "Wild Men and Spain's Brave New World." In *The Wild Man Within: An Image in Western Thought from the Renaissance to Romanticism*, edited by Edward Dudley and Maximillian E. Novak, 39–53. Pittsburgh, PA: University of Pittsburgh Press, 1972.

Rodríguez-Alegría, Enrique. "Eating Like an Indian: Negotiating Social Relations in the Spanish Colonies." *Current Anthropology* 46, no. 4 (August/October, 2005): 551–573.

Romm, James. "Biblical History and the Americas: The Legend of Solomon's Ophir, 1492–1591." In *The Jews and the Expansion of Europe to the West, 1450–1800*, edited by Paolo Bernardini and Norman Fiering, 27–46. New York and Oxford: Berghahn Books, 2001.

Roper, L. H. *The English Empire in America, 1602–1658: Beyond Jamestown.* London: Pickering & Chatto, 2009.

Rubiés, Joan-Pau. "Texts, Images, and the Perception of 'Savages' in Early Modern Europe: What We Can Learn from White and Harriot." In *European Visions: American Voices*, edited by Kim Sloan, 120–130. London: British Museum Press, 2009.

Rublack, Ulinka. "Fluxes: The Early Modern Body and the Emotions." Translated by Pamela Selwyn. *History Workshop Journal* 53, no. 1 (Spring, 2002): 1–16.

Rublack, Ulinka. *Dressing Up: Cultural Identity in Renaissance Europe.* Oxford: Oxford University Press, 2010.

Rustici, Craig. "Tobacco, Union, and the Indianized English." In *Indography: Writing the "Indian" in Early Modern England*, edited by Jonathan Gil Harris, 117–131. New York and Basingstoke: Palgrave Macmillan, 2012.

Sarson, Steven. *British America, 1500–1800: Creating Colonies, Imagining an Empire.* London: Hodder Arnold, 2005.

Sayre, Gordon M. *Les Sauvages Américains: Representations of Native Americans in French and English Colonial Literature.* Chapel Hill and London: University of North Carolina Press, 1997.

Schleiner, Winfried. "'Divina Virago': Queen Elizabeth as an Amazon." *Studies in Philology* 75, no. 2 (Spring, 1978): 163–180.

Schlesinger, Roger and Arthur P. Stabler. "Introduction." In *André Thevet's North America: A Sixteenth-Century View*, edited and translated by Roger Schlesinger and Arthur P. Stabler, xvii–xlii. Kingston, Ontario and Montreal: McGill-Queen's University Press, 1986.

Schoenfeldt, Michael C. *Bodies and Selves in Early Modern England: Physiology and Inwardness in Spenser, Shakespeare, Herbert, and Milton.* Cambridge: Cambridge University Press, 1999.

Schwartz, Stuart B., ed. *Implicit Understandings: Observing, Reporting, and Reflecting on the Encounters Between Europeans and Other Peoples in the Early Modern Era.* Cambridge: Cambridge University Press, 1994.

Seed, Patricia. "'Are These Not Also Men?': The Indians' Humanity and Capacity for Spanish Civilisation." *Journal of Latin American Studies* 25, no. 3 (October, 1993): 629–652.

Seed, Patricia. *Ceremonies of Possession in Europe's Conquest of the New World, 1492–1640.* Cambridge: Cambridge University Press, 1995.

Shammas, Carole. "English Commercial Development and American Colonization, 1560–1620." In *The Westward Enterprise: English Activities in Ireland, the Atlantic, and America, 1480–1650*, edited by K. R. Andrews, N. P. Canny and P. E. H. Hair, 151–174. Liverpool: Liverpool University Press, 1978.

Shapin, Steven. "You Are What You Eat: Historical Changes in Ideas About Food and Identity." *Historical Research* 87, no. 237 (August, 2014): 377–392.

Shapin, Steven. "Why was 'Custom a Second Nature' in Early Modern Medicine?" *Bulletin of the History of Medicine* 93, no. 1 (Spring, 2019): 1–26.

Sheehan, Bernard. *Savagism & Civility: Indians and Englishmen in Colonial Virginia*. Cambridge: Cambridge University Press, 1980.

Shell, Alison. *Catholicism, Controversy, and the English Literary Imagination, 1558–1660*. Cambridge: Cambridge University Press, 1999.

Sherman, William H. "John Dee's Columbian Encounter." In *John Dee: Interdisciplinary Studies in English Renaissance Thought*, edited by Stephen Clucas, 131–140. Dordrecht: Springer, 2006.

Siena, Kevin P. "Pollution, Promiscuity, and the Pox: English Venereology and the Early Modern Medical Discourse on Social and Sexual Danger." *Journal of the History of Sexuality* 8, no. 4 (April, 1998): 553–574.

Sim, Alison. *Food & Feast in Tudor England*. Stroud: The History Press, 2005.

Simmons, Richard C. "Americana in British Books, 1621–1760." In *America in European Consciousness, 1493–1750*, edited by Karen Ordahl Kupperman, 361–387. Chapel Hill and London: University of North Carolina Press, 1995.

Skinner, Quentin. *Reason and Rhetoric in the Philosophy of Hobbes*. Cambridge: Cambridge University Press, 1996.

Slack, Paul. *The English Poor Law, 1531–1782*. Cambridge: Cambridge University Press, 1995.

Sloan, Kim. "Catalogue: John White's Watercolours." In *A New World: England's First View of America*, edited by Kim Sloan, 93–223. Chapel Hill: University of North Carolina Press, 2007.

Small, Margaret. "A World Seen Through Another's Eyes: Hakluyt, Ramusio, and the Narratives of the *Navigationi et Viaggi*." In *Richard Hakluyt and Travel Writing in Early Modern Europe*, edited by Daniel Carey and Claire Jowitt, 45–55. Farnham: Ashgate, 2012.

Small, Margaret. "From Thought to Action: Gilbert, Davis, And Dee's Theories Behind the Search for the Northwest Passage." *Sixteenth Century Journal* 44, no. 4 (Winter, 2013): 1041–1058.

Smith, Helen and Louise Wilson, eds. *Renaissance Paratexts*. Cambridge: Cambridge University Press, 2011.

Spavin, Richard. "Jean Bodin and the Idea of Anachronism." In *Governing the Environment in the Early Modern World: Theory and Practice*, edited by Sara Miglietti and John Morgan, 67–94. London: Routledge, 2017.

Spicer, Joaneath. "The Renaissance Elbow." In *A Cultural History of Gesture*, edited by Jan Bremmer and Herman Roodenburg, 84–128. Ithaca, NY: Cornell University Press, 1991.

Sprague de Camp, L. *Lost Continents: The Atlantis Theme in History, Science, and Literature*. New York: Dover, 1970.

Spufford, Margaret. *Small Books and Pleasant Histories: Popular Fiction and its Readership in Seventeenth-Century England*. London: Methuen, 1981.

Stolberg, Michael. *Experiencing Illness and the Sick Body in Early Modern Europe.* Translated by Leonhard Unglaub and Logan Kennedy. Basingstoke: Palgrave Macmillan, 2011.
Sturgis, Amy H. "Prophesies and Politics: Millenarians, Rabbis, and the Jewish Indian Theory." *The Seventeenth Century* 14, no. 1 (1999): 15–23.
Sturtevant, William C. "First Visual Images of Native Americans." In *First Images of America: The Impact of the New World on the Old*, vol. 1, edited by Fredi Chiappelli, 417–454. Berkeley and London: University of California Press, 1976.
Sturtevant, William C. "The Sources for European Imagery of Native Americans." In *New World of Wonders: European Images of the Americas, 1492–1700*, edited by Rachel Doggett, 25–33. Seattle and London: University of Washington Press, 1992.
Sturtevant, William C. and David Beers Quinn. "This New Prey: Eskimos in Europe in 1567, 1576, and 1577." In *Indians & Europe: An Interdisciplinary Collection of Essays*, edited by Christian F. Feest, 61–140. Lincoln and London: University of Nebraska Press, 1999.
Sweet, Leonard I. "Christopher Columbus and the Millennial Vision of the New World." *The Catholic Historical Review* 72, no. 3 (July, 1986): 369–382.
Taylor, Alan. *The Divided Ground: Indians, Settlers, and the Northern Borderland of the American Revolution.* New York: Routledge, 2001.
Taylor, Alan. *American Colonies: The Settling of North America.* New York: Penguin Books, 2002.
Thirsk, Joan. *Food in Early Modern England: Phases, Fads, Fashions, 1500–1760.* London and New York: Hambledon Continuum, 2006.
Thomas, Nicholas. *Colonialism's Culture: Anthropology, Travel and Government.* Cambridge: Polity Press, 1994.
Thornton, John. *Africa and Africans in the Making of the Atlantic World, 1400–1800.* Cambridge: Cambridge University Press, 1998.
Townsend, Camilla. "Burying the White Gods: New Perspectives on the Conquest of Mexico." *The American Historical Review* 10, no. 3 (June, 2003): 659–687.
Turner, Jack. *Spice: The History of a Temptation.* London: Harper Perennial, 2005.
Valencia Suárez, María Fernanda. "The Aztecs Through the Lens of English Imperial Aspiration, 1519–1713." PhD dissertation, University of Cambridge, 2010.
Vaughan, Alden T. "People of Wonder: England Encounters the New World's Natives." In *New World of Wonders: European Images of the Americas, 1492–1700*, edited by Rachel Doggett, 11–24. Seattle and London: University of Washington Press, 1992.
Verner, Lisa. *The Epistemology of the Monstrous in the Middle Ages.* New York: Routledge, 2005.
Vincent, Susan. *Dressing the Elite: Clothes in Early Modern England.* Oxford: Berg, 2003.
Wallis, Helen. "England's Search for the Northern Passages in the Sixteenth and Early Seventeenth Centuries." *Arctic* 37, no. 4 (December, 1984): 453–472.
Walsham, Alexandra. *Providence in Early Modern England.* Oxford: Oxford University Press, 1999.
Walsham, Alexandra. *Church Papists: Catholicism, Conformity and Confessional Polemic in Early Modern England.* Woodbridge: The Boydell Press, 1999.
Walter, John and Roger Schofield, eds. *Famine, Disease and the Social Order in Early Modern Society.* Cambridge: Cambridge University Press, 1989.

Walvin, James. *Fruits of Empire: Exotic Produce and British Taste, 1660–1800.* New York: New York University Press, 1997.

Wandel, Lee Palmer. "The Poverty of Christ." In *The Reformation of Charity: The Secular and the Religious in Early Modern Poor Relief*, edited by Thomas Max Safley, 15–29. Leiden: Brill, 2003.

Warner, Marina. *Fantastic Metamorphoses, Other Worlds.* Oxford: Oxford University Press, 2002.

Weber, Max. *The Protestant Ethic and the Spirit of Capitalism.* Translated by Talcott Parsons. London: George Allen & Unwin Ltd., 1930.

Welch, Evelyn. "Art on the Edge: Hair and Hands in Renaissance Italy." *Renaissance Studies* 23, no. 3 (June, 2009): 241–268.

Wernham, R. B. *The Making of Elizabethan Foreign Policy, 1558–1603.* Berkeley and London: University of California Press, 1980.

Whatley, Janet. "Food and the Limits of Civility: The Testimony of Jean de Léry." *Sixteenth-Century Journal* 15, no. 4 (Winter, 1984): 387–400.

Whatley, Janet. "Introduction." In *History of a Voyage to the Land of Brazil*, edited and translated by Janet Whatley, xv–xxxviii. Berkeley and London: University of California Press, 1990.

White, Hayden. "The Forms of Wildness: Archaeology of an Idea." In *The Wild Man Within: An Image in Western Thought from the Renaissance to Romanticism*, edited by Edward Dudley and Maximillian E. Novak, 3–38. Pittsburgh: University of Pittsburgh Press, 1972.

White, Sam. *A Cold Welcome: The Little Ice Age and Europe's Encounter with North America.* Cambridge MA: Harvard University Press, 2017.

Whitehead, Neil L. "The *Discoverie* as Ethnological Text." In *The Discoverie of the Large, Rich and Bewtiful Empyre of Guiana*, edited by Neil Whitehead, 60–116. Manchester: Manchester University Press, 1997.

Whitehead, Neil L. "Native Americans and Europeans: Early Encounters in the Caribbean and Along the Atlantic Coast." In *The Oxford Handbook of the Atlantic World, 1450–1850*, edited by Nicholas Canny and Philip Morgan, 55–70. Oxford: Oxford University Press, 2011.

Wiesner-Hanks, Merry E. *Christianity and Sexuality in the Early Modern World: Regulating Desire, Reforming Practice.* London and New York: Routledge, 2000.

Williams, David. *Deformed Discourse: The Function of the Monster in Mediaeval Thought and Literature.* Montreal: McGill-Queen's University Press, 1999.

Williams, Glyndwr. *Voyages of Delusion: The Northwest Passage in the Age of Reason.* London: HarperCollins, 2002.

Williams, Ieuan M. "Introduction." In *Cronica Walliae*, edited by Ieuan M. Williams, 1–60. Cardiff: University of Wales Press, 2002.

Williams Jr., Robert A. *The American Indian in Western Legal Thought: The Discourses of Conquest.* New York and Oxford: Oxford University Press, 1990.

Working, Lauren. *The Making of an Imperial Polity: Civility and America in the Jacobean Metropolis.* Cambridge: Cambridge University Press, 2019.

Wright, Louis B. *Religion and Empire: The Alliance between Piety and Commerce in English Expansion, 1558–1625.* Chapel Hill: University of North Carolina Press, 1943.

Yellow Bird, Michael. "What We Want to Be Called: Indigenous Peoples' Perspectives on Racial and Ethnic Identity Labels." *American Indian Quarterly* 23, no. 2 (Spring, 1999): 1–21.

Younging, Gregory. *Elements of Indigenous Style: A Guide for Writing By and About Indigenous People.* Edmonton, Alberta: Brush Education, 2018.
Zemon Davis, Natalie. *The Return of Martin Guerre.* Cambridge, MA and London: Harvard University Press, 1983.
Zemon Davis, Natalie. "Iroquois Women, European Women." In *Women, "Race", and Writing in the Early Modern Period*, edited by Margo Hendricks and Patricia Palmer, 243–258. London: Routledge, 1994.
Zemon Davis, Natalie. *The Gift in Sixteenth-Century France.* Oxford: Oxford University Press, 2000.
Zuckerman, Michael. "Identity in British America: Unease in Eden." In *Colonial Identity in the Atlantic World, 1500–1800*, edited by Nicholas Canny and Anthony Pagden, 115–157. Princeton, NJ: Princeton University Press, 1987.

Internet sources

Baldwin, R. C. D. "Thomas Nicholls." Oxford Dictionary of National Biography. Last accessed 1 June, 2015. www.oxforddnb.com/view/article/20124?docPos=4.
Clough, Cecil H. "John Rastell." *Oxford Dictionary of National Biography.* Last accessed 21 June, 2016. www.oxforddnb.com/view/article/23149?docPos=1.
Edward VI, King of England. "My Devise for the Succession, June, 1553." Luminarium Encyclopaedia Project. Last accessed 11 April, 2015. www.luminarium.org/encyclopedia/edward6devise.htm.
English Short Title Catalogue. Search of the works of Gervase Markham. Last accessed 27 November, 2016. http://estc.bl.uk/F/RMULVCU3VFBJEG7BKDH2R97KUB735H6CDSAHJCGY3851DGR51I-15264?func=short-sub.
Fritze, Ronald H. "David Powell." Oxford Dictionary of National Biography. Last accessed 6 June, 2016. www.oxforddnb.com/view/article/22643.
Hadfield, Andrew. "Richard Eden." Oxford Dictionary of National Biography. Last accessed 10 April, 2015. www.oxforddnb.com/view/article/8454.
Henry VIII, King of England. "The Third Act of Succession, 1544." Luminarium Encyclopaedia Project. Last accessed 11 April, 2016. www.luminarium.org/encyclopedia/actsuccession3.htm.
Loades, David. "John Dudley." Oxford Dictionary of National Biography. Last accessed 11 August, 2016. www.oxforddnb.com/view/article/8156?docPos=1.
McDermott, James. "Sir George Peckham." Oxford Dictionary of National Biography. Last accessed 30 June, 2016. www.oxforddnb.com/view/article/21743.
Morgan, Basil. "Sir John Hawkins." Oxford Dictionary of National Biography. Last accessed 29 May, 2015. www.oxforddnb.com/view/article/12672?docPos=1.
Oxford English Dictionary. "Savage". Last accessed 8 July, 2016. www.oxforddictionaries.com/definition/english/savage.
Papal Bull. "Inter Caetera, 1493." American History from Revolution to Reconstruction and Beyond, the University of Groningen. Last accessed 30 June, 2016. www.let.rug.nl/usa/documents/before-1600/the-papal-bull-inter-caetera-alexander-vi-may-4-1493.php.
Payne, Anthony. "Richard Willes." Oxford Dictionary of National Biography. Last accessed 12 August, 2016. www.oxforddnb.com/view/article/29444.
Pope Alexander VI. "Inter Caetera, 1493." American History from Revolution to Reconstruction and Beyond, the University of Groningen. Last accessed

30 June, 2016. www.let.rug.nl/usa/documents/before-1600/the-papal-bull-inter-caetera-alexander-vi-may-4–1493.php.
Rapple, Rory. "Sir Humphrey Gilbert." Oxford Dictionary of National Biography. Last accessed 30 June, 2016. www.oxforddnb.com/view/article/10690.
Roberts, Julian and Andrew G. Watson. "John Dee's Library Catalogue: Additions and Corrections." The Bibliographical Society. Last accessed 30 June, 2016. www.bibsoc.org.uk/sites/www.bibsoc.org.uk/files/John%20Dee%27s%20Library%20Catalogue%204.pdf.
The Latin Vulgate Bible. Last accessed 8 September, 2016. www.latinvulgate.com.
The Official King James Bible Online. Last accessed 19 November, 2013. www.kingjamesbibleonline.org/.
"The Thirty-Nine Articles of Religion." Fordham University: The Modern History Sourcebook. Last accessed 16 November, 2016. http://sourcebooks.fordham.edu/mod/1571–39articles.asp.
Walsham, Alexandra. "Philip Stubbes." Oxford Dictionary of National Biography. Last accessed 18 June, 2016. www.oxforddnb.com/view/article/26737.

Index

Abbot, George 100–101
abundance, discourse of 58, 134, 156, 158, 169–171, 176–182, 184, 190–192, 202, 204
  see also agriculture
Acosta, José de Acosta 11
Acts of Supremacy and Uniformity 94
Adam and Eve 29, 32, 118–122, 125, 134, 144
  see also Bible; Paradise
admiralty court 83
Africa 55–56, 82, 113, 163, 170
agriculture
  abundance 58, 134, 156, 158, 169–171, 176–182, 184, 190–192, 202, 204
  agricultural trials 181, 191
  crop yields 170–171, 181, 184, 191
  ease of cultivation 180–181, 183–184, 191
  harvest failure 181, 202, 206
  Indigenous agriculture 181, 184
  see also climate; commodities; Virginia
Algonquians 184–185
  civility, potential for 50, 102, 114–115, 132–140, 145, 147, 158, 180, 186–188, 190, 203
  clothing 114, 132, 135–136, 140, 145, 147, 187
  eating habits 158, 160–161, 179–180, 183, 186–190
  primitivism 49–51, 60, 135, 140, 144–145, 147, 186–188, 190
  visual representations of 132–140, 186–189
  see also Bry, Theodore de; Roanoke; Virginia; White, John

Amadas, Philip 178, 181–182
Amazons 39–41, 43–45
  classical understandings of 41, 45
  Elizabeth I and 39–40, 44–45
  and gender 39, 44–45
  and violence 45
  see also monstrosity
ancient Britons 134, 138–139, 141–143
Antwerp 81, 130
Aristotle 26, 56
artistic gesture 135–136, 138
Asia *see* East Indies
Atlantis, America as 31–34, 59, 206
  see also theories of American origins
Australia 113

Babington, Gervase 119
Baffin Island *see* Meta Incognita
Barlowe, Arthur 49–50, 145, 178–185, 202
Barlow, Roger 58
Best, George 53–56, 87–89, 127, 129–130, 146, 169–174, 181
  see also Churchyard, Thomas; Frobisher, Martin; Meta Incognita; Settle, Dionyse
Bible 26, 38, 101
  dispersal of humankind 29–32, 38
  Garden of Eden 118–119, 121–122
  King Solomon 30–31
  and nakedness 118–121, 125
  see also nakedness; Ophir, America as; Paradise; Solomon, biblical king of Israel
Black Legend 99–101
Blundeville, Thomas 53
Bodin, Jean 162
Boorde, Andrew 57, 171, 186
Brazil 43, 118, 144, 186

Brereton, John 57–58, 97–98, 145, 155–156, 158, 191
  see also New England; Virginia
Bry, Theodore de 15, 132–143, 145, 186–189
  see also Algonquians; Virginia; White, John
Bullein, William 161, 189

Cabot, John 6, 78, 91
Cabot, Sebastian 6, 78, 91
California 125
Calvin, John 119
Canada 9, 11, 43, 46–47, 56, 119, 122, 127, 175–178, 180, 185
cannibalism 38, 40, 113, 186
  anthropophagi 41, 48, 171, 173
  and colonial justification 42–43
  and dietary desperation 172–173
  and nakedness 116–117, 135
  and savagery 46–51, 173
  wild men 46–51, 59
  see also Caribs; food; monstrosity
Cape Verde 35
Caribbean 7, 11, 30–31, 42–43, 46, 52, 82–83, 115, 122, 130, 133, 156, 163
Caribs
  and colonial justification 42–43
  etymology of 'cannibal' 43
  relationship with Taíno 42–43
  see also cannibalism; Caribbean; Columbus, Christopher; Taíno
Carleill, Christopher 9, 96–98, 102, 131, 146
Cartagena 83, 164
Cartier, Jacques 9, 47, 175–178, 180, 185
Cathay 33, 38
Cecil, William 7
Challeux, Nicholas Le 8
Charles V 30, 85
Charron, Pierre 162
Chester, John 95
Chilton, John 47–48
China see Cathay
Churchyard, Thomas 54–56, 87–89
  see also Best, George; Frobisher, Martin; Meta Incognita; Settle, Dionyse
Cibao 116

civility 7
  and appearance 113, 117, 120–124, 126–127, 131–132, 135–138, 145, 147, 203, 206
  and colonial justification 49–51, 120
  and consumption 75, 96, 102, 130–132, 146–147
  and conversion 75, 96, 98, 101–103, 126, 145, 203
  and eating habits 180, 186–188, 190
  Indigenous potential for 12, 49–51, 102, 120–121, 131–140, 145–147, 156, 158, 176, 180, 186–188, 190–191, 203, 206
  and savagery 46–51
  see also Algonquians; clothing; food; Inuit; religion
classical knowledge 27, 31–35, 38–41, 52–56, 58, 170, 206–207
climate 2, 17, 26, 28, 59, 206
  attitudes towards heat 57–58
  and clothing 128–130, 132, 146, 170
  and colonial habitability 28, 49, 54–57, 59–60, 127–130, 134, 146, 156, 159, 170, 176, 191, 204, 207
  and health 57–58, 155–156, 162, 170, 191
  humoral understandings of climate 52, 56–57, 155, 162
  and nakedness 55, 129–130
  and national characteristics 52, 55–56, 59, 170
  and patterns of colonisation 8–9, 52, 55–57, 59–60, 204
  zonal theory 52–55, 58, 60, 129, 170
  see also agriculture; Best, George; Cortés, Martín; humoral theory; Peckham, George; Settle, Dionyse
cloth industry 13–14, 81, 95, 130–132, 146, 206
clothing 18, 51, 112, 115
  and apotheosis 125
  and charity 121, 124–126, 146
  and civility 102, 120–124, 126–127, 131–132, 135–137, 146–147, 187, 206
  and climate 18, 55, 128–130, 132, 146, 170
  clothing theft 122–123, 146
  and colonial control 121, 123–124, 126, 132, 146–147
  and conversion 125–126
  costume books 112

Index

gifts of clothing 121–122, 124–126, 144, 146
and identity 112–114
and modesty 121–122, 132, 144–145
and morality 112–113, 120, 144–145
and nudity 112–116, 121, 135–136
and piety 144–145
and poverty 123–126, 128, 130, 132
and primitivism 115, 132, 135, 140, 144–145, 147, 187
and savagery 127–128, 130, 132, 135, 145, 147
and social aspiration 123, 146
as a social marker 112, 114–115, 136–137, 140, 144
sumptuary legislation 114, 144
and trade 18, 102, 113, 130–132, 146
see also Algonquians; Indigenous women; Inuit; nakedness; trade
Clothworkers of London 130
colonial investment 43–44, 60, 82, 93–94, 96, 115, 127, 137, 146–147, 184
colonisation, patterns of 8–9, 52, 55–57, 59–60, 204
see also climate
Columbus, Christopher 37, 169
as 'discoverer' of America 1, 6, 36
geographical beliefs 26, 29
Indigenous emissaries 124
religious beliefs 30–31, 124
representations of Indigenous peoples 41–43, 173
Columbus, Ferdinand 37
commercialisation as colonial and explorative objective 71–76, 79, 82, 86–88, 90–93, 96–98, 100, 102–103, 127, 129, 146
commodities 7, 8–9, 30, 33, 49–51, 57–58, 60, 73, 89, 95, 97–98, 103, 126, 129, 131–132, 134, 146, 169–170, 173, 176, 183, 186, 202
see also gold; trade
Cortés, Hernán 30, 84–86
Cortés, Martín (navigator) 53–54
Cortés, Martín (son of Hernán Cortés) 85
Countess of Warwick Island *see* Kodlunarn Island
Cuba 26, 85, 116

Darién 116
Dee, John 34, 37, 87
Drake, Francis 8, 83–84, 86, 90, 94–95, 125, 146, 182
Dudley, John 40, 76–77
Dutch Revolt 12, 14, 81, 99–100, 130

East Indies 26, 34, 87–88, 90, 113, 119, 172
Eden, Richard 16, 74, 124
approach to colonisation 76–80, 84, 92, 101, 103, 205
political allegiances 76–77, 79
religious background 79
as translator 7, 29, 31, 40–42, 76, 116, 121, 167, 185
see also Martyr, Peter; Münster, Sebastian; Willes, Richard
Edward VI 40, 77, 205
Elizabeth I 49, 90, 178, 180–181
and Amazons 39–40, 44–45
colonial investment 43–44, 60, 82, 181
colonial legitimacy 34–37, 94, 203
Dutch Revolt 12, 14, 81, 99–100, 130
Elizabethan religion 14, 72, 75, 80–81, 86, 94, 113–115, 205
relationship with Spain 80–82, 84, 99, 207
use of her image 43–44
see also letters patent; Prince Madoc; Ralegh, Walter
Elyot, Thomas 160–161, 166, 171, 189
Erasmus, Desiderius 172, 190
experience as a source of knowledge 27, 53–55, 59–60, 207

Far North *see* Meta Incognita
Fenton, Edward 87–88, 174
Ferdinand II 30–32, 77–78
Florida 8, 37, 79, 82, 119, 179
Florio, John 175–176
food 18, 51, 155, 176
and analogy 168, 183
and bodily difference 157–158, 161–162, 171, 173, 180, 190
cannibalism 171–173, 186
and civility 172, 180, 186–188, 190
and colonial settlement 18, 157–159, 161, 167, 174–175, 181–184, 186–187, 190, 192, 204
dining habits 172, 187–190

food (*cont.*)
  English diets 158, 161, 173–174, 179–181, 184
  European diets 157, 168–169
  food exchange 179–180
  food preparation 172–173, 176, 180, 186–187, 190
  gluttony 161, 189–190
  and health 156–161, 163–164, 166–168, 170–171, 173–175, 177, 179–180, 184–186, 189–192, 204
  and hospitality 180
  humoral understandings of food 56, 157–158, 160–161, 163, 169, 171, 174, 177, 184–185, 189–190
  hunger 157–158, 164–167, 192, 204
  Indigenous diets 49–50, 119, 158, 160–161, 168–169, 171–174, 179–180, 183, 186, 189
  Indigenous foods, European perceptions of 157–158, 165–168, 169–170, 174–177, 179, 183–184, 191, 204
  maize 166, 168, 181, 183–184
  and moderation 160–161, 189–190
  victualling 7, 83, 90, 122, 156, 163–165, 167, 169, 174–175, 182, 204
  visual representations of Indigenous foodways 186–189
  see also Algonquians; cannibalism; health; humoral theory; Indigenous women; Inuit
France 5, 53, 57, 118, 122
  etymology of 'savage' 50
  Huguenots 8
  influence of 28, 56, 59, 115–116, 131, 146, 206–207
  model for colonisation 3, 12, 175–178
  see also Canada; Cartier, Jacques; Florida; Léry, Jean de; Thevet, André
Frobisher, Martin 8, 49, 53–56, 87–90, 127, 156, 158, 169, 171–175
  see also Best, George; Churchyard, Thomas, Meta Incognita; Settle, Dionyse

Galen 56, 159
Garden of Eden *see* Paradise
Gilbert, Humphrey 16
  associates 35, 37, 93
  colonial projects in Newfoundland 89–93, 98, 131, 178
  death 35, 89–94, 178
  theory of the Northwest Passage 33–34, 87, 90
  see also Atlantis, America as; Hayes, Edward; letters patent; Newfoundland; Northwest Passage
gold 58, 79, 82, 84–85, 88, 100, 122, 163, 169, 173
  see also commodities
Golden Age 32, 50, 145
Grenville, Richard 182
Guiana 39–40, 43–45, 60, 100
Guzmán de Silva, Diego 163

Hacket, Thomas 8, 119
hairstyles 114
Hakluyt, Richard (the elder) 92, 97–98, 132, 146
Hakluyt, Richard (the younger) 16, 34, 47, 83, 90, 92, 97, 125, 166–167, 178
  approach to colonisation 74, 94, 96–98, 102
  association with Christopher Carleill 96
  association with the Clothworkers of London 130–131
  association with Theodore de Bry 134
  explanations for English colonial failure 71–72, 76, 92–93
  method of translation and collation 9, 15–16, 36
Harriot, Thomas 9, 15, 49–51, 57, 102, 132–145, 178, 182–192, 202
  see also Algonquians; Bry, Theodore de; Virginia
Hatton, Christopher 89
Hawkins, John 7, 82–84, 86, 94, 122, 163–165, 167
Hayes, Edward 72, 90–94, 97–98, 131, 146
health
  and climate 57–59, 155–156, 159, 162, 170, 191
  and diet 156–158, 161–164, 166–171, 173–175, 177, 179–180, 183–186, 189–192, 204
  and exploration 7, 12, 160–162, 166–167, 174–175, 180–186, 192
  humoral understandings of health 57–59, 157–163, 169, 171, 173–175, 177, 185, 189

Indigenous health 145, 155, 158–159, 161, 173–174, 179–180, 189
Indigenous remedies 163, 176–177, 179, 186, 190
  scurvy 176–177
  and sea voyages 7, 156, 164, 167
  sickness 7, 58, 162, 164, 166–167, 169, 174, 176–177, 179, 185, 189, 191
  tobacco, as cure for disease 157, 185–186, 190
  see also Algonquians; Canada; humoral theory; Inuit; tobacco
Henry VII 6
Henry VIII 7, 77
Hesperides, America as 35–37
  see also theories of American origins
Hippocrates 56, 159
Hispaniola 30–31, 41, 121
Hortop, Job 122–123, 165–167, 179, 183
Huatulco 84
humanism 6, 13, 34, 145
humoral theory 2, 56–57, 159–160, 162
  and climate 52, 56–59, 155, 162
  and diet 157, 160–161, 163, 169, 171, 173–175, 177, 184–185, 189–190
  four humours 56, 58, 159–161, 169, 174
  health regimens 57, 160–161, 166, 171, 189
  national identity 56, 162–163, 169
  regional differences 155, 162–163, 184
  six non-natural things 57, 157–160, 162, 179
  temperaments and complexions 56–59, 157, 160–162, 169, 171, 173–175, 177, 184–185, 190, 204
  see also climate; food; health

idleness 75, 95–96, 98, 103, 131
Indigenous languages 182–183, 185
Indigenous women
  appearance 114, 116, 135–136
  as emissaries and translators 48, 124
  hospitality 180
  Spanish violence 100–101
  violence of 47
  see also Algonquians; Amazons; cannibalism; clothing; food

Inter Caetera 32
Inuit 8, 88
  cannibalism 171–173
  civility, potential for 49, 89, 128, 130
  clothing 89, 127–128, 130, 146
  eating habits 49, 89, 156, 171–174, 180, 186, 191, 204
  in England 173–174
  standards of living 49, 128, 130
  violence 49, 88, 174
  see also cannibalism; clothing; food
Ireland 178
  model for colonisation 11
  Pelham, William 94
  Sidney, Henry 11, 119
  see also Gilbert, Humphrey
Iroquoians 47, 176–177
Isabella I 30, 32

James I 1, 120, 157
Jamestown 1, 6, 10, 73, 157, 192, 202, 204
Johnson, Robert 202

Kodlunarn Island 88, 174–175

Lady Jane Grey 77
Lane, Ralph 182
Las Casas, Bartolomé de 99–101
Léry, Jean de 186
letters patent 35, 90, 178
Levant 130
Llwyd, Humphrey 37
Lok, Michael 87
López de Gómara, Francisco 30–35, 84–86
  see also Atlantis, America as; Mexico; Nicholls, Thomas
lotteries 202
Low Countries 53, 72, 81, 94, 99–100

maize 166, 168, 181, 183–184
Mandeville, John 39, 41, 172
Margarita 83, 164
Marian persecutions 79
Markham, Gervase 187
Martinique 41
Martyr, Peter 7, 11, 29–31, 35, 41–42, 45–47, 80–81, 116–117, 121, 124–125, 167–169, 185
Mary I 71–72, 77, 79–80, 103, 205

Massachusetts Bay 73, 203
Mediterranean world 38, 57, 162, 170
Merchant Adventurers 130
Meta Incognita 8–9, 11, 49–51, 53–58, 87–89, 115, 127–130, 146, 156, 158, 170–175, 178–179, 182, 191, 204, 207
  see also Best, George; Churchyard, Thomas; Frobisher, Martin; Settle, Dionyse
Mexico 36, 83, 85, 164
  conquest of 48, 84–86
  Cortés, Hernán, legacy of 84–85
  English descriptions of 47–51, 122–123, 165–166, 183
  see also Chilton, John; Cortés, Hernán; Hortop, Job; Philips, Miles; Spain; Spanish America
Monardes, Nicholas 185
monstrosity 17, 26, 28, 39–48, 59, 206
  Amazons 39–41, 43–45
  cannibals 38, 40–43, 45, 48–51, 186
  and colonial justification 27, 42–43
  giants 41
  Mandeville, John 39, 41
  Plinian Races 38–39, 41, 46, 48
  wild men 40, 45–51, 119, 207
  see also Amazons; cannibalism; Caribs; Guiana; wildness
Münster, Sebastian 7, 40–41, 45, 47, 76, 78, 116, 118, 124, 167–168, 173
  see also Eden, Richard
Muscovy 14, 97, 176, 179
Muscovy Company 96, 131

nakedness 18, 38, 112, 115, 121, 124–125, 127, 130–131
  and cannibalism 116–117, 135
  and climate 55, 129–130
  meanings of 'naked' 121, 124
  and poverty 116, 118, 125–126
  and primitivism 112, 115, 135, 187
  and savagery 112–113, 115–122, 126, 138, 146–147
  and sexuality 113, 116, 118, 120, 126, 146
  and shame 118–122, 125–126, 135, 144, 146
  and sin 118–120, 126, 144, 146–147
  and social structure 113
  and trade, potential for 18, 130–131, 146

  and wildness 46–48, 119
  see also Bible; climate; clothing; trade; wildness
Netherlands see Low Countries
New England 57–58, 97, 136, 145, 155–156, 178, 191
Newfoundland
  and cannibalism 42–43, 45
  and climate 57
  and clothing 130–131, 203
  colonial settlement 9, 42–43, 45, 57, 59, 72, 89–94, 97–98, 178, 203
  Indigenous population 130–131, 203
  and trade 9, 94–97, 130–131, 146
  see also cannibalism; climate; Gilbert, Humphrey; Hayes, Edward; Parkhurst, Anthony
New France see Canada; Cartier, Jacques
New Spain see Mexico
Nicholls, Thomas 84–86
north Virginia see New England
Northwest Passage
  searches for 6, 11, 72, 87–88, 90, 173, 204
  theories of 27, 29, 33–34, 59, 87, 90, 203, 206
  see also Atlantis, America as; Columbus, Christopher; Frobisher, Martin; Gilbert, Humphrey; Meta Incognita
Nova Albion see California

Ophir, America as 30–31
  see also theories of American origins
Oviedo, Gonzalo Fernández de 7, 30, 35, 37, 121

Pánuco 48, 165
Paradise 118–119, 121–122, 134, 170
Parkhurst, Anthony 92, 94, 97
Peckham, George 9, 34–37, 42–43, 45, 57, 93–98, 102, 130–131, 146
  see also Gilbert, Humphrey; Newfoundland
Peru 119
Philip II 71, 77, 79, 205
Philips, Miles 122–123, 165–167, 179, 183
piracy 8, 72–74, 81, 83–84, 130, 156, 163
Plato 32
Plymouth colony 73, 203

Polo, Marco 26
Portugal 5, 7, 12, 28, 33, 38, 40, 56, 59, 87, 98, 102, 115–116, 146, 167
poverty
  and clothing 116, 118, 123–126, 128, 130, 132
  and emigration 73, 95–96, 98
  in England 14, 72–73, 75, 78, 95–96, 98, 103, 130–132
  and population growth 95, 103
  see also clothing
Powell, David 36–37
Prince Madoc 34–37, 59, 203
  see also Elizabeth I; theories of American origins
privateering 8, 11, 72, 74, 122, 156, 163, 167
Privy Council 82, 85
providentialism 2, 13, 30, 56, 71–72, 75, 77–78, 80, 90–96, 98, 103–104, 159, 177, 206
  see also religion

Ralegh, Walter 9, 16, 33, 39, 43–45, 100–101, 178, 181–182
  see also Guiana
Rastell, John 28–29
Reformation 3, 40, 86, 119
religion 73–74
  anti-Catholicism 35, 80–81, 94, 101
  Catholicism 14, 32, 42, 71–72, 77, 79–80, 93–94, 96–97, 101, 103, 120, 125–127, 205
  and charity 124–126, 146
  Church of England 14, 75, 80–81, 94, 119–120, 125–126, 205
  and civility 39, 75, 96, 98, 101–103, 203
  and colonial justification 37–38, 93
  and colonial objectives 17, 60, 71, 73–80, 84, 87–88, 91–98, 100–104, 203, 205–206
  critique of English piety 71–72, 76, 78–79, 86, 91–92, 100, 190
  heresy 85–86, 97, 119
  Indigenous conversion 7, 27, 32–33, 42, 47, 71–72, 75–80, 84–88, 91–93, 95–98, 101–103, 126–127, 176, 203, 206–207
  and morality 104, 113, 115, 144
  and poverty 78

providentialism 2, 13, 30, 56, 71–72, 75, 77–78, 80, 90–96, 98, 103–104, 159, 177, 206
puritanism 73, 75, 86, 144, 190
religious reform 86, 115, 144, 190
and wealth accumulation 14, 17, 71–72, 74–79, 91–92, 97, 103–104, 203, 206
  see also Elizabeth I; France; providentialism; Reformation; Spain
Ribault, Jean 8
Rio de la Hacha 83, 164
Roanoke
  colonial failure 5, 9, 132–133, 182, 191–192, 204
  see also Algonquians; Bry, Theodore de; climate; Harriot, Thomas; Virginia
Rome, ancient 119, 139
Rosier, James 136
Russell, Francis 81

San Juan de Ulúa 83, 164–165
savagery 144, 207
  and cannibalism 48–51, 116, 173
  civilising process 50–51, 132, 145, 147, 186–188, 190
  and clothing 127–128, 130, 132, 135, 140, 146–147
  as colonial justification 50–51
  etymology of 'savage' 50
  and nakedness 116–122, 146–147
  and primitivism 49–51, 145, 147, 186–188, 190
  and wildness 46–51, 119
  see also Algonquians; cannibalism; Caribs; civility; clothing; food; Inuit; Newfoundland; wildness
sea voyages
  and bad weather 90–91, 164, 174, 178
  mutiny 165, 169
  and sickness 7, 164
  victualling 7, 83, 90, 122, 156, 163–165, 167, 169, 175, 204
Secotan 135, 140
  see also Roanoke; Virginia
Segar, Francis 188
Settle, Dionyse 8, 49, 55–57, 89, 127–130, 146, 171–173

Settle, Dionyse (*cont.*)
  see also Best, George; Churchyard, Thomas; Frobisher, Martin; Meta Incognita
Shakespeare, William 112
Smith, Henry 119
Solomon, biblical king of Israel 30–31
  see also Bible; Ophir, America as
Spain 5, 7, 8, 30, 34, 40, 52–53, 57, 167
  Anglo–Spanish relations 12, 14, 44, 59, 72, 76–83, 95, 99–100, 103, 130, 133, 163, 165, 207
  anti-Hispanicism 44, 72, 82, 84–86, 90, 99–101, 207
  Armada 12, 44, 133
  colonial legitimacy 37–38, 42–43, 127
  colonial violence 12, 83, 99–101, 164, 207
  conversion projects 27, 32–33, 42, 72, 77–80, 84–86, 98, 101, 127, 206
  critique of Spanish imperialism 3–4, 10, 12, 14, 36–37, 48, 51, 72, 81, 92, 98–103, 132, 207–208
  Dutch Revolt 12, 14, 81, 99–100, 130
  greed 100–103, 207
  influence of 28–29, 34–36, 38, 54–56, 59, 115–116, 124, 127, 129, 131, 146, 167, 169, 206–207
  praise and emulation of Spanish colonisation 3–4, 14, 31, 72, 76–81, 84, 86–87, 92, 103, 205–206
  trade with 7, 81–83, 98, 163
  see also Black Legend; Mexico; religion; Spanish America
Spanish America 30, 47–52, 58, 60, 115, 163
  see also Caribbean; Mexico; Spain; West Indies
Starving Time 157, 192
Stubbes, Philip 144–145, 190
sumptuary legislation 114, 144

Taíno 42
tattoos 114
theories of American origins 17, 26–38, 59, 203, 206
  see also Atlantis, America as; Hesperides, America as; Ophir, America as; Prince Madoc
Thevet, André 8, 45, 47, 118–119, 121–123, 127, 173

Thirty-Nine Articles of Religion 75
Throckmorton, Elizabeth 44
Tilney, Edmund 180
tobacco 120, 146, 157, 183, 185–186, 190
  see also health
trade
  and alleviation of poverty 75, 95–98, 131–132
  in the Caribbean 82–83, 163–164
  and clothes 18, 113, 130–132, 146, 206
  cloth trade 81, 95, 130–132, 146, 206
  and contraction of markets 14, 95, 103, 130–131
  embargos 72, 81–82, 130
  expansion of markets 14, 74–75, 95–96, 98, 103, 130–132, 146
  and Indigenous peoples 11, 14, 75, 96–98, 102–103, 130–132, 146, 176, 204, 206
  intra-European trade 75, 81, 97–98
  and religion 97
  slave trade 82–83, 94
  see also civility; cloth industry; clothing; commodities; Muscovy Company; Northwest Passage; poverty
trade embargo 72, 81–82, 130
Treaty of Tordesillas 38
Tupi 186

Velázquez de Cuéllar, Diego 85
Vespucci, Amerigo 36, 41, 47, 118
Virginia 1, 13
  agriculture 180–181, 184, 202
  climate 57–58, 134, 158, 178
  colonial settlement 57–58, 132–134, 137, 139–140, 147, 158, 177–179, 181–184, 186–187, 190–192, 202–203
  commodities 49–51, 58, 134, 183, 186, 202
  fertility 50, 58, 134, 158, 178–182, 184, 192, 202, 204, 206
  food 49–50, 158, 179, 181, 183–184, 186–191, 204, 206
  Indigenous population 49–51, 60, 102, 114–115, 132–140, 144–145, 147, 158, 178–181, 183–184, 186–190, 203

promotion of 9, 15, 49–51, 57–58, 114–115, 133–134, 137, 145, 147, 181–184, 186–187, 190–192
visual representations of 132–140, 186–189
see also Algonquians; Elizabeth I; New England; Roanoke
Virginia Company 1, 202

Wales *see* Prince Madoc
Walsingham, Francis 84–86, 94, 131
Wateson, George 58
West Indies 31, 36–37, 47, 56, 82–83, 94, 101, 129, 163–164
see also Caribbean; Cuba; Hispaniola
White, John
governor of Roanoke 132–133
watercolours of North America 133–136, 138–139
see also Algonquians; Bry, Theodore de; Harriot, Thomas
wildness 46–51, 119, 207
see also cannibalism; monstrosity; savagery
Willes, Richard 80–81

EU authorised representative for GPSR:
Easy Access System Europe, Mustamäe tee 50,
10621 Tallinn, Estonia
gpsr.requests@easproject.com